AN EXPLORER'S GUIDE

Arizona

⑤ 5/1/08

Arizona

Christine Maxa

Photographs by David A. James

FIRST EDITION

The Countryman Press ✳ Woodstock, Vermont

We welcome your comments and suggestions. Please contact Explorer's Guide Editor, The Countryman Press, P.O. Box 748, Woodstock, VT 05091, or e-mail countrymanpress@wwnorton.com.

Copyright © 2008 by Christine Maxa

First Edition

ISBN: 978-0-88150-715-7

Cover and text design by Bodenweber Design
Cover photograph © Ron Niebrugge
Interior photographs © David James
Maps by Mapping Specialists Ltd., Madison, WI; © The Countryman Press
Text composition by PerfecType, Nashville, TN

Published by The Countryman Press, P.O. Box 748, Woodstock, Vermont 05091

Distributed by W. W. Norton & Company, Inc., 500 Fifth Avenue, New York, NY 10110

Printed in the United States of America

10 9 8 7 6 5 4 3 2 1

DEDICATION

To David, who always makes the trip so much more fun.

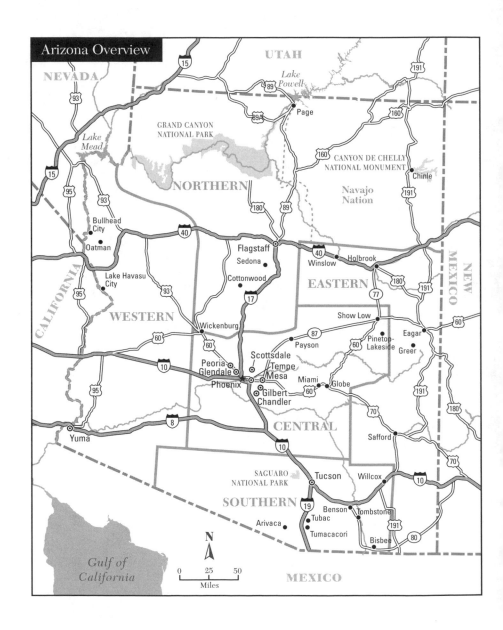

CONTENTS

1 Northern Arizona

2 Central Arizona

3 Eastern Arizona

4 Southern Arizona

5 Western Arizona

INTRODUCTION

For many native and long-term residents of Arizona, the state has come a long way since the 1980s. For decades the state lunkered along as a cowboy's workplace and a sunshine winter haven where snowbirds moved with the seasons from points north. Movie stars, politicos, and upper crusters who needed a breather from the masses nestled in the resorts clearly meant for a standard of living much higher than the locals'.

In the 1980s development happened. Populations doubled, and the slower, cowtown ways of life wobbled in the wake of city living. By the 1990s sophistication was seeping into every corner of the state. Corporate-weary professionals brought their tastes, and money, to Arizona, the nation's promised land where jobs and opportunities prevailed.

By the turn of the millennium, the scale had tipped. Gone were the tracts of open space around the bigger cities. The small towns took their turn in the cultural shift. Change remains in the air today, and the areas not yet affected are far and few between. If you haven't taken a ride around Arizona for a few years, or dismissed it because accommodations and services didn't have what you needed in the way of comfort, it's time to take another look.

Small towns with crumbling historic architecture and services that hadn't progressed since Historic Route 66 gave way to I-40 have been practically born again. Buildings are getting repaired and remodeled. Businesses have quality products with touches of luxury. And chambers and visitor bureaus actually have information on not just the major draws that everyone's seen but also

YOU WON'T SEE MANY COWBOYS ALONG ARIZONA HIGHWAYS; YOU'LL HAVE TO GO ON A BACKCOUNTRY ADVENTURE.

the unique and interesting aspects of the community that people really want to discover.

In the bigger cities things are changing so quickly, you don't want to stay away more than a few months if you have any hopes of keeping current. Phoenix has resuscitated its downtown section so valiantly, people living in the trendy Valley outskirts have moved to the city's interior "where all their friends are." Given Scottsdale's development of its Waterfront district, you can stay in a different hotel each night for a week and still not experience all the new ones—or even the newly remodeled ones. Tucson, second only to the West Coast in cool meccas for the hippie gypsy in the 1960s and '70s, has actually held on to its cultural mien while developing to the hilt. Flagstaff—always the quiet genius that shunned the limelight its neighbor Sedona adored, and content with the world coming through its doors on the way to the Grand Canyon—can't stay out of the nation's marketing limelight for too long.

A VIEW FROM THE GRAND CANYON'S SOUTH RIM.

It won't matter where you travel in the state, you will find exceptionally good food, and in the oddest places. Big cities here are on the same culinary level as New York City, Chicago, and Los Angeles. Yes, things have evolved that much. In the tiny towns, however, you are apt to find some of the best food experiences. Remember the world-weary professionals who moved to small towns? They merely continued their genius where they plopped down.

This is one of the best times to live in and visit Arizona. Admittedly, some residents are reeling from all the rocking. Others are enjoying the ride. This goes the same for visitors. With that in mind, we've endeavored in this guidebook to seek out not only places that are consistently good in services and products but also destinations, accommodations, and restaurants that have historic and/or cultural ties or personify the state's personality.

Personality? The conservative, *don't fix-it-if-it's-not-broken* state has a personality? Actually, yes. Arizona is strongly independent, stubborn sometimes to its own hurt, and an utter romantic with a passion for legends and lore. The state has embraced some of the most colorful, creative, poetic, infamous, and, at times, nefarious characters in the history of the nation . . . most of whom would have been (or were) run out of town in other states. From this colorful brew, as any chaos theory expert will tell you, comes deep beauty and awesome creativity. And while Arizona has had its messy moments in history, it always comes out smelling like a rose. With characteristics like that, no wonder Arizona's been so misunderstood.

We would like to thank Kermit Hummel for the opportunity to write this guide, Jennifer Thompson and Laura Jorstad for editing it, and all the people who graciously helped in our gathering of information for it: Rosalie Alaya, Ben Bethel, Erika Brickel, Julie Brooks, Dwayne Cassidy, Kathie Curley, Donna Eastman, Mike Finney, Ann Groves, Roy Gugliotta, Stephanie Heckathorne, Candace Kirk, Heather Koncilja, Mari Markogianis, Marjorie Magnusson, Susan Ruff, Meg Ryan, Susan Schepman, Kimberly Schmitz, Michelle Streeter, Liz Tang, and Jennifer Wesselhof.

HOW TO USE THIS GUIDE

Arizona: An Explorer's Guide is broken down into sections representing different areas of the state, then into chapters focusing on an individual city or town. Each chapter opens with a general or historical introduction to the city or town, then continues with information on destinations, accommodations, and restaurants that, largely, are quintessential Arizona.

We've tried to list independent venues as much as possible, for two reasons. Most readers, first of all, will know what to expect with the franchises. More importantly, independent businesses are a perfect example of the spirit of Arizona. We've also done our best to interweave history and fun facts into every aspect of the book, not just the introductions. This, we feel, is invaluable in getting to know a place.

Guidance lists the entities—from chambers of commerce to agencies managing public lands—that you can refer to for information on the area.

Getting There tells you, well, how to get there—what roads or other means of transport will take you to town. If public transportation or shuttles are available, we list them in **Getting Around**.

When to Come tells you not only the high season when everyone else comes but also what the rest of the year is like. That way you can decide if you want to check out the deals in the low season.

Medical Emergency lists hospitals and/or clinics. In large cities, it's 911.

To See lists attractions and points of interest you may want to visit, including museums, memorials, scenic drives, and more.

To Do features activities to keep you busy.

Wilder Places lists backcountry destinations of unique interest and/or scenic beauty.

Lodging will give you ideas of where to find unique and/or consistently good places to stay. In almost every case, if we haven't stayed there, we've paid a visit and checked it out. Often these lodgings come with some great history attached. Sometimes our listings are slim because a town offers only franchises.

Where to Eat lists venues that serve dependably good food. We've divided them into two categories—*Dining Out* (better restaurants) and *Eating Out* (very casual ones). Sometimes restaurants have off nights or suddenly change hands and morph into something totally unacceptable. Please do not blame us—but do inform us.

The Arts are featured not only because art and art walks are becoming popular and valuable sources of revenue for towns but also because these forms of self-expression often reveal the personality of the residents and a place. We tell you where to find galleries and art-centered shops, murals, or museums.

Entertainment appears now and again, especially when towns and/or their venues are renowned.

Selective Shopping usually points you in the right direction for shopping, rather than trying to critique individual stores.

Special Events is a compendium of the most important annual events going on in the community.

KEY TO SYMBOLS

⚭ Weddings. The wedding-ring symbol appears beside venues that specialize in weddings.

🏵 Special value. The blue-ribbon symbol appears at restaurants and lodging that have a consistently-good product available at a moderate or low price.

🐾 Pets. The dog-paw symbol signals accommodations that allow pets and other venues that are unusually pet-friendly. Any stipulations appear in the review.

✎ Child-friendly. The crayon symbol appears next to lodgings, restaurants, and activities that are welcoming to youngsters.

♿ Handicapped access. The wheelchair symbol appears beside lodgings and attractions that offer handicapped access.

Northern Arizona 1

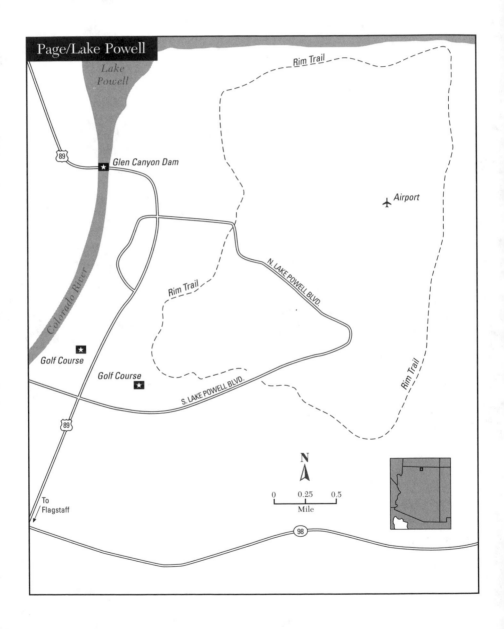

Page/Lake Powell

Lake
Powell

Rim Trail

Colorado River

89

Glen Canyon Dam

Airport

Rim Trail

N. LAKE POWELL BLVD.

Golf Course

Golf Course

Rim Trail

S. LAKE POWELL BLVD.

89

To
Flagstaff

N

0   0.25   0.5
Mile

98

PAGE AND LAKE POWELL

I f it weren't for Lake Powell, Page might not exist. However, the mesa-top town doesn't necessarily exist for the lake. The landscape, dramatic and highly attractive on its own, comes with a fascinating geological history. Once an expanse of ancient seas and freshwater lakes, the area endured the creation of mountains and plateau uplifting, resulting in a gorgeous landscape of sandstone cliffs carved by the Colorado and the Escalante Rivers. Only the most adventurous explored this beautiful but rugged area. Labyrinthine canyons were treasure chests that cached hanging gardens, dainty cascades, and relics from Native peoples out of sight from the masses.

Then things changed in the 1950s. The esoteric high-desert hideaway became a world-class water world when Glen Canyon Dam came on the scene. Built to meet western energy demands, the dam pooled the volatile Colorado River into Lake Powell. The lake totally transformed the area: Canyons were submerged; a new environment supported a different set of mammals and fish; and aesthetically, the place turned enchanting. The dam and resulting lake also turned environmentalists—the late Edward Abbey at the helm—into a formidable force that decades later would still like to see the dam go the way of the river today.

When extreme drought conditions occurred in the late 1990s and early 2000s, lake water reduced to levels that stymied larger vessels plying the lake. Environmentalists danced with glee, thinking that the environment itself was reclaiming the canyonlands. The National Oceanic and Atmospheric Administration (NOAA) explained that the lake was "doing its job" by reserving water in drought times. The curious merely put in kayaks and put on hiking boots to explore this "new" terrain of canyons that hadn't seen the light of day for decades. A new slogan appeared: "The New Lake Powell."

At the time of this writing, long-term forecasts for Arizona say drought conditions may remain for a while. The NOAA believes that the snowmelt from the northern states so necessary to fill the lake will top off, not refill, the lake. Environmentalists have their fingers crossed, and adventurers are starting to like poking around the places uncovered with falling water levels. Regardless of what happens, Lake Powell is still alive and well, and Page will always be there—an attractive and active destination to visit.

GUIDANCE **Page–Lake Powell Tourism Bureau** (888-261-7243; www.explore pagelakepowell.com), 647-A Elm St., offers information on things going on in town, on the lake, and around the Grand Circle area (northern Arizona and southern Utah). The **North Kaibab Ranger District** (928-643-7395), 430 S. Main St., Freedonia, can tell you more about trails in the national forest on the Arizona Strip. The **Bureau of Land Management** (435-688-3200), Arizona Strip Field Office, 345 E. Riverside Dr., St. George, Utah, is your source for exploring the national monuments in the area.

GETTING THERE *By car:* From points south, take US 89 out of Flagstaff. From Utah, head south and east on US 89. From the Navajo Nation, take AZ 98. *By air:* **Page Municipal Airport** (928-645-4337), 238 10th Ave., has a 5,000-foot asphalt concrete runway and service to Phoenix and Denver through Great Lakes Airlines.

WHEN TO COME Summertime is high season for lake activities. If you're looking for a bargain, plan your trip from November through March. Hikers, mountain bikers, and road bicyclists should visit during fall and winter.

MEDICAL EMERGENCY **Page Hospital** (928-645-2424), 501 N. Navajo.

✳ To See

Carl Hayden Visitors Center at Glen Canyon Dam (928-608-6404). Open daily 8–5 except Thanksgiving, Christmas, and New Year's Day. The facility has exhibits about the construction of the dam and tours through the dam and Glen Canyon Powerplant. The dam, finished in the 1960s, was built to supply electricity to western states—enough to power 400,000 households for a year. But all has not been rosy in the Colorado River since the completion of the dam. The resulting cold waters, perfect for rainbow trout, compromise the existence of the native fish, including the dour humpback chub. An aquarium lets you take a look at the endangered native fish that lurk in the Colorado River.

John Wesley Powell Memorial Museum (928-645-9496), 6 N. Lake Powell Blvd. Open Mon.–Fri. 9–5. The museum has a number of interesting things packed into it—from dinosaurs and Anasazi artifacts to present-day finds from recent Colorado River explorations—and of course a display memorializing Powell's epic journey down the Colorado River 1869–1871. $5 adults, $3 ages 62-plus, $1 for those 5–12.

✳ To Do

FISHING The hottest fly-fishing in the state happens at **Lees Ferry** (at Marble Canyon, just beyond the Navajo Bridge, turn right onto the signed turnoff for Lees Ferry and go 5 miles) in the Colorado River. It's world class in both fishing and scenery. You can employ a guide to help you land that lunker. Savvy Terry Gunn, owner of **Lees Ferry Anglers** at Cliff Dwellers, says the fishing here is the best in the Lower 48. **Ambassador Guides at Lees Ferry** (800-256-7596)

Navajo Bridge. Go south 25 miles on US 89, turn right onto US 89A, and go 14 miles. Before the original Navajo Bridge was built in 1929, the only access between Utah and Arizona was the undependable river crossing at Lees Ferry. When floods flowed or during storms, the ferry stopped, and so did traffic. The bridge was cutting-edge technology for its time—the highest steel-arch bridge in the country, rising 470 above the river. Grand Canyon National Park and Glen Canyon National Recreation Area meet on one side of the river; the Navajo Nation lies on the other.

As snazzy as this steel-frame structure was, its load limits quickly paled compared with what was needed as vehicles grew heavier with the times. Further, the original bridge was too narrow. And so a new bridge was constructed in 1995, this one even more of an engineering marvel than the first because the builders, Cannon and Associates, had to follow stringent environmental regulations and deal with intense public concern.

The mechanically inclined will be interested to know that Cannon used a method called cantilevering to building the bridge. A tieback device held up the bridge as it was built, piece by piece, from both sides of the canyon. The tieback had to accommodate the wind, temporary decking, netting for debris, a crane, and the vehicle that transported materials to the site. For each of the 20 ribs on the bridge, workers drilled 55 feet into the rock to place a rock anchor, then post-tensioned it. Taking all this into consideration, when you cross either of these steel-arch spans, know you are walking on a very special structure.

in Vermilion Cliffs can take you trout fishing on the Colorado River or fly-fishing for striped bass, the current fishing thrill on Lake Powell.

GOLF Lake Powell National Golf Course (928-645-2023), US 89 and Lake Powell Blvd. One of golf's hidden gems, this championship-quality public course is a tricky one thanks to its 300-foot elevation change and undulations that hide traps. It's one of the toughest par-4s in the nation. The signature 15th hole has you teeing from the top of the course to the hole on its lowlands. Add to the exciting golf game the exquisite scenery of azure blue Lake Powell surrounded by sanguine sandstone cliffs, and you can understand why golfers around the nation have this on their list of must-play courses. 9 holes $40, 18 holes $60.

HOUSEBOAT RENTALS The most comfortable way to experience elegant Lake Powell is by renting a houseboat. That way you can go where you like, exploring the captivating landscape by day and sleeping under the stars at night. **Antelope Point Marina** (800-255-5561) rents 59- and 70-foot houseboats for 3 to 7 days. The fee runs $5,495–8,495 for a week's rental during peak season. **Aramark**

PAGE'S GOLF COURSE HAS SOME OF THE MOST DRAMATIC SCENERY IN THE COUNTRY.

(928-645-2433 or 800-528-6154) rents 44- to 75-foot boats for 3 to 7 days: $2,200–10,595 per week, peak season. Rates drop as much as 40 percent off-season.

KAYAKING When drought conditions in recent years dropped the lake water to half its pool capacity, houseboats and yachts encountered sandbar obstacles, and kayaks became de rigueur. They're also among the best vessels for up-close exploration. **Kayak Lake Powell** (888-854-7862) takes you out on half-day to multinight tours Apr.–Oct. that include a guide (Kyle Walker, a state-certified guide and Coast Guard–certified captain with more than 10 years' lake experience), gear, and meals. You can join a scheduled trip or customize your own for three to eight people. $250–750 per person for 1–4 nights. **Lake Powell Kayak Tours** (928-645-3114), 811 Vista Ave., provides rental craft that you can use by yourself or on a 1- to 4-hour guided tour. Tours: $65–75 adults, $45–55 children; daily rates $35–55.

LAKE POWELL MARINAS Several marinas dot the thousands of miles of lakefront. The most accessible are **Wahweap Marina** (928-645-2433), 6 miles north of Page, and **Antelope Point**, the largest floating concrete structure in the world, just east of Page on AZ 98. **Bullfrog Resort & Marina** (435-684-3000) is located in Utah, near midlake; **Halls Crossing Marina** (435-684-7000), also midlake, is across from Bullfrog; **Hite Marina** (435-684-2273) is on the east end of the lake, off UT 95; and **Dangling Rope** (928-645-2969) is 40 miles uplake from Wahweap, near the canyon to Rainbow Bridge.

LAKE TOURS Lake Powell Resort offers a number of Lake Powell tours: 90-minute-long **Antelope Canyon Tour** ($31 adults, $24 ages 3–12); 3-hour **Navajo Tapestry Tour** ($51 adults, $35 ages 3–12, includes lunch); and 7-hour tours to Rainbow Bridge ($107 adults, $75 ages 3–12, includes lunch).

MOUNTAIN BIKING Page has been called the next Moab, with its slickrock surfaces and stunning red sandstone scenery. The best time to bike is fall through spring. Contact Vance at **Lakeside Bikes** (928-645-2266), 118 6th Ave., for information on routes. Watch for a new bike trail in Glen Canyon National Recreation Area in 2009.

NAVAJO CULTURE With the Navajo Nation right next door, you don't have to go far to experience the vibrant landscape and culture of the Diné. The **Navajo Heritage Center** (928-660-0304), located at Coppermine Rd. and AZ 98 behind the Big Lake Trading Post, preserves and accurately portrays the culture and traditions of the Navajo people in a captivating presentation called **An Evening with the Navajo**. Diné artisans demonstrate rug weaving, jewelry making, and dances and offer insight into why they do things the way they do; Navajo food is included. $40–55 adults, $30–40 ages 6–13.

ENTRANCE TO A SLOT CANYON NEAR LAKE POWELL.

SLOT CANYON TOURS

While the Colorado Plateau often flaunts its attractive geology in places such as the Glen Canyon National Recreation Center, Grand Canyon, and Monument Valley, it has its secrets as well. Hidden away from the casual glance lie some of the most extraordinary natural features in the state: slot canyons. Some of these canyons narrow to an arm span. Some have legends and lore. All have their own personality worth experiencing. Most tours companies travel into Antelope Canyon, the darling of slot canyons.

Check out **Chief Tsosie** (928-645-5594), 55 S. Lake Powell Blvd., for a personable and insightful tour. He also leads exclusive tours into more rugged Cathedral Canyon, as well as photographic tours, stargazing adventures, and a Navajo Healing Ritual (see p. 23). $20–35 person, $10 ages up to 12.

Overland Canyon Tours (928-608-4072), 695 N. Navajo, offers exclusive tours into Canyon X. Named for the X formed by two intersecting canyons, this slot has fewer tour groups and a quieter atmosphere than Antelope Canyon. No noise. No crowds. Photographers love it. $100 adults, $35 children.

Slot Canyon Hummer Adventures (928-645-2266), 12 N. Lake Powell Blvd. A unique 3- to 5-hour four-wheel-drive experience in the leather-upholstered and air-conditioned comfort of a screaming yellow Hummer, which takes you over slickrock, steep roads, and sand dunes to a spectacular and (as of this writing) unnamed slot canyon upstream from famous Water Holes Canyon, as well as two other canyons exclusive to this company. Still pristine, visited by wildlife, and evoking a centering feeling, the twists, turns, and sinuous forms of the water-shaped sandstone walls present an exclusive experience. $69–139.

A PANORAMA OF LAKE POWELL.

NAVAJO HEALING RITUAL **Chief Ray Tsosie** (928-645-5594) has put together a compendium of traditional Navajo healings rituals, from a sweat lodge experience to a sand rub and a hair washing with yucca root. This is a truly traditional, unpretentious experience that will give you a chance to share a cultural moment with the Navajo. Chief Tsosie, once the general manager of the Lake Powell Resort, starts the experience with a tour through his neighborhood in LaChee. The sweat lodge ceremony gives you an idea of a favorite method of keeping healthy for traditional Navajo. During the sand cleansing massage, you head for a secluded alcove with warm sandstone slabs if weather permits, or else a hogan. Chief Tsosie is an accomplished flute player and will set the healing stage with a song, then continue it with recorded music. You may finish with a yucca root hair-washing ceremony. Call for prices.

SOFT-WATER FLOAT ON THE COLORADO RIVER The **Glen Canyon Float** is exclusively offered by **Colorado River Discovery** (928-645-9175 or 888-522-6644), 130 6th Ave., Mar.–Nov. The closest you'll get to river action on this smooth-water trip is gentle riffles. The big water comes after Lees Ferry, where this trip ends; you return to Page via bus. Still, the scenery is just as impressive as the classic whitewater river trip. Side trips to petroglyph sites make a nice diversion. $70 adults, $60 ages 4–12.

✳ Wilder Places

Arizona Strip. Go south on US 89 for 25 miles, turn right onto US 89A, and continue 14 miles to Navajo Bridge at Marble Canyon. Detached from the rest of the state by the Colorado River, and left to its own devices, the Arizona Strip retains its wild and remote demeanor. If you like uncluttered wilderness where nature has the last word, you'll find it in the Strip, Arizona's largely undiscovered backcountry. Check out **Cathedral Wash**, **Soap Creek Canyon** (contact the Bureau of Land Management), and **Kanab Creek Canyon** (contact the North Kaibab Ranger District).

Glen Canyon National Recreation Area (928-608-6404). You don't always need a boat to travel in this multiarmed area that follows the Colorado (Lake Powell), Escalante, and San Juan Rivers, but you should be ready for some remote adventures. Check out their web site for hiking and mountain biking routes (www.nps.gov/glca/planyourvisit). $15 for a week.

Grand Staircase–Escalante National Monument (contact the Bureau of Land Management). The cumbersome name comes from two of the monument's natural features: a geological stairway of different-colored cliffs—the Vermilion, White, Grey, and Pink Cliffs—that eventually rise 5,500 feet to the rim of Bryce Canyon in the west; and the Escalante River, which flows in the monument's eastern end. In between the monument's namesake features sprawls the 800,000-acre Kaiparowits Plateau, which you see on the north side of Lake Powell. The plateau's austere landscape, dotted by juniper trees sometimes well over 1,000 years old, hides an extravagant lode of fossils—one of the planet's best examples of continuous late Cretaceous terrestrial life. If you don't want to explore the monument, you can get an idea of the rich cache at the Bureau of Land Management's **Big Water Visitor Center** (435-675-3200), 100 Upper Revolution Way, Big Water, UT. Open mid-Mar.–mid-Nov., daily 8–5; closed in winter.

Lake Powell Escalante Tours (928-445-9099), 18 N. Lake Powell Blvd., offers a 4-hour drive into this extravagantly wild landscape to see tropical shale embedded with shark teeth, the ancient Coal Pits smoldering with underground coal fires, and lunch atop Rachel's Knoll overlooking Lake Powell. $111.40 per person includes lunch.

✳ Lodging

OLD QUARTER HISTORIC HOTELS 🐾 **Bashful Bob's** (928-645-3919), 750 S. Navajo. Bashful Bob Wombacher has kept his rates the same for the 30-something years he's owned this historic property. Quiet, clean, and simple, each unit has a kitchen, private bathroom, large sitting area, and complimentary WiFi. The property is popular with European travelers, many of whom are repeat guests; reservations are recommended. $39 for two people.

🐾 **Lulu's Sleep-Ezee** (928-608-0273 or 800-553-6211), 105 8th Ave. Lulu Cannon completely overhauled the property into four pleasantly decorated units she keeps super-clean. The common patio has a gas grill, and the office computer gives you access to the Internet. Each room has a private bathroom and cable TV. $45–59.

RESORTS & INNS 🐾 🐾 ♂ ⅙ **Days Inn** (928-645-2800), 961 N. US 89. This franchise has pleasant rooms with great views. Double, queen, or king beds, along with free WiFi, refrigerator, coffeemaker, free local calls, and free continental breakfast. The property has a swimming pool and business center. Small pets are okay with a fee. $60–75.

🐾 ♂ ⅙ **Lake Powell Resort** (800-528-6154), 100 Lake Shore Dr. A room at this resort is the closest you can come to sleeping on the lake without being waterborne. Ask for a lake-view room. The property has two pools and two restaurants, along with a recreational lawn area, walking path, lounge, gift shop, sports shop, fitness center, and boat tour reservation station. Each room has a mini fridge, cable TV, coffee, and patio or balcony. Pets $20 a night. $59–159; $200 for suites.

🐾 🐾 ⅙ **Quality Inn** (928-645-8851), 287 N. Lake Powell. Owned and operated by Navajo, the motel has little touches that reflect the traditions of the Navajo people. For instance, each room has a packet of cedar herb to assist you in achieving serenity. The **Blue Corn restaurant** serves traditional Navajo fare. The property includes a pool, guest laundry, and business center; rooms have complimentary high-speed Internet. A hot buffet breakfast is included with your room. $74–124.

ARIZONA STRIP LODGES 🐾 **Lees Ferry Lodge** (928-355-2230), HC67—Box 1, Marble Canyon. This old stonework building fits in perfectly with the remote landscape. Furnished with the anglers who frequent the Colorado River in mind, the interiors are rustic but homey. You won't find a television in the rooms, but you will have a cozy Franklin stove to add a warm glow. Also, beds have down pillows. The Vermilion Cliffs Bar & Grille (see *Dining Out*) is on the premises. Reservations are advised, as rooms fill up quickly. $50.07–95.87.

✿ **Marble Canyon Lodge** (928-355-2225 or 800-726-1789). If the Arizona Strip has a cosmopolitan area, it would be Marble Canyon. This historic hotel right by the Navajo Bridge gets busy with rafters awaiting, or decompressing from, their rafting trips. The property includes a gas station, restaurant, and laundry facilities. Rooms have TV but no phones. Lodge rates: summer $55–75, winter $50–65.

✳ Where to Eat

DINING OUT **Bella Napolli/Italias** (928-645-2706), 810 N. Navajo. Open for lunch Mon.–Fri. 11–2, dinner daily at 5. Classic Italian fare that's consistently good. The daily dinner specials (available until 5:30) are worth an early meal, but the Italian buffet (salad bar, soups, pastas and sauces, pizza, and desserts) is the big draw. Lunch $6.99, dinner $9.99.

Fiesta Mexicana (928-645-4082), 125 S. Powell. Open daily 11–9. This regional franchise serves classic Mexican fare that is reliably tasty. They are known for the best margaritas in town. Portions are large, so come hungry. Entrées $7.25–16.95.

Rainbow Room (928-645-2433), Lake Powell Resort, 100 Lakeshore Dr. The restaurant has the best views in town, with a set of large windows showing off Lake Powell and surrounding cliffs. Inside, chef Brandon Schubert presents the best fine dining in town as well. His environmentally sensitive menu with southwestern accents includes local and organic produce. The opera-singer-turned-award-winning-chef sometimes breaks out his baritone voice, which grabs the attention of the diners. And a few times a year he puts the menus aside, does what he wants, and really wows diners. Entrées $12.95–25.95.

Vermilion Cliffs Bar & Grille (928-355-2230). Located about 5 miles west of Navajo Bridge, and practically in the middle of nowhere. The eating place of choice for fly-fishers offers dependable food in large portions, served up by attentive staff. An extensive selection of beer (about 100 different brands) is available. Servers are sometimes more colorful than the cliffs the restaurant was named for. Entrées $5.95–15.95.

EATING OUT **LeChee Flea Market**. Located about 3 miles south of AZ 98 on about Coppermine Rd. Open Sat. 9–3, and sometimes Sun. As the saying goes, "You haven't lived until you've tasted a Rez Dog" (that being a hot dog, bratwurst, or Polish sausage wrapped in frybread dough, then deep-fried). You can get one at reservation flea markets, such as the one here at LeChee (pronounced le-*chee*-ee), as well as mutton and peppers on frybread, and tamales.

✿ **Ranch House Grille** (928-645-1420), 819 N. Navajo Dr. Open daily 6–3. The best place in town for breakfast serves up tasty, freshly prepared egg dishes and pancakes all day, and they are (correctly) known for their huevos rancheros. Lunch (salads, sandwiches, and burgers) is decent. Breakfast $6.25–11.75, lunch $6.25–7.75.

✿ **The Sandwich Place** (928-645-5267), 635 Elm. Open Mon.–Fri.

10:30–8:30, Sat. 10:30–3 and 5–8:30. Serving "world famous sandwiches" and "cheeseburgers that change your life," this local favorite has a reputation that knows no bounds. The pepper steak sure is a winner, as is the pastrami burger (hamburger with onions, pastrami, and melted provolone as well as a host of condiments). Old favorites, such as BLTs, charbroiled chicken, and hot dogs, are available as well. $3.50–7.

✳ Selective Shopping

Blair's Trading Post (928-645-3008 or 800-644-3008), 626 N. Navajo. The Blair family has traded with the Navajo for more than half a century, and their trading post presents some of the Navajo Nation's best, one-of-a-kind arts and crafts, such as jewelry, baskets, rugs, and kachinas. The founders' collection, displayed in a separate area of the trading post, can be seen upon request.

✳ Special Events

July: **Hometown Fourth of July Celebration at City Memorial Park** (928-645-2741) has vendors, food, and entertainment all day, then fireworks at night.

September: **Powell Symposium: Exploring the Colorado Plateau** (928-645-9498). Lectures, field trips, receptions, and Colorado River topics.

October: The **Pumpkin Festival** (928-660-3403) features the largest gathering of carved pumpkins in the whole state.

November: **Page Lake Powell Hot Air Balloon Regatta** (928-645-2431) has balloon liftoffs every day of the weekend celebration and features a street fair and balloon glow on Lake Powell Boulevard on Saturday.

December: **Festival of Lights Parade** (928-660-3403) has a parade of decorated floats and Christmas lights.

NAVAJO NATION

The Navajo Nation is full of long views and a wealth of open spaces; it's one of the most charismatic landscapes in the state, and it inspires visits from people around the world. Its inhabitants, able to twist poetry with absurdity, are just as endearing, and famous for their sense of humor, artistry, and complex mythology. They call this high-desert country stretched between Four Sacred Mountains in three states (Arizona, Colorado, and New Mexico) the Glittering World or the Fourth Dimension. In Arizona this region stretches from Page eastward to the New Mexico border. On the south end, it curls just south of Cameron around the Coconino National Forest east of Flagstaff. It's a redrock wonderland full of shifting sands, magnificent buttes and mesas, hues and shadows that change with the whim of the sun, and legends wonderful enough to celebrate humanity and dark enough to raise the hair on the back of your neck. Those who live on the Nation say all these legends are true. Once you travel the Nation, you'll have a chance to decide for yourself.

GUIDANCE You can contact **Navajo Tourism** (928-871-6436) for general information about the Navajo Nation. Obtain permits for hiking, camping, and back country travel from **Navajo Parks & Recreation Dept.** (928-871-6647) in Window Rock; **Cameron Visitor Center** (928-679-2303), located at the junction of US 89 and AZ 64; or **Antelope Canyon Park Office** (928-698-2808) in Page. For boating, fishing, or hunting permits, call **Navajo Fish & Wildlife** (928-871-6451). Tribal offices are open Mon.–Fri. 8–5.

GETTING THERE *By car:* You can approach the Nation, located in the northeastern corner of the state, via US 89 from Flagstaff in the south and Utah in the north. From Page, take AZ 98. From Colorado, take US 160; from New Mexico, US 64 to US 160.

WHEN TO COME The best time to visit is May through October. Spring is windy and fickle, and winter brings poetic moments when snow covers the redrock cliffs.

MEDICAL EMERGENCY Dial 911.

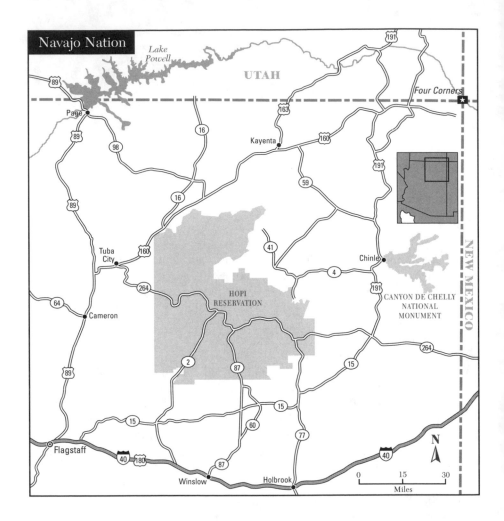

✳ To See

Code Talker Museum. Located in the Burger King restaurant in Kayenta. An unusual museum in an unlikely location, this collection of memorabilia pays homage to the Native soldiers who created a radio code from the Navajo language (spoken, never written) for the U.S. military during World War II. The code was never broken, and historians credit the Navajo Code Talkers for helping to win World War II. Outside, the fast-food spot has historic exhibits and a hogan used by early inhabitants. Free.

Diné College (928-724-6654), 1 Circle Dr., Tsaile. This school's curriculum honors the philosophy of Sá'ah Naagháí Bik'eh Hózhóón—the Diné tradition in which humanity lives in harmony with the natural world and the universe. Of particular interest is the six-story hogan-shaped **Ned Hatathli Cultural Center**. This structure houses the Hatathli Museum and Gallery, with exhibits of Native American culture as well as sales of authentic Navajo arts and crafts, and the Diné College Bookstore. Free.

Dinosaur tracks. Located in Moenave, 5 miles west of Tuba City. This natural site contains many lower Jurassic theropod tracks left around 200 million years ago, along with eggs and fossilized bones. Free.

⊘ ♿ **Explore Navajo Interactive Museum** (928-283-4545), Quality Inn, Main and Monave Ave., Tuba City. In 2002 the Navajo Nation presented the Discover Navajo People of the Fourth World Exhibit at the Winter Olympics in Salt Lake City. The tribe has now moved this exhibit to the Quality Inn complex in Tuba City. Displays include the Emergence (the Navajo creation story); the Clan Wheel (the family ancestry lines of the Navajo); a full-sized hogan and sweat lodge; rugs from across the Navajo Nation, each depicting its region's unique pattern; Seasons of the Navajo, explaining the traditional life of a Navajo family; and the Navajo Code Talker Museum, complete with small theater, authentic memorabilia, and original photos from the National Archives in Washington, DC. The museum also has interactive displays on topics such as local shepherds and weavers, and an explanation of the Diné clan systems. $9 adults, $7 seniors, $6 children under 12; children under 6 are free.

⊘ **Four Corners Monument** (928-871-6647). Located at the northeast tip of Arizona on US 160. Open daily June–Aug., 7 AM–8 PM; Sep.–May, 8–5. You can stand in Arizona, New Mexico, Utah, and Colorado at once here on the brass and granite marker where the corners of the four states meet. Navajo vendors sell handmade jewelry, crafts, and traditional foods around the monument. Inside the visitor center you can watch Navajo artisans work their crafts. $3 per person.

CULTURAL DIFFERENCES ON THE NAVAJO NATION

To avoid committing a faux pas while traveling the Nation, be aware of the following cultural differences:

- Among many Navajo, eye contact is considered impolite. Even though you have their full attention, courteous Navajo will often look down or away.
- Navajo are generally taught not to talk too much, be loud, or be forward with strangers. Engaging conversation is not their mode of operation with strangers.
- If talking is not encouraged, touching can be downright disrespectful to a Navajo. Even a strong handshake is offensive.
- Though Navajo do not own the land on which they live, they do have tribal rights. Exploring off the pavement (on foot or in a vehicle) is not allowed without a Navajo escort or permit.
- Taking a photo of a Navajo is incorrect without permission. And a small fee is expected.
- Offering to buy the jewelry a Navajo is wearing is considered gauche.
- Alcohol is not permitted on the reservation.
- The Navajo Nation observes Daylight Saving Time Mar.–Oct.

Little Colorado River Gorge. Located in a Navajo tribal park on AZ 64, 10 miles west of US 89. The Little Colorado River travels all the way from Mount Baldy in eastern Arizona's White Mountains to the Colorado River. Here, the river leaves its meandering ways behind as it plunges 2,000 feet in just 30 miles. From the overlook, the gorge presents a spectacular scene of finely layered upper limestone cliffs contrasted with ruddy sandstone below. Free.

Hubbell Trading Post National Historic Site (928-755-3475). Usually located along major highways and near chapter houses (the Navajo equivalent of a town hall), trading posts run the gamut from loosely stocked grocery stores to bustling shops with groceries, dry goods, crafts, restaurants, and gasoline. The Hubbell Trading Post, founded in 1876, remains one of the significant trading posts on the reservation and a National Historic Site. Named for Indian trader John Hubbell, the post has changed little in the last century. Old wooden floors still creak vociferously; colorful rows of foodstuffs line the shelves; frying pans, saddles, and handwoven baskets hang from the ceiling; piles of handwoven rugs are carelessly stacked in a separate room. Weavers work on woolen rugs in yet another room, their wooden picks tapping each strand into place with several quick thuds. You can purchase items here, or just admire how little time and traditions have changed. $2 per person.

Navajo Nation Administration Center (928-871-6417), Window Rock. You can slip into the meeting chambers and view a council meeting from special seating around the perimeter. A Plexiglas barrier just inside the double front doors shields noises when you enter the chambers to prevent distraction. Call to check when the council meets or to schedule a tour of the chambers.

Window Rock Tribal Park and Veteran's Memorial (928-871-6647), located near the Navajo Nation Administration Center. Open daily 8–5. You can view the mystical redstone arch for which the capital is named here, just behind the building that houses the Navajo Nation headquarters and other government offices. Recently a Veterans Memorial was added at the base of Window Rock to honor the many Navajo who served in the U.S. military. The park holds a number of symbolic features: a circular path outlining the four cardinal directions, 16 angled steel pillars with the names of war veterans, and a healing sanctuary—used for reflection and solitude—that features a fountain made of sandstone.

THE NAVAJO ARE RENOWNED FOR THEIR WOVEN RUGS.

Also see **An Evening with the Navajo** in "Page and Lake Powell."

PARKS AND MONUMENTS Canyon de Chelly (520-674-5500). Located 3 miles east of Chinle on Navajo 7. The second largest canyon on the Colorado Plateau, this deep, soulful gorge

Monument Valley (435-727-5874). Located 7 miles off US 160 at the Utah border. Open daily 7–7 Apr.–Sep., 8–5 Oct.–Mar. Before the Navajo took up residence on this land several generations ago, the San Juan Band of Paiute who frequented the area in AD 1300 also considered it sacred. They called it Valley Amid the Rocks and attributed supernatural powers to the area.

Not a valley, as its current and former Ute names imply, the landscape more aptly fits the Navajo nomenclature Tse' Bii' Ndzisgaii, or "changing of the rock." From the time an ancient ocean covered Monument Valley millions of years ago, erosional forces of wind and water have shaped this land.

The soft shales, siltstones, and slabs of sandstone here have eroded over time into pinnacles, spires, and buttes unique to Monument Valley. Iron oxide colored the rocks with hues of red, and manganese oxide painted black streaks called desert varnish on precipitous walls. The distinctive formations create a kinetic atmosphere where monoliths point to a turquoise sky, arches hollow out rock walls, and erosion-carved formations turn anthropomorphic.

Self-guided trails: The only opportunities to explore the landscape unfettered are on the 17-mile unpaved but graded road, on which you can drive a passenger car or mountain bike, and the 3.2-mile nonmotorized Wildcat Trail that loops around West Mitten Butte.

Tours: **Roy Black** (928-309-8834) provides guided 4x4 open-air, jeep, horseback, and hiking tours. At **Sacred Mountain Tours** (435-727-3218 or 928-380-4527), manager Leroy Teeasyatoh says, simply, "Just tell me what you need and I can arrange it." This traditional Navajo runs an excellent operation and is loaded with information and traditional lore. Go by jeep, horse, or hiking. Photo tours bring you to magical places in an already phantasmagorical land.

EXPLORING A SLOT CANYON ON THE NAVAJO NATION.

(pronounced *de SHAY*) in the northeast corner of Arizona lies almost at the center of the whole Navajo Nation. Ruins and rock art dating from AD 350 to 1300 appear in canyon crevices, and galleries of cottonwood trees line the stream that shimmers along the canyon floor. Some call the 26-mile-long canyon Arizona's other Grand Canyon because of its large size, but the comparison stops there. The canyon does not vaunt itself as a recreational area to the world like the Grand Canyon. Rather, it keeps a private profile. Outside the 1.25-mile-long maintained trail that travels from the rim down to White House Ruins, the canyon's interior is off-limits without a Navajo escort. Still, this canyon exudes enough of its rich atmosphere to inundate anyone peering from overlooks along its rim drives. And step below the dramatic 1,000-foot terra-cotta walls streaked with desert varnish to enter another world where tradition flourishes amid the flow of tourists and modern civilization.

There are no telephone or electrical lines in the canyon; sheep tending and farming remain the resident Indians' principal means of support. A spindly monolith known as Spider Rock remains a favorite of Indian parents, who threaten to deposit unruly children there for the mythic Spider Woman to deal with. Free.

Motorized tours: Visitors, strictly forbidden to enter the canyon without a Navajo guide, have several options. Four- and six-wheel-drive jeep tours head daily into the canyon from the **Thunderbird Lodge**. You can also hire personal guides for your own four-wheel-drive vehicle at $20 an hour at the visitor center information desk. **De Chelly Tours** (928-674-3772) will take you in your vehicle ($20 per hour, 3-hour minimum) or theirs ($125 per hour).

Horseback tours: **Twin Trails Tours** (928-674-8425), North Rim Dr., 8 miles north of the visitor center. Two-hour to multiday rides are available; call for prices. **Totsonii Ranch** (928-755-6209), located 1.5 miles past the Spider Rock viewpoint turnoff on South Rim Dr., takes you to the base of Spider Rock, 1,000 feet below the canyon's rim. Call for prices, reservations, and questions.

Mystery Valley. Located just south of Monument Valley and open only by tour (see the *Monument Valley* sidebar). This collection of swirling sandstone formations, arches, and Indian signs presents an intriguing tour. The House of Many

Hands, where whitewashed hand imprints covered the lower walls of a ruin, gave the valley its name. No one knows why the prints are there. Also, Mystery Valley is said to be haunted. The US government buried soldiers here; robbers dug up some of the graves before they were finally moved. In the night Mystery Valley is said to sometimes echo with howling from the horses of these dead soldiers.

Navajo National Monument (928-672-2700). Located at the end of AZ 564 off US 160. Open daily 8–5; till 7 May 15–Labor Day. Most pueblo villages in Tsegi Canyon stood on its floor or mesa tops. This park's Betatakin and Keet Seel ruins, however, were built in alcoves and survived the seven centuries of erosion that reduced unprotected ruins to rubble. You can visit the ruins via two trails. The visitor center has exhibits on ancient Pueblo Indians, video presentations, and books for sale. Free.

Rainbow Bridge National Monument, Navajo Parks & Recreation Department (928-871-8636). Sacred to the Navajo and the largest natural bridge in the world, Rainbow Bridge spans the teal-green waters at the confluence of Forbidding and Bridge Canyons off the Colorado River. Navajo legend says the bridge, actually a petrified rainbow, allowed a war god to cross the tumultuous, storm-racked canyon. Since the pooling of Lake Powell, most people access the national monument via a tour boat on Lake Powell. Two trails lead to the tiny monument (see *Hiking*).

RUINS Although ruins lie cached in alcoves all over the Nation, you must have a guide to approach them in most cases. You can travel without a guide to White House ruins in Canyon de Chelly (south rim) and Betatikin and Keet Seel ruins in Navajo National Monument. For an in-depth experience, Crow Canyon Archaeological Park (970-565-8975 or 800-422-8975) schedules several-day guided tours on the Navajo Nation led by informed archaeologists.

SCENIC DRIVES Because the Navajo Nation contains some of the most scenic landscapes in the world, just about every paved highway here constitutes a scenic drive. The drive from Page to Kayenta on **AZ 98** (Navajo Mountain Scenic Road) passes the cream of the canyonlands on the reservation, where the sienna cliffs of Kaibito show off an alluring canyon system and unique formations. Deep gorges, twisted by the elements, hold well preserved Indian ruins along **US 160** between Tuba City and Kayenta. Every shade of red shows itself in the domes, mesas, and buttes on the way to Monument Valley on **US 163**. At the town of **Cottonwood** (8 miles west of US 191 on Navajo 4), an unmarked northern turnoff travels the exquisite rainbow colors of the Navajo backcountry via a rugged paved road riddled with potholes that presents a combination of multi-colored cliffs, the sweet smell of piñon, and unabashed quiet. Paved **Navajo 64** and **Navajo 7** travel the north and south, respectively, rims of Canyon de Chelly. Scenic pull-offs provide good spots for photos.

✳ To Do

HIKING & BACKPACKING The Navajo Nation's combination of remoteness and scenery sealed in an envelope of quiet is most inspiring. For easy to moderate day hikes, check out the **Wildcat Trail** in Monument Valley and **White House Trail** in the Canyon de Chelly. For an up-close experience with the canyon country, plan a backpack on the north and south **Rainbow Trail**, which travels the Rainbow Plateau to Rainbow Bridge National Monument. Hidden amid an intricate maze of canyons, a hike to the bridge presents a beautiful, but challenging, 2- to 4-day round-trip backpack for experienced hikers. Contact Navajo Parks & Recreation for the required $5-per-day permits.

HORSEBACK TRAIL RIDES **Navajo Country Guided Trail Rides** (435-727-3390), mile marker 403 on US 163, 7 miles north of Kayenta. Evelyn Yazzie Jensen and Gunnar Jensen offer a range of opportunities to experience the Nation on horseback, from hourly to several-day rides. You can bring your own horses or ride theirs. Overnight rides include satisfying and good meals. $25 an hour, $125 a day, $285 overnight.

✳ Lodging

🐾 ♿ **Anasazi Inn—Tsegi Canyon** (928-697-3793), P.O. Box 1543, Kayenta. Located 11 miles east of US 163 in Tsegi. The scenery surrounding this turquoise-roofed hotel is spectacular. The rooms adjoining the lobby are your best bet; and many have views into Tsegi Canyon. Rooms have king or double beds, cable TV, and air-conditioning. The property includes grills and picnic tables at the rim of the canyon, which makes for a very special outdoor barbecue. $66–109.

🐾 ✿ ♿ **Gouldings Lodge** (435-727-3231), Monument Valley, Utah. It was Henry Goulding—owner of a trading post near Monument Valley—who opened the door of this stunning area to the world. Dealing with the Indians on everyday matters from buying their goods to acting as liaison between them and the federal government, Goulding knew how hard the Depression hit the area. When he heard that director John Ford planned to film a classic western starring John Wayne on location, Goulding grew determined to make that location Monument Valley and set out for Hollywood in 1938. Ford's staff told Goulding he might wait days before he could meet with the busy director. "I've camped out in worse places," Goulding replied, hauling out his bedroll. "I've got something you want to see, and I'm not leaving until you look at it." Goulding's verve got him an immediate audience with Ford. The "something" he had to show Ford—a portfolio of photos of Monument Valley taken by Josef Muench—wowed Ford, who eventually filmed *Stagecoach* there. Ford returned to film eight more movies in the area.

The lodge, with its comfortable rooms and tasteful decorations, has a museum memorializing Hollywood's role in the area. All rooms have views of Monument Valley as well as private balcony, cable TV, heat and air-conditioning, and mini refrigerator. The property has a year-round heated pool, fitness room, and free Internet and WiFi. $73–170 includes tickets to the museum and Earth Spirit show. Family suites and houses are available for large families.

♥ 占 **Hampton Inn** (928-697-3170), US 160, Kayenta. Built adobe style with rustic earth-toned interiors and southwestern-style appointments to meld with the Navajo Nation, this property has a walking trail, outdoor pool, and park-and-fly amenities. Rooms have TV, air-conditioning, and coffeemaker. A continental breakfast bar is included with room. The Kayenta Trading Company Gift Shop has an excellent variety of fine Native American arts, jewelry, and crafts. $66–109.

♠ **Many Farms High School Inn** (928-781-6362), P.O. Box 307, Many Farms. Open June–Aug. daily; Sep.–May, weekdays only. This School-to-Work Project turned a vacant high school into a bargain-priced inn. You'll find shared bathrooms, a game room, a public kitchen, and a TV room. The clean, simple rooms have two single beds, mini refrigerator, vanity, sofa, alarm clock, and plenty of closet and drawer space. $30 double.

占 **Navajo Nation Quality Inn** (928-871-4108), 48 W. AZ 264, Window Rock; and (928-283-4545), Main and Monave Ave., Tuba City. Owned and operated by the Navajo Nation. A franchise classic, but with Diné influences—both properties have restaurants featuring local native foods like Navajo taco and mutton stew, along with Mexican and American foods. The Tuba City version includes an exciting new museum with exhibits first presented to the world at the 2002 Winter Olympics. Rooms have double beds, satellite TV, and high-speed Internet. Breakfast buffet included. $54–132.

Thunderbird Lodge (928-674-5841 or 800-679-2473), P.O. Box 548, Chinle. Located 0.5 mile from the Canyon de Chelly Visitor Center. This historic property stands on the grounds of an old trading post and has remarkable character. Sprawling cottonwood trees, planted by the Civilian Conservation Corps in the 1930s, provide shady spots to relax under. There's a restaurant and gift shop with a great assortment of Navajo rugs. The rooms feature rustic furniture, Navajo paintings, full private bath, air-conditioning/central heating, telephone, and cable TV. You can arrange tours into the monument from the lodge. $65 Oct.–Mar., $101–106 Apr.–Sep.

✳ Where to Eat

DINING OUT Ja'di' tooh (928-645-5900), Antelope Point Marina, located just east of Page off AZ 98. Open for dinner 5–10. This new restaurant, whose Navajo name means "watering point for antelope," has a unique foundation—Lake Powell. The floating 27,000-square-foot concrete restaurant-bar (equivalent in size to 1 acre) is the first structure of its type in the country. Like a floating barge, the structure rises and falls with the water. Its site on the lake means you get awesome views of the surrounding sandstone cliffs. This is also the only establishment that serves alcohol on the Navajo Nation. Lunch entrées include a cultural collection of sandwiches and salads. Dinners include fish, chops, steaks, and specialty wood-fired pizzas, some made with frybread crusts. Lunch $9–11.50, dinner $16–31.

Stagecoach Dining Room, Gouldings Lodge (see *Lodging*). Open daily for breakfast, lunch, and dinner. With panoramic windows circling the dining area, every table has a beautiful view. You can get a decent meal here, and the Navajo tacos are some of the best around. $8–20.

EATING OUT Choohostso Indian Market. Located on the northwest corner of AZ 264 and Navajo 12 in Window Rock. There's a variety of vendors here with menus that include mutton stew, ribs, and sandwiches; corn stew; dumpling stew; squash stew; frybread; Navajo tacos; and Navajo burgers. $4.95–8.95.

Shepherd's Eyes Courtyard Coffee Shop Lounge (928-697-3368), 0.25 mile west of US 163 on US 160. Open Sun.–Thu. 7–7 (until 2 AM Fri.–Sat.). The doughnut-shaped building has several things going on at different times. Mostly, it's a coffee/espresso lounge where you can hook up to the Internet via computers ($3 for 15 minutes) or WiFi ($5). During the day Navajo set up shop and sell crafts. On weekends you may hear country-western or rock bands, or run across a powwow. Finally, you can always get traveler's information on what's going on in the Nation. Free (entertainment $3–10).

Thunderbird Lodge Café (928-674-5844), Thunderbird Motel in Canyon de Chelly. Open daily 6:30 AM–8 PM. Don't let the cafeteria-style service put you off. The Navajo dish out some tasty food here, ranging from traditional favorites to Continental fare. Authentic artwork (available for sale) crafted by local Native peoples adorns the walls. Entrées $6.50–10.

✳ Special Events

May: **Native American Arts Auction** at Hubbell Trading Post National Historic Site (928-755-3475) presents a collection of historic and contemporary Native American arts for auction; food vendors on the grounds.

June: **Sheep Is Life Celebration** (928-729-2037) in Tsaile has pre-celebration workshops, Elder and Youth Day, hands-on demonstrations, a Churro sheep show, rug auction, and presentations. The **Navajo Nation Museum Music Festival** (928-871-7941) at Navajo Nation Museum in Window Rock presents traditional and contemporary Native American music, arts, and crafts, along with vendors, book signings, and other activities.

July: **Navajo Nation Fourth of July PRCA Rodeo & Youth Celebration** (928-871-6647) in Window Rock features the Professional Rodeo Cowboys Association (PRCA) Rodeo, a carnival, traditional Navajo song and dance, concerts, arts and crafts, and fireworks.

September: **Navajo Nation Fair** (928-871-6646). The world's largest American Indian fair and multisanctioned Indian rodeo with traditional Navajo song and dance, intertribal powwow, Navajo food, concerts, parade, children's day, Miss Navajo Pageant, a fine arts competition and exhibit, agricultural and commercial exhibits, a home arts competition and exhibit, amusement rides, and a free barbecue.

GRAND CANYON NATIONAL PARK—NORTH RIM

O f the five million visitors to Grand Canyon National Park each year, only one million make it to the North Rim. When you take the extra few hours you need to visit this remote, but altogether wonderful, side of the canyon, you get a more personal experience. Like an island adrift from the rest of the state, separated 8 to 16 miles from the rest of Arizona by the Grand Canyon, the North Rim offers an outback feel and—especially in the North Kaibab National Forest—experience.

Since it's about 1,000 feet higher than the South Rim, the North Rim is cooler in summer, more colorful when autumn leaves turn, and definitely snowier in winter. Spring might not happen until May, when this side of the national park opens each year.

The North Rim doesn't have as much flash or as many activities as the South, but you will find more hiking trails above the rim, more scenic drives, fewer people milling about, no congestion, and a number of primitive camping spots. If you really want to give humanity the slip, head into the North Kaibab National Forest via unpaved road. The farther west of AZ 67 the more remote life gets. Just make sure you have enough provisions. You may not see anyone for days in these parts away from the rim.

GUIDANCE On the way to the North Rim, the **North Kaibab Plateau Visitors Center and Grand Canyon Association Bookstore** (928-643-7298) in Jacob Lake can give you information on the canyon. Inside the national park, the **North Rim Visitor Center** (open 8–6), located near Grand Canyon Lodge, has park information, interpretive exhibits, and rangers to answer any questions you may have. *The Guide*, the park's newspaper, contains current information including schedules of tours, sunrise/sunset times, and seasonal points of interest.

Get permits and information on backcountry use at **North Rim Backcountry Office**, located 11.5 miles south of the north entrance (open 8–noon and 1–5); by writing **Backcountry Information Center**, P.O. Box 129, Grand Canyon, AZ 86023; or by logging onto www.nps.gov/grca (click on *The Guide* for seasonal information about the North Rim). Contact **North Kaibab Ranger District**

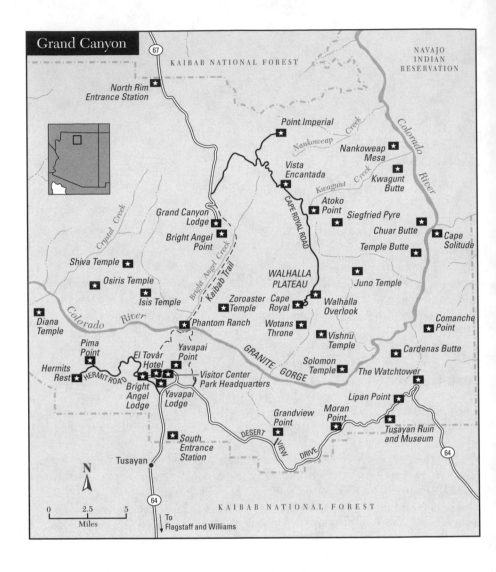

Grand Canyon

(928-643-7395), 430 S. Main St., Fredonia, for information about hiking, camping, and back roads in the North Kaibab National Forest.

FEES The park entrance fee is $25 per private vehicle; $12 per individual on foot, bicycle, or motorcycle. This fee, good for 7 days, includes both rims. The national forest does not charge user fees.

GETTING THERE Only one paved road leads to the Grand Canyon's North Rim: AZ 67.

GETTING AROUND You can take a shuttle from the lodge to the North Kaibab Trailhead for $6; it costs $4 for each additional person. **Transcanyon Shuttle** (928-638-2820) will take you to the South Rim for $65 one-way, $110 round-trip.

WHEN TO COME Because of its high elevation and propensity for snow, the North Rim season runs May 15–Oct. 15. The park remains open *for day use only* when the weather permits after October 16; however, visitor services and facilities remain closed. When AZ 67 (the road leading to the rim from Jacob Lake) closes (sometimes without notice) due to heavy snow, it does not reopen until mid-May.

MEDICAL EMERGENCY Dial 911.

✳ To See

SCENIC DRIVES The highway leading to the park (AZ 67), alone, makes a great scenic drive. The sprawling meadows and dense mixed conifer-aspen forests—the area's predominant natural feature—give a great sightseeing experience. But there's more.

The 11-mile drive to **Point Imperial**, the highest point on either rim, passes through a burn area to spectacular views of Mount Hayden, Saddle Mountain, and Marble Canyon. The 23-mile road to **Cape Royal** has a variety of landscapes, from open meadows full of watchable wildlife to cloistered old-growth forests. You can stop at several awesome viewpoints of the canyon along the way to the **Angel's Window overlook**, where California condors like to soar at road's end. If you have a four-wheel-drive vehicle, check out the 18-mile road to **Point Sublime**, considered one of the most breathtaking panoramas anywhere.

✳ To Do

BICYCLING You can ride your bicycle on paved and unpaved roads in the park. The Kaibab National Forest has a large number of unpaved roads perfect for mountain or tour bikes. The highway to the North Rim, AZ 67, is one of the best road biking routes in northern Arizona.

HIKING & BACKPACKING You can hike a wide range of trails here. The rimside **Transept Trail** is an easy trek of 1.5 miles from Grand Canyon Lodge to the North Rim Campground. The 5-mile **Widforss Trail** travels around the rim, while the rigorous 14-mile **Nankoweap Trail** treks to the Colorado River. Spending the night below the rim requires a backcountry permit: $10 per person and $5 per night.

For a remote hiking experience, check out trails on the Kaibab National Forest. The **Rainbow Rim Trail** follows

A BACKPACKER NEGOTIATES THE CANYON.

along the rim for about 18 miles, through forests and meadows, giving glimpses of the Grand Canyon (for free). The **Jump-Up-Nail Trail** and **Snake Gulch Trail** each offers a wild and remote hike in unusual canyon country.

HORSEBACK & MULE RIDES **Grand Canyon Trail Rides** (435-679-8665). From 1-hour rides on the rim to half- to full-day rides on the rim or into the canyon. $30–125.

RANGER PROGRAMS A number of ranger-led talks take place almost every day in the park. Consult *The Guide* for a schedule.

✳ Lodging

Inside the park
♿ **Grand Canyon Lodge** (888-297-2757; outside the US, 303-297-2757; same-day reservations, 928-638-2631). The only lodging in the park, this National Historic Landmark was designed to match its physical environment with limestone walls and timbered ceilings. The lodge has motel rooms and cabins, dining room, sunroom, café, saloon, gift shop, and laundry facilities. All rooms and cabins have double or queen beds, shower or bath, and telephone. Children under 16 can stay in the same room as an adult for free. Reservations recommended. $101–134.

A WISP OF A FIGURE, DISTORTED BY SPEED, SLIDES DOWN ELVES CHASM.

CAMPGROUNDS **North Rim Campground** (800-365-2267; outside the US, 301-722-1257; www.reservations.nps.gov). No hookups or dump sites. Stays are limited to 7 days. $18 per night.

Outside the park
Jacob Lake Inn (928-643-7232). Located 45 miles north of the North Rim. Open since 1923, the inn has a rustic side to it. The property has motel rooms and cabins as well as a restaurant, grocery store, and gas station. Rooms have two double beds or one king, shower, heater, and sitting area; some units have cable television, phone, and Internet access. Cabins have a double, queen, or king bed; shower; heater; and a sitting area on a deck. Rooms $100–142, cabins $85–130.

✳ Where to Eat

DINING OUT Grand Canyon Lodge Dining Room (928-638-2611, ext. 160). Open daily May 15–Oct. 15, for breakfast 6:30–10:30, lunch 11:30–2:30, dinner 4:45–9:45. You get a nice dining experience here with Grand Canyon views. Breakfast ranges from basic egg and griddle plates to a hot and cold buffet. Lunch features salads and sandwiches with a variety of burgers and wraps. The dinner menu includes pastas, aged beef, roasts, and fish with a western influence. Reservations are required for dinner, and the park recommends you make them one to two months prior to arrival. Breakfast $5.15–8.95, lunch $6.95–10.35, dinner $13.90–20.25.

Jacob Lake Inn Dining Room, Jacob Lake Inn. Open May–Oct., 6 AM–9 PM; Nov.–Apr., 8–8. Meals are decent here, made with fresh ingredients. Their fresh-baked bread shows up on breakfast and lunch items. They serve a good hamburger, and the desserts (pies, specialty cakes, and cookies) are house-made. Entrées $5.95–12.95.

EATING OUT Deli in the Pines, Grand Canyon Lodge. Open daily 7 AM–9 PM. Grab a muffin or sandwich for the trail, snack on a hot dog, or order a whole pizza. The kind of convenience and comfort food you richly deserve after a day on the trail. $2–20.

GRAND CANYON NATIONAL PARK—SOUTH RIM

"There's this thing called *canyon magic*," a riverboat pilot named Okie said as he leaned back on his elbow and watched the Colorado River course peacefully around a distant bend. "Running the rapids is a hoot. But that's just part of the reason us boatmen keep coming back. It's the canyon magic. It gets into your blood."

No matter what your experience here—looking at distant panoramas from viewpoints on the rim, hiking down the wall of the canyon from the enchanting Supai Group into the shiny dark mounds of the ancient Vishnu Schist cradling the river, riding hair-raising rapids on a rafting trip—the Grand Canyon will captivate you, just as it does all its nearly five million annual visitors.

Most of these folks never get any farther than the edge of the rim. The deeper, and longer, you go below the rim, the more the canyon gets into your blood. You don't necessarily have to travel to the heart of the canyon (the Colorado River) to know its soul. You can feel its heartbeat by hiking even a short distance on the routes between the rim and the river. Once you step below the rim, your whole perception of the grandest of canyons changes: Views become more detailed, smells more pungent; the weather varies; feelings of remoteness and isolation set in. The deeper and farther you go, the more exciting and wild your world gets. That's all part of the canyon's magic.

GUIDANCE **Grand Canyon Park Headquarters** (928-638-7888) will connect you to the right extension. The web site www.nps.gov/grca has a wealth of information. *The Guide*, the park's newspaper, contains current information including schedules of tours, sunrise/sunset times, and seasonal points of interest. You can obtain permits and information on backcountry use at the **Backcountry Information Center** in the Maswik Transportation Center (open 8–noon and 1–5) or by writing **Backcountry Information Center**, P.O. Box 129, Grand Canyon, AZ 86023. When you get to the park, head to the bustling **Canyon View Information Center** near Mather Point. From the east entrance, go to **Desert View Park Information Center**, located at Desert View Point (this center has a passport stamp cancellation station). Contact the Kaibab National

Forest's **Tusayan Ranger District** at 928-638-2443 for information about points outside the park in the national forest.

FEES The park entrance fee is $25 per private vehicle, and $12 for an individual on foot, bicycle, or motorcycle. This fee, good for 7 days, includes both the North and South Rims.

GETTING THERE *By car:* The South Rim has two entrances: the main entrance, off AZ 64 from Williams, and the east entrance, also off AZ 64 from Cameron (on US 89). *By bus:* You can take the **Greyhound Bus** (800-231-2222) to Flagstaff or Phoenix, then a shuttle via **Open Road Tours** (928-226-8060 or 877-226-8060). *By air:* The **Grand Canyon Airport** (928-638-2446) has service from Las Vegas. *By train:* From Williams, hop on the vintage **Grand Canyon Railway** (800-843-8724).

GETTING AROUND Free **shuttle buses** (pets not allowed) cover three routes indicated by different colors. The Hermits Rest Route (red) travels 8 miles from Village Route Transfer and Hermits Rest (stopping at overlooks). The utilitarian Village Route (blue) travels among the Canyon View Information Plaza, Yavapai Point, hotels, restaurants, campgrounds, and parking. The Kaibab Trail Route (green) heads from the Canyon View Information Plaza to South Kaibab Trailhead and Yaki Point.

Taxi service is available 24 hours a day from lodging to trailheads and the Grand Canyon Airport (928-638-2822 or 928-638-2631, ext. 6563).

May 15–Oct. 15, you can travel to the North Rim via the **Transcanyon Shuttle** (928-638-2820) for $65 one-way, $110 round-trip.

WHEN TO COME The busiest time in the national park is summer. Next are the spring and fall shoulder seasons (best for hiking). Winter offers a fine opportunity to miss the crowds and have a reasonably good chance to eat and sleep where you want without planning months in advance.

MEDICAL EMERGENCY The **North Country Grand Canyon Clinic** (928-638-2551) is open 8–6; Nov.–May, hours are 8–5. A dentist (928-638-2395) is available Mon. 8–4, Tue.–Wed. 7–4.

☀ **KENNELS** (928-638-0534). Open daily 7:30–5. Note that pets are not allowed on shuttles or below the rim, and must be leashed at all times in the park.

✴ To See

Bright Angel History Room, Bright Angel Lodge. This compendium of memorabilia features the Fred Harvey legacy in old menus, a carriage, pictures, and plates. Check out the geological fireplace designed by architect Mary Colter, who also designed many of the public buildings on the rim. Free.

Desert View Bookstore, Desert View Point. Open daily 9–5. Just about everything you wanted to know about the Grand Canyon, but were afraid to ask during a ranger-led talk, is available in books here.

Kolb Studio, Village Historic District, Bright Angel Trailhead. Open daily 8–6. The home and studio for Grand Canyon photographers Emory and Ellsworth Kolb goes five levels below the rim on the canyon wall. You can peruse free art exhibits and take a tour (free, but reservations are required) of the studio.

Tusayan Museum, 3 miles west of Desert View. Open daily 9–5; check winter schedule. A self-guided trail through the remains of an Ancestral Puebloan village gives you an idea of how Native Americans lived in the canyon about 800 years ago. The museum displays artifacts and art and has a gift shop.

Yavapai Observation Station (located at Yavapai Point). Built in 1928 with the goal of observing and understanding the canyon's bold geology, this station lives up to its mission. Panorama windows present unabashed views of the canyon, and a museum features geology and physiography.

SCENIC DRIVES Hermit Road allows only shuttles during most of the year (except Dec.–Feb.), but **Desert View Drive** (AZ 64) presents gorgeous canyon views all year round. The highway travels the canyon rim east of Grand Canyon Village for 26 miles.

A HIKER RUBS HIS FEET ON BRIGHT ANGEL TRAIL.

✳ To Do

AIR TOURS They may infringe upon the sanctity of the landlubbers' experience in the national park (to the point that the Arizona legislature limited their flight space), but air tours over the stunning terrain sure are sensational. Tours originate from Grand Canyon Airport, Flagstaff, Sedona, Las Vegas, and Phoenix. **Air Grand Canyon** (928-638-2686 or 800-247-4726), located in Grand Canyon Airport, presents the most tours; they last 50–100 minutes. $109–189 adults, $75–169 under 13. **Papillion Grand Canyon Helicopters** (702-736-6322) offers 45-minute helicopter tours from the Grand Canyon Airport. $168 adults, $148 children.

BICYCLING You can ride your bicycle on paved and unpaved roads and the Rim Trail. You may not ride on any trail below the rim. If you plan to cycle the Hermit Road, make sure you give the shuttle buses the right of way (pull off the road and dismount if need be). With the heavy shuttle traffic in summertime, best to avoid this road then.

HIKING & BACKPACKING One of the most intimate ways to experience the canyon, foot travel requires adhering to a few guidelines for a successful venture: Drink enough water (at least a gallon a day in the summer), take electrolyte supplements, eat salty foods, wear a hat and sunscreen, and rest often. (Also note that pets are not allowed below the rim.) The National Park Service strongly advises against hiking from the rim to the river and back in one day. Hikers should not attempt such treks unless they can finish marathon-length hikes with 5,000-foot elevation loss and gain. Saner day hikes include a segment of the 12-mile **Rim Trail**; **Bright Angel Trail** to 1.5-Mile Resthouse or 3-Mile Resthouse; **South Kaibab Trail** to Ooh Aah Point (1.8 miles) or Cedar Ridge (3 miles); **Hermit Trail** to Waldron Basin (3 miles) or Santa Maria Spring (5 miles); and the **Grandview Trail** to Coconino Saddle (2.2 miles) or Horseshoe Mesa (6 miles).

Spending the night below the rim requires a backcountry permit: $10 per person and $5 per night. You can purchase the permit in person or by mail from the Backcountry Information Center.

MULE TRIPS (928-638-2631). As long as you're in average physical condition, over 4-foot-7, weigh less than 200 pounds, and speak fluent English, you can delve below the rim on a day ride to Plateau Point or 2-day overnight trip to Phantom Ranch (3-day trips are available in winter). $136.35 per person per day; call for multiday prices.

RAFTING TRIPS A whitewater rafting trip, the quintessential canyon experience, usually requires a reservation made well in advance. Trips run from 3 to 21 days. Cancellations occur often, so take heart: It's not an impossible dream. **Wilderness River Adventures** (928-645-3296 or 800-992-8022); **O.A.R.S.** (800-386-6277).

RANGER PROGRAMS A number of ranger-led talks take place almost every day in the park. Consult *The Guide* for a schedule.

WALKING TOURS The **Grand Canyon Village Historical District** takes you back to the turn of the 20th century when the Grand Canyon first got the world's attention. It includes structures ranging from the Santa Fe Railway Station (circa 1909) to the oldest standing structure on the rim: Buckey O'Neill Cabin, built in the

A RAFT NEGOTIATES CLASS 10 HERMIT RAPIDS.

THE CANYON SEEN FROM THE GRAND VIEW TRAIL.

1890s. Get a map at one of the visitor centers. Take a stroll on the paved section of the **Rim Trail** between Pipe Creek Overlook and Kolb Studio for a look at one of the world's most awesome object lessons in natural history.

✴ Lodging

The Grand Canyon National Park has six lodges (operated by Xanterra Resorts & Lodges). To make reservations, call 888-297-2757 (outside the US, 303-297-2757; same day reservations, 928-638-2631) or contact Xanterra South Rim, LLC, 10 Albright, Grand Canyon 86023.

On the rim

Bright Angel Lodge. There's nothing more thrilling than walking into this rustic lodge when there's a cold enough bite in the air to warrant a fire in the lobby's great fireplace. Here backpackers and sightseers congregate, and a mélange of languages

fills the air. This lodge, a National Historic Landmark, personifies the rugged essence of the canyon. Architect Mary Colter designed the lodge; her projects always emanate grace and inspiration. The property includes the Bright Angel and Arizona Room restaurants (see *Dining Out*), a gift shop, and the History Room. Lodge rooms have a telephone; some have private bath and/or fireplace. Historic cabins have television and private bath. Rooms $50–134, cabins $89.

El Tovar. This grande dame of the park's lodging, and a National Historic Landmark, recently passed the century

GRAND CANYON LODGING TIPS

As long as you don't have your heart set on staying at El Tovar or in a historic cabin at the Bright Angel Lodge, you *can* land a room on the rim. While summertime sees the most visitors to the park, you can expect a pleasant experience if you follow these few tips:

- Be flexible with dates and avoid multiple-night stays.
- Try to plan 30 days ahead.
- Every lodge has sudden cancellations and/or a few unreserved rooms. The chances of getting a room early in the morning on the day of your intended stay are good.
- Park at the lodge and take the shuttle, an efficient alternative to hunting for parking spots.
- Eat breakfast at the El Tovar after 9 AM; eat lunch at the Arizona Room before noon and dinner before 6 PM.
- Everything becomes available during the winter season, Nov. 1–Feb., excluding Christmas week.

mark and got a remodel to celebrate. Elegant and popular, the rimside hotel stays booked, and you want to plan early if you simply must stay here during your visit to the park. There's a fine dining room (see *Dining Out*) and concierge. Rooms have double, queen, or king beds, cable television, telephone, full bath, and air-conditioning, as well as turndown and room service. $134–304.

Kachina and Thunderbird Lodges. Located on the rim and more modern, these lodges' rooms work well for families. Some have canyon views. Rooms have two queen beds or one king bed, private bath, mini fridge, telephone, television, and safe. $125–136 for two, $9 per extra person.

Maswick Lodge. Located 0.25 mile from the rim in a ponderosa pine forest with several options: basic motel-style rooms (two queen beds,

private bath, telephone, and television), more spacious rooms (two queen beds or one king, private bath, telephone, television, refrigerator, air-conditioning), and cabins (summer only—two single beds or one double bed, private bathroom with shower, telephone, and television). The lodge has a cafeteria, sports bar with wide-screen TV, curio shop, and transportation/activities desk. $76–124 for two, $9 per extra person.

Yavapai Lodge. Located 0.5 mile from the rim in a townlike atmosphere next to the Market Plaza (which has a general store, bank, and U.S. post office) and near a laundry facility, this makes a perfect family base. The lodge also has a cafeteria, curio shop, and transportation/activities desk. Rooms have two queen beds or one king bed; all have private bath, telephone, and television. $96–113 for two, $9 per extra person.

Below the rim

🐾 **Phantom Ranch**. Another Mary Colter design, the only accommodation below the rim resides beside Bright Angel Creek on the north side of the Colorado River. You can only approach Phantom Ranch via foot, mule, or rafting the Colorado River. If you can nab a reservation for Christmas week, consider it a prize. Dormitory space (men and women sleep separately) has heat in winter and evaporative cooling in summer, 10 bunk beds, a shower (bring your own soap), and restroom. Cabins have a set of bunk beds with bedding, cold-water sink, toilet, liquid soap, and towels. Showers in separate area. Remember to order a meal if you don't bring your own food ($10–31 for breakfast, sack lunch, or a stew, steak, or veggie dinner). $29 for dorm space.

CAMPING (800-365-2267; outside the US, 301-722-1257; http://reservations .nps.gov). Pets must be leashed and attended at all times.

Mather Campground. Open year-round for tent and RV camping (no hookups). Restrooms available. Wood and charcoal fires are permitted in provided campsite grills only. Laundry and showers nearby. Mar. 1–mid-Nov. (reservations recommended), $18 per site per night; mid-Nov.–Feb. 28, $12 per site per night on a first-come, first-served basis.

Desert View Campground. Located 26 miles east of Grand Canyon Village. Open mid-May–mid-Oct. No hookups, first come, first served. $12 per site per night.

✳ Where to Eat

The Arizona Room, Bright Angel Lodge. Lunch 11:30–3 (closed Nov.–Feb.), dinner 4:30–10 (closed Jan.–Feb.). Popular because it's good, this restaurant gets busy, especially at dinnertime. The lunch menu offers salads, pasta, and sandwiches; at dinner it's aged, hand-cut steaks, BBQ ribs, chicken, and fish with southwest accents. Signature margaritas and decent wine complement the meal. First come, first served; waiting list during peak times. Lunch $7.75–11.50, dinner $11.25–25.60.

Bright Angel Restaurant, Bright Angel Lodge. Open for breakfast 6:30–11:15, lunch 11:45–4, dinner 4–10. Get a good breakfast here, a salad or sandwich for lunch, and a decent meal for dinner. First come, first served. Ask, and you might get a window table. Breakfast $5.25–10.50, lunch $7–8.95, dinner $9.20–16.

El Tovar Dining Room (928-638-2631), El Tovar Hotel. Open for breakfast 6:30–11, lunch 11:30–2, dinner 5–10. Reservations recommended (up to 6 months in advance). This might be the only elegant restaurant in the state with a dress code casual enough that you can practically plop down right off the trail (providing this is not after a weeklong backpack and/or your aroma doesn't overpower the food's) for a gourmet meal. The classic native stone and Oregon pine create a warm atmosphere. The menu blends regional and classical flavors in a nice blend of meat, fish, and vegetarian dishes. Breakfast $8.45–11.55, lunch entrées $12.25–15.50, dinner entrées $18.25–26.25.

FLAGSTAFF

For centuries, travelers and cultures have considered Flagstaff a hub in the Southwest. Native peoples made seasonal camps in mountain meadows. Pioneers struggling through their westward journey considered the town a good place to camp. Historic Route 66 put it on the map. Northern Arizona University and the Grand Canyon keep it there.

More than just a point on the map, university town, or city on the way to the Grand Canyon, however, Flagstaff has the kind of cool, high-country hip alluring to a variety of personalities: outdoor adventurers, academicians, students, artists, Hollywood names. Though it's considered the high desert, Flagstaff has several ecosystems: piñon-juniper plateau lands, mountain meadows, mixed-conifer sub-alpine forests, and barren tundra. It's one of the state's ultimate cool spots that still sports snowcapped peaks when temperatures start to hit novel numbers in the desert cities.

Outside the backcountry, the historic section east of Route 66 has the most happening: buildings rumored to be haunted that have histories splashed with colorful anecdotes, restaurants, bars, and shopping. It's a mix of generations here, with students tipping the scale during the school year. It doesn't necessarily quiet down in summer, either, though the bars may be a bit less raucous. That is, if they're not one of the haunted spots. . . .

GUIDANCE **Flagstaff Visitor Center** (928-774-9541 or 800-842-7293), 1 E. Route 66 (in the historic train station), offers maps, brochures, up-to-date information on events, and a small gift shop. Open daily (except Christmas and Thanksgiving), Mon.–Sat. 8–5, Sun. 9–4. If you plan to head out into the backcountry and need information on fishing, hiking, or mountain biking, call **Peaks Ranger District** (928-526-0866), 5057 N. US 89, or **Mormon Lake Ranger District** (928-774-1182), 4373 S. Lake Mary Rd. For information on the city's multiuse trail system, contact **City of Flagstaff** (928-779-7632).

GETTING THERE *By car:* Flagstaff is a hub for three major highways: I-17 runs south to Phoenix; I-40 runs east to Winslow and New Mexico and west to Williams and California; and US 89 runs north to Page and Utah. *By train:* **Amtrak** (928-774-8679), 1 E. Santa Fe Ave. *By bus:* **Greyhound Bus**

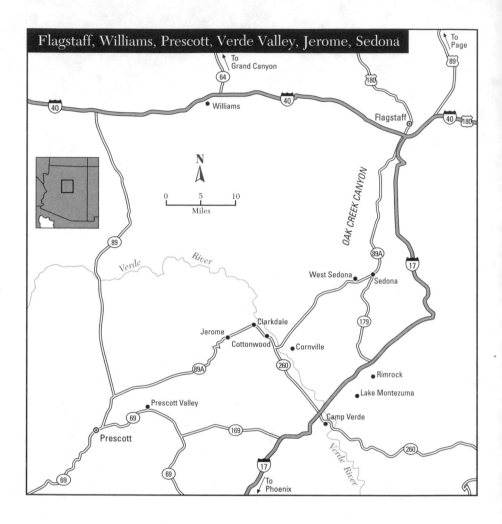

(928-774-4573), 399 S Malpais Lane. *By air:* **Flagstaff Pulliam Airport** (928-556-1234), 6200 S. Pulliam Dr., offers daily flights and service for corporate and private aircraft.

WHEN TO COME Sitting at the feet of Mount Humphreys, Arizona's tallest peak, Flagstaff enjoys mild summer days that finish off with cool nights; bring rain gear for daily thunderstorms. In autumn the aspens glow gold and draw residents from around the state into the high country to admire them. Also, during fall the town swells with the return of students to the university. If you plan a fall visit, make sure you have a reservation. When the winter storms arrive, the mountain turns white—perfect for downhill skiing, cross-country skiing, and snowboarding.

Beaver St.; **Concentra Medical Center** (928-773-9695), 120 W. Fine Ave.;
Walk-in Clinic (928-527-1920), 4215 N. US 89.

✳ To See

The Arboretum at Flagstaff (928-774-1442), 4001 Woody Mountain Rd. Open
Apr.–Oct., daily 9–5. View the native wildflowers that appear in this area from
the high desert to alpine meadows. The Arboretum is also the place of choice for
birders around Flagstaff. Attracted to the avian necessities of life—a pond that
gathers surface water, trees in which to roost or nest, and seeds and insects to
feed upon—more than 100 different species of birds have made an appearance
at the garden. Seasonal events include a Live Bug Zoo, wildflower walks,
evening bat program, and Live Birds of Prey Demonstration Program. $5 adults,
$2 ages 6–17; under 6 free.

Lowell Observatory (928-774-3358), 400 W. Mars Hill Rd. Open Nov.–Feb.,
noon–5; Mar.–Oct., 9–5. Open evenings: Sep.–May, Wed., Fri., and Sat. at 7:30;
June–Aug., Mon.–Sat. at 8. One of the oldest observatories in the United States.
Scientists first noticed signs of an expanding universe between 1912 and 1915,
but the planetarium got its claim to fame when astronomers here discovered
Pluto in 1930. Later, astronomers co-
discovered the rings of Uranus in
1977. An anti-light-pollution cam-
paign keeps Mars Hill and its five
observatory telescopes sufficiently in
the dark to let astronomers keep tabs
on Pluto, Jupiter's moon Io, and aster-
oids and trans-Neptunian objects.
Tours take you through the planetarium each hour. There's also nighttime
telescopic viewing, weather permitting. $5 adults, $4 seniors, $3 stu-
dents, $2 ages 7–17.

Museum of Northern Arizona
(928-774-5213), 3101 N. Fort Valley
Rd. Open daily 9–5. Everything you
wanted to know about the Colorado
Plateau—and more—is found here.
The plateau has the greatest diversity
of geology, biology, and culture in the
world, attracting scientists from across
the globe. It's also a repository for
several Native American tribes, and
has about 600,000 artifacts. Displays
present information on dinosaurs, volcanoes, fossils, and prehistoric people.
Check out the museum founders'

A SCENE FROM FLAGSTAFF'S HISTORIC DISTRICT.

home, the Colton House. Keep in mind that you can rent it for an event. There's a museum shop and bookstore on site, too. $5 adults, $4 seniors and students, $2 ages 5–17.

Walnut Canyon (928-526-3367). From Flagstaff, take I-40 east to exit 204, then continue 3 miles south. Open Dec.–Feb., 9–5; Mar.–May and Sep.–Nov., 8–5; June–Aug., 8–6. Overcrowding at the nearby Wupatki site probably precipitated the move of some prehistoric Native peoples to this canyon just east of Flagstaff. More than 300 small cliff dwellings nestle in the 400-foot-deep canyon. With a dependable supply of water, good soil, and a protective environment that has a soothing and peaceful feeling, the canyon hosted Native Americans for 200 years, and then they disappeared suddenly. Several trails explore the canyon and its ruins. Call for information on ranger-escorted tours. $5 ages 17-plus; under 16 free.

✳ To Do

BMX PARK The Basin (928-779-7690), corner of West and 6th Sts. This state-of-the-art 2.2-acre park has 900 tons of concrete and 8-foot-deep bike bowls. Free.

COOKING CLASS The **Cottage Place Restaurant** (see *Dining Out*) offers a cooking class every Sunday from noon–3:30. This class, a huge hit, includes instruction, a packet of recipes, sampling of the featured creations, and wine tasting. $45 per person. Reservations required.

THE CLIFFS AT WALNUT CANYON HOSTED NATIVE AMERICANS FOR 200 YEARS.

DOG PARKS 🐾 When Fido needs to stretch his legs and let off steam, head for the city's two off-leash areas: **Thorpe Park** at 600 N. Thorpe Rd. and **Bushmaster Park** at 3150 N. Alta Vista Rd. Water is available May–Oct.

FISHING Flagstaff's mountains don't have the trout streams that others of their size might, but there are a few area lakes in Mormon Lake Ranger District that get stocked by Arizona Department of Game & Fish, such as **Mormon Lake**, **Upper** and **Lower Lake Mary**, and **Kinnickinnic Lake**. You can access these lakes by taking exit 337, Lake Mary, from I-17 and heading south.

GOLF Continental Country Club (928-527-7999), 2380 N. Oakmont Dr. Opens at 8 AM in May and Oct.; at 7 AM, June–Sep. Narrow fairways braced by ponderosa pines, open meadows, fresh air, and fast greens present an exciting but enjoyable golf game in the mountains. The 18-hole, 6,014-yard course presents what the management calls "fun-to-play" par-5s, along with demanding par-3s. Pro shop and driving range. PGA professional on hand for private lessons. $22–69.

HIKING (See also *Volcanoes*). Above the **San Francisco Peaks** have almost two dozen trails—eight of which travel more than 8,000 feet inside the **Kachina Peaks Wilderness**. **Humphreys Trail** takes you to Arizona's citadel (but don't take this one unless you're in good physical health and not prone to altitude sickness). Several accesses to the **Arizona Trail** are located near the city. If you don't want to venture into the backcountry, try the **Flagstaff Urban Trail System** that meanders right around town, starting in **Buffalo Park**, 2400 N. Gemini Rd. You can get a map and more information from the City of Flagstaff.

MOUNTAIN BIKING This is the land of the fat tire. You'll see them on the street as well as the back roads and trails. You can ride anywhere that is not a designated wilderness area; the most popular trails travel around Mount Elden and Schultz Pass Road. Call Peaks Ranger District for information. Check out the **Flagstaff Urban Trail System** that meanders right around the town. You can get a map and more information from the City of Flagstaff. Stop at **Absolute Bikes** (928-779-5969), 18 N. San Francisco St., if you need to rent a bike, acquire more gear, or find more information on area routes.

ROCK CLIMBING Experienced climbers gather at **The Pit** off St. Mary Rd., 2 miles south of the Mormon Lake Ranger Station. Beginners can start at the **Vertical Relief Climbing Center** (928-556-9909), 205 S. San Francisco St., where they don a hard hat and muster up a good dose of intestinal fortitude to climb the walls of the indoor gym. After they're comfortable with the indoor fun, they can graduate to an outdoor guided climb. Open Mon.–Fri. 10 AM–11 PM, Sat.–Sun. noon–8. Free.

SKIING Once the snow starts falling, the city's surrounding countryside gives you several ski options.

ⓧ ♦ **Arizona Snowbowl** (928-779-1951), US 180 and Snowbowl Rd., is open for downhill skiing and snowboarding from mid-December through mid-April. Black-diamond runs are big here among its 32 trails thanks to 2,300 feet of vertical drop. The average yearly snowfall measures up to 260 inches. Four chairlifts, full-service rental shop, repair shop, ski school.

Cross-country ski trails at **Flagstaff Nordic Center** (928-220-0550) traipse through more than 40 kilometers of groomed cross-country trails in the Coconino National Forest. Open Dec.–Apr.; rentals, lessons, snowshoeing, and group packages available.

SKY RIDES Arizona Snowbowl (928-779-1951, ext. 115), US 180 and Snowbowl Rd. Open end of May–Labor Day, 10–4. Hop on a chairlift and rise up to 11,500 feet while you take in eagle-eye views of northern Arizona. $10 adults, $8 seniors, $6 ages 8–12 and 70-plus.

VOLCANOES Flagstaff sits right atop the San Francisco Lava Field—which harbors more than 600 volcanoes. You can bet things weren't always cool, calm, and collected around town! These relics of volcanism create perfect venues for outdoor recreation. You can climb them, view them, and even enter chambers formed by them. Contact Peaks Ranger District for information on the following: Hikers who head for the 2-mile-long **Inner Basin Trail** in **Lockett Meadow** can stand in the palm of the caldera formed when Mount Humphreys blew its top. **Lava River Cave** gives you a subterranean view of volcanism via a lava tube about 0.75 mile long, with some places as big as a subway tunnel and others you have to crouch to pass through. With peaks and spires reminiscent of Bryce Canyon National Park, **Red Mountain**'s surreal amphitheater of orange-tinged volcanic stone has eroded fantasy forms that look as aesthetic as a volcano can get. **Strawberry Crater Wilderness** has a mile-long trail that winds around a beautiful cindered area up to almost the top of a crater shaped like its name.

Sunset Crater National Monument (928-526-0502), 12 miles north of Flagstaff on US 89. Open Dec.–Feb., 9–5, Mar.–May and Sep.–Nov., 8–5; June–Aug., 8–6. You can see just how wild and beautiful a postvolcanism landscape can be at Sunset Crater. Rising 1,000 feet above a cinder-covered landscape, Sunset Crater's near symmetrical cone overlooks a landscape of cinder hillsides that slope casually like swells of the sea, their ruddy brown or jet-black colors contrasting austerely with gaunt stands of ponderosa or colorful dots of wildflowers. $5 per person 17-plus; under 16 free (Wupatki National Monument included).

Wupatki National Monument (928-679-2364). Located about 22 miles north of Flagstaff off US 89, at the opposite end of horseshoe Sunset Crater–Wupatki Rd. Open Dec.–Feb., 9–5; Mar.–May and Sep.–Nov., 8–5; June–Aug., 8–6. The ancient Sinagua people—along with several other cultures—migrated here when the Sunset Crater volcano erupted. The largest set of ruins in the Flagstaff area lie just behind the visitor center. Basalt mesas, formed from older volcanic eruptions, rise from the ruddy Moenkopi sandstone formation. Some mesas have exquisitely mortared pueblos still standing upon them. $5 per person 17-plus; under 16 free (Sunset National Monument included).

WALKING TOUR Memorial Day–Labor Day, local historians and authors Richard and Sherry Mangum, dressed in period costumes, lead a 90-minute Flagstaff Historic Walking Tour. The Mangums talk about the colorful history of Flagstaff. The tour meets at the visitor center and is limited to 60 people. Reservations suggested (928-774-8800). Free.

✳ Wilder Places

Kachina Peaks Wilderness. The highest peaks in the state present subalpine forests, mountain meadows, and some of the earth's oldest trees. Ferns deck aspen forest floors, where Basque sheepherders carved their initials and names in the trees' argentine bark decades ago. Hikers who climb the highest peaks can see panoramas of the Grand Canyon, Painted Desert, and Sedona.

✳ Lodging

HOTELS & HOSTELS ⚜ **DuBeau Route 66 International Hostel** (928-774-6731 or 800-398-7112), 19 W. Phoenix. One of the oldest hostels west of the Mississippi has Young Boomer Retro interiors. You get private and dormitory accommodations, with a bathroom in every room. The property boasts a large party room, complimentary pool and foosball tables, two kitchens, high-speed Internet, and complimentary breakfast; no lockout, curfew, or chores. Local calls are free. You can also sign up for a tour to the Grand Canyon and Sedona here. $16–18 dorms, $34–41 private rooms.

⚜ **Grand Canyon International Hostel** (888-442-2696), 19 S. San Francisco St. This homespun hostel with a quiet demeanor has a hotel feel with outside entrances. You'll find two kitchens, high-speed Internet, a TV lounge with video library, and complimentary breakfast. There's free shuttle transport to and from the Greyhound station, and you can walk to the Amtrak station only a block away. Sign up for a tour to the Grand Canyon and Sedona. $16–18 dorms, $34–41 private rooms.

🐾 **Hotel Monte Vista** (928-779-6971), 100 N. San Francisco St. In its heyday this hotel attracted the likes of Zane Grey, Esther Williams, and Bing Crosby. This gave locals a chance to rub shoulders with the world as it passed through the frontier town. Like an aged relative who can get away with eccentric behavior, the hotel (more than 80 years old) has accumulated some quirky habits over the years: A rocking chair in Room 305 insists on facing out the window no matter how many times it's turned toward the room. A bar stool in the hotel's lounge sometimes whizzes past patrons across the room. And the hotel's whole second floor seems to give some people the creeps. The hotel is rife with spooky phenomena. $65–170; pets $25, phone deposit $25.

⚜ **Little America Hotel** (928-779-7900), 2515 East Butler Ave. The roomy, sunny oversized rooms and suites make great bases, especially if you plan to spend a few days in town. Classy, with French provincial furniture, they also have mini fridge, large flat-screen plasma TV with movies and games on demand, free Internet access, coffeemaker, down pillows, and big bathroom. The 500-acre property has a swimming pool, hiking trail, outdoor hot tub, and fitness center. Its Western Gold Dining Room is legend for Sunday brunches. Server Eleanor Gardner has gotten quite a following in her 30 years with the restaurant and even got a governor's service award. But be prepared to wait up to 2 hours (!) for her. $109–149.

BED AND BREAKFASTS England House Bed and Breakfast (928-214-7350 or 817-214-7350), 614 W. Santa Fe Ave. As soon as you look at this house, built in 1909, you sense something special. Made from stones hewn for a stonemason, the craftsmanship is impeccable, down to the basalt fireplace and fireproof ceiling in the parlor. Owner-innkeepers Laurel and Richard Dunn put some elbow grease into the home and finished the inside with period furnishings and decor they call "anti-doily" (mostly 1850–1860 French antiques). Each room has its own bath; beds have ironed sheets and pillowcases, along with down feather beds or memory mattress. Guests can use the Jacuzzi on the premises. On arrival, guests can decompress with a complimentary shoulder massage and a glass of wine or ale. Fresh-baked treats and fruit are available all day; ice cream bars are always available for late-night snacks. In the morning Laurel makes a very healthy, and very delicious, full breakfast (included with room). No pets, and no children under 10. $125–195.

Starlight Pines Bed and Breakfast (928-527-1912 or 800-752-1912), 3380 E. Lockett Rd. Innkeeper-owners Richard and Michael are delightful hosts in this Victorian-style home decorated with period furniture and appointments. It's high romance here, with period colors, 12-foot ceilings, wood-burning fireplaces, claw-foot tubs, unique antiques (including a 650-pound china bathtub and a fainting couch), fresh flowers, Tiffany lamps, and original skeleton keys for every door. The hosts call it "Victorian with an Edge." You will call it very cool and utterly comfortable. Michael makes gourmet breakfasts (which appear in national magazines, for good reasons) while Richard makes sure everything is there at your disposal—including an amenities drawer that contains everything you might need but forgot. $125–165.

COTTAGES & LODGES 🐾 🦴 **Comfi Cottages of Flagstaff** (928-774-0731

or 888-774-0731), 1612 N Aztec St. Pat and Ed Wiebe's collection of cottages all have a retro homey feel. Pat stocks each one like a doting mother, including a generous supply of fixings for breakfast, including bacon, eggs, bread, butter, muffins, cream cheese, milk, and OJ. It's everything that travelers who prefer to make their own meals or want a home base could want, as each home is a real one, with bedroom(s), kitchen, and bathroom. One cottage has a loft that kids will adore. The cottages are within walking distance of the historic section. All cottages have complimentary WiFi, cable TV, gas barbecue grill, and telephone. Bicycles, tennis rackets, and picnic baskets are provided on request. $120–260. Children under 6 free.

🦴 **Montezuma Lodge at Mormon Lake** (928-354-2220). From Lake Mary Road, drive about 4 miles on Mormon Lake Road to the signed turnoff. You may remember staying at a classically retro cottage like one of these built in the 1930s and '40s. The property has several cottages clustered in a pine forest where herds of elk roam and raptors perch for their next meal. Just down the road pools Mormon Lake. $105–125 per night and $650 weekly. Two-night minimum stay.

∞ 🐾 🦴 **Mormon Lake Lodge** (928-354-2227), Main St., Mormon Lake. Situated in a pine forest next to a lake that draws wildlife, the lodge is one of the places of choice for Arizonans to cool off from the infamous desert heat. From its very start 80-plus years ago, it was popular: the true Wild West, where loggers, ranchers, and hunters hung out. Nowadays team roping and rough stock cowboy events spice up the atmosphere. Cowboys come from all points in the Southwest to compete. And as their reputation goes, they work hard and play hard. The lodge sells T-shirts bragging I SURVIVED A WEEKEND AT MORMON LAKE LODGE. The property has a restaurant that serves excellent steaks, a fishing pond, campsites, and horse-back rides, a petting zoo, and buffalo. Cabins $45–140, rooms $45–90; campground and RV park $10–24 per night.

✴ Where to Eat

DINING OUT ♿ **Cottage Place Restaurant** (928-774-8431), 126 W. Cottage Ave. Open for dinner Tue.–Sun. 5–9:30. Private dining rooms make the atmosphere cozy. The AAA Three Diamond menu presents American and Continental cuisine featuring rich classics such as lobster, smoked salmon, duck, chateaubriand for two, and—as vegetarian dishes—*fettuccine e pomodore* and forest mushroom ravioli. The wine list has earned the Award of Excellence from *Wine Spectator* magazine since 1996. Executive chef Frank Branham is consistent in his attention to food and service details. Entrées $18–29.

Dara Thai (928-774-0047), 14 S. San Francisco St. Open Mon.–Fri. 11–10, Sat. noon–6, Sun. noon–9. Red-orange walls, floral upholstered booths, and wooden floors and tables blend tastefully like the food's pungent and floral spice notes of chile pepper, kefir lime leaves, basil, lemongrass, ginger, mint, and fish sauce. The authentic meals are done well. The whole experience gives you a true taste of the graceful Thai culture. Entrées $11.95–16.95.

🐌 ♪ **Granny's Closet** (928-774-8331), 218 S. Milton Rd. Open daily 11 AM–1 AM. Still going strong after three decades, this Flagstaff favorite serves up big portions of decent homemade food. Nothing in the salad bar gets scooped from a can. The prime rib comes from a family recipe. The Italian food has the same roots and some zip in its sauce. The family's granny makes apple pie every morning. The place has two dining areas: one for Lumberjacks (aka Northern Arizona University students), which is where it's all happening, and one for those who like it quiet. You can choose. Entrées $9.95–20.95.

Josephine's Modern American Bistro (928-779-3400), 503 N. Humphreys St. Open Mon.–Sat. (Sun. during summer): lunch 11–2:30 (closed in winter), dinner 5:30–9. The restaurant is named for owners' Jill and Tony Consentino's mother, who taught them all they know about food. They learned well enough to earn the restaurant a AAA Three Diamond award and the Award of Excellence from *Wine Spectator* magazine. The building, on the National Historic Register, was one of the first in the area constructed with volcanic rock. The utilitarian Craftsman bungalow design has battered rock columns on the porch, a sculpted rafter with diamond sash windows, coffered ceilings, and plenty of wainscot paneling. You'll find classic dishes here with creative twists. The osso buco comes with green chile and chive sweet potato cake. You'll have to go to Boston to get the seared diver scallops done any more perfectly. The champagne vinaigrette salad features a perfect blend of sweet candied pecans, creamy goat cheese, and tart grapefruit with a tease of curry. Don't pass up the velvet-textured home-made ice cream. Entrées $21.50–27.50.

La Bellavia Restaurant (928-774-8301), 18 S. Beaver St. Open daily 6:30–2. A favorite breakfast spot for locals. If you do as the locals do, you'll order the wonderful Swedish oat-cakes. Don't make the mistake of thinking they're like regular pancakes. These are *big*: in texture, taste, and size. You can also get eggs in a variety of special dishes of the eggs Benedict ilk. Bread is fresh baked—if you see cranberry and hazelnut French toast as a special, don't hesitate to order it. Espresso drinks and local art avail-able. Entrées $4.75–7.75.

ALONG A FLAGSTAFF STREET.

EATING OUT Macy's European Coffee House (928-774-2243), 14 S. Beaver St. Open daily 6 AM–10 PM. True international cities always have a restaurant like this one, where you'll find an eclectic crowd that spans the social and cultural strata. The shop has a coffeehouse feel but serves excellent vegetarian fare that can be altered to vegan. Besides an excellent variety of coffees and teas, you can get healthy and delicious breakfast and lunch, too. Entrées $6.25–7.

New Jersey Pizza Company (928-774-5000), 2224 E. Cedar. Open daily 11–10. The best pizzeria in town serves an incredible variety of pizzas. Their claim to fame is serving "thou-sands upon thousands of pizza combi-nations over the years." With more than 30 veggie toppings, a variety of meats, and rich cheeses, you can understand the possibilities. Desserts (including the gelato and cannoli shells) are homemade, with ingredi-ents like Sedona apples, Camp Verde peaches, pumpkins, and pecans, and local organic farm eggs. Pizzas $7.47–18.67.

Tybo's BarBQ (928-714-0678), 5877 Leupp Rd. Open Mon.–Thu. 11–9 (till 10 Fri.–Sat.); Sun. brunch 10–4. This family-owned restaurant started as a saloon with a water tank that served hamburgers from a wood-burning stove in the 1920s. Men would bring their kids—they'd have a "couple" while the kids filled contain-ers from the water tank. Hopi and Navajo Indians stopped by, as this was the halfway point between the Rez and Flagstaff. Things got wild enough for some patrons to ride their horses through the bar. These days, locals park their horses outside, but the food hasn't changed. You can get some great food here at great prices: hand-cut steaks, barbecue, chops, and pizza piled so high with toppings and cheese, the menu asks you "What Crust?" Entrées $8.69–17.99.

✳ The Arts

First Friday Art Walk at the Artists Gallery (928-773-0958), 17 N. San Francisco St. Monthly art walks (held 6:30–9) give visitors a chance to see why Flagstaff is listed in art critic and author John Vallani's book *100 Art Towns in the U.S.* The free art walk is ongoing year-round.

✳ Selective Shopping

You'll find a number of boutique and specialty shops in the historic section of the city.

✳ Special Events

April: **Northern Arizona Book Festival** (928-380-8682). Acclaimed authors participate in readings, panel discussions, and workshops.

May: **Movies on the Square** (928-607-2347). Free family-oriented movies every Friday night in Heritage Square through mid-Sep.

June: **Corvette'n America Road Tours** (928-527-8388). "Show & Shine" Corvette show and tour for Corvette owners to northern Arizona. **Pine Country Pro Rodeo** (928-526-3556). Top cowboys compete in rodeos.

July: **Museum of Northern Arizona Heritage Program** (928-774-5213). Hopi and Navajo festivals of arts and culture celebrate Native American culture.

September: **Coconino County Fair** (928-679-8000). Exhibits, livestock, rides, food, and entertainment. **Route 66 Days** (928-607-2347). Live music, vintage and hot rod car show, and a parade all celebrate the Mother Road. **Flagstaff Festival of Science** (www .scifest.org). All things science celebrated by field trips, exhibits, and scientific and open houses.

December: **New Year's Eve Pinecone Drop** (928-779-1919, ext. 430). Who needs a glittering ball when you have a giant pinecone?

WILLIAMS

L ocated at the foot of Bill Williams Mountain, named for the colorful fur-trading mountain man Bill Williams, the city of Williams couldn't help but enjoy the same rugged individualism and love of the backcountry the mountain man displayed. Known for his creative thinking and unconventional wisdom, Bill Williams eluded demise several times while traipsing the wilds.

The tall, slim redhead for whom the city is named had some colorful characteristics. Some pages of Old Bill's personal history have him wobbling between itinerant preacher and whiskey aficionado. Regardless, Old Bill was a master in the backcountry, and he earned the respect and friendship of some of history's more infamous mountain men, such as Antoine Leroux and Zebulon Pike. Old Bill's independent personality and sense of adventure have trickled down into the city of Williams.

Williams prospered in its early days via the railroad and lumber, then took a cosmopolitan turn when the Santa Fe Railway built a spur line to the Grand Canyon at the turn of the 20th century, bringing the world to Williams's doorstep. The town turned downright rowdy trying to entertain humanity with saloons, bordellos, gambling houses, and opium dens. It took awhile for some of these eyebrow-raising vices to wane, even by 1936 when Route 66 put Williams on the Main Street of America. When I-40 bypassed the city in 1984, Williams held tightly to its Grand Canyon connection by registering its trademarked claim, "The Gateway to the Grand Canyon."

The city endured a tired spell in the 1990s—to the point that some old buildings felt the breeze from the swing of the demolition ball. Old Bill's creative spirit came through, however, and innovative business people took the initiative to dust off the business section's marvelous old architecture (listed on the National Register of Historic Places), renovate with pleasant upscale interiors, and offer quality products.

Today Williams has become an attractive destination in itself by blending its colorful history with today's comforts. Plus, it still has the only train to the Grand Canyon, the longest segment (2 miles) of Historic Route 66, and that marvelous backcountry where Old Bill Williams once roamed. Once? His spirit has never really left.

GUIDANCE Pick up a map of the historic buildings and information about the town and surrounding area, including the Grand Canyon, at the **Williams–US Forest Service Visitor Center** (928-635-4061 or 800-863-0546), 200 W. Railroad Ave. Open 9–5. You can also get information on, and maps of, the South Kaibab National Forest backcountry surrounding the town.

GETTING THERE *By car:* Take I-40 right to Williams, located between Flagstaff to the east and Ash Fork to the west. *By air:* **H. A. Clark Memorial Field** (928-635-1280), 3501 N. Airport Rd., has a 6,000-foot runway and 16 transient tie-downs.

WHEN TO COME High season happens from Memorial Day to Labor Day when temperatures range from the 80s in the day to the 50s at night; then once again from Thanksgiving to mid-Jan., when you should dress for winter's 40-degree days and freezing nights.

MEDICAL EMERGENCY **Flagstaff Medical Center** (928-779-3366), 1200 N. Beaver St., Flagstaff.

✳ To See

Cataract Creek Gang Gunfight Every day in summer, around sundown, someone gets killed on Main Street (Route 66). The same ne'er-do-wells who rob the Grand Canyon Railway (see *To Do*) come back into town to raise a ruckus around 7 PM.

✐ **Grand Canyon Deer Farm** (928-635-4073), 6769 E. Deer Farm Rd. (I-40, exit 171). Open daily Oct. 16–Mar. 15, 10–5; Mar. 16–Oct. 16, 9–6. This petting zoo has a fun variety of animals. Several kinds are in perfect proportion to pint-sized kids, such as pygmy goats and miniature donkeys, monkeys, mini cattle, baby bison, and a baby camel. They also have llamas, peacocks, several species of deer (including reindeer), talking birds, wallabies, coatimundi, and marmosets. Here kids can learn up close and personal all about the animals and how to approach them. $7.50 adults, $4.50 ages 3–13, $6.50 ages 62-plus; children under 2 are free.

✳ To Do

CROSS-COUNTRY SKIING Located off Spring Valley Rd. north of I-40. Contact Kaibab National Forest. The **Chalender X-Country Trails** feature a network of three trails totaling 21.9 miles created especially for cross-country skiing. The trails range from easy **RS Hill Trail**, to intermediate **Spring Valley Trail**, to difficult **Eagle Rock Trail**.

ALONG HISTORIC ROUTE 66.

GOLF **Elephant Rocks Golf Course** (928-635-4935), 2200 Country Club Dr. Named for the pachyderm-sized lava boulders situated along the road into the course, the city golf course rates as one of the most scenic in the state. The course, built in the 1920s, developed problems such as fairways without grass and oil-sand greens. In 1989 the city took over the 9-hole course and had Gary Panks redesign it; in 2000, another 9 holes were added to make it into an 18-hole beauty. Driving range, practice greens, pro shop, and clubhouse. $39–49 includes cart.

FISHING Several area lakes (**White Horse**, **Dogtown**, **Cataract**, and **Kaibab**) get stocked with trout. You can use a boat in **White Horse** and **Dogtown Lakes**. Contact the **Williams–US Forest Service Visitor Center** for more information.

HIKING There are almost three dozen day hikes in the national forest around Williams, including the Grand Canyon. Check out the **Bill Williams**, **Sycamore Rim**, and **Bixler Saddle Trails**. Also, you can access the **Arizona Trail** from nearby trailheads. Contact the **Williams–US Forest Service Visitor Center** for more information.

HORSEBACK RIDES **Stables in the Pines** (928-635-0706), 117 S. 3rd St. Open May–Sep. Saddle up for a half-hour or all-day trail ride through the Kaibab National Forest. You can make reservations for night rides and cookouts, as well.

MOUNTAIN BIKING Kaibab National Forest has created several official mountain bike routes, including 12.4-mile-long **Ash Fork Hill Route 66**, the 6.9-mile **Devil Dog Bike Tour**, **Old Perkinsville Road** (9.3 miles), **Round Mountain Loop** (18.3 miles), and 15.9-mile **Stage Station Loop**. Contact the **Williams–US Forest Service Visitor Center** for more information.

RAILROAD **Grand Canyon Railway** (928-773-1979 or 800-843-8724). Vintage trains with restored 1923 Harriman coaches leave the historic 1908 depot every day (except Dec. 24–25), climbing hills and winding around valleys for 2¼ hours up to the Grand Canyon. Along the way stowaway musicians play old tunes and bandits wait along the tracks in an attempt to rob the train. Once you're at the Grand Canyon, you have almost 4 hours to take in the sights. Packages available for several-day trips. $60–155 adults, $35–130 youths, $25–85 children.

ROCK CLIMBING Some of the country's choicest climbing routes scale the walls of Sycamore Canyon, especially at Sycamore Falls—where you can often see climbers just about any day all summer. Contact the **Williams–US Forest Service Visitor Center** for more information.

SKIING **Elk Ridge Ski Area** (928-814-5038), 418 W. Franklin (Bill Williams Mountain). Open Thu.–Sun. in-season, when snow permits. It's a small area, but it works well for beginners or advanced skiers who need a downhill run in a pinch. The area focuses on families and has a snow play and snow tubing slope.

✳ Wilder Places

The Grand Canyon, only an hour's drive away, makes a spectacular destination.

Sycamore Canyon Wilderness Contact the **Williams–US Forest Service Visitor Center**. One of the wilder canyons in northern Arizona lies just south of Williams. Its premier multiuse trail, the Sycamore Rim Trail, is one of the state's most diversified. Check out the Rocky Mountain iris spread in spring. In summer wildflowers dot meadows, and boggy areas have water lilies. You get views of the dramatic redrock canyon walls, mountain climbers at Sycamore Falls, and the historic Overland Trail. No mechanized equipment allowed.

Bill Williams Mountain. Contact the **Williams–US Forest Service Visitor Center**. The 9,264-foot-high peak has a network of multiuse trails with pine-oak to aspen-fir forests. The most popular is the Bill Williams Trail, as rough-and-tumble as Old Bill himself.

✳ Lodging

⚓ ♿ **Grand Canyon Railway Hotel** (800-843-8724), 233 N. Grand Canyon Blvd. Large rooms decorated in classical French Revival with a Southwest flair have queen beds and cable TV. Southwestern suites have a sleeper couch, chair, TV, and kitchenette with microwave, mini refrigerator, coffeemaker, and wet bar. The property has a lounge, an indoor swimming pool and Jacuzzi, basketball and volleyball courts, and a small children's playground. $98–200; call for specials.

The Lodge (928-635-4534 or 877-563-4366), 200 E. Route 66. The old adobe-style building is an attractive blend of cheeky exteriors full of kitsch and recently remodeled interiors leaning toward luxury. Single rooms and suites have wood and travertine flooring, solid wood furniture, and ultracomfortable bedding. Rooms have queen or king beds, cable flat-screen TV, radio, and complimentary continental breakfast. Suites have upgraded flat-screen TV and video, microwave, refrigerator, and dining table; some have fireplace. $139–159.

BED AND BREAKFASTS ✤ **Canyon Country Inn** (928-635-2349), 442 W. Route 66. The inn's homey country decor features quilts and stuffed bears. The rooms are quiet, clean, and have their own bathroom. Continental breakfast is included. No pets. $49–85.

Red Garter Bed and Bakery (928-635-1484 or 800-328-1484), 137 W. Railroad Ave. The two-story Victorian Romanesque–style bed and breakfast, once considered the rowdiest abode on Williams's Saloon Row, was constructed in 1897 as a saloon and bordello that remained in service until the 1940s. A steep flight of steps known as the "Cowboy's Endurance Test" led to the girls upstairs. Owner-innkeeper John Holst transformed the seamy saloon into a classy B&B now listed on the National Register of Historic Places. Holst serves homemade pastries (scones, cinnamon rolls, croissants, and Danish), fruit, juice, and gourmet coffee for breakfast (included with the room) in the bakery downstairs and shares tidbits of history about the building. No pets. $120–145.

✳ Where to Eat

DINING OUT **Bella Donna Italian Restaurant & Night Club** (928-635-5378), 106 S. 9th St. Open daily for dinner, Apr.–Sep., 4–11; till 10 Oct.–Mar.). Though the restaurant specializes in Sicilian-style cuisine, the food has a light, fresh taste. It's one of the best places to eat in town. The ravioli, handmade every day, comes with several different fillings and sauces; the shrimp scampi is excellent, and the ribs popular. You can eat a gourmet pizza there, or have it delivered to your room. You might hear a lot of whistling going on during your dinner. This tradition started

🍽 **Old Smoky's Restaurant and Pancake House** (928-635-1915), 624 W. Route 66. Open 6 AM–1 PM; closed Wed.–Thu. in winter. One of the area's classic diners opened in 1946 as a 24-hour-a-day café. Over the years, the diner evolved into a BBQ eatery and then its current incarnation—a country-style breakfast venue, and a darn good one. The rustic exterior reminds you of an old cozy cabin; inside, its old diner style feels like the good ol' days. The food is burley breakfast at its best, including all-you-can-eat biscuits and gravy or pancakes for less than $5. You can build your own omelet, or order a health-conscious meal, too. At lunchtime the main fare is sandwiches. Entrées $4.99–7.99.

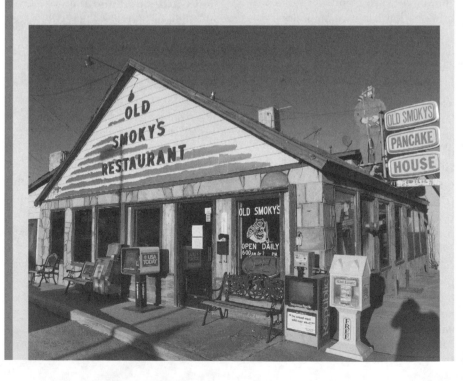

with the owner's Sicilian grandfather: When he sent his adolescent children down to the cellar to fetch him a cup of wine from the cask, he would have them whistle. This whistling assured him that the kids were not sipping. When a bottle of vino gets opened in the dining room or kitchen for cooking, the event comes with whistling. Entrées $9.95–25.95.

Red Raven Restaurant (928-635-4980), W. Route 66. Open Tue.–Sun. 11–9. This recent addition to the Williams restaurant scene is gathering nothing but rave reviews from locals. Owner David Haynes attributes his success "to good, fresh ingredients, and some of the best steaks around." The remodeled building looks fresh and balanced inside, especially with tables dressed in linens and fresh flowers. The fine-dining menu lists about a dozen thoughtfully prepared items featuring pasta, fish, steaks, and wraps. Tempura pops up around the menu. Lunch $6–7, dinner $10.95–19.95.

EATING OUT ❧ ♪ **Twisters** (928-635-0266), 417 E. Route 66. Open daily 8 AM–8 PM (10 PM in summer). Pure Route 66, from the malt-shop fare to the 1950s music to the Route 66 Place gift shop. The fare—hamburgers, hot dogs, onion rings, fries, milk shakes, phosphates—makes this one of the best comfort-food joints around. And for $5, you can get a sandwich and one of seven sides (fries, potato salad, coleslaw, and more).

✳ Special Events

May: **Rendezvous Days** (928-635-4061) celebrates the town's western heritage with buckskinners, a black powder shoot, a parade, and family activities.

June: **Renaissance in the Pines** (928-635-4061) reenacts a more romantic era; come in costume or as you are to watch jousting, entertainment, and fair maidens and handsome knights.

July: **Cowpuncher's Reunion Rodeo** (928-632-7680). Working cowboys in the area get together and rodeo.

August: **Cool Country Cruise-In & Route 66 Festival** (928-635-0266). This celebration of Route 66 features a variety of activities such as an open car and bike show, a poker run, a '50s dance, and a battle of the bands.

September: **Labor Day PRCA Rodeo** (928-635-4061) brings the Professional Rodeo circuit to town with a parade and dances.

October: **Family Fun Fall Festival** (928-635-4061) features a carnival, major recording act, and live entertainment.

November–January: **Mountain Village Holiday** (928-635-4061) lasts from Thanksgiving to New Year's, with Christmas lights, hayrides, craft sales, art show, holiday activities, and shopping. **The Polar Express** (800-843-8724), through mid-Jan., is based on the classic children's book by Van Allsburg.

PRESCOTT

W hen Joseph Walker led a group up the Hassayampa River to prospect for gold in the river's tributaries, a spot along Granite Creek caught his interest enough that he made camp there in 1863. Fueled with storied sayings—"If ya wash yer face in the Hassayampa River, you can pan four ounces of gold dust from yer whiskers"—the Walker party hit pay dirt, and big.

Rustic and raucous, this mining camp soon traded its generic name of Granite City for the more respectable Prescott, in honor of historian William Hickling Prescott. Shortly afterward, when the newly designated Arizona Territory needed a nonpartisan capital, Prescott fit the bill and became the only wilderness capital in U.S. history.

The ragamuffin capital quickly filled with the ilk so common to boomtowns— prospectors, cowboys, merchants, shady ladies, and shysters. As the town grew, so did its caliber of citizens, whose names of Gurley, Groom, Goldwater, and Hall became memorialized in streets, buildings, and nature. Intertwining local color with class, ingenuity with personality, and wit with wisdom, Prescott endured to become one of Arizona's most endearing cities, coined "Everyone's Hometown."

The city also earned the title "One of America's Dozen Distinctive Destinations" from the National Trust for Historic Preservation. And for good reason: The town has more than 700 buildings on the National Historic Register, including Victorian homes, a huge courthouse square, and old-time saloons. A number of antiques shops allow you to take a piece of history home with you.

GUIDANCE **Prescott Chamber of Commerce & Tourist Information Center** (928-445-2000), 117 W. Goodwin St. Open Mon.–Fri. 9–5, Sat.–Sun. 10–2. You can get maps, a schedule of events, and answers to questions about the Prescott area. A walking tour pamphlet ($1) lists 34 different historic buildings. **Bradshaw Ranger District** (928-443-8000), 344 S. Cortez St., can give you information on backcountry use in the Prescott National Forest.

GETTING THERE The majority of visitors enter Prescott by way of I-17: From the north, take No. 217 (AZ 169), drive 12 miles, turn right onto AZ 69, and drive 19 miles. From the south, exit at AZ 69 and drive 34 miles. Heading from Sedona, take AZ 89A all the way, about 61 miles. From I-40, take AZ 89 (exit 144) south for 50 miles. *By air:* **Ernest A. Love Field** has three paved runways. **Prescott Airport Shuttle** (800-445-7978) makes 16 trips a day from Phoenix.

WHEN TO COME It's mild all the way around the calendar in Prescott: Snow hardly lasts a day, and hot days evanesce into cool nights. The season starts in March, intensifies by June, peaks on the July 4th weekend—when lodging is booked months ahead of time—then relaxes after Labor Day. December is a big month, since another of the town's nicknames is Arizona's Christmas City.

MEDICAL EMERGENCY **Yavapai Regional Medical Center Hospital** (928-445-2700), 1003 Willow Creek Rd.

✳ To See

Courthouse Plaza, Gurley and Montezuma Sts. A time line chiseled in the plaza concrete measures the county's history with events between 1581 and 1985. Readers following the time line will end up at a bronze sculpture dedicated to the most glamorous fighters in the United States Calvary, the Rough Riders, designed by Solon Borglum—whose brother worked on Mount Rushmore. Every night in summer the plaza has some kind of entertainment.

The Phippen Museum (928-778-1385), 4701 AZ 89 N. Open daily 10–4, Sun. 1–4. Named for the first president of the Cowboy Artists of America, George Phippen. The art museum correctly describes itself as the most beautifully located museum in Arizona, standing in the mist of the stunning outcroppings of Granite Dells. It features western and Native American art and has a marketplace of authentic Indian items. $5 adults, $4 seniors; 12 and under free.

Sharlot Hall Museum (928-445-3122), 415 W. Gurley St. Open Mon.–Sat. 10–4, Sun. noon–4. The largest museum in the area is an educational adventure— much like its namesake founder's life. Prescott's poet and former state historian Sharlot Hall traveled Arizona's mining camps to collect oral histories. With captivating exhibits that change frequently during the year, a research library, and historical plays enacted in the Blue Rose Theater, you get an entertaining dose of the area's lively past. The campus contains the territorial governor's mansion, a gazebo, a rose garden, and other buildings dating from the frontier days. $5; free under 18.

WHISKEY ROW.

The Smoki Museum (928-445-1230), 147 N. Arizona St. Open Mon.–Sat. 10–4, Sun. 1–4. Perhaps one of the most unusual museums in America. Designed to resemble an Indian pueblo, and full of Native

American artifacts, the museum was built in 1935. Native stone and thousands of pine logs were used to create the inside columns, window enclosures, slab doors, vigas, and latillas. Filled with priceless Native American artifacts, art, and a research library, the museum presents an overlook of Native American mystique, legends, and history. The name came from the Smoki People, a group of Prescottonians so captivated by the Hopi Indians, they took to enacting Hopi ceremonies and dances—including the controversial Hopi snake ceremony—as well as those of other southwestern tribes. The faux ceremonies and dances ended in 1990 when the Hopi people actively protested against the group in downtown Prescott. $4 adults, $3 seniors, $2 students; under 12 free.

SCENIC DRIVES Take a look at surrounding ranch country on the 50-mile-long **Iron Springs Road Loop**. This is also a popular road biking route. Go north on Montezuma, and continue as it turns into Iron Springs Road out of town and south to Skull Valley. At Thompson Valley Road, turn left. Go about 4 miles to AZ 89 and turn north. This road will wind up into the Bradshaw Mountains and bring you back into Prescott. To tour the backcountry, take the **Bradshaw Mountains Motor Tour**—a 25-mile loop that takes you on a backcountry route (high clearance is required for some segments) into a historic world of mining deep in the national forest. Go east on AZ 69, turn south onto Mount Vernon Street (Senator Highway), continue south to FR 197, and turn left, back to AZ 69. A high-clearance vehicle may be needed on the lower portion of FR 197.

✳ To Do

DOG PARK ✿ **Willow Creek Dog Park** (928-777-1122), 3181 Willow Creek Rd. Open 7 AM–10 PM. Open to dogs over 4 months old. Walking path, dog fountain, tables, benches, shade ramada, small-dog area.

GAMING Bucky's Casino (928-776-5695), 1500 E. AZ 69. The Yavapai-Prescott tribe's casino has 300 slots machines and live poker. Across the street is the **Yavapai Casino** (928-445-5767), 1505 E. AZ 69. The smaller of two Yavapai casinos, this one has 175 slot machines, including Wheel of Fortune and Jeopardy! progressives, and bingo. Free bus rides from Phoenix.

GOLF Prescott offers a number of courses, from affordable to state-of-the-art. Each gives you a challenge with its varying terrain of rolling hills, tree-lined fairways, and granite outcroppings balanced with tremendous views.

Antelope Hills Golf Courses (928-776-7888 or 800-972-6818), 1 Perkins Dr. Among Arizona's best affordable courses, the two par-72 courses at Antelope Hills rank among the favorites. Not only are their views some of the most stunning golfers can set their eyes upon, looking toward the Granite Dells and Mogollon Rim, but they're both 18-hole championship courses. Lawrence Hughes designed the North course, and Gary Panks the South course.

It's like having resort golf at public prices. The facility has a natural-turf driving range and full-service golf shop, **Manzanita Grille** (good food), and lounge. Dress code calls for a shirt with collar and no cutoffs. $40–55 with cart.

Prescott Golf & Country Club (928-775-3941), 1030 Prescott Country Club Blvd., Dewey. Located just down the road from Prescott, out in the countryside where the spaces are open and mountain views impressive, this course spreads in the valley between the Mingus and Bradshaw Mountains. The 7,200-yard, 18-hole course has a tree-lined fairway and fast bent greens. A double-sided practice facility has driving tees and chipping and putting greens. The country club has a golf shop, restaurant, and lounge. Fees include golf and cart. $35–45.

StoneRidge (928-772-6500), 1601 N. Buff Top Rd., Prescott Valley. This 18-hole championship golf course gets its name from its location among granite boulders and deeply carved washes—particularly around hole 12, where pockets of boulders, rocks, and ridges follow you. The par-72 course runs 7,052 yards with 350 feet of elevation changes from lowest tee to highest green. Jan.–Apr., $22–41; May–Oct., $22–65. Rates include cart.

HIKING Right in town you have **Thumb Butte**, the locals' trail of choice for a short fitness hike, at the end of Thumb Butte Road, as well as the 4-mile-long **Peavine Trail**. Get information from the visitor center. National forest footways, like the **Granite Mountain** and **Groom Creek Loop Trails**, wind through mixed-conifer canyons, around weather-smoothed granite boulders, past ancient rock art, and up bald-rock peaks. Contact the Bradshaw Ranger District.

HISTORIC TOURS In a city whose motto is *Where History Lives On*, you don't have to look too far to dip into the past. More than 700 Prescott buildings appear on the National Register of Historic Places. From May through October at 10 each morning, the Prescott Chamber of Commerce (928-445-2000 or 800-266-7534), 117 W. Goodwin St., presents an hour-long docent-led **Historic Walking Tour of Downtown Prescott**. Prescottonian Melissa Ruffner— **Melissa Ruffner's Prescott Historical Tours** (928-445-4567)—takes you on a colorful spin through Everyone's Hometown, elucidating upon the town that created her family heritage since 1867. You'll see some of the best examples of Victorian-style homes on a **Mount Vernon Stroll**. The self-led stroll will take about an hour to view beautifully restored buildings.

HORSEBACK RIDING **Smokin' Gun Adventures** (928-308-0911). Smokin' Dave Wrangler gives an entertaining trail ride in several areas around Prescott, ranging in length from an hour to all day. Three-day vacations for cowpokes who don't want to leave the trail.

KAYAKING & CANOEING There are several lakes in the area, and they all present perfect kayak conditions (see *Wilder Places*). **Prescott Outdoors, LLC**, runs concessions at Watson and Goldwater (canoe only) Lakes. All boats are rented on a first-come, first-served basis; no reservations. Apr.–Sep., weekends 10–4.

MOUNTAIN BIKING Prescott has hundreds of miles of trails to ride within minutes of the downtown area. The trails range from easy to technical, and from popular to the kind you won't see a soul upon all day. For information on trails, stop at the chamber of commerce for a bicycle map. For more information on more remote trails, contact the Bradshaw Ranger District. To rent a bicycle, go to **Ironclad Bicycles** (928-776-1755), 710 White Spar Rd.

ROCK CLIMBING The perpendicular granite walls of the Granite Mountain Wilderness are prime rock climbing haunts. **Rubicon Outdoors** (800-903-6987) leads half- and full-day ascents.

✳ Wilder Places

Goldwater Lake (928-777-1100), city of Prescott, 201 S. Cortez St. Go 4 miles south on Mount Vernon to the signed turnoff and turn right. This sweet little lake sits in a cozy of ponderosa pines. A trail with benches rings it; picnic sites overlook it. $2 parking fee. Boat rentals and fishing available.

Granite Mountain Wilderness Contact the Bradshaw Ranger District for information. No mountain bikes or mechanized machinery are allowed in the wilderness. The golden granite boulders stack up to produce aesthetic moments with far-reaching panoramas. Higher up in the mountain, the forest becomes ponderosa pine. The wilderness has world-class rock climbing and favorite hiking trails. The Little Granite Mountain Trailhead is located about 8 miles north of downtown Prescott on Iron Springs Road. Free.

Lynx Lake. Go east about 3 miles on Gurley St., and turn right onto Walker Rd.; go 2 miles to the lake. $2 day-use permit to park. Wednesdays are free. Peaceful Lynx Lake has hiking trails, camping, and fishing.

Watson Lake/Granite Dells, about 5 miles north on AZ 89. One of the most scenic spots in the area was a hiding place for the nefarious a century ago. Erosion-carved granite outcroppings make for an aesthetic scene amid sapphire-hued water. If you have a kayak, bring it to explore the lake and channels, or rent one at the lakeshore. Watch for rock climbers scaling granite walls.

Watson Woods Riparian Preserve (928-777-1100), city of Prescott, 201 S. Cortez St. Go east on Gurley St., and turn left onto AZ 89; go 2.2 miles, and turn right onto Prescott Lakes Pkwy.; turn left at Sun Dog Ranch Rd., then left again into the parking lot. This preserve gives you an opportunity to view watchable wildlife in a cottonwood-willow riparian forest on a very short trail. $2 donation.

✳ Lodging

BED AND BREAKFASTS AND INNS

⊙ & **Hassayampa Inn** (928-778-9434 or 800-322-1927), 122 E. Gurley St. Like the river it's named for (the Apache word *hassayampa* means "the river that loses itself"), the hotel started out as a "first-class hostelry" and lost itself for a time before returning to its hotel roots and claiming an AAA Three Diamond rating. Built in 1927 as The Grand Hotel, the property hosted the upper crust and Holly-wood. A child of the Jazz Age, Prohi-bition, and gangsters, it took its wayward turn in the 1970s and dallied as a boardinghouse, retirement home, and interim campus for Prescott College. It was born again when it found a place on the National Register of Historic Places and went through a multimillion-dollar renovation in 1985. Since then, the hotel has remained the classiest act in the town, with a gorgeous lobby full of original Castillian oak furnishings, a tiled fireplace, and a hand-operated original Chinese red elevator. Art deco has a strong say here, and it's well done. Rooms have central AC, WiFi, TV, private bathroom, and phone. $129–219 includes complimentary breakfast at the hotel restaurant, the Peacock Room (see *Dining Out*).

The Pleasant Street Inn Bed and Breakfast (928-445-4774), 142 S. Pleasant St. The century-old Victorian home was moved from a location a few blocks away to the historic district in 1990 then remodeled. Modern interiors keep the feel of the place light, and sun-filled rooms add airiness. There's plenty of parking, and you can walk the three blocks to the downtown stores and Whiskey Row from here. Of the four available rooms, two are suites and two are large rooms. All have queen or king beds; three have in-room private bath and one offers private use of a hall bathroom. One is connected to an outside deck. Children over 12 years old are welcome. No pets. Owner-innkeeper Jeanne will fix you a full breakfast with quality ingredients, or you can have a quick continental breakfast if you plan to eat and run early in the morning. $110–150.

Prescott Pines Inn (928-445-7270), 901 White Spar Rd. The inn, located on the southern edge of town away from Whiskey Row, comes with a historic lineage. It first came on the scene in 1863 as the Brookside Ranch. In the 1930s it became the Haymore Dairy. In 1987 it was remodeled and restored as a comfy, but not stuffy, Victorian inn. There are 11 guest rooms plus the three-bedroom chalet—a 1,300-square-foot A-frame house that sleeps 8 to 10. In summer the air wafts with the smell of roses and peonies in the garden. Located closer to the national forest than downtown, the inn has a relaxed feeling in the surrounding pines. Rooms $79–89 (add $10 for breakfast for two); guest houses $109–119 (add $10 for breakfast for two); chalet (self-service only) $289.

Rocamadour Bed and Breakfast (928-771-1933), 3386 N. Hwy. 89. Located 4 miles north of the city, the Rocamadour—meaning "rock lover"—takes its name from the enchanting rock formations of the Granite Dells in which it's located. The labyrinthine collection of granite formations, which attracted Hollywood stars such as Tom Mix and John Wayne, spreads around the property and creates some gorgeous views. Innkeepers Mike and Twila Coffey attend to every detail savvy travelers appreciate. Rooms have private bath,

THE PLEASANT STREET INN B&B.

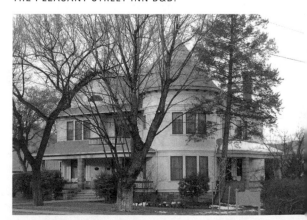

cable TV, fireplace (some), and Internet. Gourmet breakfasts are included. The property is a favorite of national and world travelers. $139–189.

HOTELS ∞ 🏆 **Hotel St. Michael** (928-776-1999 or 800-678-3757), 205 W. Gurley St. Advertised as having "modern electricity" and being "the only absolutely fire proof building in Prescott" when it was first built in 1891 as the Hotel Burke, the building promptly burned to the ground during the Great Fire of 1900. Rebuilt a year later, the hotel was subsequently named Hotel St. Michael and continues as one of Prescott's most beloved properties. Check out the cartoon faces along the top of the building. They're said to be the architect's rendition of some of the city's local officials, presiding during the construction of the hotel. Situated on the north end of Whiskey Row and across the street from the Courthouse Square, it's right in the middle of all the action. You'll have some of the best views in town from these rooms. Rooms have double, queen, or king bed; cable TV; direct-dial phones with free local calls and air-conditioning. Breakfast at the Caffe St. Michael (see *Dining Out*) is included in rates. $59–119.

Hotel Vendome (928-776-0900), 230 S. Cortez St. Clara Worthen advertised her newly built hotel in 1918 as "a place where particular people will be satisfied." The hotel's parlorlike lobby and European style are particularly attractive. The hotel, restored to its horse-and-buggy days interior, has another particular point of interest: ghost Abby Byr, who died in Room 16, and her cat, Noble. Abby plays pranks and Noble mews. Current

owner Frank Langford says Abby's a friendly ghost. Continental breakfast included in rates. Beer, wine, coffee, and WiFi available in lobby.

✳ Where to Eat

DINING OUT **129½ An American Jazz Grille** (928-443-9292), 129½ N. Cortez St. Open for lunch Tue.–Fri. 11–2, for dinner Tue.–Sat. at 5. This combination restaurant–jazz club has the cool warmth of an expatriate club in France with a menu that flirts with a French infusion. It also has some of the best jazz in the city. You'll find an eclectic crowd here, from 20-somethings doing the social scene to baby boomers nodding their heads and cowboys tapping pointed toes to the music. The food is as good as the music and as decadent as the red-and-black decor. The fare leans toward hearty, with some lean dishes for lighter eaters. Entrées $17.95–26.95.

Caffee St. Michael (928-776-1999), 205 W. Gurley St. Open Fri.–Sat. 7 AM–10 PM, Sun.–Thu. 7–7. Known for its plate-glass floor-to-ceiling windows, this restaurant has some of the best ground-level seats in town. The cognac wooden trim lavished all around and metal ceiling pull you back, with a friendly tug, to the turn of the 20th century when the building was constructed. The chef keeps a refreshingly light touch with seasonings to allow the flavor of the food to reign. Breakfasts lean toward bistro style, with eggs Benedict, Belgian waffles, and huevos rancheros. Lunch sees unusual sandwiches, burgers, and pastas. Special menu on holiday. Entrées $9.95–16.95.

El Chorro Restaurant (928-445-7130), 120 N. Montezuma St. Open daily 11–9. This Mexican favorite has been around since 1959. The chefs use decades-old recipes of classic Mexican fare. Entrées, such as combination plates of El Charro Grande (foot-long tortilla) and *Boracho* (Drunken) Burrito, are satisfying; daily specials are a great buy. Plus, they have free delivery. Entrées $6.59–13.50.

El Gato Azul (928-445-1070), 316 W. Goodwin St. Open Mon.–Thu. 11–9, Fri.–Sat. 11–10. The chef here braids a bit of Mediterranean with a strand of Spanish and a dash of Southwest. You end up with a creative and tasty menu. Meals like prickly pear stuffed toast, open-faced rellenos, vegan tamales with roasted vegetables, and blue corn pancakes make this restaurant as fun as its decidedly Latin décor. When the weather's right, outdoor dining places you right alongside the banks of Granite Creek. Tapas are served 3–5. Entrées $14.95–23.95.

✐ **The Palace Restaurant and Saloon** (928-541-1996), 120 S. Montezuma St. Open daily for lunch 11–3, dinner Sun.–Thu. 4:30–9 (till 10 Fri.–Sat.). Some of the West's most notorious characters stopped in for a drink here at the town's historic bar. In the late 1870s the famous trio of Wyatt Earp, Virgil Earp, and Doc Holliday showed up. The good doctor locked into a winning streak on Whiskey Row, rumor has it at The Palace, where he won $10,000 just before he left for Tombstone. Enough about the saloon, gamblers, and infamous patrons; you're interested in food, right? Steaks are big here: all hand cut—from a pound T-bone to cut-it-with-your-fork fillet—but balanced with fish from salmon to cat. Lunchtime serves gourmet sandwiches. Kids order from the

Cowpoke's Menu for $5.95. Entrées $12.95–26.95.

Peacock Room (928-778-9434), Hassayampa Inn, 122 E. Gurley St. Open for breakfast Mon.–Sat. 7–11 (Sun. brunch 11–1:30), lunch Mon.–Sat. 11–2, dinner daily 5–9. Prescott's popular fine-dining establishment made an appealing change in 2005 when Steve Helland came on board. This creative chef takes the time to make everything fresh, from the hollandaise sauce for the morning's eggs Benedict to the jalapeño pepper jelly demiglaze of the Sonoran pork osso buco at dinner. You'll get grape salsa with your huevos rancheros and roasted corn pudding and creamed spinach with the Black Angus prime rib. Breakfast is labeled A Gala Affair, which it certainly feels like with the piped-in classic music and sterling silver and crystal appearing here and there. Entrées $16–32.

Prescott Brewing Company (928-771-2795), 130 W. Gurley St., Suite A. Open Sun.–Thu. 11 AM–midnight; till 1 AM Fri.–Sat. This is where you'll find the best beer in town/Arizona/the nation/the world—depending on what kind of brew you order. Showing off a wall full of coveted first-place national and international beer awards, owner John Nielsen says this is the only brewpub in Yavapai County. Three award-winning brews remain on tap year-round; other winners appear seasonally. The food served with this celebrated beer is pub fare with a flair. Kids' menu available. After a meal here, you just might end up agreeing with Poor Richard when he said, "Beer is living proof that God loves us and wants to see us happy." Entrées $8–15.

SweetTart (928-443-8587), 125 Cortez. Open Tue.–Sat. 7–4, Sun.

8–3; closed Mon. Prix fixe dinner on Sat. by reservation. In patisserie style, this little gem of a restaurant serves some pretty sumptuous items. First, the tarts, created artisan style in a tasty variety of flavors from fruit to cream with almond sugar dough (much like shortbread, but more crumbly), and nothing artificial. Then there's cake—milk chocolate hazelnut (favorite) to triple mousse—as well as Danish, brioche, and croissants. Next, the sandwiches, as special as the sweets: prosciutto with mozzarella, Mancini chicken panini, and Black Forest ham and cheese. Entrées $6.50–8.50; Sat. dinners $45 per person; you may bring your own wine.

EATING OUT ❦ **Annalina's** (928-776-1277), 126 S. Montezuma. Open daily 10–8; closed Tue. in winter. The food at this colorfully decorated eatery is about as authentic as you can get, and it has some Mexico City influences. Menudo is a daily occurrence, tacos are delightfully soft shelled, and the beans are downright soulful. Corn tortillas are made fresh daily, and the chips fried throughout the day. Entrées $7.50–8.75.

❦ **Cattlemans Bar and Grill** (928-445-4300), 669 E. Sheldon St. Open daily 11–10. Part of Prescott for almost 100 years, this is where you go for a great steak—porterhouse, rib eye, top sirloin, or filet mignon—at a great price. Lamb and pork chops are just as good. Popular items include the flat iron steak sandwich, filet mignon, and 24-ounce porterhouse. Entrées $6–8 at lunch, $8–20 at dinner.

❦ **Dinner Bell, Inc.** (928-445-9888), 321 W. Gurley St. Open Mon.–Fri. 6 AM–2 PM (1 PM Sat.), Sun. 7 AM–1 PM. No checks or credit or debit

cards. ATM machine inside. This local favorite—where every stratum of society meets, from retro hippies to their suit-and-tie grandparents—has two sides. The front brings you back a step or two into time with its 1960s decor; the back room overlooks Granite Creek with floor-to-ceiling windows that open up like a garage door in warm weather. Both have fresh and natural ingredients, filtered water, and low prices. Breakfast (like special waffles and omelets you build yourself with a boat-load of ingredients from which to choose) is served all day. Lunch is home-cooked sandwiches and specials. Beverages range from specialty coffee drinks to frappe freezes, fresh fruit smoothies, and Italian sodas. Unlike the rest of the menu, choosing dessert remains simple—there's only one item, homemade apple pie, plain or à la mode. Entrées $4.75–6.95.

Pangaea Bakery & Café (928-778-2953), 220 W. Goodwin St., Suite 1. Open Mon.–Fri. 7–5:30, Sat. 8–3. Nicole Marshall has been making artisan bread products here for more than a decade, along with interesting-but-intensely-good sandwiches, not-your-typical pizzas, and organic coffees and teas. Also, this is where you get bubble tea—a chai-like concoction (inasmuch as it has dairy, but with a variety of flavors) with tapioca pearls settled on the bottom. You sip the drink with a superwide straw, and when a pearl pops up, it chews like a gummy bear. Very cool. Entrées $5.95–11.95; pizza $21 or $2.75 a slice.

Prescott Coffee Roasters (928-717-0190), 318 W. Gurley St. Open Mon.–Fri. 6–2, Sat.–Sun. 6:30–2. Richard Gregory's coffee shop/restaurant, with its laid-back, cutting-edge blend of folky funk, would have fit right in on Tucson's 4th Avenue in the 1970s. The ambience invites you to make yourself at home and enjoy the stream of humanity that stops by from every corner of town for some of the freshest coffee this side of Central America. Richard likens his brew to fresh-made cookies compared with store-bought. He's got a great lineup of unusual sodas and teas, too. You can watch him roast coffee, which he does daily. Better yet, you can take a batch of fresh roast home with you. $3.95–5.95.

The Raven Café (928-717-0009), 142 N. Cortez. Open Mon.–Thu. 8:30 AM–11 PM, Fri.–Sat. 7:30 AM–midnight, Sun. 8 AM–9 PM. One of the town's hottest meeting spots serves up politically correct coffee, gourmet teas, an incredible line of beers (30 on tap and more than 200 labels in total), and some nice wines. They randomly hold special theme nights, but you can count on classic/cult movies every Tuesday night. All the interiors were designed and created by local artists and craftsmen. The food is organic, and the practices as green as the owners can get. Entrées $6.25–8.50.

Scout's Gourmet Grub (928-442-3336), 1144 Iron Springs Rd. Mon.–Fri. 7–7, Sat.–Sun. 8–3. Scott Simmons, a former park ranger, has created a national-park-themed restaurant with meals named for the outdoor greats—such as the Grand Canyon Grinder, rugged Rocky Mountain Meatball, Yummy Yosemite, and Canyonlands Classic. There's a nice variety of veggie sandwiches, too, as well as salads. Gourmet pizza comes in individual sizes. A local favorite for sandwiches. Entrées $5.69–6.99.

DOWNTOWN PRESCOTT'S ART FOR ALL MURAL IS NOW COMPLETE.

✳ Entertainment

JAZZ You can hear jazz nightly at **129½ An American Jazz Grille** and the **Peacock Lounge** at the Hassayampa Inn. **The Palace Restaurant and Saloon** has honky-tonk piano every Sunday 2–5, dinner theater every other Monday (a play or musical group), country music on Friday and Saturday nights. See *Dining Out* for more information on all three.

✳ The Arts

Prescott's ART the 4th Dimension connects people to the arts. Each month, their **4th Friday Weekend Long Art Walk** presents Prescott's diverse art experience from Friday evening through Sunday afternoon. Currently, 17 galleries in an area that Art the 4th Dimension calls the Square Squared take part in the walk.

✳ Selective Shopping

If you like to shop until you drop, head straight for Cortez Street, where you'll find antiques, collectibles, folk art, Indian jewelry, and funky fashions. After that, you can move on to the art galleries on Montezuma Street and McCormick Arts District, then the boutique shopping malls on Gurley Street and in the Hotel St. Michael.

✳ Special Events

Call 928-445-2000 for more information.

June: **Territorial Days** is an art and craft show on Courthouse Plaza. **Folk Arts Festival**.

July: **Frontier Days and World's Oldest Rodeo** include the Frontier Days Parade. **Indian Art Market** (Sharlot Hall Museum) presents quality Native American art and crafts.

Old Town Square Arts and Crafts Festival (Courthouse Plaza).

August: **Arizona Cowboy Poets Gathering** (Sharlot Hall Museum).

September: **Faire on the Square Art & Craft Show** (Courthouse Plaza). **Yavapai County Fair** has a rodeo, food, vendors.

October: **Folk Music Festival**.

December: **Christmas Parade and Courthouse Lighting**. During the **J. S. Acker Musical Showcase**, businesses provide caroling, music, hot beverages, and snacks.

In Mexico and some points in Southern California, you'll hear the event pronounced *roh-DAY-oh*. Most everywhere else, it's ROH-dee-oh. But here in Prescott, it's not just a ROH-dee-oh, it's the World's Oldest Rodeo. Claiming that you've got the world's oldest rodeo (and continuous on top of that) isn't easy, nor a trivial matter as the makers of the game Trivial Pursuit found out when rodeo town Pecos, Texas, challenged one of their question and answers that read: "What rough-and-tumble Western sport was first formalized in Prescott, Arizona? Answer: rodeo." You must meet the following important criteria:

1. Have a committee to plan and stage the rodeo.
2. Invite cowboys to compete.
3. Charge admission.
4. Give prizes and trophies.
5. Have the contests documented.

   Over the years Prescott has gotten protests from other rodeo towns, too, namely its neighbor down the road, Payson. After careful scrutiny and given the lack of the documented proof that Prescott can ante up, the title always lands back in Prescott's hand. So Prescott finally patented the event. They now have the government's blessings—and hopefully, if begrudgingly, Pecos's and Payson's.

VERDE VALLEY (COTTONWOOD, CAMP VERDE, CLARKDALE, CORNVILLE, PAGE SPRINGS, RIMROCK)

"Cottonwood," one businessmen in the Verde Valley pragmatically explained, "and its next-door neighbor, Clarkdale, exist because of the mines at Jerome. The single miners who liked to party a lot lived right in Jerome. Clarkdale was built for the mine's executives, and the blue-collar workers lived in Cottonwood."

But the history of these towns goes beyond copper mines to the beginning of the Arizona Territory in 1863, when Anglos started streaming into the Verde River Valley at its confluence with West Clear Creek. Trouble started because the valley already had inhabitants—the Apache. Within two years Camp Verde (first known as Fort Lincoln) was established as a war outpost.

After a decade the army prevailed and impounded the tribes in the Rio Verde Reservation, near present-day Cottonwood. Two years later Tucson businessmen successfully demanded that the army uproot and transport the tribes to the San Carlos Agency near Globe. In another two years miners and ranchers moved into the area.

The towns started to cater to Jerome mining during the teen years of the 20th century. Cottonwood supplied vegetables to the miners (as well as some pretty hot bootleg booze that brought imbibers from neighboring states), and Clarkdale became the oldest master-planned community when John Clark developed it into a residential community with state-of-the-art homes to house mining executives. In the 1930s and '40s, tiny Rimrock (next to Camp Verde) attracted a curious mix of ranchers, movie stars, and gangsters on the lam.

When Jerome went bust in the 1950s, Cottonwood prevailed and continued as the leading marketing center for the area. Clarkdale got caught in a retro pocket for several decades, and the smaller communities like Page, Cornville, and Rimrock slumbered. By the 1990s these towns started to get outside attention. Cornville became a renaissance area for artists of all types, Camp Verde wiped the sleep from its eyes and is on its way as a family and nature-lover's destination, and Page Springs captured the eye of vintners. Like many little Arizona towns, they have all attracted entrepreneurs with extraordinary talent who like open space and serenity.

GUIDANCE **Camp Verde Chamber of Commerce** (928-567-9294), 385 S. Main St., Camp Verde; **Cottonwood Chamber of Commerce** (928-634-7593), 1010 South Main St., Cottonwood; and **Clarkdale Chamber of Commerce** (928-634-9591), P.O. Box 308, Clarkdale. For information about backcountry use in the national forest, contact **Coconino National Forest** (928-527-3600) and **Prescott National Forest** (928-771-4700).

GETTING THERE Camp Verde (to the east) and Cottonwood (in the west) are located like bookends on opposite ends along the banks of the Verde River along AZ 260. Clarkdale lies just north of AZ 260, and Cornville and Page Spring are located just south of AZ 89A on Page Springs Road along Oak Creek.

WHEN TO COME Mild weather (60 degrees) draws visitors here in winter. The simmer of summer days (98 degrees) cools down comfortably by midnight (60s).

MEDICAL EMERGENCY **Verde Valley Medical Center** (928-634-2251), 269 S. Candy Lane, Cottonwood.

✳ To See

⚷ ✿ **Fort Verde State Park** (928-567-3275), 125 E. Holloman St., Camp Verde. Open daily 8–5; closed Christmas Day. Located east of I-17 just off AZ 260. Once an active military post, the fort had 22 building on 55 acres. It still has the original parade grounds and four original buildings on 22 acres. You can check out the officers' quarters and peruse a museum house furnished in 1880 style. $2 ages 14 and older; under 14 are free.

⚷ ✿ **Montezuma's Castle National Monument** (928-567-3322), 2800 Montezuma Castle Rd., Camp Verde. Located off I-17, exit 289. Open daily 8–5 (till 7 May–Sep.). It never had a visit from Montezuma. And it doesn't have a castle, either. But Montezuma's Castle National Monument does have one of the best-preserved cliff dwellings in the Southwest. The five-story, 20-room cliff dwelling, located along Beaver Creek in the Verde Valley, once housed about 50 Sinagua Indians between AD 1100 and 1400. Another ruin, called Castle A, lies just south of Montezuma Castle. $2 adults, children free.

Montezuma's Well (928-567-3322). Located about 11 miles north of Montezuma Castle; I-17 exit 293. Open 8–5 (till 7 May–Sep.). Once you see Montezuma's Castle, take a look at one of the Indians' main water sources in the area. Actually a sinkhole (a collapsed underground limestone cavern) filled with water, this was the main water source for the Indians who stayed in Montezuma Castle. The well at the "lake" pumps out 1.5 million gallons of 76-degree water daily. The well's carbon-dioxide-rich water sustains several forms of plant and animal life not found anywhere else in the world. Free.

Old Town Cottonwood. Located at the north end of town along historic AZ 89A, Old Town Cottonwood has a museum, unique shops, restaurants, and galleries. Most of the shopping area's buildings were constructed at the turn of the 20th century.

✎ **Tuzigoot National Monument** (928-634-5564). Open daily 8–5 (6 in summer). Located off Broadway between Cottonwood's Old Town and Clarkdale on old AZ 89A. The red sandstone pueblos once housed more than 200 Native people in about 100 rooms. Archaeologists have stabilized the ruins to give an idea of what they might have looked like. The visitor center has a museum full of artifacts: ollas, pottery, tools, and shell/stone jewelry to peruse. $5 per person, 16 and under free.

✳ To Do

BIRDING Though the Verde Valley has become an object of ardor among birders in the last several years, the area has always been a hot spot with birds. Since Dr. Edgar Mearns, who lived at Fort Verde, started cataloging the area's avian life in the area in 1889, 340 species have shown up. The hot spots are trails along the **Verde River**, **West Clear Creek**, and **Oak Creek**. Contact the national forests for trails. More than 100 species have been sighted in and immediately around the **Dead Horse Ranch State Park**. During winter watch for bald eagles along the Verde River. The Audubon Society named Arizona Department of Game and Fish's **Page Springs Hatchery** (928-634-4805), 1600 N. Page Springs Rd., Cornville, an Important Bird Area. More than 100 birds have been sighted at the fish hatchery.

GAMING **Cliff Castle Casino** (800-381-7568), 55 Middle Verde Rd., Camp Verde. The Yavapai-Apache casino has a cosmic bowling alley (with fluorescent-colored lights), arcade, Kids Club for children 6 weeks to 12 years old, Dragonfly lounge for adults with nightly entertainment, and a lodge and restaurant just off the premises. The casino offers 570 slot machines, keno, live poker, blackjack, and bingo.

HIKING The high-desert countryside of the Verde Valley presents some intriguing trails that are best hiked from early fall through late spring. The most exciting trails travel the **Sycamore Canyon Wilderness** (Coconino National Forest), especially **Parsons Trail** or **Dogie Trail**; and the **Woodchute Trail** in the Mingus Mountains (Prescott National Forest). More experienced hikers should check out the historic **Mail Trail** that starts around Camp Verde and travels to Payson (Coconino National Forest).

HORSEBACK RIDING **M Diamond Ranch** (928-592-0148 or 928-300-6466) is a 100-year-old working cattle ranch in Rimrock. You can take a 1- to 2-hour trail ride, cook out, or take part in a cattle drive. Call for reservation and prices.

KAYAKING With 18 miles of the Verde River flowing through Camp Verde, you can put in for a paddle that can range from a gentle float to a lively Class II ride from Feb. through May. Contact Tonto National Forest (602-225-5200) for a Verde River guide.

PETROGLYPHS **V-bar-V Heritage Site** (928-284-5323). Open daily Fri.–Mon. 9:30–3:30; closed Thanksgiving and Christmas. From I-17, go south on AZ 179 past Beaver Creek Campground to the signed turnoff. The largest-known and best-preserved petroglyph site has more than 1,000 glyphs in 13 panels that show perfect examples of the Beaver Creek Style. No pets allowed. Free.

RAILROAD **Verde Canyon Railroad** (928-639-010 or 800-293-7245). Vintage FP7 engines pull cars along a historical route along the Verde River between Clarkdale and Perkinsville. Each season has its sensational features: Spring reveals wildflowers coloring the banks and waterfalls flowing (if the winter had enough rain); black hawks and night herons show up in summer; cottonwood and willow trees glow gold in fall; and bald and golden eagles migrate here in winter. Travel via coach, first class, and caboose with access to the open-air viewing car. Coach: $54.95–79.95 adults, $34.95–49.95 ages 12 and under, $49.95 for those 65-plus.

WINE TASTING Who would imagine Arizona, especially tucked-away Page Springs, could produce quality wines? People thought the same when Napa Valley settlers planted vineyards with cuttings snipped from Sonoma and San Rafael vines in 1861. **Page Springs Vineyards & Cellars** (928-639-3004), 1500 N. Page Springs Rd., Cornville, is producing world-class wines. Callaghan fans will be interested to know it gets Kent's nod. Winemaker Eric Glomski, formerly from David Bruce Winery in the Santa Cruz Mountains, specializes in Rhône-style wines. Tasting room open daily 11–6.

✳ Wilder Places

Dead Horse Ranch State Park (928-634-5283), 675 Dead Horse Ranch Rd., Cottonwood. One of the few remaining Fremont cottonwood/Goodding willow forests in the state runs along the Verde River. This state park includes a portion of this richly diverse riparian forest that draws wildlife, especially birds. Several multiuse trails—including the 1.5-mile-long Verde River Greenway, which meanders along one of the state's best nesting habitats—network around the park. In winter the park's lagoon gets stocked with trout, a big draw for bald eagles that migrate to the river. $6 per vehicle, $2 per bicycle.

✳ Lodging

BED AND BREAKFASTS AND INNS

∞ ❀ ૬ **Luna Vista Bed and Breakfast** (928-567-4788 or 800-611-4788), 1062 E. Reay Rd., Rimrock. Innkeeper-owners Kala and Frank have warm personalities that match their home: a sophisticated yet safe haven. Themed suites are aesthetically balanced, roomy, and comfortable. The property has a heated pool and spa, game room, business center, library, complimentary WiFi, private patios, gardens, outside facilities for pets, and horse and trailer facilities.

Nearby are private hiking trails with cultural interest. A generous happy hour with snacks welcomes you. Breakfasts (brunch on Sunday) are hearty and included in rates. Children 8 years or older are preferred. $125–235.

HOTELS & MOTELS **Cottonwood Hotel** (928-634-9455), 930 N. Main St., Cottonwood. The oldest hotel in Cottonwood (built in 1925), and listed on the National Historic Register, has upper-level rooms that overlook the heart of Old Town. Rooms are neat, clean, and full of history. If the walls could talk, you might hear some details about ol' Duke and Gail Russell, his squeeze at the time he stayed here; or the antics of Mae West, who roomed here before her star rose in the Hollywood skies. Each apartment has its own unique decor. The property includes a gift shop, coin-op laundry, and TV/VCR area. Rooms have queen beds and private bath; (most) fully stocked kitchen with (all) refrigerator and microwave; TV, some with VCR, and views. $65–105.

🐾 🐾 **Pines Motel** (928-634-9975 or 800-483-9618), 920 S. Camino Real, Cottonwood. Clean and simple, and perfect as a casual base if you plan on tooling around. There's a heated pool (seasonal); rooms have cable TV, WiFi, microwave, mini fridge, in-room coffee, and free local calls. Pets $10. $49–79.

✳ Where to Eat

DINING OUT 🐾 **Adobe Café** (928-567-5640), 567 S. Main St., Camp Verde. Open Tue.–Sat. 7–3. This old stagecoach stop from the 1870s serves some decent, home-cooked foods. Breakfast features biscuits and gravy and egg sandwiches. At lunch, salads, sandwiches, and a special. $4.75–6.95.

Mai Thai on Main (928-649-2999), 157 S. Main, Cottonwood. Open Mon.–Sat. for lunch 11:30–2:30, dinner 5–9. Noi Olson's wonderful, authentic restaurant serves traditional food from her Thai homeland. The food matches the distinctive harmony of flavors you would find in a restaurant in Chiang Mai. This is an enduring favorite. Entrées $8.25–11.95.

Manzanita Inn Restaurant and Lounge (928-634-8851), 145 E. Cornville Rd., Cornville. Open for dinner Wed.–Sun. 4–8. Arizona's small towns often attract talented artists and professionals with their alluring aura and slow pace. Manzanita's original owners, Albert and Isabelle Kramer, fell under tiny Cornville's spell more than 15 years ago and stayed to create a loyal following. Chef Albert, winner of a number of cooking awards and prestigious honors, once prepared meals for the queen of England and several U.S. presidents and drew regulars from all over the state (even the country) to feast in Old World elegance on his fare. Locals Randy Hale and his wife were regulars who turned owners the end of 2006. Chef Albert still consults on, and his chefs still prepare, the meals (specialty German dishes, fish, steaks, pasta, exotic game, homemade soups, fresh organic veggies, savory sauces, and decadent desserts). Customers continue to give the nod of approval. Reservations suggested. Entrées $14.95–22.95.

Su Casa (928-634-2771), 1000 Main, Clarkdale. Open daily 11–9. Located in Clarkdale's historic section where retro culture comes on thick. This friendly restaurant serves authentic

Sonoran and Arizonan food that's fresh and well made. The menu has several vegetarian meals, and the chiles rellenos has a following. Entrées $6.95–11.95.

EATING OUT Sweet Jill's (928-649-2779), 1750 E. Villa Dr., Cottonwood. Open for breakfast and lunch Mon. plus Wed.–Sat. 8–4; lunch only Sun. 8–1. The fresh, gourmet food here has no preservatives or alien-sounding ingredients. Breakfasts are made by Camille, who has earned a near-cult status with her specialties. Hot traditional and gourmet sandwiches, panini, and salads for lunch. The decor's fun, wild art is for sale. Breakfast $6.95–8.95, lunch $5.95–8.95.

✳ Selective Shopping

Check out the Old Town section of Cottonwood for specialty stores. In Camp Verde, **Ancient Bear Gallery** (928-567-2288), 546 Main St., Suite 113, open Wed.–Mon. 10–6, has authentic Native American fine jewelry, crafts, and art at reasonable prices.

✳ Special Events

February: **Wine & Pecan Festival** (928-567-0535) in Camp Verde features local wines, more than 3,000 pounds of pecans—the fruit of century-plus-old pecan trees—and jazz.

April: **Verde Valley Birding ansd Nature Festival** (928-282-2202). Spotlighting the birds of the Verde Valley and natural history through field trips, talks, and workshops at Dead Horse State Park.

May: **Verde Valley Fair** (928-634-3290) in Cottonwood features animals, artwork, baked goods, and

more, with a carnival, rodeo, and entertainment. **Cottonwood Auto, Aeroplane & Cycle Show** (928-634-7593). From classics to curiosities, whether it flies or drives, they'll gather for it at the Cottonwood Airport.

June: **Arizona Crawdad Festival** (928-567-0535) at Camp Verde cooks crawdads in the most delicious ways with music, vendors, and fun.

July: **Cornfest** (928-567-0535) in Camp Verde cooks up a ton of sweet corn from Hauser & Hauser Farms with other foods, contests, vendors, and music.

September: **Verde River Days** (928-634-5283) at Dead Horse Ranch State Park in Cottonwood honors the preservation and care of the Verde River with exhibits and a lot of water fun. **General Crook's Pioneer Days & Mule Show** (928-567-0535) in Camp Verde steps back into time with an antique-tractor engine show, tractor pull, mulepacking and trails competitions, Dutch oven cook-off, and music.

October: **Fort Verde Days** (928-567-0535) in Camp Verde looks at the fort's past with cavalry drills, a carnival, a parade, and other events. **Fall Harvest Carnival** (928639-3200) in Cottonwood presents an evening of costumes, candy, and hayrides.

December: **Cottonwood Christmas Parade** (928-634-7593) on Main Street, Cottonwood, has floats, music, entertainment, candy, and Santa. Later that evening head to Old Town for the **Chocolate Lovers' Walk**. **Parade of Lights** (928-567-0535) in Camp Verde beams with decorations, floats, music, and fun.

JEROME

T eetering atop Cleopatra Hill, the City in the Sky can be seen from miles away—especially at night, when the lights of its handful of streets twinkle. In the early-morning light it glows like burnished copper—the mineral that made it famous and earned its other nickname of Billion Dollar Copper Camp.

Jerome had two copper kings who kept thousands of miners busy: William Clark, who owned the United Verde Mine and created Clarkdale; and "Rawhide" Jimmy Douglas, who owned the Little Daisy Mine. At its height (1914–1920), Jerome had 15,000 residents stuffed into enough mountainside shacks for only a third of them. They worked (and played) in shifts around the clock, so one room could house three miners, who took turns sleeping in it. Like every mining town, the miners played as hard as they worked. With one bar for every 100 people, you can imagine how the atmosphere rocked from more than mining equipment.

Over the years, mining took its toll on the mountain: Smelter smoke smothered the vegetation, dynamite rankled foundations, and raucous behavior attracted extra attention and stern laws. By 1953 the copper market had dropped too low for profits, and Jerome pretty much closed down. In the 1970s the counterculture took to the funky ghost town, and Jerome started to come to life again—this time with art as its mainstay. The town has tidied itself up over the last few decades, but the funkiness remains.

In this hilltop town where canyon wrens drop their glissando cry and agave blossoms, beaming like lemon lanterns, angle boldly from the rocky slopes, the gray hardship of the miners' lives gets overshadowed by color. Weird is wonderful in Jerome. WE ARE ALL HERE, signs appear around town, BECAUSE WE ARE NOT ALL THERE. JEROME, ARIZONA, another sign proclaims, POPULATION: STRANGE.

While the rest of the world rushes along in conformity and standards, Jerome backflips into its own state of mind. Some say it's just being high-spirited. Speaking of which, spirit sightings are rife. But let's be clear about this: Jerome is not haunted, nor does it have ghosts. Jerome has spirits. Hang around Cleopatra Hill long enough, and you just might have your own spirit-filled encounter.

GUIDANCE **Jerome Chamber of Commerce** (928-634-2900), 310 Hull. Run by volunteers, this trailer office usually opens by 10 AM, especially Thu.–Sun. Stop by to get info and a Jerome Historic Building and Business Map, which lists the original names of historic buildings and the businesses that currently reside in them. If the office isn't open, they usually leave maps in an outside bin. For information on backcountry use in Prescott National Forest, contact **Verde Ranger District** (928-567-4121), 300 E. Hwy 260, Camp Verde.

GETTING THERE Jerome lies right on AZ 89A, almost equidistant between Prescott and Sedona. From Phoenix, take I-17 north, exit at AZ 260, then head northeast to Cottonwood to link up with AZ 89A.

GETTING AROUND This tiny mountainside town has few parking opportunities along the streets—many as narrow as an old European village's. Best to park your vehicle in the public lots on the east end of town, put on a pair of walking shoes, and stroll.

WHEN TO COME The height of humanity gathers here in Oct. when all things spooky are celebrated, Halloween being the main event. Aug. and Jan. are slow, and some shopkeepers go on vacation (that would be physically). All other months draw crowds on the weekends. With only about 60 rooms to accommo-date everyone, it's best to make reservations if you plan to spend time here.

MEDICAL EMERGENCY **Verde Valley Medical Center Sedona Campus** (928 639-6000), 269 S. Candy Lane, Cottonwood.

✳ To See

Gold King Mine (928-634-0053). Located off AZ 89A on Perkinsville Rd. (fol-low the signs). Open daily 9–5 except Christmas Day. Looking for copper, the Haynes Copper Company dug 1,200 feet and struck—gold! The camp grew into the town of Haynes, with a population of just over 300. Now the 100-plus-year-old ghost town (population: 1) remains alive and well as a living museum with a collection of antique trucks, tractors, and construction and mining equipment dating back to the turn of the 20th century. $4 adults, $3 ages 62–74, $2 ages 6–12.

Jerome State Historic Park (928-634-5381), Douglas Rd. Open daily 8–5. Learn the professional side of the Billion Dollar Copper Camp when you tour the Douglas Mansion, built in 1916 by mining magnate James S. Douglas on the hill overlooking his big ore-producing Little Daisy Mine. Douglas designed the property as a hotel for mining officials and investors, with a residence for himself and his family. True to mining-town tastes, the adobe property had the best of everything—a wine cellar, billiards room, marble shower, steam heat, and central vacuum system. The state has turned the property into a museum presenting exhibits of photographs, artifacts, and minerals. $3 for ages 13 and up.

SCENIC DRIVES **AZ 89A**, traveling in either direction, makes a scenic paved drive. Heading south to Prescott takes you through the pass near Mingus Moun-tain; heading north, you go into the red rocks of Sedona. Go 43 miles north on **Perkinsville Road** to Williams (23 miles unpaved, but graded).

✸ To Do

HIKING There are a handful of trails in the Prescott National Forest just outside town along AZ 89A. The best time for hiking them is Mar. through Nov. Contact the Verde Ranger District. Check out the 5.5-mile-long **North Mingus Trail** on Mingus Mountain.

✸ Wilder Places

Mingus Mountain. One of the area's high points stands at just over 7,700 feet about 7 miles south off AZ 89A. Several trails take you around the mountain, through forests of Gambel oak trees up into ponderosa pines laced with bigtooth maple and aspen trees. This makes for some gorgeous autumn color hikes. Contact the Verde Ranger District.

Woodchute Wilderness. Another high point, Woodchute Mountain, at 7,800 feet, lies in a designated wilderness. Its popular Woodchute Trail takes you to its heights. It's a great place for wildflowers after a wet winter. Contact the Verde Ranger District.

✸ Lodging

HOTELS 🐾 **Conner Hotel** (928-634-5006 or 800-523-3554), 164 Main St. You can simply walk out the door into the hub of activity in Jerome when you stay here. The restored hotel has a balance of antiquity with some modern-day luxuries. Rooms have antiques, overstuffed furniture, and local artwork and photographs celebrating Jerome's history. Each room has a king or queen bed, private tiled bath, satellite TV, telephone, coffeemaker, microwave, and mini fridge. Rooms 1–4 are located above a bar; all others are quiet. $85–145.

♿ **Jerome Grand Hotel** (928-634-8200 or 888-817-6788), 200 Hill St. What used to be the ultramodern United Verde Hospital that opened in 1927 is now a restored hotel with the best views in town. The highest public structure in the Verde Valley stands solidly on a 50-degree slope, built to withstand mining blasts of up to 100,000 pounds of dynamite. A 1926 Otis elevator provides service to all five floors. The 50-horsepower

Kewanee boiler provides steam heat to all 23 rooms. Each has queen or twin beds, TV and VCR, private bath, and telephone serviced by an antique switchboard. No pets. The views from the Balcony Rooms are worth the little extra they cost. $100–230.

BED AND BREAKFASTS **Ghost City Inn Bed and Breakfast** (888-634-4678), 541 Main St. (AZ 89A). One of Jerome's most popular places to stay, for good reason, has the best of both worlds, blending history and comfort. Built as a boardinghouse around 1890 and remodeled in the 1990s, the building still has quirky lines and original bead board ceilings—not to mention gorgeous views of the Verde Valley. Six themed room interiors range from period to outdoor. Rooms have private bath, TV, VCR, ceiling fan, and air-conditioning; breakfast included. $95–145.

🐾 **The Surgeon's House Bed and Breakfast** (800-639-1452). This Hill Street home, built in 1916, was once

THE SURGEON'S HOUSE B&B.

owned by a doctor. The home has a decor akin to a kaleidoscope with colorful, curious, and creative items and artifacts. Owner-innkeeper Andrea Prince, as distinctive as her home, has a ready story about all the interesting things in her bed and breakfast and life in Jerome. Andrea has created a number of little niches on the property for you to enjoy, from a lively patio to a hidden garden. Breakfast is a real treat here, because, not only is Andrea an excellent cook, but she adds creative touches to produce a meal that's a meld of gourmet and yummy. Plus, the view from the dining room is awesome. Nonguests can join the breakfast hour for $15 and 12 hours' notice. Pets are okay with prior notice and a $35 fee. $100–150.

❋ Where to Eat

DINING OUT The Asylum (928-639-3197), 200 Hills St. (in the Jerome Grand Hotel). Open daily for lunch 11–3, dinner 5–9. The restaurant motto—*We're not just a restaurant, we're an adventure!*—fits. The wine-red interiors set off by white table-cloths and black napkins celebrate the menu's bold elegance, which appears from the wine to the desserts. The restaurant often earns the *Wine Spectator* Award of Excellence for their selection of wines. Professional wait staff tend gracefully to your needs. The prickly pear pork is perfect. The butternut squash soup, which lures people back for return visits, is silken good; the homemade bread, distinctively doughy; the brûlée cheesecake, exquisite. The short tips special had pockets of saltiness. This news utterly astounded our waiter when we told him. The short tips never made it on the check (and the staff had no idea of our identity)—a classy move that's classically Asylum. Lunch entrées $9–14, dinner entrées $17–38.

Flatiron Café (928-634-2733), 416 Main St. Open Thu.–Mon. 8:30–4. Situated at the fork of the main road, where traffic starts its wind through the town of Jerome from the highway, the Flatiron is easy to find. The menu runs from healthy (maple-nut granola with yogurt) to basic (two thick slices of sourdough toast with butter and jam) to comfort gourmet (bagel and lox) food here. Lunch reads the same (albacore tuna to roast beef to smoked salmon quesadilla). Beverages include espresso drinks, teas, and chai. $2.50–9.50.

Red Rooster Café (928-634-7087), 363 School St. Open weekdays 11–3, weekends 11–4. With colorful interiors as eye-opening as a rooster's crow at first light, fresh food, and desserts practically hot out of the oven, Red Rooster is, as their motto states, *worth a trip up the hill*. Chef Kim Hollow believes being bold with spices, and it works. The homemade salads, soups, and sandwiches turn out excellent, which brings a good turnout of diners. She always has a cache of good vegetables and fruits, garlic, chili paste, and a unique cheese. Desserts are house-made each day. Entrées $5–8.

EATING OUT English Kitchen (928-634-2132), 119 Jerome Ave. Open Tue.–Sat. 8–3. This is Jerome's version of a local diner. Food is simple and basic here in this pert white building with a wooden patio. It's the oldest restaurant in Jerome. Its history starts with Chinaman Charley Hong; the Chinese were famous for giving their restaurants literal Anglo names. With dependable hours of operation and decent food, it's usually busy, especially the patio during warm weather. Entrées $5.79–8.79.

Haunted Hamburger (928-634-0554), 410 N. Clark St. Open daily 11–9. You can get many different items here, from hamburger to ribs and steak, or you can choose french fries or a salad side. Everything is dependably good. Hamburgers, however, are the stars of the show, and the more oozing with trimmings, the better. The celebrated burgers draw people from all over the country. The only thing better than the hamburgers is the view from the porch. But you might have to wait for it. Entrées $6.95–17.99.

✳ The Arts

When Jerome turned ghost town, the ramshackle buildings looked good to the freethinkers who took up residence in the 1970s. Though the culture was creative, and especially expressive, they all weren't necessarily artists. Over the years the visual arts have maintained a role in the community. Lately the art has matured, and it is at the point collectors may find some great buys.

✳ Shopping

The whole town is a shopping fest, from the kitschy to the collectible.

THE RED ROOSTER CAFÉ.

SEDONA/OAK CREEK CANYON

T hey were warned not to stay, the legend about Palatkwapi says. Spirit guides sternly directed them not to indulge themselves in the idyllic atmosphere of Palatkwapi, the "place of the redrocks." But the early Hopi ignored the spiritual guidance of their deities and pursued their life of leisure with abandon. Finally a few virtuous Hopi entreated the deities to bring a flood.

Before the flood forced the early Hopi to higher ground, and their eventual settlement at First Mesa, legend says the people built Palatkwapi into a thriving cultural and religious center. Palatkwapi, now called Sedona, was a meeting and healing place for Indians all over the Southwest 1,000 to 2,000 years ago. Now a town with more than 40 art galleries and 22 public art landmarks packed into 15 square miles—and enough seers, crystal shops, and New Age centers to reek havoc at a séance—things haven't changed much. The redrocked town has the world passing through its doorways, to the tune of around four million visitors a year. And for good reason: The city got the top slot on *USA Today*'s list of the 10 Most Beautiful Cities in the United States.

THE RED ROCK–SECRET CANYON WILDERNESS BORDERS SEDONA TO THE NORTH.

Situated at the mouth of Oak Creek Canyon, where erosion has carved the Mogollon Rim into a jigsaw of colorful sandstone mesas and formations that stretch for several miles along the creek, Sedona is the area's hub—though Oak Creek Canyon, with its awesome riparian forest and slickrock formations, has also racked up some impressive accolades, ranking among the nation's most beautiful drives (AZ 89A). Residents claim the canyon has its own set of vortexes, and it will take you down a notch or two (to which visitors will testify) no matter how hectic your lifestyle.

Though its appearance has changed since its recent cowtown days, Sedona hasn't really hasn't strayed too far. You can still buy a pair of custom-made boots. The same characteristics of the cowboy founding fathers show up in modern-day residents: These are some independent, iconoclastic, community-minded, informal folks, not to mention some out-and-out characters. Neither has the town veered from its legendary Hopi spirituality. Beyond the vortexes and metaphysical hype, you can still feel a special inspiration when you visit. If it's not enough to change your life or heal you—it's certainly enough to get you centered and relaxed.

GUIDANCE Uptown Visitor Center (928-282-7722 or 800-288-7336; www .visitsedona.com), 331 Forest Rd. Contact **Coconino National Forest Red Rock Ranger District** (928-282-4119), 250 Brewer Rd., for information on trails, picnic areas, and back roads. Open 8–4:30.

GETTING THERE *By car:* Sedona is located at the intersection of AZ 89A and 179. You can take the scenic route from Flagstaff via AZ 89A. From I-17, exit at AZ 179 to Sedona; or take AZ 260 to Cottonwood then AZ 89A east to Sedona. *By air:* **Sedona Airport** (928-282-4487), 235 Air Terminal Dr., has transient hangers.

GETTING AROUND **Sedona RoadRunner** (928-282-0938). This daily free city transit service runs every 10 minutes 9–6:30 on the 1.3-mile corridor between Hillside Galleries on AZ 179 and the north end of uptown Sedona on AZ 89A.

Sedona Trolley (928-282-4211), 276 N. AZ 89A, Suite B (in the Uptown Depot at the traffic light), offers two tours—one heading uptown, the other to West Sedona. $10 adults, $5 ages 12 and under.

WHEN TO COME Sedona's a busy city every month of the year, except for Aug. and Jan. The best weather happens in the spring and fall, along with the biggest influx of tourists. Summer sees near-daily thunderstorms, which locals consider an attraction not to miss. December, like the shoulder seasons, is crowded; make sure you have a reservation if you plan on staying.

MEDICAL EMERGENCY **Sedona Urgent Care** (928-203-4813), 2530 W. AZ 89A, Bldg. A, for minor emergencies. **Verde Valley Medical Center Sedona Campus** (928-204-3000), 3700 W. AZ 89A.

✳ To See

Chapel of the Holy Cross (928-282-4069), 780 Chapel Rd. Open daily. Built by artist Marguerite Brunswig Staude in 1956 as a nondenominational monument to God. Staude considered art to be the search for the spiritual side of the universe. Besides spiritual, beautiful panoramas make it inspirational. Free.

Sedona Heritage Museum (928-282-7038), 735 Jordan Rd. Open daily 11–3. This founding family's home and apple orchard, now a redrock Historic Landmark, gives you a look into Sedona lifestyles back in its pioneer and ranching days. Exhibits change in the main room a few times a year. Several other rooms have neatly arranged displays. Take one of the scenic pathways through the fruit orchard and past vintage farm implements to the museum. The 4,000-square-foot Apple Barn houses a 40-foot-long apple-sorting machine from the 1940s. $3.

✳ To Do

AIR RIDES **Red Rock Biplane Tours** (928-204-5939). Located at the Sedona Airport. Fully narrated tours give a fun side of Sedona by air. From the mouth-stretching (g-force-induced) takeoff to the smooth-as-silk glide around the redrocks, with a few tummy-tickling moments in between through vortexes (aka updrafts). $89–159 per person; $459 for a private hour-long tour for two; $250 for 30 minutes of "stick time."

Arizona Helicopter Adventures (928-282-0904), 235 Air Terminal Dr. Located in the Airport Main Terminal Building. For 12 to 35 minutes you can glide around the folds of spectacular redrock canyons along the Mogollon Rim, enjoying eye-level glances into Indian ruins and dramatic sweeps along curious rock formations that seem only a touch away. Sure, the world tilts when the helicopter banks around canyons, and the bottom falls out when you zoom back down crevices, but who cares about updrafts and tilts with scenery this pretty? $58–138 per person.

If you're looking for a more docile aerial experience, your best choice is the oldest form of aviation—a ride in a hot-air balloon. Drift 1,000 feet above the ground in a basket held up by a balloon eight stories high. **Arizona Balloon Works** (928-399-9833) has sunset flights and travels above the Prescott National Forest. **Northern Light Balloon Expeditions** (928-282-2274) travels at dawn nearest the redrocks above the Coconino National Forest. **Sky High Balloon Adventures** (928-204-1395) floats above the Prescott National Forest.

Skydive Sedona (928-649-8899), 1001 W. Mingus Ave., Cottonwood. If a biplane, helicopter, or hot-air balloon isn't enough, maybe an exhilarating free fall toward the redrocks will do? $220 per person.

FISHING Rainbow Trout Farm (928-282-5799), 3500 N. AZ 89A, No. 88. Open Mon.–Fri. 9–5, Sat.–Sun. 9–6. Even if you don't fish, the scenery here is gorgeous—ruddy Oak Creek Canyon sandstone walls in a riparian forest. The $2 admission fee includes fishing equipment, bait, use of grill and picnic tables; children under 6 free.

GOLF Oak Creek Country Club (928-284-1660 or 888-703-9489), 690 Bell Rock Blvd. Sedona's original championship course was designed by Robert Trent Jones. The 145-acre course looks more midwestern than arid southwestern with its three lakes. The player-friendly links features tree-lined doglegs with strategically placed fairway bunkers in the landing areas, and slightly elevated greens surrounded by large, swirling bunkers. $69–125.

Sedona Golf Resort (928-284-9355), 35 Ridge Trail Dr. This is the course that lures golfers from around the world to its emerald greens winding around jaw-dropping redrocks. The 6,646-yard, par-71 course presents one of the most unforgettable golf experiences in the world. Designer Gary Panks worked in a number of challenges that demand your attention, no matter how you rank in the game. Rates include green fee, cart, and range balls. $69–105.

SEDONA'S PINK JEEP PLAZA.

HIKING In this enchanting landscape full of legends and lore, hiking takes on new meaning, if only being bedazzled by the redrock cliffs and sensual smells of the canyon forest. Check out the **Secret Canyon**, **Bell Rock**, or **Loy Canyon** trails. The **West Fork Trail** is the most popular (and beautiful) in Oak Creek Canyon. $5 parking pass required to park on national forest land; $8 parking fee at Call of the Canyon parking area for West Fork Trail.

HORSEBACK RIDING See *Jeep Tours*.

INDIAN RUINS/ROCK ART Sinagua Indian signs appear all around the area. You may serendipitously spot a ruin in a tucked-away alcove during a canyon hike, or relics on a road or trail. Look, but don't take. Guided tours are the best way to guarantee sightings. Also, you can see an excellent site at the **Palatki Heritage Area** (928-282-3854), managed by Coconino National Forest Red Rock Ranger District; open daily 9:30–3. You must make reservations to visit the site.

JEEP TOURS A number of tour companies will accommodate your every whim when it comes to exploring redrock country. Usually each tours a particular area exclusively. Iconic **Pink Jeep Tours** (928-282-5000), 204 N. AZ 89A, for instance, exclusively visits the Broken Arrow area. Only **Sedona Red Rock Jeep Tours** (800-848-7728), 270 N. AZ 89A, visits Soldier Pass Trail area. Both offer everything from jeep tours (adrenaline rushes included) to guided horse-back rides, as well as spiritual and archaeological tours. Tours start at $45.

MOUNTAIN BIKING Though much of the national forest area is designated wilderness where nothing mechanized (as in motorized vehicles or bicycles) is allowed, there are still a number of trails you can cycle on. Contact **Coconino National Forest** for more information. **Absolute Bikes** (928-284-1242), 6101 AZ 179, Suite C, village of Oak Creek, rents bicycles and has information on where to ride.

✳ Spas

New Day Spa (928-282-7502), 1449 W. AZ 89A, Suite 1. Nurturing and sooth-ing, the luxury starts in the waiting area when a meltingly warm pillow filled with calming and restorative herbs gets wrapped around your neck. In the treatment rooms, therapists use natural products, from Alpine goat butter to Yon-Ka facial products from Paris to high-quality herbal products made in town by Body Bliss. Several dozen treatments—from simple massage to Ayurvedic and exclusive body therapy—are tailor-made to fit your needs. Aura-Soma therapy uses color for internal insights. Nail care and waxing available. The spa plans to expand in 2007 with a steam room, cold plunge pool, and outdoor Jacuzzis on the rooftop. Body treatments $125–240, massages $55–140, facials $95–140.

The Spa at Sedona Rouge (928-203-4111), Sedona Rouge Hotel, 2250 W. AZ 89A. Dedicated to calming the mind, balancing the emotions, and connecting the body to the rhythms of nature. Though the spa offers a menu, albeit short and sweet, the sky is the limit when it comes right down to the treatment, inas-much as each 60- or 90-minute session is tailor-made to the needs of the guest and administered with some of the best hands in the Southwest. Therapies include deep tissue, craniosacral, energy work, and reflexology; hot stones, essential oils, brown sugar, or fresh fruits (depending on the season); facials, cou-ples, and exclusive treatments. The signature olive oil lemon-mint soap is a hit—even men come to buy it at the spa shop. Men's and women's steam rooms, outdoor whirlpools, and Tranquility Room and Garden. Call for spa retreat pack-ages. Sixty- to 90-minute sessions cost $95 to $150; couples, $180–270.

☙ **Stillpoint . . . Living in Balance, Inc.** (928-301-0830), 415 Juniper. Call for appointment. Most spa therapies cater to relaxing the body. Stillpoint . . . Living in Balance provides a more therapeutic experience in a quiet atmosphere dedicated to their clients' personal space. Owners and therapists Joy and Cynthia mix massage with energy therapies to produce a powerful experience. Their signature, The Stillpoint, is a blend of therapeutic massage and energetic balancing with the use of essential oils, crystals, and hot basalt stones. The intriguing menu includes a variety of therapies, including aroma, lymphatic drainage, and craniosacral; reflexology; and integrative massage that includes Swedish, deep tissue, neuromuscular, and polarity. They also offer a menu of other therapies, including clairvoyant readings and chakra balancing. $75–115.

DESTINATION SPAS Mii Amo Spa (928-282-2900), Enchantment Resort, 525 Boynton Canyon Rd. Situated in a redrock canyon sacred to the Apache, and containing a powerful vortex, this destination spa has that distinctive Sedona atmosphere of peace and contentment. The spa deservedly rates among the top in the world. You can get a number of classic treatments here from top therapists, including facials, massages, and popular body treatments, as well as sessions that incorporate energy; or you can choose from a menu of "journeys" with different emphases (de-stressing, losing weight, anti-aging, spiritual, and more). Whatever you decide, it feels somehow more redemptive because of that special Sedona aura. There are a number of classes and activities you can partake in during the day, such as a session in a meditation room with a large amethyst crystal to coax you into a more intuitive state. Mii Amo even makes three squares a day more special: The restaurant serves delicious healthy meals with a gourmet touch from an exhibition kitchen. Call for reservations and prices.

> **VORTEXES**
> In the mid-1970s a medium channeled information describing four major electromagnetic energy sources called vortexes near Sedona. The town has never been the same.
> **Boynton Canyon**: Go west on AZ 179 to Dry Creek Rd., turn right, and follow the signs to the canyon and the 2-mile-long Boynton Canyon Trail, just outside the entrance to the Enchantment Resort.
> **Airport Mesa**: Go west on AZ 179 W and turn left onto Airport Rd.; drive about 0.5 mile to reach a trailhead for 3.5-mile-long Airport Mesa Trail.
> **Bell Rock**: Located in the village of Oak Creek along AZ 179 just north of Jacks Canyon Rd.
> **Cathedral Rock**: Take the Red Rock Crossing Trail in Crescent Moon Picnic Area (see *Wilder Places*).
> **Sedona Heart Center** (928-282-2733), 1385 W. AZ 89A, gives vortex tours in air-conditioned vans twice a day for $75 a tour; $130 for both. If the vortexes inspire you, the Heart Center offers individual energy work sessions as well.

✳ Wilder Places

Crescent Moon Picnic Area (contact the Coconino National Forest). Open 8–8; till dusk from Memorial Day through Labor Day. Many visitors come to this pretty space to see one of the most photographed scenes in the Southwest: Cathedral Rock reflected in the waters of Oak Creek at Red Rock Crossing. You can also fish, swim, and wade in Oak Creek, and picnic on its banks. $7 per car; $1 for walk-ins.

Red Rock Secret Mountain Wilderness (contact the Coconino National Forest). One of the state's most charismatic designated wilderness areas has several memorable hiking trails. Some lead to vortexes, others travel distinctive canyons, and some climb up to extraordinary panoramas. All travel through the distinctive redrocks that made Sedona famous.

∞ ⊘ & **Red Rock State Park** (928-282-6907), 4050 Red Rock Loop Rd. Open year-round: Oct.–Mar., 8–5; Apr., 8–6; May–Aug., 8–8; Sep., 8–6. This 5-mile network of trails presents excellent light hikes for families. The park offers guided nature hikes. No pets allowed. $6 per car, $2 per bicycle.

Slide Rock State Park (928-282-3034). Once a homestead owned by the Pendley family, this streamside park provides a grandiose experience along the slickrock shelves that brace Oak Creek; you can ride the water as it blasts through a chute. For a more mild-mannered experience, peruse the grounds and the apple orchard that Frank Pendley planted in 1912. The trees still supply enough fruit for bears and humans to enjoy—self-service for the bears, while whole fruit and containers of fresh juice are sold at the park's Slide Rock Market to humans. $8 per car, $2 per bicycle.

✳ Lodging

BED AND BREAKFASTS ∞ **Briar Patch Inn** (928-282-2342 or 888-809-3030). The 9-acre creekside grounds drip with natural opulence and serenity. The property has 18 cottages, decorated in a southwestern style with Indian art and crafts. Each cottage has king or queen bed(s), radio, CD player, and private entrance, bath, and patio. Most cottages have full kitchen or kitchenette, some have mini refrigerator, and three have a TV; all include a hearty and home-made buffet breakfast. In summer a classical duet plays music on the lawn where breakfast is served. Yoga happens during summer weekends. The inn's gentle and kind atmosphere inspires your personal celebrations to bubble up: People fall in love, children dance barefoot, and professional dancers take a few impromptu swirls during breakfast. An on-site aesthetician gives marvelous facials in the creekside gazebo or your cottage. The inn has a long list of loyal guests; plan your stay early to be sure to get a room. Two-night minimum on weekends, 3-night on holidays. No pets. $195–385.

∞ **Sedona Cathedral Hideaway** (928-203-4178 or 866-973-3662), West Sedona. This ultraboutique hideaway has up-close views of Cathedral Rock, one of Sedona's vibratory centers. Whether you believe in the power of vortexes or not, the views are magnificent and inspiring. The trail to the formation is only a few minutes' walk away. However, the formation is only one facet of this hidden gem. When you don't want anyone else to know where you are, you want total romance, and/or you just want to bask in some self-indulgent doting, this hideaway can become a destination in itself. Open space, so attractive to the human spirit, plays a big role here. The home's huge rooms have a line of windows that bring the outdoors in. Room amenities like comfort-number king-sized beds, fireplace, double shower, Jacuzzi tub, WiFi, surround sound, iPod jacks, DVD player, flat-screen TV, mini fridge, microwave, and personal safe match those found in any large resort. But the 4,500-square-foot hideaway has only two rooms. Innkeeper-owners Kathy and Larry attend to your every need and request, from a gourmet breakfast (included with accommodations and served where you like) to facials, massages, and anti-aging treatments (extra). The 1-acre property has a bocce ball court, labyrinth, and sundecks for you to soak in rays from the sun, energy from Cathedral Rock, or your own glow from all things wonderful. $240–295; $20 for each additional person.

HOTELS AND INNS 🐾 **El Portal** (800-313-0017), 95 Portal Lane. This one-of-a-kind 12-room inn was built of recycled wood, handmade adobe, vintage art tiles, and 200-year-old wood beams to replicate a 1900 Spanish hacienda while staying true to original style and construction methods. Decorated with Frank Lloyd Wright in mind, the inn is a mecca for architectural aficionados. Gracious innkeeper-owners Steve and Connie Segner and part owner Lynda Bour-

geois make the rounds with guests in the inn's great room, which converts into a dining area that serves gourmet breakfasts and exquisite weekend dinners (meals extra) prepared by Eden Messer. The trio elucidate upon the inn's fascinating architecture and its special location—it was built on a piece of land that a water diviner claimed has vortexes—as long as your interest holds. Make sure you know if you want to relax or have energy, because one vortex energizes and the other relaxes you. $225–495; specials July–Sep.

🌸 🐾 **Iris Garden Inn** (800-321-8988), 390 Jordan Rd. Located two blocks from the main highway in Uptown. If you don't plan to spend a lot of time in your lodging, these neat, clean, and pleasant rooms may work perfectly for you. All rooms have a mini refrigerator, microwave, coffeemaker, TV, phone, and free WiFi. Two pet rooms are available for $15 a day extra. Roll-away bed, $10 extra.

∞ 🐾 ♿ **L'Auberge Inn** (928-282-1661 or 800-272-6777), 301 L'Auberge Lane. This quiet, wooded Sedona classic offers the height of relaxed Old Word class and romance. The property mixes rustic opulence with a storybook atmosphere on the banks of Oak Creek. Its new boutique spa, open to guests only, meets the sensuous standards of the inn and has experienced service-minded therapists. You'll also find the four-star L'Auberge Restaurant (see *Dining Out*) and a business center; fresh scones, coffee, and tea are served daily 7–9 AM, and cocktails and wine each evening 6–7 in the lobby. There's astronomy on Friday evenings. Individually decorated lodge rooms have king bed and private patio or balcony.

Garden and creekside cabins look like French country cottages with their wooden details, rustic wood-burning fireplaces, and covered porches that soak in the sweet spicy smell of Arizona sycamore trees along Oak Creek; each has mini refrigerator. $20 daily service fee covers most tips, WiFi, and use of business center. Pets get spoiled with a dog bed, mat, feeding bowl, and host of gourmet goodies. $275–475.

⊗ 🐾 ♿ **Sedona Rouge Hotel & Spa** (928-203-4111), 2250 W. AZ 89A. Quiet and peaceful even though it's situated right along Sedona's main highway, this luxury boutique hotel sidesteps any hint of southwestern influence with a full-spectrum Mediterranean style inspired by Roman, French, and North African cultures prominent in Andalusia—the Venice of Moorish Spain. The highly tactile decor drips with saturated colors on organic appointments of wood, metal, and glass. The owners' vision for a classy, trendy, sexy, and fun hotel works; children are welcome, but adults prevail. You'll find 77 guest rooms, heated lap pool, fitness room with state-of-the-art equipment and personal trainer available, yoga and tai chi classes, 2,500 square feet of meeting space, conference room, complimentary WiFi, and cable TV, along with complimentary bottled water and light snacks. $139–249.

LODGE ⊗ 🐾 🐾 **Sky Ranch Lodge** (928-282-6400 or 800-708-6400). Located just before the airport, near the end of Airport Rd. The same family has owned this property since 1982, and it's one of the best deals in town. The grounds have mature landscaping full of gardens with winding

paths, bridges, creeks, ponds, and little secluded niches, as well as a swimming pool and spa. A variety of rooms have deck, private patio, beamed and vaulted ceiling, kitchenette with microwave, and/or fireplace. Each room includes a king or two queen-sized beds, cable TV, and complimentary bottled water. Pets $10 each. $75–185.

RESORT Enchantment Resort and Mii Amo Spa (928-282-2900), 525 Boynton Canyon Rd. The resort sits in its own private canyon, sacred to the Apache, from which a major vortex emanates. It wears its name well, as guests have repeatedly commented. It's the kind of place where you start to wear a smile for no reason, and find yourself staring at the magnificent cliffs for a long time. Even Type As can't resist the chance to just relax and enjoy the elegance of nature. The property includes two restaurants (Yavapai is four star), the world-renowned Mii Amo spa, a clubhouse, a gift shop, a game room, meeting rooms, seven championship tennis courts (thanks to former owner and tennis guru John Gardiner), five pools, an outdoor whirlpool spa, a par-3 golf course and putting green, and croquet. Rooms have king or queen beds, sitting area, full bath and dressing area, deck with views; studios have a beehive fireplace, kitchenette and dining area, and gas grill; hacienda studios feature full kitchens. $295–425 for a Casita Bedroom, $640–900 for a one-bedroom Casita Suite, and up.

✳ Where to Eat

DINING OUT El Rincon (928-282-4648), Tlaquepaque Village. Open Mon.–Sat. 11–9 (till 8 Sun.). The family-run restaurant has held the admiration of the locals for more than 30 years with their blend of traditional Mexican cuisine and Navajo influences. There are many reasons for the success: The wait staff have remained the same for years—the true sign of a successful establishment. Too, there's no lard in the house; they use fresh ingredients and make each meal individually. The food has won several awards. And they make their own sweet-and-sour base for the margaritas! The house specialty is chimichangas made with masa dough instead of a tortilla and served enchilada style with sour cream. The chocolate chimi (made with Ghirardelli chocolate) and light-as-clouds sopaipilla are the most popular desserts. Dinner reservations suggested. Child plates available. Entrées $10.75–15.

Heartline Café (928-282-0785), 1600 and 1610 W. AZ 89A. Open for lunch daily 11–2:30 (closed Tue. in summer months) and dinner 5–9:30. Quintessentially Sedona with its eclectic menu of entrées served in a casual atmosphere, this restaurant is a local favorite. Consistently good

Cowboy Club (928-282-2400), 241 AZ 89A. Open daily for lunch 11–4, dinner 5–10. If the walls could talk, we'd know a whole lot about goings-on during the last 50 years in Sedona. The place, established as the Oak Creek Tavern, was once *the* hangout of choice for cowboys, movie actors, celebrities, and locals. Now it's one of the popular haunts for residents and visitors alike. Wood plank walls, a rock wall fireplace, a scenic mural, and prints of cowboy scenes by local artists create a cowboy atmosphere. The menu of high-desert cuisine revels in it. You can try something unusual and order rattlesnake, or get an excellent cut of buffalo. The steaks and ribs rate among the best in town. And it's pure comfort food when it comes to sides, such as garlic or sour cream mashed potatoes. Desserts are house-made, and your waiter will let you know which are the best that night. For finer dining, try the **Silver Saddle**—same restaurant, different room, and a more upscale menu. Entrées $9–17 for lunch, $10–43 for dinner.

AT THE COWBOY CLUB.

entrées range from vegetarian choices to Kobe beef. Thai touches appear in the flower petals on the salad and curry sauces; pastas and gnocchi feature Mediterranean influences; spices show up all over the place, with pleasing results. The wine list has consistently won the *Wine Spectator* Award of Excellence since 1998. The dessert plate for two is generous enough to feed four. Lunch entrées $9.75–15, dinner entrées $15.50–25.50.

L'Auberge de Sedona (928-282-1667), 301 L'Auberge Lane. Open daily 7:30 AM–9 PM. A brief description of this Four Diamond restaurant would read: Entrées include fish and meat dishes served in gourmet French style. But once you talk with the wait staff, attentive and pleasant, or restaurant manager Maury Kepley, you start to understand why this spot is held in such high regard. The ingredients—from the French butter to the meat and fish—are of the utmost quality, whether you order sea bass or roast pheasant, butter-basted opah or beef tenderloin. An assembly

DESSERT AT THE REDSTONE CABIN.

line of chefs make everything from scratch, from the bread in the pan-seared foie gras and huckleberry bread pudding to the rolled chocolate candy garnish alongside the triple chocolate mousse. In quintessential French style, sauces are big here—some take up to 17 hours to prepare. Finally, the wine list gets the nod from *Wine Spectator*, which has designated it one of the best in the nation. The more casual **Terrace Bistro at L'Auberge de Sedona** has the same menu, but served outside along the banks of Oak Creek (same hours, too, weather permitting). Entrées $29–39.

Redstone Cabin (928-282-4200), 260 Van Deren. Just off the main drag with a special secluded ambience, this fine-dining restaurant has a rustic elegance. A river rock fireplace in the dining room and soothing water feature on the patio bring a natural feel to the place. Heat lamps and wool blankets make outdoor dining, with the redrocks in view, possible even when the weather turns cold. The menu is hearty and delicious, from the pistachio halibut to the prime rib. Meals change seasonally, but the steaks are always excellent, and the menu has some of the tenderest buffalo you'll taste. The wine list, a selection of steady favorites and interesting finds, has character. Entrées $14–40.

Troia's (928-282-0123), 1885 W. AZ 89A. Open Tue.–Sat. at 5 PM. Rosanne and Sam Troia have created a warm, open dining space serving classic Sicilian food. Locals are often busy meeting and greeting neighbors and friends when the place fills (reservations are recommended). The magic happens in the exhibition kitchen. Lasagna and shrimp scampi are the most popular entrées, and the olive tapenade appetizer is a favorite. The veal is butter tender, the fettuccine Alfredo rich and sensuous; the minestrone soup is like a garden—thick with beans and pasta and full of veggies. Pizzas are made with fresh dough and house-made sauce. Save room for one of the desserts, many of which are homemade; the spumoni is excellent. Entrées $12–23.

The Yavapai Restaurant (928-282-2900), Enchantment Resort (see *Resorts*). Open daily for breakfast 6:30–11:30, lunch 11:30–2:15, dinner 5:30–9:15. Leave your cell phones behind and get ready to commune with food in a most delicious and extravagant way. The first course is enough to make a mini meal. The pan-seared foie gras is over the top. Carpaccio of beef comes with quail eggs, and gnocchi practically melts in your mouth. Second-course salads are artful and fresh. The main course presents classics such as duck, Colorado lamb, and seared scallops. Creative desserts—more an exclamation point than a rich final course—make a perfect ending. The venue holds the *Wine Spectator*'s Award of Excellence. End-to-end picture windows make twilight dining highly desirable; be sure to make a reservation. $19–29.

EATING OUT ❧ ♪ **Black Cow Café** (928-203-9868), 229 N. AZ 89A. Open daily 8 AM–9 PM. At first blush you think this is an ice cream parlor specializing in gooey sundaes—from classic tin roof to caramel Snicker and the Chocolate Lover's Dream. But it's more. First, it's not just ice cream they sell. It's some of the best ice cream you'll ever taste. The confection, made on the premises, shows up

on menus at better local restaurants. Next, the house-made cinnamon rolls and Danishes melt in your mouth. Then the World's Best Hot Dog carries its title well. Pastas and veggie sandwiches are available, too. $3.95–6.25.

❧ **Garland's Indian Gardens Trading Post** (928-282-7702), 3951 N. AZ 89A. Open daily 8–6. This specialty grocery has all the fixings for a gourmet picnic: great-tasting deli sandwiches and salads, sumptuous sweets, locally grown fruits and vegetables. Take your goodies across the street to eat along the banks of Oak Creek, or have a seat on the outside patio. A lagniappe: The property has a soothing vortex. $6.95–8.95.

❧ **Kaiser's West** (928-204-2088), 2920 W. AZ 89A. Open Mon.–Fri. 7 AM–8:30 PM, Sat. 8–8:30, Sun. 8–2. Expect to find a packed place during the prime mealtimes here. The staff usually go the extra mile to serve everyone in a timely manner. And what they serve is good basic favorites with innovative ingredients that make them a little different than the diner experience you expect. The Finest French Toast lives up to its name. At dinner the brisket and barbecue ribs are favorites. Desserts have names like Judi's Famous Pecan Pie and Homemade Ice Cream. Entrées $7–20.

❧ **Sally's Mesquite Grill** (928-282-6533), 250 Jordan Rd. Open daily 11–7. Owner Mike Sally got interested in barbecue when he was the general manager for the Ottawa (Canada) Rough Runners football team and on a recruiting trip in Dallas, Texas. He toyed with recipes, fed friends and neighbors, then opened up Sally's. Everything is smoked fresh (ribs for 3 to 4 hours, beef and pork for 12 hours, and chicken for 3 hours) and melts in your mouth. The (secret) sauce has a homemade taste, the beans carry only a kiss of sweetness and (secret) flavors, and the coleslaw contains other (secret) vegetables and spices. $7.25–19.95.

✳ The Arts

When surrealist painter and sculptor Max Ernst moved to Sedona in 1950, a trail of other artists and writers followed. The Cowboy Artists of America started here in 1965 (at the present Cowboy Club). Today more than 200 artists in every medium and style, contemporary to Native American, live in Sedona. Galleries cluster in **Tlaquepaque Arts and Crafts Village**, **Hillside Sedona**, and **Hozho Shops and Galleries** (see *Selective Shopping*). The **Sedona Arts Center** (928-282-3809), AZ 89A and Art Barn Rd., holds regular exhibits.

✳ Selective Shopping

Shops line the main highway here, congregating especially in uptown and a few shopping areas. **Hillside Sedona** (928-282-4500), 671 AZ 179, and **Hozho Distinctive Shops & Galleries** (928-204-2257), 431 AZ 179, have distinctive shops, world-class galleries, and award-wining restaurants in a multilevel marketplace.

Hoel's Indian Shop (928-282-3985), 9589 N. AZ 89A. Open daily 9:30–5; best to call first. You'll find one of the finest selections of quality Indian jewelry, fetishes, pottery, baskets, kachinas, and rugs here, made by Navajo, Hopi, Zuni, and Santo Domingo artists.

Tlaquepaque Arts & Crafts Village (928-282-4838), 336 AZ 179. Open daily 10–5. You'll find more than 45

galleries, shops, and restaurants in this open-air shopping venue of Spanish-style buildings.

✳ Special Events

January: **Sedona International Film Festival** (928-282-1177) presents more than 100 features, documentaries, and shorts from around the world, plus workshops.

February: **The Sedona Marathon** (800-775-7671) brings runners from around the nation to *fartlek* through the redrocks.

June: **Sedona Taste** (928-282-0122). Fine food and drink at Los Abrigados Resort & Spa benefits the Boys & Girls Clubs of Northern Arizona.

August: **Red Rocks Music Festival** (928-733-7257). This weeklong classical music festival features world-class chamber music, orchestral performances, master classes, and workshops.

September: **Sedona Jazz on the Rocks** boasts internationally known vocalists, musicians, composers, and conductors at indoor and outdoor venues throughout the town.

October: The **Sedona Arts Festival** (928-204-9456) is rated as one of the top in the nation and features fine arts and crafts, cuisine from Sedona's finer restaurants, and continuous entertainment at Sedona Red Rock High School.

Mid-November through New Year's Day: **Red Rock Fantasy** (928-282-1777 or 800-521-3131). More than a million lights are used in almost 50 displays made by families.

December: **Festival of Lights** (928-282-4838) shows off thousands of luminaries at Tlaquepaque Arts and Crafts Village; entertainment, too.

Central Arizona 2

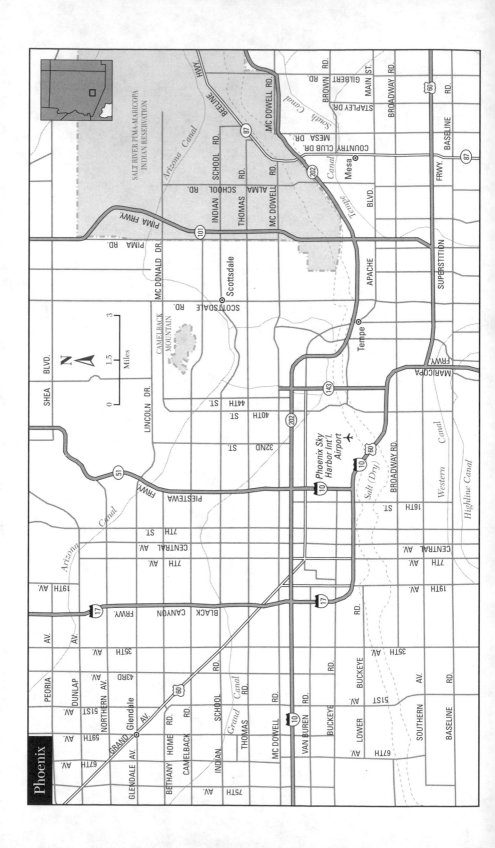

Phoenix

GREATER PHOENIX AND THE VALLEY OF THE SUN

A t first blush you might never guess that the nation's fifth largest city lies in one of the world's principal deserts, averaging only 7 inches of rain a year. Lushly landscaped, bejeweled with swimming pools, and gushing with fountains, Phoenix is an oasis in a sear landscape. With 325-plus sun-soaked days each year, this city's winters are what many folks might call a good summer day. The temperate shoulder seasons feel Edenic. This weather, and the gorgeous natural Sonoran vegetation, has attracted royalty, actors and actresses, politicos, and artists for decades. Greater Phoenix has consistently ranked among the nation's top cities in the number of AAA Four and Five Diamond resorts.

The name *Phoenix* was bestowed by Darrel Duppa, one of the founding fathers, who prophetically named the Salt River Valley settlement for the mythological bird that rose from its own ashes. The prehistoric Hohokam Indians, whose archaeological sites and intricate canal system are continually unearthed all over the Valley, prospered in the area centuries earlier, then mysteriously vanished in the 14th century. Duppa declared that this prosperity would rise again. Historians claim history has never witnessed a metropolis grow from barren desert to the cosmopolitan status of Phoenix in such a short period of time.

The Valley of the Sun has Phoenix as its centerpiece; the 22 surrounding incorporated cities include Scottsdale, Tempe, Mesa, Chandler, and Glendale. While growth continues each year in the Valley, sprawling closer to the ring of mountains that defines the Valley's borders, burgeoning urban life in central Phoenix, Scottsdale, and Tempe also has people turning their heads (and sometimes spinning them) with its surge of upscale condominiums and lofts, restaurants, hotels, and gathering places all centering on water. With tourism the second largest industry in the metropolitan area, Greater Phoenix clearly exists for your pleasure.

GUIDANCE **Arizona Office of Tourism** (602-364-3700 or 866-806-8228; www
.arizonaguide.com), 1110 W. Washington St., Suite 155 (open 8–5), and **Greater
Phoenix Convention and Visitors Bureau** (602-452-6282 or 877-225-5749;

www.visitphoenix.com), 50 N. 2nd St. (open 8–5), have a wealth of information. Call **Echo Canyon Recreation Area** (602-256-3220), **Phoenix Mountains Preserve** (602-262-7901), 2701 E. Squaw Peak Dr., and **South Mountain Park** (602-262-7693), 10919 S. Central Ave., for information on trail use. **Arizona Public Lands Information Center** (602-417-9300), 1 N. Central Ave., Suite 800 (open 8–4), is a clearinghouse of information for destinations and activities on public lands.

GETTING THERE *By car:* Downtown Phoenix lies at the intersection of I-17 and I-10. *By bus:* **Greyhound Bus** (602-389-4200), 2115 E. Buckeye Rd. *By air:* **Phoenix Sky Harbor International Airport** (602-273-3300), 3400 Sky Harbor Blvd., is served by more than 20 airlines, including Aeromexico, Air Canada, Alaska Air, America West/U.S. Airways, American, British Airways, Continental, Delta, Frontier, Northwest, and Southwest JetBlue.

GETTING AROUND The **Valley Metro** (602-253-5000) system runs buses throughout the day. **Metro Light Rail** service is scheduled to start at the end of 2008. The rail will connect Phoenix Sky Harbor International Airport to the downtown area (along Central Ave.), including the convention center and other venues. Until then, construction along Central will slow traffic.

DOWNTOWN PHOENIX.

WHEN TO COME Admittedly, the triple-digit-degree summers seem to get hot enough to make the asphalt soften, sending Phoenicians into the high country (especially in August); of course, that's when you'll find the best deals. The heat starts to ebb by mid-Sep., and the city resuscitates by Oct. when temps drop into the 80s. Outdoor events start in Nov. The high season, with perfect weather (high 60s to mid-70s), runs from Jan. through Mar.; make reservations for all you plan to do then. Whenever you come, plan to dress in layers, even in the heat of summer—indoors are air-conditioned.

MEDICAL EMERGENCY Dial 911.

✳ To See

🖋 ♿ **Arizona Mining and Mineral Museum** (602-255-3795), 1502 W. Washington St. Open Mon.–Fri. 8–5, Sat. 11–4, closed Sun. and state holidays. Minerals quickened the hearts of the settlers who came to Arizona, as well as the visitors who come today. Besides information on gold panning to rockhounding, this museum offers fascinating displays of over 3,000 mineral specimens from around the world. Arizona copper takes up a sizable corner of the collection. A section showcases lapidary arts and glamorous fluorescent minerals. $2 adults; under 18 free.

✍ ♿ **Arizona Science Center** (602-716-2000), 600 E. Washington St. Open 10–5. What started as a hands-on learning center for children in the Valley in 1984 has evolved into a full-blown science center that will interest folks of every age. More than 300 hands-on exhibits, a computerized planetarium, a five-story giant-screen theater, and live demonstrations deliver enough information to please anyone; a gift shop and food service fulfill appetites. $9 adults, $7 ages 3–7 and 62-plus.

∞ 🐾 ✍ ♿ **Desert Botanical Garden** (480-941-1225), 1201 N. Galvin Pkwy. Open daily, Oct.–Apr., 8–8, May–Sep., 7–8; closed July 4, Thanksgiving, and Christmas Day. The garden, actually a one-of-a-kind museum accredited by the American Association of Museums, has several themed trails, indoor and outdoor exhibits, and 139 rare, threatened, and endangered plant species from around the world. Volunteers lead guided trail tours each day from October through mid-May; bird walks occur weekly all year, and sunrise and flashlight tours take place in the summertime. Trailside Discovery Stations give you a chance to use most of your five senses to learn about desert plants from October through April. When gardening happens in the Valley (Oct., Nov., Mar., and Apr.), a stop at the Ask a Gardener Station might get the answer to your desert gardening conundrums via knowledgeable volunteers (weekends 10–1). Kids have a blast with Desert Detective games and interactive seasonal exhibits. Garden shop, patio café, and library on grounds. $10 adults, $9 seniors, $5 students, $4 ages 3–12; under 3 free.

Heard Museum (602-252-8848), 2301 N. Central Ave. Open daily 9:30–5; closed holidays. World renowned and a local favorite, the Heard Museum grew from a private collection of Dwight B. and Maie Bartlett Heard in 1929 to about 39,000 works of Native American cultural and fine art. The museum especially describes the culture of southwestern Native peoples through exhibits and special events, such as Indian markets and hoop-dancing competitions. Exhibits include jewelry, textiles, basketry, kachina dolls, pottery, cradleboards, paintings, and sculpture. $10 adults, $9 seniors, $5 students with ID, $3 ages 6–12.

Heritage Square (602-262-5029), 115 N. 6th St. Open Tue.–Sat. 10–4, Sun. noon–4; closed mid-August through Labor Day. The compendium of eight historic buildings here date back to the very beginning of Phoenix (the late 1880s) and appear on the National Register of Historic Places. Styles range from utilitarian regional style (The Duplex)—where the porch often doubled as the bedroom on summer nights—to elegant Victorian.

✍ ♿ **Phoenix Zoo** (602-273-1341), 455 N. Galvin Pkwy. Open daily 9–5 (summer 7–2 weekdays, 7–4 weekends); closed Christmas Day. One of the nation's largest privately owned nonprofit zoological parks has about 1,300 animals, including 200 endangered or threatened birds, mammals, and reptiles from the globe. The zoo has several interesting habitats, including the Wallaby Walkabout, Monkey Village, Desert Lives (bighorn sheep), Baboon Kingdom, and African Savanna. The Harmony Farm petting zoo and Enchanted Forest is great fun for kids. Its ZooLights holiday lighting event is wonderful—see the zoo at night during the holiday season amid thousands of miniature lights (early Nov.–early Jan.). $14 adults (13–59), $9 seniors 60-plus, $6 ages 3–12; those 2 and under are free.

*⃝ ♿ **Mesa Southwest Museum** (480-644-2230), 53 N. Macdonald, Mesa. Open Tue.–Fri. 10–3; Sat. 11–5, Sun. 1–5; closed Mon. and holidays. The museum has an impressive 48,000-piece collection of information on Southwest cultural and natural history. Kids will cry *"Awesome!"* over Arizona's largest collection of dinosaur fossils. $8 adults, $7 seniors 65-plus, $6 students 13-plus with ID, $4 ages 3–12; under 3 free.

*⃝ ♿ **Pioneer Village** (623-463-1052), 3901 W. Pioneer Rd. Open Wed.–Sun. 9–5 (in summer 8–2). Located just off I-17 at exit 225, 1 mile north of the Carefree Hwy. exit. As Arizona started to grow up in the mid-1950s, historic buildings were demolished to make way for the new. In an effort to preserve the history lost to development, the city created this village and moved 27 vintage buildings and structures here. It's the state's largest collection of historic buildings, from log cabins to stores—and they all have a story attached. In living history fashion, Pioneer Village focuses on life and living conditions in Arizona's territorial days (1863–1912, the year Arizona became a state). $7 adults, $6 seniors 60-plus, $5 students 6–18; 5 and under free.

*⃝ ♿ **Pueblo Grande Museum** (602-495-0900), 4619 E. Washington St. Open Mon.–Fri. 9–4:45, Sun. 1–4:45; closed on major holidays. Hard to imagine that you can step centuries back into the ruins of a 1,500-year-old Hohokam village while standing in the heart of a very modern Phoenix. The city has dedicated this park to the study and interpretation of the Hohokam culture through ruins and exhibits, both ongoing and changing. The Hohokam built irrigation canals that inspired the current canal system in the Valley; you can see some of the last remainders of still-intact irrigation canals as well as an excavated ball court and full-scale reproductions of Hohokam-style homes. A special program called *Dig It* shows you how archaeologists study clues and piece together information from artifacts and gives you a chance to build your own version of a Hohokam village like Pueblo Grande. $2 adults, $1.50 seniors 55-plus, $1 ages 6–17; kids under 6 get in free.

*⃝ ♿ **Rawhide** (480-502-5600), Wild Horse Pass, 5700 N. Loop Rd. Open daily (except Christmas) Mon.–Thu. 5–10, Fri.–Sun. 11–10 (summer hours are Sun.–Thu. 5–9, Fri.–Sat. 5–10). Celebrating all things Wild West, Rawhide will take you back to an authentic Arizona 1880s town, where the streets popped with gunfights and clamored with townsfolk activities. You can watch musicians entertain and Native Americans share their legacies at an informal seating area, or experience fun burro- and camel-back and stagecoach rides that take you around the park. Test your skills with activities like the mechanical bull and climbing wall. You might even get arrested, all (hopefully) in good fun. **Rawhide Steakhouse and Saloon** excels in cooking up mesquite-grilled cowboy steaks,

surprises with deep-fried rattlesnake, and rewards with fresh-baked apple pie. The whole attraction is a special place to experience Phoenix when it didn't even have its name yet. Free. Assistance pets only.

✳ To Do

DAIRY TOUR ✔ **Shamrock Farms** (602-477-2462), 40034 W. Clayton, Stanfield. Reservations required. Join the herd as a tractor-pulled wagon shows you the ins (the different components of the farm) and outs (how milk gets delivered around Arizona) of one of the nation's largest working dairy farms. Everyone gets to participate in interactive displays and games. You learn about the nutritional values of dairy products, then see how the ladies (the dairy's 10,000-cow stable) lead a life of luxury as they produce milk. There's a sweet treat at the end of the tour. Call at least 48 hours in advance.

DOG PARKS ✾ **Steele Indian School Park** (602-495-0739), 300 E. Indian School Rd. A gated area on the northeast corner of the park has a drinking fountain and two sections: one for dogs under 20 pounds, the other for larger pooches.

✾ ♿ **PETsMART Dog Park at Washington Park** (602-261-8559), 6455 N. 23rd Ave. This 2.65-acre park has a 6-foot-high fence, two double-gated entrances, a water fountain, two doggy watering stations, benches, mutt mitt dispensers, and garbage cans for dog waste. Large trees provide shade. Fenced area for smaller dogs.

✾ **Phoenix Sky Harbor International Airport** (602-273-3300), 3400 E. Sky Harbor Dr. Bone Yard at Terminal 4 is a shaded, bone-shaped gravel area with mutt mitts plus two water faucets with buckets. Terminal 3 Paw Pad has water spigots and bowls, mutt mitts, and a red fire hydrant.

FISHING Greater Phoenix has some great fishing holes. This is not a fisherman's tale. The Department of Game and Fish stocks lakes and ponds (1 big fish for every 20 little ones) with rainbow trout Nov.–Mar., channel catfish Mar.–July and Sep.–Nov., and sunfish three times a year. Bass, crappie, bluegill, white amur, tilapia, and carp roam the waters as well. Most lakes get stocked biweekly from Sep. 20–July 10 on an arbitrary day between Monday and Saturday. This includes Incentive Stocks with 2- to 4-pound lunkers. Contact the Arizona Department of Game and Fish (602-942-3000) for more information. You will need a

DOWNTOWN PHOENIX.

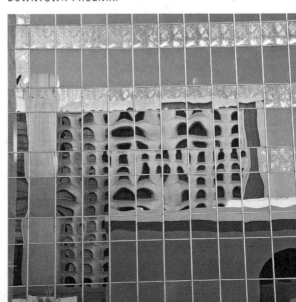

fishing license if you're 14 or older. Spend $16 on a Class U urban fishing license that's good for the calendar year, or get a Class D 1-day-only license for $8.50.

GLIDER RIDES & PARASAILING Turf Soaring School (602-439-3621), 8700 W. Carefree Hwy. (AZ 74), Peoria. Open daily 9–5. You can take flight in the Arizona sky in a glider. The experience is basically your first lesson in piloting a glider plane, and it's entered in your official logbook. You can choose to be released from the tow plane anywhere from 3,000 to 5,000 feet (the higher the altitude, the longer your ride); also select what type of ride you want, from smooth and scenic to a hair-raising loop-de-loop aerobatic deluxe. $95–175.

GOLF Golf may not be the sole reason people come to Phoenix. The mild fall through spring weather and scenery may have something to do with it. But maybe not. From its start as a resort town, Phoenix has always enjoyed golf, and today you'll find some of the world's best courses here. The National Golf Foundation dubbed Greater Phoenix the Golf Capital of the World.

Arizona Biltmore (602-955-9655), 24th St. and Missouri. Few golf courses can match what this time-honored course has in spades: tradition. The stately **Adobe**, second oldest in Phoenix, came on the scene long before modern designs. Its architecture—a triumph of beauty over trickery—forces you to think through your game. The par-71 course provides a relaxing yet challenging round with a couple dozen rugged bunkers with bays and grassy capes and several water traps. Watch that 60-year-old Aleppo pine tree on the 15th hole. The younger **Links** adds some glam to its capricious personality. Pine-lined fairways roll past some of the most stunning homes in Phoenix. Water hazards are big in this course, and well-bunkered greens are reminiscent of the deep and well-set seaside links of the British Isles. No two holes are alike here, so you'll always have a different game that requires thoughtfulness and precise shot selection. No denim allowed; collared shirt and Bermuda shorts required. Championship putting course included in fees. Award-winning golf shop. Private lessons and daily clinics offered. $75–175.

🏌 **ASU Karsten Golf Course** (480-921-8070), 1125 Rio Salado Pkwy., Tempe. This championship classic Pete Dye Scottish Links produces champions. Arizona State University's 18-hole, par-72 course has rolling hills, railroad ties, and greens partially hidden by bunkers and water. In keeping with scholarly tradition, you will be tested on this college course. The 16th tee is the major challenge. Besides the distraction from its beauty, a lake that runs the entire length of the hole guards the hole's right side while mounding the left and backsides. It takes a 217-yard carry over the water to reach the greens. To bogey or birdie, that is the question. Golf cart and locker included in fees. $48–105.

Gold Canyon Golf Course (480-982-9449), 6100 S. Kings Ranch Rd., Apache Junction. You have a choice of two 18-hole championship courses here. Both are challenging, both are scenic. The one that gets all the attention and high-profile ratings is the elevated **Dinosaur** (par-71/72). Once you wind your way a few holes up the mountain, the scenery gets phenomenal. Signature hole 4 is the most picturesque; hole 5 comes with a challenge. Sibling course, the

Sidewinder, also a par-71/72, is flatter and about half the price. Sidewinder winds through canyons and arroyos. Both are impeccably groomed, both carry enough stars from *Golf Digest* to form a constellation, and both give you good golf and plenty of views. Cart included in fees. Dinosaur $55–160, Sidewinder $40–140.

Papago Golf Course (602-275-8428), 5595 E. Moreland St. This hot municipal course will have you arriving in the early hours of the morning to get a tee time. William Bell (think Torrey Pines in San Diego) designed the challenging course with large mature trees and traditional undulating fairways; it has a 132 slope rating from the back tees. This is where golfers qualify for the Phoenix Open. Like most of the Valley's difficult courses, it's beautiful, too: set next to the distinctive Papago Buttes. $50 riding, $38 walking.

The Phoenician Golf Course (480-423-2449; 24-hour reservation line, 480-423-2450), The Phoenician Resort, 6000 E. Camelback Rd. With three championship 9-hole courses named for the type of terrain in which they spread, the game here mixes challenge with diversity. The **Oasis Nine**, designed by Homer Flint, boasts a tropical setting loaded with water features. The **Desert Nine**, designed by Ted Robinson Sr., who calls it one of the prettiest courses in the Southwest, hugs the base of Camelback Mountain. Quintessential desert vegetation decks the greens. The **Canyon Nine**—a combined effort of Flint and Robinson—features lush landscapes overlooking panoramas of the Valley. The dress code is strictly enforced here: collared shirts, slacks, or Bermuda-length shorts for men; for women, sleeveless shirts must have a collar, and slacks or Bermuda-length shorts are required. Denim, tank tops, and T-shirts are never permitted. Green fees include golf carts and practice range balls prior to play. Callaway Rentals clubs with two sleeves of Callaway golf balls and FootJoy rental shoes are available upon request. $90–199.

⊙ **The Raven Golf Club** (602-243-3636), 3636 E. Baseline Rd. If you play this, the highest-rated golf course in Phoenix, you may be rubbing shoulders with some professional baseball players, as it's also the Official Home Golf Course of the Arizona Diamondbacks. Impeccably manicured to be tournament-ready, the course gets overseeded with poa and bent grasses; tees, fairways, and approaches have overseeded winter rye. *Impeccable* applies to the guest service here, too, which makes your experience just a little sweeter no matter how your game turns out on this par-72 course. If you plan to play during the hotter months to nab a bargain, the course provides mango-scented cooling towels. No denim allowed, but golf mocs are okay. $115–180.

Whirlwind Golf Club (480-940-1500), Sheraton Wild Horse Pass Resort & Spa, 5594 W. Wildhorse Pass Blvd. You won't find houses surrounding this golf course, but you may see wild horses. This Troon-managed facility has two 18-hole courses designed by Gary Panks. **Devil's Claw** has a combination of fairway elevations changes, signature bunkering, and superb course conditioning. Every hole carries the name of a significant legend or landmark of the Pima and Maricopa Indians. **Cattail** has you navigating over and around several water features and deep canyons. Because this club utilizes the G2, a climate-controlled device that changes the air temperature in and around golf carts more than 40 degrees,

THE SUPERSTITION MOUNTAINS RISE OUTSIDE PHOENIX.

you can take advantage of the low summer rates and live to talk about the fabulous play you made at Dragonfly Falls. Green fees include golf cart practice balls, bag tag, and yardage guide; $95–150.

The Wigwam Golf Club (623-935-3811), 300 Wigwam Blvd., Litchfield Park. This course, opened in the 1930s, is synonymous with golf in Arizona. The **Gold Course**, nicknamed Arizona's Monster, showcases designer Robert Trent Jones Sr.'s love of heroic shot-making that produces, in his words, "Easy bogies and hard pars." Even though the course will beat you up unless you're an excellent golfer, the waiting list for tee times is often l-o-n-g. Jones went easy on the **Blue Course**. This short but tricky links has an array of deep and perilous bunkers, ponds, and dogleg fairways. Plus, it's full of contradictions—a roller coaster of golf holes presenting different obstacles and challenges. The **Red Course** is a parkland-style course. The Wigwam even has something for pint-sized beginners: **Little Wigwam Golf Link** has three different holes to help little ones learn to hit the ball, get familiar with strategy, and develop a love for the game. A new state-of-the-art practice range is one of the largest in Arizona. The Village Green, a 2-acre putting green and garden, is the American version of the famous Himalayas putting green at St. Andrews, Scotland. The golf club also has a full-service golf shop and Jim McLean Golf School. The only resort course with 54 holes on site, the Wigwam is one of the best golf resorts in the state. $63–162.

HIKING The city parks have some great trails; locals use them all year long, all day long. If you are not acclimated to the desert, drink a quart of water with electrolyte mix every hour in the warmer weather, and every couple of hours in winter; always wear a hat and sunscreen; and hike during the cooler morning hours in warmer weather. The most popular trail is the **Piestawa Peak Summit Trail** in the Phoenix Mountains Preserve, which climbs about 1,200 feet in 1.2 miles. The **Circumference Trail** takes you about 4.5 miles around the mountain. Another popular route, and more technical, is the **Summit Trail** on Camelback Mountain—but you will have to wait for a parking space in cooler weather. If you want to get away from the masses and experience desert remoteness, hike the **National Trail** in South Mountain Park. Also see *Wilder Places*.

HORSEBACK RIDING You can ride in any of the mountain parks if you saddle your own steed. Rent a horse from **Ponderosa Stables/South Mountain**

Stables (602-268-1261), 10215 S. Central Ave., and ride in South Mountain Park for 1–4 hours for $25–75 (open Mon.–Sat. 8–4, Sun. 9–4).

MOUNTAIN BIKING **South Mountain Park** has a reputation for its premier mountain bike routes. The Desert Classic Trail presents a signed route; it's the best for all levels of experience. The Mormon and National Trails, full of technical moments, demand experience and will give you a run for your money. **Dreamy Draw Park** in Phoenix Mountain Preserves and **Papago Park** in Tempe draw fat tires, too.

PARKS **Papago Park** (602-256-3220), Van Buren St. and Galvin Pkwy. You can't miss the curious ruddy mounds called Papago Buttes for which the park is named. These geological formations, pocked with openings, have drawn many cultures, starting with the Hohokam Natives. The park has three urban fishing lagoons lined with palm trees that give an oasislike effect. Also in the park, check out the pyramid tomb of Arizona's first governor, George Hunt. Follow the bike trail along the Hunt Bass Fishery, a cottonwood-willow riparian area with a secluded feel. Arizona Department of Game and Fish stocks this waterway. Watch for giant blue herons here that wade in the shallows looking for aqueous life to munch.

❀ **Steele Indian School Park** (602-495-0739), 300 E. Indian School Rd. One of the Valley's most aesthetic green spaces honors Arizona's Native peoples and open space. The design was inspired by the late-19th-century City Beautiful movement, which promoted the idea that city dwellers need open green space to develop civic pride and community. This park celebrates the state's Native American history with design elements that feature Indian concepts of life, earth, and the universe. The park has gardens, Native American poems etched into the concrete walkways, water features, and a dog park.

SUNSET VISTAS Phoenicians know one of the best points to view a sunset sits at the top of **Dobbins Lookout** in **South Mountain Park**. Though not the tallest peak in the park/preserve, the lookout gives the best views of the Valley. The road up to the lookout—a winding, twisting route with tight hairpin turns—is an interesting drive in itself.

✳ Spas

Aji Spa (602-385-5759), Sheraton Wild Horse Pass Resort & Spa, 5594 W. Wild Horse Pass Blvd. Open daily 5:30 AM–8 PM. *Aji* means "sanctuary," and the Gila River Indian Community has created one in a way that invokes the spirit of their traditions and faith, as well as their values of serenity, tranquility, simplicity, freedom, and authenticity. These traditions show up tangibly. The flute music you often hear in spas actually fits here culturally. Round corners and curves, along with placement of things in groups of fours, represent the cyclical nature of life. Artwork of tribal legends appear in every room. Treatments showcase the language and philosophies of the spa's owners. For instance, the *Wihosha* facial includes *Tashogith*, the Purifying White Clay Facial, which uses the same white clay important to the Gila River Indian Community for centuries; Blue Coyote Wrap, the spa's signature treatment, personifies the Pima legend of the coyote and the bluebird. Each massage takes place on heated tables with warm towels wrapped around your feet and across your back. Treatments $125–195; $75 per hour for personal training in fitness center.

Alvadora Spa (602-977-6400 or 800-672-6011), Royal Palms Spa and Resort, 5200 E. Camelback Rd. Open daily 9–6. The Mediterranean cultures believed that each new dawn offered a special opportunity for rejuvenation. The ancients called it *Alvadora*. Mirroring the romance and beauty of the Old World in style and treatments, this spa features the herbs, flowers, oils, and minerals indigenous to the Mediterranean in a setting akin to it. Water treatments are big, too. Sitting areas with fireplaces and fountains offer quiet interludes between treatments in which to relax; sip a cup of tea, elixir, or lemon water; and nibble on fruits and nuts. These small spaces bring an intimacy into the 9,000-square-foot facility. Two recently completed spa suites ensure total privacy for multiday destination spa packages (call for more information). $125–260.

Arizona Biltmore Spa & Fitness Center (602-955-6600 or 800-950-0086), 2400 E. Missouri. Open daily 8–8. World class like the resort in which it's located, this spa has seen a lot of beautiful bodies over the years and excels in attention to details. The staff, gifted with "healing hands" and at least a decade, sometimes two, of experience, apply the purest and most natural spa products; you can't help but come away renewed, if only in attitude. The spa features products made from locally harvested ingredients used by Native Americans in many of its treatments (such as Chaparral Clay Wrap) and draws on ancient treatments from different cultures as well: Europe, medieval China, the Pacific Islands, and Native tribes of the Sonoran Desert. Several treatments are specifically designed for teens and men. Hydrotherapies take place in two wet rooms. Your visit includes use of three spa pools, steam rooms, saunas, separate men's and women's locker rooms, power shower, and outdoor retreat areas. The fitness center has state-of-the-art cardiovascular and weight-training equipment and an aerobics room. Treatments $135–205; personal training $65 for 30 minutes. The salon has nail, hair, and waxing services.

Narande (602-225-9000), Wyndham Buttes Resort, 2000 Westcourt Way. At a time when so many of our lives are full of overwhelming details and dramas, Narande takes a minimalist approach. Its decor, simple but elegant, right away makes you feel less burdened and life less complicated. *Narande* means "alongside flowing water." This poetic name honors the tradition of water as a key to relaxation. Treatments range from classic massages, such as aromatherapy, sports, and maternity massages, to ancient treatments like Reiki, craniosacral therapy, reflexology, and shiatsu. In between are scrubs, wraps, and facials. The signature Narande Red Flower ritual incorporates Japanese tradition to care for the body with conscious intent in relaxing, luxurious steps: cleanse, polish, energize, and replenish. The final step is to hydrate with a warm blend of lime oil and SilkCream. Facilities include saunas, swimming pool, fitness center, and locker rooms. Nail, hair, makeup, and waxing services are available. Treatments $120–170; it costs $15 to use spa facilities without a treatment.

Suddenly Slimmer Wellness Center & Day Spa (602-952-8446), 3313 E. Indian School Rd., Suite 8. Open, Mon.–Sat. 9–5 (Tue.–Fri. until 7), Sun. 10–3. This family-run spa/wellness center got its roots about 10 years ago when the owner started her acupuncture practice. She always envisioned a complete wellness center as a service to the community, and her dream has come true. What started as an 1,800-square-foot facility is nearing the completion of a remodel that will see it transformed into an 8,000-square-foot space loaded with stained-glass windows, plants, healing music, and a friendly staff. One of the treatments the owner has used to help her clients detox turned out to be successful in helping them shed inches of fat as well—hence the name Suddenly Slimmer. The nondehydrating mineral wrap is a signature therapy. The spa menu has a thorough variety of modalities, and if you're looking for something different or unique, you'll probably find it here. For instance, the Body Bliss Massage incorporates the chakras with classic massage. Other treatments range from traditional relaxing massages to powerful healing therapies from all over the world and very cool facial therapies. Body wraps $110–200, massages $110–155, facials $60–210, waxing $35–75, acupuncture $95 per hour.

✳ Wilder Places

Echo Canyon Recreation Area (602-256-3220), Tatum and McDonald Dr. Open daily 5 AM–11 PM. One of the premier hikes in the Valley, the Summit Trail on Camelback Mountain, is not an easy trail, but it will get you to a vantage point that shows you some upscale surrounding neighborhoods and beautiful Valley panoramas. A cluster of easier trails wind around the mountain park, too.

Phoenix Mountains Preserve (602-262-7901), 2701 E. Squaw Peak Dr. Open daily 5 AM–11 PM. This is where Phoenix outdoor mavens meet, from hoi polloi to world-class athletes. The fairer the day, the more folks come out to play. The large park actually has several trailheads in different locations; this one will take you to the Summit Trail on Piestawa Peak, as well as a handful more trails not as extreme. Also check out the 32nd St. (and Lincoln) access. The whole park has classic desert scenery at its best, with wildlife sightings (coyotes, owls, ringtails, and snakes) common occurrences. Drink plenty of water, wear sunscreen, and watch where you put your hands and feet. Free.

South Mountain Park (602-262-7693), 10919 S. Central Ave. Open daily 5 AM–11 PM. One of the largest parks in the nation, this park gets three million visitors a year—second to the Grand Canyon. The South Mountain system comprises three distinct ranges—Ma-Ha-Tauk to the north, Gila Mountain to the south, and Guadalupe Range in the east. In typical Sonora Desert fashion, the ranges run diagonally across the desert floor. Among them a network of multiuse trails travel into canyons, up slopes, and across ridgetops. Free.

✳ Lodging Pets

HOTELS ∞ 🐾 ♿ **The Clarendon Hotel Suites** (602-252-7363), 401 W. Clarendon Ave. This boutique hotel, situated in a neighborhood setting in uptown Phoenix, keeps you close to the city's hot spots. The Phoenix owners have kept the spirit of the 1970s-built hotel alive by creating a retro decor with a modern twist that turns out utterly hip, yet pleasing. Rooms display work from local artists and offer complimentary WiFi, telephone calls (including international), newspaper, and covered parking. They also boast locally roasted coffee, loose-leaf teas, cable TV, triple 310-thread-count sheets on the same brand of bed you'll find at the Ritz Carlton and Sheraton, down pillows, L'Occitane amenities, and tons of character. For an extra C-note, the Pimp My Fridge! service will gussy up your mini fridge with any decadent dainty you want, from designer chocolates to a gourmet cheese plate and figs. Several nearby restaurants provide delivery service. The property has an 80-degree swimming pool surrounded by a cobalt-blue deck, whirlpool, and access to a rooftop fitness center with personal trainer available Mon.–Sat. It also features **C4 at The Clarendon**, just opened. The restaurant specializes in Japanese food with a Southwestern touch (including sushi).

RESORTS ∞ 🐾 ✂ ♿ **Arizona Biltmore** (602-955-6600), 2400 E. Missouri. When it comes to Arizona's evolution into a world-class tourism destination, this is where it all started. Called Jewel of the Desert when it opened in 1929, the AAA Four Diamond Award winner (it's also garnered a pages-long list of other awards) has hosted royalty, every president from Herbert Hoover through George W., and an array of Hollywood stars and sports figures. With a location to die for, a design by Frank Lloyd Wright, and ever-improving service to meet guests' trendy needs, the Grande Dame of Arizona is still one grand resort and a pleasure to experience at least once.

The property has eight swimming pools; two PGA 18-hole championship golf courses; a spa and fitness center; seven night-lighted tennis courts; a lighted basketball court; lawn chess with life-sized pieces set out at 9 AM; croquet and bocce ball; a business center; six restaurants, including Wright's (see *Dining Out*); and Kids Korral and Kids Korral Playground. Large guest rooms have king or two queen beds, cable TV, in-room movies, WiFi access, mini bar, safe, spa amenities, and music suites featuring iPods and Bose SoundDock. Preferred Pet Pals provides pets up to 50 pounds a welcome treat, room service pet menu, walking tours, and room to run. A $100 pet deposit is required, $50 of it refundable on good behavior. Classic room $295–875.

∞ 🐾 ✂ ♿ **The Buttes—A Marriott Resort** (602-225-9000), 2000 Westcourt Way, Tempe. Historically, the Buttes were the central point in the Valley and used as a lookout. Showcased atop the West Twin Buttes, this property has one beautiful view of the Valley and all its natural landmarks. Its restaurant, **Top of the Rock**, is a community favorite. The 25-acre grounds include a stunning pool area carved into the mountain with two free-form swimming pools (one the size of a football field and the largest in the Southwest) and four mountainside spas, four lighted tennis and sand courts, a business center, a fitness center, a pool bar and grill, jogging and hiking trails, and Narande Spa. Rooms have down comforters with duvets laundered for each guest, cable TV, WiFi access, mini bar, and weekday newspaper. $239–429.

∞ 🍷 🐾 ♿ **Crowne Plaza San Marcos Golf & Conference Resort**

(480-812-0900), 1 San Marcos Plaza, Chandler. Back in 1912 when it opened, this facility wasn't just the epitome of class and opulence but also Arizona's first golf resort. Listed on the National Register of Historic Places and newly remodeled, it remains a beloved and classy hotel. Its 18-hole USGA golf course lures players back again and again; you'll also find a pool, a whirlpool, three restaurants, and a tennis court. Rooms are large, and each has a patio; amenities include weekday delivery of *USA Today* and the *Arizona Republic* on the weekends; an hour of free local calls; incoming faxes (first two pages); bottled water replenished every day; two hours' free time on the tennis court; and an overnight shine of one pair of shoes per night. High season $150–339, low season $71–179.

◯◯ ☻ ⚶ **Royal Palms Resort and Spa** (602-840-3610 or 800-672-6011), 5200 E. Camelback Rd. This Mediterranean- inspired AAA Four Diamond resort gushes with solar colors and elegant Old World charm. The grounds are so intimately wrapped in mature landscaping, you'll forget you're in the city. In Mar. the heady scent of orange blossoms from property trees and surrounding groves saturates the air. Recent renovations created an all-new enclave of 70 rooms that surround the intimate Montavista, a romantic Mediterranean-style courtyard with a colorful tiered garden, tranquil reflecting pools, and fireplaces for a taste of ultraluxury. Romance thrives here and is celebrated unabashedly. Romantically challenged guests can get personal coaching from the resort's Director of Romance Paul Xanthopoulos. Grecian-born Xanthopoulos claims a lineage dating back to Eros, the mythical god of love. Impromptu weddings at the resort are becoming his specialty. The property has T. Cook's restaurant (see *Dining Out*), the Alvadora spa, a pool, and a fitness center. Each room and suite includes a private patio or balcony, custom furnishings, a 25-inch TV, and WiFi. $389–3,200. Daily $22 service fee covers general expenses such as gratuities for all but restaurant or room service, valet parking, daily newspaper, business services.

◯◯ ☻ ⚶ ⚶ **Sheraton Wild Horse Pass Resort & Spa** (602-225-0100 or 888-218-8989), 5594 W. Wild Horse Pass Blvd., Phoenix. This resort literally lives up to its name: Native American owned and operated, it lies in the Gila River Indian Community, where wild horses still roam. Basically out in the middle of nowhere, but only a few minutes' drive to the Valley, the resort remains pristine. Couple that with the authentic renditions on the property of the Akimel O'otham and Maricopa Indian cultures, and the result is a unique upscale stay in a rugged and beautiful land. Along with typical Sheraton amenities come unusual tribal associations. The domed lobbies of the main resort, golf clubhouse, and the spa represent *Olas kih*, the native roundhouse. Native American art (mostly from the Community) decks the walls in a variety of media, and murals color the ceilings. Outside, a convincing 2.5-mile-long replica of the Gila River, replete with wetlands, winds through the resort; a riverside pool has cascading waterfalls and bridges after the ancient (nearby) Casa Grande Ruins. A cultural concierge offers guests a wealth of authentic tribal information and tours of the property. Amenities include high-speed Internet, the Aji Spa, several dining venues including Kai restaurant (see *Dining Out*), Whirlwind Golf Club, Koli Equestrian Center, Love That Dog program for pets up to 40 pounds, two tennis courts, a riverside jogging and hiking trail, three pools with wheelchair access, Wild Horse Pass Casino (adjacent to the resort), and one very real cultural experience. $289–429.

Wigwam Resort & Golf Club (623-935-3811), 300 Wigwam Blvd., Litchfield Park. While some Arizona inns and resorts are veering away from classic Southwest styling, the Wigwam is relishing it. The resort has even trademarked its slogan, Authentic Arizona, and celebrates its Santa Fe styling, adobe casitas, and cowboy culture.

If it weren't for the boll weevil, this classic resort might not exist. When the weevil decimated cotton crops in South Carolina, Goodyear Tire and Rubber Company looked elsewhere for a perfect spot to raise long-staple cotton. They found it in today's towns of Goodyear and Litchfield. The resort, built in 1918, originally provided a place for Goodyear executives to stay when they came to visit the cotton ranches. Soon family members joined them. On Thanksgiving Day 1929, the resort opened to the public.

Casitas are spread over 463 acres landscaped with gardens and manicured lawns. The property has three 18-hole championship golf courses, nine outdoor lighted tennis courts, two swimming pools with fire pits, Red Door Spa, putting green, croquet, Ping-Pong, billiards, and bike rentals. Oversized rooms have private patio, southwestern decor with ceramic tile, 27-inch remote-control

television with cable programming, in-room movies, video games, computer hookups, and enlarged bath with walk-in closet. The resort hosts special events during the year, including jazz concerts in summer. $319–549.

BED AND BREAKFASTS AND INNS

🏵 🐾 **The Honey House Bed and Breakfast** (602-956-5646), 5150 N. 36th St. It's hard to believe this B&B is located in the middle of three million people. Ensconced in an acre of mature landscaping including century-old trees and colorful gardens (some snowbird guests come back just to work in the garden), the property feels like it's in its own world. It's been designated a National Wildlife Habitat, and the only sounds you hear are from animals and birds (birders with life lists usually get to check off a few names).

A Mormon beekeeper homesteaded this land in 1895; he and the missus lived in the house, while the other missus lived in the outbuilding. When the other missus died, the beekeeping equipment landed in the outbuilding she lived in. Decades later the son sold the compound to the innkeepers Jeanette and Larry Irwin, and they have restored and remodeled it into a cozy place to stay—two rooms in the house and the Honey House outbuilding. You can use the hot tub anytime you like, and bikes are available for visiting the Arizona Canal Bike Trail just down the block. $89–109.

✳ Where to Eat

DINING OUT **Barrio Café** (602-636-0240), 2814 N. 16th St. Open for lunch Tue.–Fri. 11–2:30; for dinner Tue.–Thu. 5–10 (till 10:30 Fri.–Sat.);

and Sun. 11–9. You'll think you're at the beach in Mexico at this neighborhood venue featuring southern Mexico cuisine interpreted by chef Silvana Salcido Esparza. Chef Silvana culled back-road and village experiences during a two-year foray into Mexico and melded them with modern culinary expertise to create one of the hottest (as in *caliente*, not necessarily *picante*) Mexican menus in the Valley. Fresh concoctions include fish tacos, lobster quesadillas, and chiles rellenos stuffed with shrimp and scallops. Start your meal with guacamole made tableside and end it with goat's milk caramel stuffed churros for dessert. Barrio serves about 200 top-shelf brands of nectar of the gods (aka tequila) and wine made from Baja California vineyards, coined a mini Napa Valley. Entrées $12–28.

Cheuvront Wine & Cheese Cafe (602-307-0022), 1326 N. Central Ave. Open Mon.–Wed. 11–10 (till 11 Thu., midnight Fri.); Sat. 4–midnight; Sun. 4–9. Arizona senator Ken Cheuvront "fell in love with the whole concept of cheese and wine" when he went to school in Paris. The state's native son decided to invest some of the earnings from his construction company into his two favorite pastimes and started the downtown café known around town simply as Cheuvront's. You'll find the best cheese menu in the city here, with about two dozen varieties from around the world—from butter-rich soft cheeses to English Stilton and Cheuvront's favorite nutty Italian Taleggio. The wine menu is the result of meticulous tasting. Cheuvront has three tasters sampling wine all the time, and about 100 make it to his palate each week. Some diners focus totally on the cheese or pâté

(duck or goose) plates, but there's more. The house-made vegetable lasagna and Parmesan-crusted chicken are favorite entrées. Though the menu may change with the seasons and availability of ingredients, the pumpkin bread pudding with caramel rum sauce—a secret recipe handed down from his grandmother—stays on the menu all year. The restaurant packs in the diners (often politicos), so it's best not to come if you're in a hurry. $14.50–25.

Durant's (602-264-5967), 2611 N. Central Ave. Open for lunch Mon.–Fri. 11–4; for dinner Mon.–Thu. 4–10, Fri. 4–11, Sat. 5–11, Sun. 4:30–10. Not much has changed here since founder Jack Durant opened the steakhouse in 1955, including Durant's motto: "Good friends, great steaks, and the best booze are the necessities of life." You still enter through the kitchen, power lunches reign, and the meals still contain some of the best beef around. Nor do the wait staff change often here; many have made a career serving at this bastion. Meals are full of moxie, and as hale and hearty as the motto. Lunch entrées $11.95–29.95, dinner entrées $20.95–45.95.

Fez on Central (602-287-8700), 3815 N. Central Ave. Open daily 11 AM–midnight; closed 2–4:30 Mon.–Thu. Cool, chic, and ultramodern, Fez steadies itself with the old axiom that the best way to the heart is through the stomach. Fez's wonderful menu (traditional American favorites with Mediterranean or Moroccan twists created by award-winning chef-partner Tom Jetland) has won the hearts of people of all ages, cultures, and colors. The dining room is a melting pot of humanity. This is not the place for a quiet evening meal. Life happens here, and it's rollicking. But do come hungry, because portions are as generous as the food is good. The *kisras* (like a pizza) are popular items; lamb *kisra* looks beautiful and tastes excellent. The hamburgers, considered the best in town, are big and juicy. Signature dishes (with *Fez* in the name) include poached pears, nuts, and heady spices. Check out the wine fusions: Pomegranate Cabernet and Apricot Chardonnay. Signature drinks make it a meeting place, too. Entrées $9.25–18.

Kai (602-225-0100), Sheraton Wild Horse Pass Resort & Spa, 5594 W. Wild Horse Pass Blvd., Phoenix. Open Tue.–Sat. 5:30–9. Kai serves up an authentic Native American culinary experience that features cuisine from the Pima and Maricopa tribes and locally farmed ingredients from the Gila River Indian Community. Seeds and spices make a strong statement here. It's a one-of-a-kind cuisine created in a gourmet way and, at the time of this writing, the only AAA Five Diamond venue in the city. Native American chef Jack Strong incorporates traditional Native plants such as beans, corn, and squash as well as Sonoran Desert ingredients like saguaro blossom syrup, cholla buds, and agave lacquer in his menu. If you taste influences from James Beard Award–winning chef Janos Wilder, it's because he's the consulting chef. The waiters take the time to explain every dish you order—listing ingredients and traditions attached to them. The staff's low-key, polite approach has incredible appeal—a perfect foil for the strong, attractive menu with iconoclastic ingredients that marry well: frybread with lobster;

smoked tomato risotto; candied scallops; apple tabbouleh; and buffalo with saguaro and cholla. Entrées $21–34.

Monti's La Casa Vieja (480-967-7594), 100 S. Mill Ave., Tempe. Open Sun.–Thu. 11–10 (till 11 Fri.–Sat.). The birthplace of Carl Hayden, a prominent historical figure in the Valley, has harbored several restaurants since it was built in 1872. The house, which still has the original latilla mud ceiling in the oldest section, is listed on the National Register of Historic Places as well as historic registers for the state and the city of Tempe. The family's hacienda had a diner for weary travelers until the Depression. And there was a restaurant/bar during WWII. When Leonard Monti opened his steakhouse in 1956, naming it for the Haydens' homestead (known as *La Casa Vieja*, or "the old house"), who could have guessed that the place would rate among the favorites a half a century later with half a million people dining here each year? You get a good steak (seafood, chicken, or chops) at a good price at the Old House. This includes their infamous Roman bread circa 1970 (rosemary focaccia). Daily specials hover around $10. Entrées $13–23.

Mucho Gusto Taqueria & Mexican Bistro (480-921-1850), 603 W. University Dr., Tempe. Open Mon.–Thu. 11–10 (11 Fri), Sat. 4–11. Not just a Mexican eatery, Mucho Gusto has style, and it racks up local awards consistently. The menu presents gourmet authentic Mexican dishes—several vegetarian—with a simple but flavorful wine list that features selections from Spain and South America. Favorites include *picaditas* (thick corn tortillas), gaucho steak, shrimp in a spicy amaretto garlic sauce, and chiles rellenos puebla style. The food is prepared with as much local organic products as possible. Lunch $6–8.50, dinner $10–16.

My Florist Café (602-254-0333), 534 W. McDowell Rd. Open daily 7 AM–midnight. Owner David Lacy started his elegant but casual venue in the bakery next door, named for the Willo Historic District in which it's located. Lacy expanded the Willo Bakery to include this building, a former flower shop still sporting a huge neon-light sign fresh out of the 1960s announcing MY FLORIST. The café has become a neighborhood meeting place and serves excellent sandwiches (made with wonderful Willo Bakery breads), salads, and some of the best desserts around. Willo Bakery, by the way, has evolved into a fine-foods grocery store/bakery with exquisite breads and desserts. Jazz happens nightly on the Steinway piano. Entrées $7.25–10.75.

Pizzeria Bianco (602-258-8300), 623 E. Adams. Open Tue.–Sat. 5–10. The only thing better than a good, hand-made pizza baked in a brick oven is one made by a James Beard Award recipient—a first for a pizza chef. Chris Bianco makes these wonderful pizzas, one at a time, which turn culinary heads all around the nation. He also uses the best local ingredients, serves house-made bread with the salad and antipasto, and uses hand-made mozzarella. Be prepared to wait for a table (no reservations except for six or more). Pizzas $10–14.

T. Cook's (602-840-3610), Royal Palms Spa and Resort, 5200 E. Camelback Rd. Open for breakfast daily 6:30–10; lunch Mon.–Sat. 11–2, (Sun. 10–2; dinner daily 5:30–10. Every meal is special and excellent,

including breakfast (a favorite for area professionals) and lunch. At dinner-time the dining room becomes a savory scene. Executive chef Lee Hill-son takes Tuscan traditions to new levels, simple but bold. Not many chefs can serve that Italian mainstay, pork belly, and get away with it. Pair it with pork tenderloin, a tomato onion tart, green apples, and sautéed spinach, and you have a favorite. Mussels come from Cape Cod's Snug Harbor, and scallops from Georges Bank. If that's not enough, chocolate maestro Pierino Jermonti, the pastry chef, creates grand finales that bring people to their feet. His Cathedral of Chocolate, complete with stained-glass windows, and his pairing of white chocolate with Brie cheese are peerless. Entrées $24–32.

Wild Thaiger (602-241-8995), 2631 N. Central Ave. Open Mon.–Thu. 11–9, Fri.–Sat. 11–10, Sun. 5–9. Those who crave the perfumed flavors of lemongrass, galangal, ginger, and mints and the piquancy of peppers will feel like they are sitting in Thailand here. The food is cooked fresh, and the two Thai chefs tailor Thai specialties the way you want them—from mild and delicate to flaming hot. Culinary wags agree that this small-sized venue serves some of the biggest and best flavors in town. Lunch entrées $6.95–9.95, dinner entrées $8.95–19.95.

Wright's at the Biltmore (602-955-6600), Arizona Biltmore Resort, 2400 E. Missouri. Open for dinner Mon.–Sat. 6–10, Sun. brunch 11–2. Still glowing from menu and interior changes made in the fall of 2006, Wright's has maintained its traditions of quality and class. Executive chef Michael Cairns and chef de cuisine

Matt Alleshouse created a menu called American Lodge Cuisine that leaves food critics smiling and other restaurants going and doing likewise. Chef Michael's experience studying under Japanese chef Masahide Nishiyama taught him reverence and aesthetics—a theme that consistently shows up in the harmonious tastes and presentations of each course. Besides leaning toward fresh, local ingredients, Chef Matt gathers foods from around the nation's boutique, dairy, and game farms, then crafts the oft-changing menu to reflect what's available. After growing up in his mother's kitchen and spending the last six years in the Biltmore's, Matt marries flavors so well that no one ingredient upstages another—though he will admit to being a "grill guy." This favored cooking technique shows up in the prime fillet of beef tenderloin with caramelized onions and blue-cheese-crusted pan-roasted marble potatoes, brussels sprout petals, and demiglaze (also one of Chef Michael's favorites). The most elegant dessert on the menu is still the chocolate soufflé with Grand Marnier crème anglaise. As for interiors and service, the gold leaf ceiling and Frank Lloyd Wright influences remain, and the staff are still a benchmark for service; they've just become more personal. In other words, you can put your elbows on the table, but you can't dance on it. This is, after all, the Biltmore. Entrées $29–39.

EATING OUT City Bakery at Bentley Projects (602-253-7200), 215 E. Grant St. Open Mon.–Sat. 7–3. One of the favorite breakfast and lunch spots in the Valley now has a venue in the trendy downtown arts district. Assorted pastries greet you in the

morning, along with homemade granola and cranberry walnut French toast. At lunch you can get the standard favorites such as strawberry chicken, veggie melt, and curried chicken, along with the exclusive PLT sandwich: prosciutto, organic tomatoes, and arugula with artichoke aioli on focaccia. The desserts remain decadent as ever. Breakfast $5–7, lunch $7.50–10.

Fry Bread House (602-351-2345), 4140 N. 7th Ave. Open Mon.–Thu. 10–7 (till 8 Fri.–Sat.). If you have heard of, or better yet tasted, a Navajo taco, you will know the deliciousness that awaits at this small Tohono O'od-ham–owned eatery. You can sample this traditional pillowy, chewy fried treat with a variety of toppings. For a meal, red or green chili is best. If you have room for dessert after finishing off one of these huge meals, try the frybread topped with honey or chocolate and butter. Entrées $3.50–6.50.

The Gelato Spot (602-957-8040), 3164 E. Camelback Rd. When you were in Rome, you did as the Romans did and imbibed in the sweet frozen confection once made of the snow gathered from the Alps. One taste of the silken substance offered here might put you back at the Spanish Steps. Some of the staff even speak a bit of *Italiano*. Dozens of gelato flavors made fresh every day line up in display cases. You can also order a cup of exotic tea. Next door is **Hava Java**, a coffee shop that attracts all sorts of interesting folks, from professional cyclists to movie stars to neighborhood java junkies. $2.50–4.50.

La Grande Orange (602-840-7777), 4410 N. 40th St. Open Sun.–Thu. 6:30 AM–9 PM (10 PM Fri.–Sat.). From breakfast (think giant muffins, house-made English muffins, fresh fruit, whole-grain cereals, and fresh egg dishes) through lunch (distinctive salads and fresh sandwiches made on artisan bread), and from 4 PM when the pizza starts baking (make that specialty pizzas with toppings like oyster mushrooms, prosciutto di San Danielle, avocado, and caramelized fennel) until closing, this neighborhood venue does not stop. Commuters line up for coffee, mothers bring in their young tykes, professionals sip and forge deals, and regulars help themselves to upscale items lining shelves and coolers. This is where you want to come to people-watch; you'll see every culture to match the world music playing in the background. Breakfast $4–7.25, lunch $6.95–8.25, pizza $11–14-plus.

🐾 ✐ **Luke's Italian Beef** (602-264-4022), 1604 E. Indian School Rd. Open Mon.–Sat. 10–8; closed Sun. Travelers from cities with an Italian neighborhood know how important it is to know where to find the best Italian beef. Luke's shows its Windy City roots with memorabilia from Chicago and Italian beef good enough to hail straight from Taylor Street. Be sure to get peppers and a double dip of natural juice (and extra napkins) for the perfect nepenthe. Entrées $4.95–6.95.

Matt's Big Breakfast (602-254-1074), 801 N. 1st St. Open Tue.–Sun. 6:30–2:30. The orange, cream, and yellow colors of the '50s diner motif mirror the colors of prior decade's propaganda posters hanging on the wall encouraging Americans to drink milk, eat eggs, and slather real butter onto their foods to boost their flailing health. This wholesome idea is taken a step farther in Matt's simple menu, where free-range eggs raised

humanely, fresh milk, and real butter are used, as well as organic ingredients whenever possible. You'll get a pitcher of warm real maple syrup to pour over handmade waffles and pancakes. The bacon is meaty grain-fed natural Iowa pork. The beef is all-natural. You'll also get a glop of jam in a condiment bowl, rather than a peel-back packet, to put on thick slices of country toast. The meals don't stray from the comfort level when lunch rolls around at 11. Hamburgers (Angus beef) get fried in butter, tomato sauce has cream, and the chili has chunks of cheese melted in it. Entrées $5–7.95.

✳ The Arts

ASU Art Museum (480-965-2787), Herberger College of Fine Arts at Arizona State University, southeast corner of 10th St. and Mill Ave., Tempe. Open Tue. 10–9, Wed.–Sat. 10–5. An impressive and innovative art venue exhibiting more than 10,000 pieces of contemporary art, American ceramics, American and European prints, and southwestern art with a heavy emphasis on Latino artists. Free.

First Fridays Art Walks (602-256-7539). One of the most beloved events in the city teeters between a fine arts soiree and raw-edged social scene. Art venues vary from distinguished galleries to homes and businesses that display exhibits; or you can just hang out in street parties to experience the art of living. On the first Friday of every month, thousands converge in the Roosevelt Historic District up to Indian School Road to view every medium and form of artistic expression. Artlink Phoenix provides shuttles through the evening for each First Friday, and many galleries cluster close enough to walk to.

Phoenix Art Museum (602-257-1880), 1625 N. Central Ave. Open Tue. 9–5, Wed.–Sun. 10–5; closed Mon. and major holidays. With a constant temperature of 72 degrees and 50 percent humidity to protect the art, it doesn't matter what time of the year you come to visit here; it's always cool. And so are the exhibits. The collection of more than 17,000 works of American, Asian, European, and Latin American artists includes modern, contemporary, and western American art. Classics include works by Monet, Picasso, Frida Kahlo, and Georgia O'Keeffe. Some innovative exhibits have you interacting in the ArtWorks Gallery, viewing historic interiors of the Thorne miniature rooms, and learning about great fashion designers and their work in the fashion design gallery; a sculpture garden gives you space to rest and relax. $10 adults, $8 seniors and full-time students with ID, $4 ages 6–17. Free to all on Tue. 3–9.

SCULPTURE IN THE PHOENIX ART MUSEUM PLAZA.

✳ Spectator Sports

Only seven other cities in the nation have top professional teams in all four major sports.

Arizona Cardinals (602-379-0102 or 800-999-1402). One of the two charter members of the National Football League plays at their own stadium in Glendale.

Arizona Diamondbacks (602-462-6500), 401 E. Jefferson St. The 2001 World Champion baseball team began playing the majors in 1998.

Phoenix Suns (602-379-7867). Basketball games at U.S. Airways Center in Phoenix often sell out.

Mercury Basketball (602-252-9622). The WNBA team also plays at U.S. Airways Center.

Coyotes Hockey (480-563-7825). The NHL team plays at the Glendale Arena.

SPRING TRAINING Cactus League Spring Training games start in Mar. Twelve Major League Baseball teams make Arizona their home in spring. The nine teams that play in the Greater Phoenix area are spread throughout the Valley at the following locations. You can purchase tickets direct from the stadium or call Ticketmaster (480-784-4444).

Chicago Cubs, Hohokam Park (480-964-4467), 1235 N. Center St., Mesa. **Kansas City Royals** and **Texas Rangers**, Surprise Stadium (623-594-5600), 15960 N. Bullard Ave., Surprise. **Los Angeles Angels of Anaheim**, Tempe Diablo Stadium (480-350-5205), 2200 W. Alameda Dr., Tempe. **Milwaukee Brewers**, Maryvale Baseball Park (623-245-5500), 3600 N. 51st Ave. **Oakland Athletics**, Phoenix Municipal Stadium

(602-392-0074), 5999 E. Van Buren. **San Diego Padres** and **Seattle Mariners**, Peoria Sports Complex (623-878-4337), 16101 N. 83rd Ave., Peoria. **San Francisco Giants**, Scottsdale Stadium (480-990-7972), 7408 E. Osborn Rd., Scottsdale.

✳ Selective Shopping

You'll find a collection of **antiques and collectible shops** on 7th Ave. south of Camelback and north of McDowell. Also head to the city of Glendale's historic district.

🐾 **Biltmore Fashion Park** (602-955-8400), 2502 E. Camelback Rd. Open Mon.–Sat. 10–6, Sun. noon–6. Exclusive, chic, and *the* place to see and be seen, this open-air pet-friendly mall has some exquisite appointments, from the floral landscaping in its courtyard setting to the hacienda fountains. Shopping leans toward the lap of luxury here; shops like Saks Fifth Avenue, Ralph Lauren, Gucci, Cole-Haan, and Godiva Chocolatier have merchandise you won't find elsewhere. There are also several upscale restaurants.

Chinese Cultural Center (602-244-8600), 668 N. 44th St. Unless you've studied the Chinese influence in Arizona, you would never know that this culture was once represented in just about every community in the state. Most cities razed their Chinatowns. This cultural center has the most advanced facilities in the Americas featuring Chinese architecture. The property has Chinese gardens, replicas of ancient Chinese pagodas and statues, retail stores featuring Oriental merchandise, restaurants, and the incredibly intriguing **99 Ranch Market**. If you have a hankering for any type of Asian food, you'll find it here,

from durian to salted duck eggs; fresh crabs to live eels; lime leaf to bunches of basil. It's a fascinating spot to peruse.

Phoenix Public Market (www .phoenixpublicmarket.com), 721 N. Central. Open Sat. 8–1; slow or closed in Aug. Often farmer's markets become a happening. This one gives you a look at the best of Arizona produce, products, and talents in a historic neighborhood. Pick up something to eat—from pulled beef to seafood gumbo or a pastry—or a piece of art. Of course, you can always get some fresh produce, too.

✳ Special Events

January: **P. F. Chang's Rock 'n' Roll Arizona Marathon & Half Marathon** (800-311-1255). Bands, cheer squads, prizes, and a finish-line party makes this Boston qualifier a big bash.

February: **Hoop Dance Festival** (602-252-8848) at the Heard Museum presents top Native hoop dancers from North America who compete for cash prizes and the international title.

March: **Art Detour** (602-256-7539) is a yearly art happening in which artists open their studios and galleries showcase top local artists. **Heard Museum Guild Indian Fair & Market** (602-252-8848) presents museum-quality arts and crafts made by Native American artists. **Tres Rios Nature Festival** (623-204-2130) is a 2-day outdoor event focusing on the rich natural and cultural diversity of the Gila River.

April: **Arizona Asian Festival** (602-307-0050). Asian cultures are celebrated here in dance, music, and food. **Arizona Book Festival**

(602-257-0335, ext. 28) celebrates all things book—from featured authors to exhibitors selling books to 20,000 bibliophiles in attendance. **Maricopa County Fair** (602-252-0717) features food, games, exhibits, livestock, and a carnival.

July: **Fabulous Phoenix Fourth** (602-262-7176), Steele Indian School Park.

October: **Arizona State Fair** (602-252-6771) features food, games, exhibits, livestock, entertainment, and a carnival. **Cowboy Artists of America Sale & Exhibition** (602-307-2007) is a Phoenix Art Museum fund-raiser featuring new works by Cowboy Artists of America members.

November: **ZooLights** (602-273-1341) shows you the Phoenix Zoo decked out in miniature lights for night viewing. **Las Noches de las Luminarias** (480-941-1225). Stroll the Desert Botanical Gardens by the light of thousands of hand-lit luminaries with entertainment, food, wine, and hot beverages.

December: **APS Fiesta of Light Electric Light Parade** (602-262-7176) draws thousands to Central Avenue to see hundreds of light-decorated floats. **Christmas Mariachi Festival** (480-558-1122) presents the greatest mariachis in the world. **Fiesta Bowl Parade** (www.tostitosfiestabowl.com). Early comers will get grandstand seating, and thousands line up standing-room-only to see floats, helium balloons, marching bands, and equestrian units on Central Avenue.

SCOTTSDALE

Some cities know their calling. Scottsdale, founded in the late 1890s by Rhode Island banker Albert Utley—whose goal was to create a Utopian community—has fulfilled it in a world-class way. Scottsdale's resort scene indulges the senses with everything from cutting-edge spas to championship golf courses; sumptuous lodging to fine dining. Its urban élan has come from a recent growth spurt that has redefined its downtown. Once a strictly tourist haunt specializing in cowboy art and Native American crafts that rolled up its sidewalks after sunset and flirted with ghost-town status in the depths of summer, Scottsdale's downtown has become an ever-more-active place to live, work, and play. *Play* is the operative word here. With service venues multiplying to meet every whim you might have as you read this, you should never have to leave Utopia wanting.

Not one to forget its roots, Scottsdale blends its urban sizzle with the Old West. Amid new trends and latest styles in food, art, and architecture, cowboy hats still pop up, equestrian paths memorialize the town's enduring equine love affair, and western art makes a big statement in the gallery scene. It's still one of the best places to procure museum-quality Native American arts and crafts.

Whether your leanings are contemporary or cowboy, Scottsdale knows you still have to eat. The town has restaurants that rub shoulders with the best in the world, run by chefs who continually appear in the best-new-chef pages of *Food & Wine* magazine, receive James Beard Foundation Awards of Excellence, or earn AAA diamonds. From Sea Saw's shushimi to La Hacienda's four-star Mexican food, Acacia's exquisite steaks and seafoods to Lon's menu of eloquence and perfection—with the eclectic fare of local favorite Cowboy Ciao and Café ZuZu in between—food is big in Scottsdale.

Finally, for those of you who think the best part of the day begins when the sun sets, the best nightlife in the Valley happens at its world-famous nightclubs, Axis/Radius and E4, which draw A-listers. Kazimierz's World Wine Bar, owned by self-titled "Wino" (and fabulous restaurateur) Peter Kasperski, has become an archetype for wine bars in other cities. But remember, what's said and done sub-vino does not always remain sub-rosa, even in a Utopia like Scottsdale.

GUIDANCE **Scottsdale Convention & Visitors Bureau** (480-421-1004 or 800-782-1117) has in-depth information for the types of experiences you want to

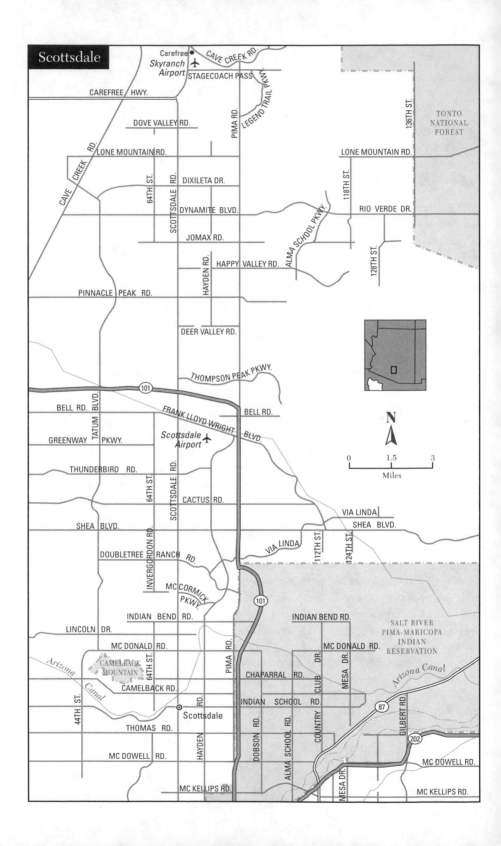

tailor your visit around: shopping, golf, spas, art, and food. Call **McDowell**
Mountain Regional Park (480-471-0173) **Pinnacle Peak Park** (480-312-
0990), 26802 N. 102nd Way for information on trail use. The State Lands
Department (602-364-2753) provides permits for entering state lands.

GETTING THERE *By car:* From Phoenix, take Camelback Rd. east to downtown
Scottsdale. From Loop 202, exit at Scottsdale Rd. and go north. The 101 Free-
way takes you to the far north and eastern edges of town. *By air:* **Phoenix Sky
Harbor International Airport** (602-273-3300), 3400 E. Sky Harbor Blvd.,
Phoenix, is about 15 minutes from downtown. If you have your own craft, fly in
to the **Scottsdale Airport** (480-312-2321), 15000 N. Airport Dr.

GETTING AROUND Scottsdale Trolley (480-421-1004) runs every 10 minutes
11 AM–9 PM (free), hitting all the high spots from Scottsdale Fashion Square
south to downtown and beyond. For a map, log onto www.scottsdaletrolley.com.

WHEN TO COME Peak season lasts from Jan. to late Apr.; rates are high, rooms
are filled, and streets buzz with activity. Summertime, from June to late Aug.,
lures visitors with restaurant specials and the best deals in accommodations. You
can get a room at the toniest resorts for budget prices. The locals know this, too,
so plan ahead even in summer.

MEDICAL EMERGENCY Dial 911, or **Mayo Clinic Hospital** (480-301-8000),
13400 E. Shea Blvd.

✳ To Do

BIKING ABC/Desert Biking Adventures (602-320-4602), 7119 E. Shea Blvd.,
Suite 109-247, offers mountain and cross-country downhill adventures. They
provide support vehicle, equipment, and water. **Bike Haus** (480-994-4287),
located downtown at 7025 E. 5th Ave., rents mountain and road bikes by the
half ($25) and full ($35) day, providing helmet, lock, and water bottle.

DOG PARKS 🐾 **Chaparral Park** (480-312-2331), 5401 N. Hayden Rd. Open
dawn–9 PM. The largest dog park in the city has drinking fountains and seating
areas. It's divided for passive and active dogs.

🐾 **Horizon Park** (480-312-2331), 15444 N. 100th St. Open dawn–dusk. Two-
thirds of an acre with a 10- by 20-foot shade ramada and a people/dog drinking
fountain. When the canines kick up too much dust, just push a button and the
dust-control feature waters the area to settle the dirt.

GAMING The Salt River, Pima, and Maricopa Indian Community has two casinos
in Scottsdale. **Casino Arizona** (480-850-7777), 524 N. 92nd St., has around 500
slot machines, a poker room, $100,000 live play keno, a 500-seat bingo hall,
Racebook/OTB betting, and Players 21. Its world-class show lounge presents top
acts; there are five restaurants, including fine dining at the **Cholla**, which has

SCOTTSDALE GOLF

Golf transcends game status here; it's a way of life. Some of the best courses in the world splay across Scottsdale soil, and the green meccas attract all things golf from every corner of the world: pro players, schools, equipment manufacturers, and legendary tournaments. Not all the best courses will set off alarms on your credit card, especially if you follow the good advice of Harry Vardon: "Don't play too much golf. Two rounds a day are plenty."

Camelback Golf Club (480-596-7050 or 800-242-2631), 7847 N. Mockingbird Lane. Playing one of the two courses here can turn into an adventure. The **Club Course**, designed by Jack Snyder in 1978, is typical American links style laid out in a landscaped natural wash. The 7,014-yard, par-72 course gives no little challenge to the best of golfers with its secluded sand traps, gently rolling terrain, and abundance of water holes—not to mention great mountain panoramas bold enough to distract the most disciplined pro. One of the state's best water holes lies at the **Resort Course**'s ninth hole. This Arthur Hills course is known for its water holes and strategic layout. Tall tress, subtle topography, and challenging bunkering make an interesting game. More than 20 PGA golf professionals will help you get through all the challenges. If that's not enough, you can sign up for the John Jacobs Practical Golf School (one of the most innovative in the country) located on the grounds. Other services include club and shoe rentals, driving range, putting greens and chipping areas, club cleaning, golf shop, and grill. Low season $39–99, high season $79–169.

Grayhawk (480-502-1800), 8620 E. Thompson Peak. Listed as one of the top 100 courses to play in the United States, Grayhawk stands out among the 200 links in the Valley. It has two courses—Talon and Raptor. Both are 18-hole desert courses with a par 72. **Talon**, designed by U.S. Open and PGA champion David Graham and architect Gary Panks, offers an exciting landscape full of par-3s to give you drama, challenge, and views—the McDowell Mountains to the north and the city of Phoenix to the south. The 7,001-yard facility plays well enough to have been listed as one of *Golf Magazine*'s Top 10 You Can Play in US. The **Raptor Course**, designed by Tom Fazio, plays with your pluck. Take a risk, get a reward. Maybe. See how close you come to its par-72, 7,108 yards from the back tees. Just remember to double-check your first impressions of shots. Green fees include golf cart, practice balls, yardage card, pin placement sheet, and bag tag. $75–210.

Kierland Golf Club (480-922-9283), 6902 E. Greenway Pkwy. Golf has always been big in the Kierland family, and the club goes out of its way to equip golfers with great greens and the tools to tackle this course. First, the course (rated one of the most women-friendly in the nation) plays with adventure. Designer

© Scottsdale Convention & Tourism Bureau

Scott Miller put 300 bunkers, lakes, washes, and classic desert vegetation between you and 27 holes on the Audubon-friendly rolling greens. Next, instructors high on the golf-industry-lauded ladder present a fitness training system guaranteed to increase driving distance while improving overall fitness and stamina. Even weekend warriors have no more excuses. The husband-and-wife teaching team of Mike and Sandy LaBauve of LaBauve Golf Academy are available for instruction. The club's exclusive FORE-MAX Training Systems, developed by fitness director Steve Heller melds traditional golf tips, on-course play, fitness, training, nutrition, and custom club fitting. For your ambulatory comfort, you can zoom around the course on a Segway or an air-conditioned golf cart. Finally, you can rest under 83-foot-long Callaway Cool Shade canopies after chasing Callaway Golf Big Bertha Blue range balls driven by the latest Callaway woods and irons. Kierland calls it "start to finish golf." Everyone else calls it "very cool." $75–180.

Legend Trail Golf Club (480-488-7434), 9462 Legendary Lane. One of the North Scottsdale beauties (nearby views include Pinnacle Peak and the McDowell Mountains; to the south are Camelback and Mummy Mountains, with the city of Phoenix beyond), this championship 18-hole course will give you a run for your money, inasmuch as the large undulating greens are a challenge to read. Rees Jones designed the par-72 course to follow the lay of the land, and so it winds through stands of paloverde trees and saguaro cacti. Hole names like Water Chant, Good Medicine, and Stones That Speak might evoke some good juju. The course doesn't really start going until its signature hole 7, where a cascade tumbles into a pond hidden from the tee box. From there, the variety continues. Four sets of tees match your skill level. Golf shop (rated in the top 100 of a Zagat survey), restaurant, and home of Golf Digest Schools. $70–185.

Sanctuary Golf Course (480-502-8200), 10690 E. Sheena Dr. Hard to believe environmentalists and golfers can shake hands, but they did over this course. Designer Randy Heckenkemper made golf history by transforming the Bureau of

Reclamation's stormwater retention area into one hot par-71 golf course with a range of 4,096 to 6,624 feet. And he did it by following the environmental guidelines established by the staid Audubon International Institute. As an Audubon Signature Status Golf Course, Sanctuary has to manage its effluent usage, pest control, water quality, and storm-runoff storage to Audubon's standards. Heckenkemper remained true to the lay of the land of the sexy rolling desert foothills of the McDowell Mountains; vegetation and washes often interlope into your play. Wildlife makes a big show here, especially coyotes, roadrunners, jackrabbits, and quail; sometimes you'll see mule deer, javelina, or bobcats. The end product is a nature sanctuary that requires intense accuracy from its players. Fees include golf cart. $40–119.

Talking Stick (480-860-2221), 9998 E. Indian Bend Rd. Ben Crenshaw and Bill Coore designed two completely different but user-friendly golf courses for the Salt River Pima and Maricopa Indian tribes. Worlds away from the target golf so predominant in the area, these courses present traditional play for golf purists. The 7,133-yard **North Course** has a par-70 rating; chip-and-run is a valuable tool here. Views of Camelback Mountain, the McDowell Mountains, and Pinnacle Peak surround the slightly crowned course, which has no trees. It's landed in top state and national ratings by various golf venues. The **South Course** is 6,833 yards with a par of 71 and is more straightforward regarding plays. Parkland style and full of cottonwoods and water, the course has slight elevation changes, fingered bunkers, and tiered landscaping. Fees include carts; soft spikes only allowed. $110–180.

Tournament Players Club of Scottsdale Stadium Course (480-585-4334 or 888-400-4001), 7575 E. Princess Dr. This over-the-top 18-hole course rests like an emerald in a gold-plated mountain setting. Known for numerous history-making moments by the world's greatest players during the PGA Tour's FBR Open (formerly Phoenix Open), the course is rife with class standards and excellence. This is where Tiger Woods made his famous hole-in-one on hole 16. Tom Weiskopf and Jay Morrish created a course that blends challenge with playability. Additions of an award-winning golf shop, practice facilities, full-service men's and women's locker room facilities, and ESPN Golf School keep this course on the national lists. If you're a guest at the Scottsdale Fairmont Princess, the resort's Golf Concierge program (an extra service that attends to all the details of arranging itineraries, locker facilities, lessons, rentals, and transportation for tee times, not to mention supplying iced aromatherapy towels, lip balm, sunscreen, and water) gives you even more reason to become one with this course. Fees includes green and cart fees, practice balls, yardage book, bag tag. Dress code: No denim or gym shorts; no T-shirts, halter tops, or bathing suits. **Stadium Course** $68–245, **Desert Course** $33–70.

Troon North Golf Club (480-585-7700), 10320 E. Dynamite Blvd. Described as "the best course ever built," with a price tag and list of awards to prove it, the immaculate greens wind through natural ravines and hillsides in the Sonoran Desert. Compelling panoramas, slinky slopes, and desert vegetation are the natural features this club's two championship courses (**The Monument** and **The Pinnacle**) center on. Designers Tom Weiskopf and Jay Morrish added technical features that require five sets of tees for both courses. The 18th hole of the Pinnacle gives you the illusion of teeing off directly into the area's landmark Pinnacle Peak mountainside. Tim Mahoney, who rates among the country's top 100 instructors, heads the Golf Academy. Green fees include golf car, bag tag, yardage book, divot tool, and practice balls. $85–295.

We-Ko-Pa Golf Club (480-836-9000), 18200 E. Toh Vee Cir., Fountain Hills. It didn't take long for the **Cholla** course, located on land owned by the Fort McDowell Yavapai Nation, to achieve global status. Two days after it opened in 2001, it was named one of the best 10 new courses in the world. Things have not changed here. With no homes, no roads, and plenty of desert vegetation to give some holes an isolated feeling, this course is about you, nature, and the game of golf. Mountain scenery rubs shoulders with challenges on this pristine course, from bunkers to double-doglegs. Four sets of tees give you a choice of yardages that range from 5,289 to 7,225 with a par of 72. Regular back tees play to 6,644 yards. The **Saguaro** course was still in planning at the time of publication. Designers Bill Coore and Ben Crenshaw anticipate a course that will provoke golfers to play different shots and be open to thinking out new challenges. Nonresident $80–195, resident $50–120.

exceptionally good food in large portions. **Casino Arizona II** (480-850-7777), 9700 E. Indian Bend Rd., has over 200 slot machines known to pay big. Locals crowd for specials served at its **Wandering Horse Bar and Café**.

HIKING Check out the **Scenic Trail** in McDowell Mountain Park and the **Pinnacle Peak Trail** in its namesake park, both in North Scottsdale. Hiking here requires drinking much more water (fortified with electrolyte mix) than you anticipate; plan on a quart every hour or two, depending on the temperature. Make sure your hike ends by 10 on summer mornings, and wear sunscreen and a hat.

HORSE SHOWS Horse events happen all year long in Scottsdale, but the big ones—the **Arizona Sun Circuit Quarter Horse Show** and the **Scottsdale Arabian Horse Show**—take place around Jan. and Feb., featuring a variety of world-championship performance competitions and traditional rodeo events. Glamour still prevails at the Arabian horse show. While more than 2,000 spirited Arabian horses from around the world compete with each other in two big arenas, movie stars, over 400 commercial exhibitors, food vendors, and showgoers garbed in several-thousand-dollar outfits grab attention on the rest of the grounds. Most all of the events take place at **WestWorld** (480-312-6802), 16601 N Pima Rd.

HOT-AIR BALLOONING Adventures Out West/Unicorn Balloon (480-991-3666), 15001 N. 74th St., takes off every day at dawn with a champagne breakfast. Dusk flights are available Nov. through mid-Mar. $165 adults, $125 children 12 and under with adult.

RAILROAD ✐ **McCormick-Stillman Railroad Park** (480-312-2312), 7301 E. Indian Bend Rd. Open 10 AM; call for closing times. This small-scale reproduction of the Century Narrow Gauge Railway equipment caught the eye of Walt Disney, who offered to buy it for one of his theme parks. You can ride the train along its mile-long tracks, peruse the museum, and then stop by the general store for hot dogs and ice cream. Kids (of all ages) can head for the playground

---

ARABIAN HORSES, DARLINGS OF THE EQUINES

The Arabian horse—a symbol of wealth—carried great prestige in ancient Arabian communities. This tradition has trickled down through the centuries and peaked during the 1970s, especially in Scottsdale, which boasted the biggest, finest horse market in the world.

At that time horses in general were an investment. Arabians, in particular, were promoted heavily; the best horses sold for $1 million or more. Since a change in tax laws, however, all horses became more affordable. This included the darling Arabian, which has since evolved into a family-oriented horse.

or spin on the park's carousel. Rides cost $1 per person; they're free for those under 3 (with a paying adult).

✳ Spas

Agave, The Arizona Spa (480-624-1500), Westin Kierland Resort & Spa, 6902 E. Greenway Pkwy. Open daily 6 AM–8 PM. Indigenous plants and oils are big here, especially the namesake agave plant, which is used in spa products, treatments, and even the complimentary energy drink. The signature skin treatment is Agave Enchantment; *Tui' Na* is the spa's signature massage treatment, which establishes harmonious Qi (energy) and blood flow. The Agave Signature Oil custom-blends agave with hazelnut, lemon, and lime oils for some ultrasmooth skin and shiny tresses. The spa treatments include some interesting work with basalt (True LaStone Therapy) and gemstones, as well as hypnotherapy. The wet room has a sun ceiling that gets a dousing of light so enticing guests often pull up a chair and relax to the sound of water features. Treatments (Never-Too-Soon Teen Facial and Razzle-Dazzle Manicure/Pedicure) cater to the whole family. Facilities include 20 treatment rooms, a full-service beauty salon, a movement studio, a weight training/cardio studio, and men's and ladies' locker rooms (each with whirlpool, sauna, and steam room). $125–210 for body treatments and massages, $125–210 for facials, and $85–100 for training sessions.

Centre for Well-Being (480-941-8200 or 800-843-2392), The Phoenician Resort, 6000 E. Camelback Rd. Open every day 7–7. One of the world's most innovative spas, and very high on must-experience lists, the Centre for Well-Being presents a whole cadre of treatments from traditional Swedish massage to cutting-edge energy therapies. The treatment menu is pages long. Experienced therapists with a propensity to nurture create an extraordinary spa experience. This was one of the first spas in the country to offer optimal aging and wellness medicine; you can get naturopathic and homeopathic consultations, an exclusive Optimal Aging and Wellness Consultation, and anti-aging Facial Rejuvenation Acupuncture from licensed naturopathic physician Dr. Amy Whittington. The spa's Circle of Intuitive Guides leads guests into metaphysical realms with remarkably accurate Tarot, astrology,

AT THE HYATT SPA AVANIA.

and guided meditation. Treatments $140–250; $100 for a 50-minute personal training in the fitness center.

Eurasia Spa Scottsdale Athletic Club (480-922-8855), 8235 E. Indian Bend Rd. True to its name, the spa features decor and treatments from all over Asia. The Hing family put great thought into the spa interiors. While you wait for your therapist in the Tranquility Room, meditation tables of sand and stone allow you to do finger writing and arranging of the stones to clear your mind and calm your soul. The fresh bamboo plants lining the windows represent energy and strength. Each treatment room is named for an Asian flower to represent a different strength: the Peony represents longevity and nobility; Lotus, purity and truth; Wisteria, cascading beauty; Orchid, an elegant floral ballet. Brush artist Joyce Hing painted the floral art. If you get a couples massage, you might notice headless warriors statutes—a traditional token to ward off evil spirits. The couples room is designed to create and maintain harmonious relationships. Arcosanti bells add tone therapy to help soothe your psyche. House-made products customize treatments. If you have time, indulge in a traditional Japanese soak. $175–220 for signature body treatments, $115–165 for massages, and $115 for facials; nail care, waxing services, and men's treatments available.

Jurlique Spa (480-424-6072), Fire Sky Resort & Spa, 4925 N. Scottsdale Rd. Open daily 8–8 (till 7 in summer). Decorated with rustic knotty-pine floors in the treatment room, slate ones in the bathroom, and glass and metal all around, this spa has an earthy feeling balanced by dainty, colorful chandeliers. Therapists use Jurlique's organic products grown in the Adelaide Hills of South Australia (the most mineral-rich spot on earth) in fabulous facials, polishes, wraps, hot stone therapies, and glows. Jurlique makes unique herbal, antioxidant blends that are free of chemicals, animal content, and artificial fragrances and colors. The products have an intense aromatherapy influence. All this becomes important when you consider that what goes on the skin seeps into the body. Each treatment room is a private, self-contained refuge. That means no locker rooms. No sharing dressing space. No stall showers. A private bathroom. The rooms are big enough to add breathing space between the treatment table, an elegant curtained-off tub, and the workstation where those wonderful-smelling oils get mixed (often your choice of which ones). This makes any treatment ever so special and luxurious. $70–190.

The Lamar Everyday Spa (480-945-7066), 5115 N. Scottsdale Rd. Open daily 9–7. Often (correctly) described as an oasis in the desert, this day spa is one big find. The Caribbean theme prevails in names of treatment rooms and decor and extends into the whole of the spa, whose casual but sensuous demeanor has that subtle element of elegance found on tropical islands. A coed area has a private garden with fireplace, water features, ballroom dancing classes, and views of Camelback Mountain from the patio,. Your treatments can run from a chair massage or mini mani to a full day of luxury—facials to body treatments. The spa uses Yon-Ka products for facials and offers an oxygenated one that just might keep you from plastic. A variety of body treatments include shiatsu, Swedish massage, body buffs, and hot rock therapy. The best part is that the price is right. The locals once had the spa to themselves, but now the secret is out; make reservations early if you want a weekend or night treatment. Massage and body treatments $50–150, facials $50–125.

Sanctuary Spa (480-607-2330), 5700 E. McDonald Dr., Paradise Valley. Open 6 AM–8:30 PM. Sitting at the feet of the Praying Monk formation atop Camelback Mountain, the spa has an East meets West mind-set. The environment has classic Oriental leanings, gracefully balancing the five elements with rugged western elegance. Instead of windowless treatment chambers, indoor–outdoor treatment rooms bring the outside in, and you outside if you wish. This alone makes any spa treatment you choose special—and the menu is pretty exclusive. The services include a selection of Asian-inspired treatments; Watsu; facials: salon services; and consultations, such as Tarot from Valley expert Cindy Nichols (who reads for all the A-names), astrology, and numerology. After your treatment, you have full use of the vitality pool, steam room, and Zen meditation garden. In-room treatments and personal training available. Treatments $135–245, facials $135–235, consultations $155–230.

Spa Avania (480-483-5558), Hyatt Regency Scottsdale Resort and Spa at Gainey Ranch, 7500 E. Doubletree Ranch Rd. Open daily 8 AM–10 PM. You won't find another spa like this one, with its slate, black granite, and solid cherry hardwood details and a Grecian name that means "an ideal state of being." Every detail of the spa experience is based on the science of time and your body's internal clock. The spa menu is divided into morning (awakening and rejuvenation), midday (restoration and balance), and evening (relaxation and renewal) offerings that work with your body's metabolism and biorhythms. Treatment rooms have natural light, rare exotic teas from Mitea are offered, mineral water from Macedonia is served, men have their own treatment room with flat-screen TV and mini bar, couples can reserve oversized treatment suites, garden treatment suits have private entrances, a French Celtic mineral pool (no chlorine) provides the ultimate soak, hot- and cold-water immersion pools add elements of Kneipp Therapy, a dry inhalation room infuses eucalyptus oils, outdoor storm showers give an alternative to the oversized showers in the men's and women's changing areas, a yoga studio teaches YogaAway to restore and recoup your clarity and balance, and a state-of-the-art fitness center stays open all day. After all this, *avania* is almost a guarantee. $120 for rituals, $115–180 for massages, $130–160 for body wraps, $150 for aromatic Vichy, $135–180 for facials, $20–75 for waxing services, $30–75 for gentlemen's grooming.

The Spa at Camelback Inn (480-596-7040 or 800-922-2635), 5402 E. Lincoln Dr. Open daily 6:15 AM–7:30 PM. The biggest and the first comprehensive spa in the Southwest is perennially voted among the best spas in the Valley by the locals. With that in mind, you won't necessarily find the lobby to be a cool, calm sanctuary, but one bustling with people. People like this spa because it has what they want—great treatments from great therapists (all the movie stars ask for Harrison) at great prices. The journey starts outside the spa doors in the garden courtyard where aromatherapy scents waft from open doors, music plays, and flowers color the grounds. Once you're through the lobby and separate from the rest of the spa, peace happens. Treatments range from traditional Swedish and shiatsu massage to more meditative therapies that precipitate awareness of self and a sense of inner balance. Facilities include a heated outdoor lap pool, coed Jacuzzi, men's hot tub and cold plunge pool, women's hot tub, complete men's and women's locker rooms, separate Turkish steam rooms, and Finnish saunas. Salon services tend to hairstyling, cuts, weaving, and coloring and nail services. The fitness gym is hot—the latest equipment, classes, personal training, nutritional counseling, Pilates, water, and lavender towels to cool your brow. $115–135 for bodywork, $135 for facials, and $45–80 for training sessions.

The Spa at Four Seasons Resort Scottsdale (480-513-4145), 10600 E. Crescent Moon Dr. Southwestern elements play prominent roles at this spa: adobe-style architecture, southwestern decor, and treatments using mud, herbs, hot stones, and honey. Therapists and aestheticians use 14 treatment rooms, including two spa suites, to work their magic. Spa director Lia Rowland trained at the Paris headquarters for the spa's new product line, Academie Scientifique. The skin care line promises to restore and refresh feminine beauty—which means facials are de rigueur here. As a lagniappe, therapists give guests a Tip to Take Home, techniques to assuage dry skin, relieve tension headaches, and exfoliate skin. The state-of-the-art fitness center includes every type of machine you think you need, and more. Personal trainers assist with tai chi, yoga, stretching, and Pilates, as well as sport-specific training to improve performance for golfers, tennis players, and joggers. $80–264 for bodywork, $130–210 for facials, and $50–120 for training sessions.

VH Spa (480-248-2000), Hotel Valley Ho, 6850 E. Main St. You won't get the dose of tranquility and Om-like peace most spas exude when you make yourself at home in the lounge. Oh, it's quiet—no cells phones are allowed, and whispers are preferred—but the colors remain vibrant light green and turquoise, urging guests in color-therapy language to speak from the heart. This spa caters to the stressed-out business person, presenting massages and shiatsu. You can even customize your treatment with guided massage. And if that's not enough, you can give your consciousness a treatment with quantum biofeedback. Acupuncture Facial Rejuvenation, given by Victoria Mogilner, author of *Ancient Secrets of Facial Rejuvenation*, makes the ultimate facial. VH Spa also offers exercise training sessions, guided hikes, and special classes such as Belly Dancing with Veils, Pool Scuba, Yoga, and Yamuna Body Rolling. $95–185 for massage, $185 for body treatments, $125–150 for facials, and $65–85 for training sessions.

Willow Stream—The Spa at Fairmont Princess (480-585-2732), 7575 E. Princess Dr. Like the rest of the resort, this spa has a magnificent layout. Patterned after the western Grand Canyon's Shangri-la, redrock-walled Havasu Canyon, the spa wraps itself in a natural environment. Even products have local traditions and ingredients. Three years in the making, the spa interior has natural elements and specially chosen colors to reflect its philosophy of discovering your internal pool of energy. No assembly-line therapies here. Treatments are original, schedules liberal (1–2 hours with 15 minutes in between), and therapists doting. A rooftop pool replete with waterfalls is the epitome of elegance. Schedule your session at night when you may end up having the spa to yourself; the after-dark beauty when the water features light up add to the experience. Fitness facility, salon services, meditation gardens, men's and women's spa and lounge areas. $149–309 for bodywork, $149–209 for massages, $149–259 for facials, and $49–69 for training sessions.

✳ Wilder Places

McDowell Mountain Regional Park (480-471-0173), 16300 N. McDowell Mountain Rd. Open Sun.–Thu. 6 AM–8 PM, Fri.–Sat. 6 AM–10 PM. Considered one of the most scenic of Maricopa County's mountain parks, this one stretches along the eastern edge of the Valley to offer views of the famous Superstition Mountains. The park has 50 miles of trails crossing mountains rising 3,000 feet for every experience level. $5.

McDowell Sonoran Preserve (480-998-7971), end of Alma School Rd. north of Dynamite Rd. Some trails require a $15 State Lands Department permit.

Pinnacle Peak Park (480-312-0990), 26802 N. 102nd Way (a mile south of Dynamite and Alma School Rds.). The bouldery, low-lying ridges at the north end of the Valley makes a scenic spot to get outdoors and enjoy the desert. You may see rock climbers, loaded with gear, heading for a favorite route via the manicured Pinnacle Peak Trail.

✳ Lodging

∞ 🐾 ✎ ♿ **FireSky Resort & Spa** (480-945-7666), 4925 N. Scottsdale Rd. Located right in the thick of things on the other side of a hedge that muffles the sights and sounds of the city, FireSky, a recent AAA Four Diamond winner, is one of the city's hidden treasures. Big on romance, the whole resort is filled with niches wrapped in mature vegetation and soothed by fireplaces or water features. The sand-bottomed pool and strip of beach makes a fun place for kids or a cozy fireside spot for adults. The Jurlique Spa (which specializes in its own organic products) is the only Jurlique-branded spa in the state. **Taggio Restaurant** flew in an Italian chef who uses local ingredients, plus a few esoteric ones specially ordered from his homeland. Guest rooms have marble and tile in the bath, luxurious linens, sexy sheers, WiFi, and plasma TV with yoga and meditation TV channels. The resort also has a wine hour each evening, in-room spa treat-

ments, and welcome treats for pet guests. $199–359.

∞ 🐾 ✎ ♿ **Camelback Inn** (480-948-1700 or 800-242-2631), 5402 E. Lincoln Dr. The Marriotts were so enamored of this desert resort, they finally bought it after repeated vacations there. It remains the favorite of Bill Marriott Jr.—son of the late hotel chain founder, chairman of the board, and president of Marriott Corporation. And for good reason: It's been the lodging of choice for presidents, Hollywood legends, and travelers since original owner Jack Stewart opened it in 1936. For those who demand the threefold braid of privacy without seclusion, posh without pretense, and friendliness without familiarity—kick off your shoes and stay awhile; like Marriott, you may not want to leave. The inn, currently being remodeled is totally Southwest inside and out; Native American, authentic adobe architecture, and nature are big here. Some bellmen don't mind donning a cowboy hat. The blend of cultural tradition and glamour works. The resort shares the distinction of earning AAA's Five Diamond status for the last 31 years—the only Arizona property and only one of three properties nationwide to do so. The resort has six all-weather tennis courts (five lit for night play, one screened for privacy, and the inn will match unpartnered players with others of equal skill level); the largest spa in the Southwest; championship golf; basketball and volleyball courts; three swimming pools; several restaurants; and a 24-hour fitness center. A renovation project should be completed in 2008. Low season $199–629, high season $399–900.

⊕ 🐾 🗡 ♿ **Doubletree Resort** (480-947-5400), 5401 N. Scottsdale Rd.

THE TRADEMARK HORSE SCULPTURE IN FRONT OF DOUBLETREE RESORT TURNS HEADS.

Known as "the resort with the horses," this property turns heads as people pass by on Scottsdale Road. The bronze sculpture *My Friends* by Snell Johnson—three Arabian horses at full gait in a fountain—evokes energy. Inside the grounds, life decompresses to match the resort status. You would never know you're *this close* to the best shopping, restaurants, and entertainment venues in the Valley. The Frank Lloyd Wright architecture, manicured lawns, and fountains bring a lush touch to the desert. The gray stone walls of the buildings are textured to look like the bark of the 200 palm trees planted on the property. The 22 acres hold two swimming pools (adult and children's with playground), tennis courts, a nine-hole PGA regulation putting green, a health club, and racquetball courts. Inside each room, all oversized, you have a private balcony with a pool, courtyard, or fountain view, wet bar, WiFi access, cable TV, and movies on command. There's no resort fee, and you get free parking. A Kid's Club takes place in summertime. Pets up to 25 pounds are welcome for a $50 nonrefundable fee. Low season $99–249, high season $189–299.

⊕ 🐾 🗡 ♿ **The Fairmont Scottsdale Princess** (480-585-4848), 7575 E. Princess Dr. The resort's Spanish Colonial–style buildings steeped in terra-cotta color spread like a southwestern ranch over wide-open spaces. An impressive array of water features spout fountains, cascades, and refreshing streams appear around the grounds, creating an atmosphere reminiscent of a Roman plaza. The outlay marries casual with class, comfort with style. A five-star rating promises over-the-top service. Seven tennis courts are the site of the ATP/ Franklin Templeton Men's Tennis Tournament; five heated pools and a waterslide present great aqueous moments; the neighboring Tournament Players Club hosts the PGA Tour's FBR Open (formerly Phoenix Open). The resort's restaurants collectively have enough diamonds to light up the sky, and its spa, Willow Stream —The Spa, mirrors the red rock walls of Havasu Canyon replete with waterfalls. Aesthetic and special, the resort is ideal for guests who like an air of elegance mixed with southwestern style. Low season $149–229, high season $359–579; up to two pets under 25 pounds are welcome, $30 each.

① ✿ ✍ � **Four Seasons Resort Scottsdale at Troon North** (480-515-5700), 10600 E. Crescent Moon Dr. Situated on the northern edge of Scottsdale, where the edges of the city blur with the desert. Regardless of how close it lies to the backcountry, you still stay spoiled with AAA Five Diamond service. The staff members don't just meet guests' needs; they anticipate them. The resort presents stunning views of the Valley from its aerie in the boulder-strewn High Sonoran Desert. Unpretentious territorial-style buildings and suites keep a low profile to the beautiful desert surroundings. Inside, understated but elegant appointments make comfort a natural. All rooms have a fireplace; suites have an outdoor garden shower, private plunge pool, and outdoor kiva fireplace. Besides a swimming pool and four tennis courts (two lit for night play), the resort's association with Troon North Golf Club just down the road makes it a hit with golfers. Its spa always appears on best lists and maintains a Mobil Four-Star rating. Kids will love it for its Kids for All Seasons program, not to mention the potential outdoor adventures waiting all around. There's also a complimentary laundry and a toaster in each room (no more cold toast from room service). Pets (dogs and cats under 15 pounds) get special amenities upon arrival. Low season $185–425, high season $495–795.

① ✿ ⅙ **Hermosa Inn** (602-955-8614 or 800-241-1210), 5532 N. Palo Cristi Rd. One of the few remaining authentic southwestern haciendas, this boutique inn majors in seclusion and romance, taking after its original owner, cowboy artist Alonzo "Lon" Megargee, who liked his women and regularly applied his rawboned charm to woo them. The artist's paintings, Old West scenes brimming with personality, hang throughout the inn. What started as Megargee's art studio evolved into a full-blown guest ranch hand built by Megargee in the 1930s and correctly named Casa Hermosa (handsome house). The current owners, who restored the hacienda to maintain an authentic sense of Arizona's history, added an underground wine cellar, library, and boardroom, designed with salvaged barn wood, vintage bricks, and stone. The property includes AAA Four Diamond LON's at the Hermosa restaurant (see *Dining Out*) and a heated swimming pool with cabanas (you can schedule a massage in a cabana). Guest casitas have exclusive interiors, including separate sitting areas with beehive fireplaces, wood-beamed ceilings, skylights, shutters, wet bars, and a courtyard setting with a semiprivate whirlpool spa. Casita 147, Lon Megargee's, may even have a bit of the old charm lilting in the air. Rumor has it he comes back to visit every once in a while. Casitas include WiFi, high-definition TV, and CD player. Continental breakfast buffet included in rate. Low season $110–510, high season $299–689.

Hotel Valley Ho (480-248-2000), 6850 E. Main St. When it first opened in 1956, celebrities couldn't stay away from this desert property. Over the years it lost its footing in the world of resorts and finally closed. Reopened and remodeled to reflect its 1950s heydays, this once trendy resort has regained its standing in the community as one of *the* places to see and be seen. It's pure retro made hip. Guest rooms have color schemes of turquoise and goldenrod and black, red, and white; geometrics; and creative baths. Signature guest rooms have baths with frosted glass walls and

PONDS ON THE GROUNDS OF THE HYATT REGENCY.

an azure blue light above large tubs. In studio guest rooms, the tub stands behind a curtain, rather than a wall, and the executive suite has a circular bathtub large enough for two. Rooms have suede platform beds with quality linens, carpet tiles, flat-screen TV, WiFi, and large and wonderful patios (terrace rooms have glassed-in patios). Low season $149–319, high season $209–389.

🦐 ☃ **Hotel Indigo** (480-941-9400), 4415 N. Civic Center Plaza. One of the best deals in the town sits right next to where everything happens in downtown Scottsdale. Taking a cue from the Fibonacci Sequence, the hotel's logo is the nautilus shell, and murals of the sequence found in nature, such as the agave, hang on the outside. Inside, the owners display photography in the hallways taken by up-and-coming local artists using abstract indigenous imagery. The hotel works with Arizona State University students, awarding them scholarships if their art is chosen. The property includes the open-room **Phi Bar/restaurant**, a heated pool, Phitness room, and parking. Rooms have king or two double beds, 32-inch flat-screen TV, complimentary WiFi, MP3 player hookup, spa-inspired shower, Aveda amenities, windows that open, and a sitting area. The hallways have an emerald glow from low green lights. $69–229.

⊕ ☃ 🐾 & **Hyatt Regency Scottsdale Resort** (480-444-1234), 7500 E. Doubletree Ranch Rd. Expansive, active, elegant but playful, this Hyatt has a multiple but appealing personality. Known for its picture-perfect view of the McDowell Mountains, the resort offers a compendium of interesting features many locals don't know about. In all-things-to-all-people fashion, the resort entertains cross-generationally. Its double-H design provides courtyards in which to relax. Nightly entertainment brings crowds to the open-air courtyard. A 2.5-acre water playground provides 10 pools, a three-story waterslide, and sand beaches where adults and kids play. Hard-surfaced tennis courts, three nine-hole golf courses, and jogging and cycling trails keep guests active. The Lost Dutchman Mine has kids digging in a sandpit for semiprecious stones, while Camp Hyatt Kachina teaches them about the flora, fauna, culture, and geography of Arizona. A Native American and Environmental Learning Center feeds the mind, a Native American Sculpture and Mineral Garden feeds the soul, while environmentally friendly wetlands and a Native Seed Garden honor the land and its people. Also on the premises are four restaurants and Spa Avania. Rooms offer a taste of the Southwest in copper, eggplant, and sand hues, along with cable TV, private balcony, mini service bars, and WiFi access. $190–350.

⊕ 🐾 ✐ ♿ **The Phoenician** (480-941-8200 or 800-325-3589), 6000 E. Camelback Rd. This 250-acre resort spreads at the feet of the Valley's trademark Camelback Mountain. Created solely for luxury and pleasure, this AAA Five Diamond facility culls comfort from several cultures—warm southwestern colors; haute European accents of marble, gold leaf, and crystal; a $25 million art collection; and island-inspired landscaping. Centre for Well-Being Spa, nine pools, three USGA-approved golf courses (one a championship course designed by Homer Flint and Ted Robinson Sr.), a

12-court Tennis Garden featuring four surfaces, Funician Kid's Club, three restaurants (including Four Diamond **Mary Elaine's**, whose chef Bradford Thompson won the 2006 James Beard Award for best chef in the Southwest), and private dining in **The Praying Monk** working wine cellar keep guests busy inside the resort. Guided tours to places of interest around the state accommodate those who like an adventure. Even if you don't rent the presidential suite ($3,500–5,000 per night includes a personal butler, limousine transportation, someone to unpack and press your clothes, a choice of cotton or satin linens, and a poolside cabana), the staff go way beyond the call of duty to make each guest's experience a special one with a *your-wish-is-my-command* attitude. Bellmen have been known to personally buy a teddy bear for a distressed child. Rates for a Super Room (standard 600 square feet): $375–675. Log onto www.thephoenician.com for special packages.

⊕ 🦞 🐾 ♿ **Renaissance Scottsdale Resort** (480-991-1414), 6160 N. Scottsdale Rd., Scottsdale. This may be the only resort with a popular shopping mall, **Borgata Shopping Village**, in its front yard. This makes for some interesting sojourns, if only to peruse and listen to Friday-night jazz. The property sits in the center of spas, hiking, golf, and shopping (beyond Borgata). The Scottsdale Trolley will take you in the right directions. Shopping aside, this tucked-away property will give you privacy and romance, if that's what you'd prefer. It's a place where you kick back and relax. The rooms, casita-style suites, have a rustic blend of wood-beamed ceilings, an arched

DIAMONDS ARE A RESORT'S BEST FRIENDS

Achieving Four or Five Diamond status is no small event. The awards, started by Arizona Automobile Association in 1977, recognize accommodations and restaurants for exceptional quality, outstanding customer service, and first-class amenities. The Five Diamond winners represent a fraction of 1 percent of about 60,000 properties throughout North America.

"Service is what distinguishes Four and Five Diamond facilities," says Jim Prueter, AAA Vice President of Travel. "Anticipating a guest's need before the guest expresses—or even realizes—that need, greeting the guest by name, quickly answering the phone—all these things make a visit more pleasurable and more memorable."

At the time of this writing, Scottsdale has four Five Diamond hotels. The number equals that of Las Vegas and is higher than you'll find in Chicago, Miami, San Francisco, Washington, DC, and the entire state of Hawaii.

THE PHOENICIAN.

© Scottsdale Convention & Tourism Bureau

niche wet bar, and a sunken outdoor hot-tub spa on their private patio; cable TV, WiFi access, a newspaper delivered to your room, and shoeshine service are included. Many rooms have real functioning fireplaces. Mature landscaping surrounds the rooms, two pools, four tennis courts, croquet green, putting green, and Ping-Pong tables. A complimentary restaurant, **Courtyard Tapas**, is open Oct.–May. More than 40 tapas are offered on the menu (meat/poultry, seafood, vegetable, and dessert), along with a Spanish cheese cart and Spanish and Californian wines. $75 nonrefundable sanitation fee for pets. Low season $129–369.

Sanctuary on Camelback Mountain (480-948-2100), 5700 E. McDonald Dr., Paradise Valley. Tucked away on a spot the Hohokam revered as sacred, this 53-acre resort lives up to its name in the aesthetic sense and in essence. Threaded with Asian hues, the whole resort plays with yin–yang design concepts. The AAA Four Diamond property has a pleasing graceful demeanor, so common to Oriental hospitality, without pretentiousness. Cathy Hayes, of Hayes Architecture Interiors, Inc., balanced mindfulness with beauty during a recent remodel of the property's 98 casitas terraced on a mountainside. The interiors blend Zen architecture with the original clean lines from the 1960s and '70s, colored with hues of the desert. The resort features **elements restaurant** with its gorgeous views of the Valley, a negative-edge and lap pool, Sanctuary Spa, and a fitness room. Casitas include flat-screen TV, featherbed and down pillows, Mascioni linens, large bath, high-speed Internet, and in-room safe. $225–620.

ⅻ 🦞 ✎ ♿ **Scottsdale Resort & Athletic Club** (480-344-0600 or 877-343-0033), 8235 E. Indian Bend Rd. Alice and Bob Hing, tennis players for several decades, started this boutique resort with their favorite sport in mind. It's one of the best tennis resorts in the nation and hosts several tournaments. Whether tennis is a passion or you never play, the rooms alone are enough reason to stay here: They're big, have great interiors, and are a bargain for the area—tucked moments away from downtown Scottsdale. The property includes the Eurasia Spa, restaurant, lounge, two outdoor pools, world-class Athletic Club with daily complimentary fitness classes, 11 championship tennis courts, and meeting rooms. Guest rooms (350 square feet) have king beds, kitchenette, entertainment center with TV and DVD player, desk, and complimentary high-speed Internet access; suites (700 square feet) add a den with queen sofa bed and private patio or balcony. Villas (900–2,500 square feet) include a full gourmet kitchen. Guest rooms $149–249, suites $179–359, villas $249–399.

ⅻ 🐾 ✎ ♿ **The Westin Kierland Resort & Spa** (480-624-1000), 6902 E. Greenway Pkwy. With a mind to make Arizona's history come to life, Westin titled this property with the theme Treasuring the Essence of Arizona. And it works, thanks to Arizona state historian Marshall Trimble, who wrote narratives to explain the names for rooms and areas in the hotel, as well as assisting with historic artwork displayed throughout the property. The property sits right next door to Kierland Commons shopping area. Kids may actually say thank you when they see the water park that gushes 575,000 gallons of water for two large pools (the main pool—8,000 square feet—is heated and 4 feet deep, with a zero-entry sandy beach), two hot tubs, 900-foot-long flowing "river" for "tubing," and a 110-foot-long waterslide. Kids 4–12 can head for the Tumbleweed Kids' Club. The resort also features eight dining venues; Agave—The Arizona Spa; the Kierland Golf Club; and, of course, that Heavenly Bed. $129–549.

✳ Where to Eat

DINING OUT **Acacia** (480-515-5700), Four Seasons Resort Scottsdale at Troon North, 10600 E. Crescent Moon Dr. Open nightly 6–10 (till 10:30 Fri.–Sat.). Rustic meets elegant here, with a latilla and beamed ceiling, travertine fireplace, and etched-glass room panels. The double-sided fireplace opens onto the patio, which looks upon one of the best views in the Valley. These natural elements create a relaxed atmosphere in which the staff dote upon you with over-the-top service and food. Executive chef Mel Mecinas, comfortable cooking for world-renowned personalities and stars, serves modern American steak house fare of exquisite prime beef, fresh seafood, and seasonal specialties. The bread practically melts in your mouth; the tenderloin is fork-tender, strip steaks ooze with flavor, the lobster is sweet as fresh surf. The signature dessert is chocolate soufflé, but you won't go wrong with anything you order to finish your meal. Dress is resort-formal (collared shirts, long pants, and close-toed shoes for men). Entrées $32–42.

Café ZuZu (480-421-7711), 6850 E. Main St. Open daily for breakfast 6–11:15, lunch 11:30–2:30, dinner 5:30–10. One of the hot meeting places of the Valley, where the edges of the sophisticated Hotel Valley Ho lounge spill into the café on a busy night. This makes for fascinating people-watching. Inside the restaurant's line of demarcation, you almost expect the Rat Pack to come swaggering in, martinis in hand, for a comfort-food dinner. It's Frank Sinatra all the way here—from the predominant color of orange (Sinatra's favorite) to the modern decor he so preferred. Chef Charles Wiley, who has racked up kudos from *Food & Wine* and televisionland, takes quintessential comfort food and turns it into delightful dishes, from macaroni and cheese to beef stroganoff; grilled cheese to the Famous ZuZu Burger; tuna steak to rib-eye steak. Wiley does all things well. All these entrées come as upscale versions with rich and wonderful ingredients. The wait staff here are young and, refreshingly, come with few or no airs. Entrées $10.25–26.

La Hacienda (480-585-4848), Fairmont Scottsdale Princess, 7575 E. Princess Dr. Open for dinner 5:30–10 Thu.–Tue. As soon as you step into this restaurant, you might think you've crossed a time warp and entered a gracious Mexican hacienda full of warmth and richness. It's one of two AAA Four Diamond Mexican restaurants in North America. The restaurant features a variety of *antojitos* (appetizers) and signature spit-roasted suckling pig carved right at your table. Executive chef Reed Groban and La Hacienda's chef de cuisine Tom Riordan travel in Mexico (a different region for every trip) to search for interesting new ideas for the classic dishes. This helps to keep the menu fresh and interesting. If the strolling mariachis (strumming soft ballads *sans* trumpet) don't make you feel you're in the land of beauty where gardenias grow, the margaritas might help. Tequila margaritas are the restaurant's specialty drink, and they offer a bedazzling array. The 24K margarita features premium liquors and real 24-karat gold leaf. Patrons who can't make up their mind what flavor margarita they want can order a flight of five different mixes. Entrées $25–39.

LON's at the Hermosa (602-955-7878), 5532 N. Palo Cristi Rd. Serving "artful American cuisine," chef Michael Rusconi weds the classic with the Southwest to create delicious, award-winning creations at this AAA Four Diamond venue. The melt-in-your-mouth Prince Edward Island mussels (a favorite with ladies), scallops, and fish specials come from Foley Fish in Boston. Meats—natural, organic, and humanely raised—come from ecologically sound sources. The cheeses have a rich creaminess. And many of the vegetables and spices come right out of the chef's half-acre garden. Chef Rusconi double-checks each plate before it leaves the kitchen, making consistency the venue's invaluable element. The grilled beef tenderloin with white truffle scented macaroni and cheese and two-pepper crusted natural pork tenderloin with prickly pear braised red cabbage, green beans, and garlic-mashed potatoes are the standing favorites, but coriander and honey lacquered breast of duck with sweet potato pie is the chef's favorite. LON's is a Valley favorite for Sunday brunch. If you have a high-end or romantic dinner in

mind, consider reserving the working wine cellar. The restaurant has an award-winning wine list featuring 750 selections and a 6,000-bottle inventory. Entrées $21–34, brunch $20.

Olive & Ivy (480-751-2200), 7135 E. Camelback Rd. Market open daily 7–3:30; restaurant Mon.–Fri. 11–11; Sat.–Sun. 10–10. Arizona restaurateur Sam Fox combines Old World Mediterranean with new at this trendy hot spot. The huge venue has several different areas, from its community dining bar to patio nooks to private dining rooms. The fare has Mediterranean names and ingredients, and the wine list is large. The small plates and flat breads shine. Grab some house-made gelato in the market for dessert. The market also makes a quick stop for baked goods, specialty quiches, rustic loaves, and gourmet espresso and coffee. Entrées $16–30.

Sea Saw (480-481-9463), 7133 E. Stetson Dr., Scottsdale. Open daily 5:30–10 (till 11 Fri.–Sat.). Chef Nobuo Fukuda named his small venue by blending the word *seafood* with *wabi-sabi*—a Japanese philosophy that finds beauty in the imperfect, incomplete, and unconventional. He then created the perfect unconventional menu, blending food, flavors, and techniques from his Japanese homeland with styles from around the world to produce a menu that has the world's best chefs sitting adoringly at his table enjoying what Nobuo calls Tapanese food (Japanese tapas). Order a handful of these small plates to make up your meal. Chef Nobuo likes to seesaw between cool and warm plates—for instance, the edamame soup (chilled soybean puree and ginger crème fraîche) and whitefish carpaccio (sliced with ginger, sesame seeds, yuzu juice, and roasted garlic oil); or sashimi so artfully presented, diners often sit and stare several moments before digging in, and lamb with curry coconut milk marinade, grilled with red pepper coulis. Or do an *omakase* (chef's pleasure): Chef Nobuo's eight-course tasting menu with paired wines and sake for $125. For $175, Chef Nobuo will prepare a customized six-course meal and pair each course with the perfect wine— an anomalous talent among Japanese chefs. Chef Nobuo won the 2007 James Beard award for best South-western chef. Dessert plates, created by chef Tracy Dempsey, are outstand-ing and thoughtfully compiled. The wine list features more than 3,300 wines, including saki and champagne. The decor is cool and oceanlike, with silver shimmers in sky blue and seafoam green; low-key global music adds a cosmopolitan suggestion. The best part of this experience is simply watching Chef Nobuo and his staff prepare your meal with precision, dis-cipline, and reverence. Tapanese plates $14–22.

Windows on the Green (480-423-2530), 6000 E. Camelback Rd. Open for dinner Thu.–Mon. 6–10; closed Tue.–Wed. Named for the emerald views you see of the Phoenician Golf Course through giant windows, this AAA Four Diamond restaurant sim-mers. The rich meld of gold, cream, and caramel colors create a cushy set-ting for chef de cuisine Roberto Sanchez's gourmet dinners with folky accents from his Mexican homeland. His father grows and blends the spices Sanchez uses for his fun but elegant southwestern cuisine. The rack of lamb and scallops are favorites,

but the undecided can look to Sanchez for a tasting of four entrées. Guacamole made tableside is an ongoing tradition here. The wine cel-lar—shared with Four Diamond sister restaurant Mary Elaine's—won a *Wine Spectator* Award of Excellence. Recently director of wine Sean Mar-ron hand selected more than 50 exclusive rare tequilas and mescals from artisan distilleries in Mexico, each complete with its own fascinat-ing story. You can get some snazzy infusions made with them or down them neat in flights of three. Entrées $27–44.

EATING OUT The Breakfast Club (480-222-0055), 4400 N. Scottsdale Rd. Open Mon.–Fri. 6–3, Sat.–Sun. 8–3. Come breakfast time—the tradi-tional time for breakfast, that is—this is one of the hottest spots in town. Good enough to earn a Mobil star. Breakfast is served all day here, so if you don't want to stand in line, you can merely check out the menu and return when things quiet down a bit . . . though that might not necessarily happen on the weekends. With several TVs, music, and newspapers scattered here and there, you can catch up on the latest buzz, too. Choices run from distinctive Bar Harbor flapjacks (the king of blueberry pancakes) to deli-cious Belgian waffles (with a variety of toppings), Southwest-style eggs to Benedict-style eggs (both featuring a number of versions), and steak and eggs to omelets—as in build your own with a couple dozen different choices of ingredients. Portions come big. $5.95–12.95.

Frank and Lupe's Old Mexico (480-990-9844), 4121 N. Marshall. Open Mon.–Sat. 11–10. One of the locals' favorites, especially when the weather suggests that sitting on a patio is the best place to dine. The New Mexico cuisine, all house-made, has endured the test of time since 1980. The favorite is Lupe's Enchilada Plate, made with homemade corn tortillas. The chicken mole enchiladas and open-faced chile poblano (stuffed with chicken) rates right up there, too. If you want, you can substitute regular corn for blue corn tortillas. Entrées $6.75–10.75.

Mandala Tearoom (480-423-3411), 7027 E. 5th Ave. Open daily for lunch 11–2:30, dinner Sun.–Thu. 5–9, Fri.–Sat. 5–10; brunch Sat.–Sun. 10–3. Teas, it's true, are big here: black teas, yerba mate, chai types, oolongs, green teas, white teas, medicinal teas, rooibos, and herbal teas—all certified organic (often biodynamic, single-estate teas, sustainably grown, and fair trade) made with the Swiss water process. Along with your beverage you can order from their organic vegetarian kitchen. The tearoom serves fresh seasonal organic nongenetically-modified vegetarian ingredients in their soups, salads, sandwiches, and entrées. Live teriyaki lettuce wraps are all raw. Tempeh fajitas might make you forget about the steak version. Mandala macro platter gives you a soiree into the world of macrobiotic, and *ziti al forno* brings you back to hot meal heaven, albeit vegan style. It's all vegan here, even the desserts. Entrées $9–13.

Sugar Bowl (480-946-0051), 4005 N. Scottsdale Rd. Open Mon.–Thu. 11–11 (till midnight Fri.–Sat., 10 Sun.). One of the Valley's favorite places for ice cream yummies was immortalized in Bil Keane's cartoon, *The Family Circus*. Keane was a neighbor of the Huntress family owners. Truly a sugar plum daydream, the retro ice cream parlor, dressed in pink vinyl booths and a wooden soda-fountain-style counter lined with chrome stools, has not changed much since the day it opened—Christmas Eve 1958. This includes some of the staff, who see "kids of the kids" coming back to satiate their sweet tooths. The Sugar Bowl serves Dreyer's Grand ice cream, has the best hot fudge in town, and serves up sodas of all kinds and Top Hats (a cream puff filled with ice cream and topped with a sauce) like they were going out of style. There are also meals—things besides peanut butter and jelly sandwiches—on the menu, along with daily specials. Entrées (ice cream) $3.75–6.95, meals $3.95–8.50.

✳ The Arts

Ranked as a top art destination in the country, Scottsdale has visual arts scene full of variety and talent. Some of the best displays appear in the five-star resorts, with the Phoenician at the top of the list. Though art pops up all over the city, it's concentrated in the downtown area, especially Main Street and Marshall Way. Here, the predominance of western and Native American art has made way for a strong contemporary scene that even lets some photography in now and again. Join the locals at the **Scottsdale ArtWalk**, every Thursday 7–9 PM, where galleries offer special receptions, demonstrations, and exhibits. Several themed ArtWalks happen during the year.

Scottsdale Museum of Contemporary Art (480-994-2787), 7374 E. Second St. Open Tue., Wed., Fri., and Sat. 10–5, Thu. 10–8, Sun. noon–5; closed Sun.–Mon. (and Tue. in summer). The museum has a collection of contemporary art from around the globe presented in a variety of venues—interactive, changing exhibits, art nights—and goes a step farther by hosting programs with a social twist, such as discussion panels, yoga nights, and artist talks and performances. $7 adults, $5 students; free to members and children under 15.

Taliesin West (480-860-2700), 12621 N. Frank Lloyd Wright Blvd. The great FLW built homes in beautiful places all over the country. The Valley has several such domiciles. Taliesin West is the queen—the repository of Wright's lifetime efforts. You can take a 1- to 3-hour tour to see how the master blended genius with nature. The property also headquarters the Frank Lloyd Wright Foundation and is home to the Frank Lloyd Wright School of Architecture. Tours $18–45.

✳ Selective Shopping

Kierland Commons (480-951-1100), 15210 N. Scottsdale Rd. Open daily; shop hours vary. Open air and perfect for just strolling, this shopping area is one of the hottest in the Valley, full of uncommon shops and dining. You can have an enjoyable time whether you take out your wallet or just take in the sights.

Old Town Scottsdale, 7201 E. Indian School Rd. Open daily; shop hours vary. The 2-mile-long strip of Scottsdale Road blends Scottsdale's roots with where the city's at today. Hitching posts and wood-front shops remind you of the days when sheep were herded down the main drag (Scottsdale Road) and open space prevailed. It still exudes an Old West flavor through a variety of shops that offer traditional, southwestern, and trendy

merchandise. You'll also find a number of dining, entertainment, and spa venues, as well as historical districts.

Scottsdale Fashion Square (480-994-8048), 7014 E. Camelback Rd. Open Mon.–Sat. 10–9, Sun. 11–6. The queen of shopping malls brings you all kinds of shopping adventures, from exclusive boutique designer shops like Boss Hugo Boss, Louis Vuitton, and Tiffany & Co. to department stores like Macy's, Neiman Marcus, and Nordstrom, with just about all of the popular franchises in between. The largest mall in Arizona (and growing) has a food court, seven restaurants, two theaters, a full-service concierge desk, valet parking, and taxi and limousine services.

✳ Special Events

January: **P. F. Chang's Rock 'n' Roll Arizona Marathon** (800-311-1255) is an annual 26.2-mile race through Scottsdale, Phoenix, and Tempe with live music at every mile. **Celebration of Fine Art** (480-443-7695) features more than 100 artists selling gallery-quality work. **Barrett-Jackson Classic Car Auction** (480-421-6694) draws more than 1,000 collector automobiles from around the world as well as 200,000 admirers who can buy (or salivate over) them. **Arizona Sun Circuit Quarter Horse Show** (877-730-0212) presents about 1,500 of the country's best quarter horse athletes, who compete for $200,000 in prizes. **Indian Artists of America Show** (866-398-2226) celebrates the music, fashions, cultures, and unique artistic mastery of indigenous North American peoples. **FBR Open** (602-870-0163) has gained near-legendary status over the past 72 years as one of the five oldest events on the PGA Tour.

February: **Arizona Sun Circuit Quarter Horse Show** (877-730-0212). The country's best quarter horse athletes compete at this 8-day event. **Prada del Sol Parade** (602-996-8289) is the world's largest horse-drawn parade. **Scottsdale Fine Art & Chocolate Festival** (480-837-5637). More than 150 world-class, jury-selected artists vie with the world's favorite confection for your attention.

March: **Celebration of Fine Art** (480-443-7695). More than 100 artists show and sell their gallery-quality work. **Giants Spring Training** (480-312-2586). The San Francisco Giants practice all month at Indian School Park. **Scottsdale Arts Festival** (480-874-4686). This weekend-long event—one of the premier arts festivals in the country—draws 40,000 visitors.

April: **Championship Arabian Horse Show at WestWorld** (480-741-5830). The annual event showcases world-class Arabian horses competing in all disciplines.

October: **Scottsdale Classic Futurity & Quarter Horse Show** (480-860-1544). Horse competition. **Scottsdale**

International Film Festival (602-410-1074). The best in current international films are shown at Harkins Camelview Luxury Cinemas. **Tour de Scottsdale** (480-460-5052). More than 1,000 bicyclists circumnavigate the McDowell Mountains to raise money for McDowell Sonoran Land Trust and Rebuilding Together. **Bon Appétit ArtWalk** (480-990-3939) combines food, drinks, and art in an event hosted by Scottsdale Gallery Association, *Bon Appétit* magazine, and the Scottsdale Convention & Visitors Bureau.

November: **Arabian Horse Association Fall Festival & Futurity Horse Show** (480-515-1500). Arabians compete. **Artfest of Scottsdale** (888-278-3378) is the highest-rated fall art festival in Arizona, featuring more than 220 fine artists from around the country.

December: **Holiday Lights** (480-312-2312). McCormick-Stillman Railroad Park lights up with more than 100,000 holiday lights. **Scottsdale's Ultimate Block Party** (866-443-8849). Evolving into a sophisticated event, the night offers food, drinks, and entertainment, including a midnight fireworks display.

MINING COUNTRY: GLOBE, MIAMI, AND SUPERIOR

L ike three pearls strung together by US 60, Globe, Miami, and Superior are gems that all have much more to offer than first meets the eye. Minerals have always played a big part in their history, but life goes on: Superior leans toward art and movies, Miami antiques, and Globe exquisite architecture with European craftsman influences.

With gold strikes foremost on their minds, prospectors were swooning in this mineral-rich mining country by the 1860s. Fueled by reports of "silver-streaked rocks, silver nuggets, and ledges of precious metals" by a New Mexico doctor who treated the Apache peoples for an epidemic eye infection, activity centered on Sombrero Butte in the Sierra Ancha Mountains north of Globe. A strange mix of drifters, cowboys, preachers, unlucky prospectors, merchants, and investors gathered.

The Sombrero Butte lead was suddenly dropped when a soldier named Sullivan found a chunk of silver near Camp Pinal (Superior). All eyes turned toward finding Sullivan's silver lode. And what a lode it was: enough to call the area Arizona's silver belt and the mine, the Silver King. But before that happened, silver claims had been filed in the present-day Globe area two years earlier; one, the Globe Ledge, by the group that discovered the Silver King Mine. The Apaches delayed any further development of the Globe Ledge, so the group groped for that elusive Sullivan find and found it.

The Silver King Mine drew hundreds of miners to the Superior area in 1875. Among the brood came famous opportunists Wyatt Earp and Doc Holiday. It was a boom situation. As the ore ebbed by 1888, so did the people. However, the town didn't actually appear on the map until the turn of the 20th century, and then as a tent city for several years. Copper brought the miners back in 1910 when it was discovered beneath the silver cap.

Meanwhile, back in Globe, claims multiplied, the Apache relented, and the Globe Mining District formed by 1875. A year later, Globe got its start as Globe City and eventually became the county seat, with the state's first school district. In the downtown, Mesquite Street marked the boundary of respectability. Fair ladies never ventured south, where brothels abounded. The town was so raucous, the original 16-cell jail wasn't big enough to house the clientele. The sher-

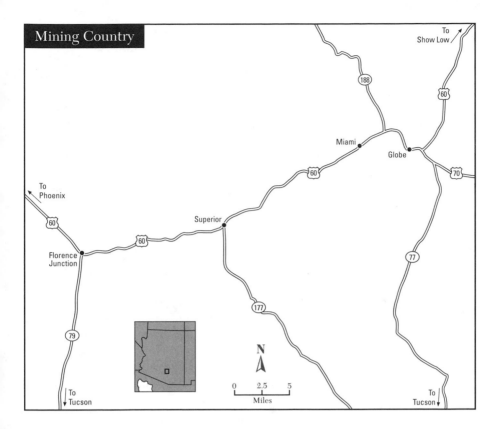

Mining Country

iff's office looked more like a revolving door—men never lived long in the position, and unmarried men need only apply.

During this silver boom, claims spread out to present-day Miami. The commute to work from Globe became drudgery, as all modern-day commuters can understand. After no little resistance, Miami developed into a separate city continually promoted by sly businessman Cleve Van Dyke. Years down the road, the minerals in Miami kept Globe alive.

Today Superior's sensational setting along the perpendicular ridge, Apache Leap, and old historic buildings makes it a natural for Hollywood. Almost a dozen movies and several commercials have been filmed there, including *How the West Was Won*. You can take walking tours in Globe to view the exquisite architecture built by Italian masons who worked on the Roosevelt Dam, walk the red-light district, and tour the jail where things were always hopping. In Miami, ever the merchant like its founding father, antiques shops give you a chance to peruse past generations' treasures.

The Apache built a casino on their land, providing an outlet for modern-day gold diggers to test their luck. Perhaps the surer treasure is the backcountry they own—pristine, beautiful, and full of watchable wildlife. All the land around

Mining Country is that way—a rich, untrammeled landscape of mountains and desert canyons. Metaphorically, it's the Mining Country's gold that the old prospectors never found.

GUIDANCE **Globe-Miami Regional Chamber of Commerce and Economic Development Corporation** (928-425-4495 or 800-804-5623), 1360 N. Broad St., Globe. **Superior Chamber of Commerce** (520-689-0200), 300 Main St., Superior. Contact the **Globe Ranger District** (520-402-6200), 7680 S. Six Shooter Canyon Rd., or the **Globe and Tonto Basin Ranger District** (928-467-3200), Roosevelt, for information on national forest backcountry, and the **Bureau of Land Management Tucson Field Office** (520-258-7200), 2661 E. Broadway, Tucson, for information on public lands south of US 60 not in the national forest.

GETTING THERE US 60, AZ 88, AZ 77, and US 70 meet in Globe. Miami lies only a few miles west on US 60, and Superior 24 miles west on US 60 at AZ 77.

WHEN TO COME Cooler than the lower deserts, Mining Country gives a reasonable reprieve from the summer heat. Spring and fall offer the best weather and the most activity. Winter days hover around the 60s, and the nights flirt with the freezing mark.

MEDICAL EMERGENCY **Cobre Valley Hospital** (928-425-3261), 5880 S. Hospital Dr., Globe.

EXQUISITE STONEMASONRY CAN BE FOUND THROUGHOUT THE TOWN OF GLOBE.

✳ To See

🐾 ✍ ♿ **Boyce Thompson Arboretum** (520-689-2723), US 60, 13 miles east of Florence Junction. Open daily Sep.–Apr., 8–5 (closed Dec. 25); May–Aug., 6–3. Mining magnate and philanthropist William Boyce Thompson opened Arizona's oldest and largest arboretum in 1923 as a center for research. The arboretum has about 2,000 different species of plants from arid climates around the world, including a mature eucalyptus forest; boojum trees; and rose, wildflower, butterfly, hummingbird, and cactus gardens. Queen Creek's sliver of a stream that runs through the arboretum beneath a dramatic backdrop of volcanic tuff cliffs attracts more than 250 bird species throughout the year, and staff- and volunteer-led bird walks take place each weekend, along with wildflower and plant hikes. Two trails wind around the grounds: One takes you above the ground and the other in the desert gardens. $7.50 adults, $3 ages 5–12; children under 5 free.

Gila County Jail and Sheriff's Office (928-425-9340), 149 E. Oak St. Open Mon.–Fri. noon–4. The town built four jails, each one bigger than the previous, and somehow still couldn't keep up with the rowdy clientele. Historian Kip Culver tells you all about the people and history related to the jail and Globe. $2 per person, $3 per couple.

San Carlos Apache Cultural Center (928-475-2894). Located in the town of Peridot (mile marker 272) off US 70 between Globe and Safford. Open Mon.–Fri. 9–5. The San Carlos Apache tribe tells history their way here. Exhibits describe the tribe's spiritual beginnings, the Mountain Spirit Dancers (*Ga'an*), and the Sunrise Ceremony, once called the Changing Woman Ceremony. Historic exhibits explain the Apache's cultural legacy, their forced confinement on the reservation, and their future vision for the tribe. Apache art and crafts include peridot jewelry, handmade dolls, and baskets. The center has a gift shop. $3 adults, $1 students and seniors; under 12 free.

INDIAN RUINS ✇ **Besh-Ba-Gowah Archaeological Park** (928-425-0320 or 800-804-5623), 150 N. Pine St., Globe. Open daily 9–5. One of the Southwest's largest single archaeological sites sits at the confluence of Pinal Creek and Ice House Canyon Wash. The 600-year-old Salado ruin (a ceremonial, food storage, and redistribution complex) is one of the most significant finds of the century. The Salado culture lived from 1150 to 1450 on the Tonto Basin. $3 ages 12–65, $2 over 65; under 12 free.

🐾 ✇ **Tonto National Monument** (928-467-2241), 3 miles southeast of Roosevelt Dam on AZ 88. The Lower Cliff Dwelling is open daily 8–5, except Christmas; guided tours of the Upper Cliff Dwellings are by reservation only, Nov.–Apr. Two sets of cliff dwellings constructed in natural alcoves were occupied by the Salado Indians AD 1300–1500. Farmers of the Salt River Valley, the Indians also produced some of the most exquisite polychrome pottery and meticulously woven textiles in the Southwest. You can see their handiwork displayed in the visitor center museum. To get to the ruins, you walk a 0.5-mile-long paved trail to the Lower Cliff Dwelling. Leashed pets are permitted on this trail. You can only view the Upper Cliff Dwelling via a guided tour (reservations required; pets not allowed). The 3-mile round trip takes 3–4 hours. $3 per person.

SCENIC DRIVES The **Apache Trail**, one of the state's classic scenic drives, winds between Roosevelt Lake and Apache Junction. Always keeping its eye on the string of azure-colored lakes pooled along the Salt River, the road actually follows an old Apache footpath. During construction of Roosevelt Dam, the road provided transportation of equipment and supplies. The narrow, hairpinned, unpaved (but graded) track has no guardrails, which tends to give novices white knuckles. They are advised to drive it from west to east, with the reassuring cliffs right next to the vehicle; an east–west crossing puts your wheels inches from a precipitous drop. There's plenty of scenery; some excellent hiking trails; and Tortilla Flats, with a single-digit population, has a restaurant to refresh you.

✳ To Do

BOATING The largest of the reservoirs, Roosevelt Lake, pooled from the Salt River, gives you a chance to partake in a rather anomalous desert activity—boating. You can rent craft ranging from a 14-foot fishing boat to a 56-foot-long houseboat from **Roosevelt Lake Marina** (928-467-2245 or 602-977-7171), AZ 88, open daily 7:30–5.

FISHING Roosevelt Lake, located about 30 miles northwest off AZ 88, has 88 miles of shoreline and a variety of fish just itching to put up a fight—largemouth and smallmouth bass, crappie, sunfish, catfish, bluegill, and carp. Contact the Tonto National Forest or Arizona Department of Game and Fish (602-942-3000) for information.

GAMING Apache Gold Casino (928-475-7800), about 17 miles east of Globe on US 70 in San Carlos. Named for a lost treasure of gold known only by the Apache. The casino has 500 video and progressive slot machines, live bingo, $50,000 keno, blackjack, and "one of the West's most liberal Poker Rooms."

GOLF Apache Stronghold (928-475-7800), about 17 miles east of Globe on US 70 in San Carlos. Legend says a deity named Usen created a mystical area in the midst of the Chiricahua, Aravaipa, Superstition, and White Mountains that the Apache call the Stronghold. Here tribe members could walk invisibly among their enemies. The San Carlos placed an award-winning golf course in this area. Now, that doesn't necessarily mean you can pick up those sand-trapped balls without anyone seeing you, but it does mean you will play golf in a landscape like no other. Cliffs, rather than swanky homes, surround you, and archaeological sites, not hotel rooms, appear among the desert vegetation. $45–55.

HIKING See also *Wilder Places*. You can take your pick of what kind of environment you like to hike in, and how close, or far, from civilization you want to get. Globe's in-town **Round the Mountain Park** has a small network of trails that can give you a good workout and take you away from the city's sights and sounds. If you want to get into the backcountry and the higher elevations, the **Pinal Mountain Recreation Area** has several trails. **Picketpost Mountain** (contact the Globe Ranger District) calls for experience if you want to hike its unmaintained route, which climbs almost 2 miles (sometimes requiring hand-over-foot work) to a 4,375-foot peak. The 360-degree view makes the climb worth it.

ARIZONA TRAIL. There are several segments of trail you can hike in this general area that take you through cloistered canyons, up desert mountains covered with saguaro cactus forests and wildflowers in spring, and across desert flats. Contact the Globe and Tonto Basin Ranger Districts.

ROAD BIKING Located among some of the most thrilling mountain ranges as far as road biking goes, Superior understands those road bicyclists who live for rollers and challenging slopes. There are several annual road biking events. In

Mar. the **Mining Country Challenge** —and it is a challenge—tests your cycling mettle on a 66- or 96-mile route through the surrounding mountains. In early April the 62-mile **OMYA/Superior Road Race** begins in Superior and travels to Winkelman and back, paying a cash purse of $2,000; the next day the **OMYA/ Superior Criterium**, a 0.7-mile loop, earns a cash purse of more than $1,200. For information on these events, call 520-689-0200.

ROCK CLIMBING **Devil's Canyon**, located along US 60 about 4 miles west of Superior near Oak Flat Campground, is a premier climbing spot that draws climbers from around the world. Contact the Globe Ranger District.

A STREET SCENE IN MIAMI, ARIZONA.

✱ Spas

Adobe Ranch Wellness Spa (928-425-3632), 138 S. Broad St., Suite 2. Open Mon.–Fri. 10–5 (till 2 Sat.); extended hours available. While spas naturally lean toward luxury, not all have luxury prices. You can get a nice spa package here and feel just as pampered as you would in an upscale resort spa for half the price. Packages here cost about as much as a single spa treatment elsewhere, and a 90-minute session costs half what you'd pay for a 60-minute treatment elsewhere. The reason? You're in the best-kept secret of the state's historic Mining Country. Enjoy. Massages $45–85, facials $40–80, special treatments $25–65, nail services $25–45.

✱ Wilder Places

Pinal Mountain Recreation Area (contact the Globe Ranger District). The sky island Pinal Mountains vary in vegetation from scrubby chaparral mix along mountain slopes to quaking aspen trees on the peaks. In between, the landscape ranges from high-country pines to New England–style hardwood forests and classic high-desert vegetation. Trails travel several miles and climb several thousand feet. The most scenic are **Six Shooter** and **Ice House Trails**.

San Carlos Apache Reservation (928-475-2344 or 888-475-2343). Located about 17 miles east of Globe on US 70. World-class for big-game hunting, the Apache reservation also has some great backcountry routes perfect for exploring. Even if you don't hunt, those trophy animals make good wildlife-watching. You can fish, camp, hike, and bike on the land for $10 a day.

✳ Lodging

Noftsger Hill Inn Bed and Breakfast (928-425-2260 or 877-780-2479), 425 North St., Globe. Built in 1907 as the North Globe Schoolhouse, the school immediately underwent expansion. It was *the* place for education until 1981, when its last class graduated. Ten years later owner-innkeepers Dom and Rosalie Ayala started renovation on the building to convert it to a B&B. The classrooms-turned-guest-rooms have become huge studios furnished with antiques, double, king, or queen beds, sitting area, TV, and private bath, formerly a cloakroom. Chalkboards have messages from former guests, many of them students with fond memories of the school. Each room has a view from windows you won't see crafted quite so beautifully these days. In the morning Rosalie makes sure you won't go hungry with a delicious southwestern-style breakfast. Birding specials in May include a "lesson" given by a birding expert on Friday nights with a complimentary bird walk on Sunday morning. Breakfast is included with all accommodations; pets not allowed. $65–90.

Apache Gold Casino Resort (928-475-7800 or 800-272-2438), US 70, San Carlos. The San Carlos Apache give this Best Western a cultural spin. The property includes a heated outdoor pool, meeting facilities, a bar/lounge, a restaurant, golf, a hot tub, a sauna, a fitness center, a game room, an arcade, and a guest laundry. Rooms include free local calls, cable TV with in-room movies, high-speed Internet, and coffeemaker. The **Apache Grill** features authentic Apache and southwestern cuisine,

and the gift shop offers Apache basketry and bead work. $59–109.

☃ **El Rey Motel** (928-425-4427), 1201 Ash St., Globe. This vintage motel, built in the late 1930s and remodeled with modern comforts, perfectly answers the call for something cozy, fun, and clean. It has kept its southwestern style and added some personality to the rooms. Enjoy the use of business machines (fax and photocopies), free coffee and computer use in the lobby, and laundry facilities. Rooms have cable TV, refrigerator, microwave, and free newspaper. Pets are okay with a fee. $35–43.

✳ Where to Eat

DINING OUT Back 9 Bistro (928-473-4442), Cobre Valley Country Club, 2 Pinal Canyon Dr., Globe. Open for lunch Mon.–Fri. 11–2, dinner Wed.–Fri. 5–8. In a town that excels in Mexican food served from family-run kitchens, this bistro makes a find if you're looking to go non-Mexican. They are known for their various half-pound burgers, including chipotle blue cheese and green chile cheeseburgers, as well as pastas; the blackened halibut is a nonmeat-eater's favorite. Meals are simple and fresh, with a special every day. Friday nights (prime rib night) get crowded; best to make a reservation. Entrées $9.95–17.95.

🍲 **Café Piedra Roja** (520-689-0194), 507 W. Main St., Superior. Open Mon.–Sat. 10–4. Colorful and serving consistently good Mexican food, this café upholds the town's propensity to support the arts. Its bold-colored walls have local artwork that you can purchase. The food is cooked with canola oil; no animal fat. Refried beans are homemade. And the salsa is *pico d'gallo* (tomato, onion, cilantro, and chiles). Along with a daily special, the menu has salads (the chicken salad with mango has grilled chicken strips and mango on lettuce with chips and salsa, tomatoes, and lime); Mexican dishes (burritos, tostada, and nachos); and sandwiches (hamburgers, grilled chicken, and ham or turkey tortas). There's always a special, and the enchiladas are exceptional. So are the prices. Entrées $3.75–6.45. BYOB for a $1 setup fee.

Guayo's on the Trail (928-425-9969), 1938 Hwy. 188, Globe. Open Wed.–Mon. 10:30–9; closed Tue. An enduring Globe favorite that's been around since 1938. Eddie *y* Karen Esparza cook up classic Mexican delights, including *albondigas* and menudo, every day. The traditional bowl of chips (the first one's free) come hot and homemade, like everything else. Beer is served in frozen mugs. Seniors get a 10 percent discount. Entrées $6–14.

EATING OUT Burger House (928-473-9918), 812 Live Oak St., Miami. Open Mon.–Sat. 5:30 AM–8 PM. Mexican at its fast-food finest. The made-to-order food is dependably good, and you can get it on the fly or sit down for a quick, simple meal. $2.50–5.95.

El Ranchito (928-402-1348), 686 Broad St., Globe. Open Tue.–Fri. 11–9, Sat.–Sun. 8–9; closed Mon. As the name says, it's a tiny restaurant, but the food has big flavor. All of it's made on the premises, and the green chili is the town favorite. On weekends a breakfast of *pozole*, menudo, *huevos con jamos*, and *machaca* is served in addition to the regular menu. Entrées $4.95–7.50.

❋ The Arts

Blue Mule (928-425-4920), 656 N. Broad St., Globe. Open Tue.–Sat. 10–5, Sun. 10–4. Artist-owners John and Laurie have created a space for themselves and local artists to show their creativity. The floor is a work of art in itself—pieces of wood John glued down, sanded, and varnished; a tedious process with gorgeous results. Besides painting, Laurie specializes in cat adoptions. If you love cats, take your armor with you if you don't want to walk out with one of the cute, forlorn homeless critters.

❋ Selective Shopping

The biggest finds in the Mining Country are antiques and art. Globe still has a working, operating downtown with all the basics you need in life from clothes to auto repairs and a saddle shop. Broad Street (named for

GLOBE'S BROAD STREET.

the number of broads working in the whorehouses) in the downtown historic section has a number of collectible and antiques shops. Miami has a national reputation for its antiques business on Sullivan St., just northwest of US 60. Plan your shopping for the weekend, however; stores tend to be closed during the week or open by appointment only.

Copper Mine Picture Café (928-473-4367), 418 Sullivan St., Miami. Open Thu.–Sun. 11–5. For a small town, an honest-to-goodness gallery is a rare find. This one, located in an attractive old building among a line of antiques stores, gives you a chance to view some quality art from local artists. Owner Jim Coates a native Arizonan who has lived in several places around the country, has new shows monthly. You can get a cup of coffee and shoot the breeze with Coates, too.

✳ Special Events

February: **Historic Home & Building Tour and Antique & Quilt Show** (928-425-4495) in Globe features architecture and antiques via tours around town (admission) and exhibits at the Cobre Valley Center for the Arts (free).

March: **Apache Leap Days and Mining Festival** in Superior celebrates mining with food, contests, and a bungee jump ride over the town's backdrop ridge, Apache Leap.

December: **Festival of Lights** (928-425-4495). Luminaria and Native American performers at Besh-Ba-Gowah Archaeological Park.

WICKENBURG

With its appealing meld of classic Sonoran scenery, mining history, and dude ranches, Wickenburg correctly calls itself "Arizona's Most Western Town." Cowboys, the steeds they ride, and the open spaces where they roam are key to what Wickenburg is all about. With that in mind, and the fact they just got their first Starbucks last year, you can see how succinctly the chamber of commerce sums up its town as one that "hearkens back to a different time and place."

Life doesn't get much simpler than here in Wickenburg. That is, until you take a walk along a trail in its backcountry, just a short few minutes from town, and experience the magnificence of the Sonoran Desert in bloom. Or visit an old mining site strewn with relics on a hardscrabble hillside and pause to wonder how strong the drive for riches must have been to keep prospectors working under a broiling summer sun. Or watch a 60-year-old cowboy in a rodeo beat the buzzer in a bull-riding event, then limp out of the area with a smile on his face.

Unless you know the hard knocks of life personally, value the views of an unhindered horizon, or can identify with Baxter Black's poetry, you may not quite understand Wickenburg. No problem. Just stick with the high points of enjoying an untrammeled backcountry trail with hardly a sign of another human being, enjoying scenic drives as close and easy as they used to be in Arizona's bigger cities three or four decades ago, and getting a look at a cowboy at work without going too far off the highway.

If you just plan to stay in town, perusing it takes you a step back in time. Century-old buildings fill Frontier Street. You get a dose of cowboy humor if you espy the NO FISHING FROM BRIDGE sign over the Hassayampa River. It's right next to the LEGEND OF THE HASSAYAMPA sign, which goes on to tell you that one drink from the Hassayampa River will compel imbibers never to tell the truth again. Visitors will be hard pressed to get a drink from the Hassayampa, which flows mostly underground, unless they head to the chamber offices and pick up a bottle of "genuine" Hassayampa River water—probably a by-product of that silly miner's legend. But don't trust us. We've had a drink of the water. Go see for yourself.

GUIDANCE **Wickenburg Chamber of Commerce** (928-684-5479), 216 N. Frontier St. Open Mon.–Fri. 9–5, Sat.–Sun. 10–2 (call for summer weekend

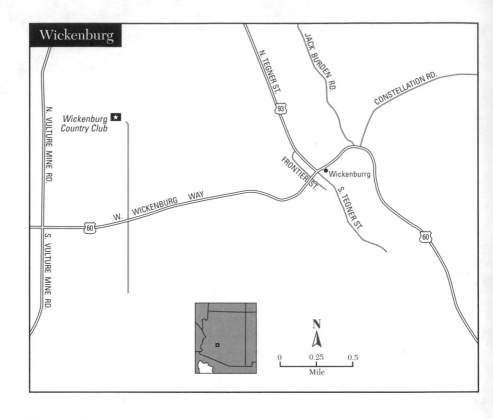

Wickenburg
Country Club

N. VULTURE MINE RD.

S. VULTURE MINE RD.

N. TEGNER ST.

JACK BURDEN RD.

CONSTELLATION RD.

93

FRONTIER ST.

Wickenburrg

S. TEGNER ST.

W. WICKENBURG WAY

60

60

N

0   0.25   0.5
Mile

hours). Get information on backcountry use on public lands in the area from
Bureau of Land Management—Phoenix Field Office (623-580-5500),
21605 N. 7th Ave., Phoenix, open 8–4; or **State Trust Land Department** (602-
364-2753), 1616 W. Adams, Phoenix.

GETTING THERE *By car:* It's an hour's drive from Phoenix on US 60, and an hour
south of Prescott via AZ 89. The **Valley Metro** has a commuter bus along US 60
that travels between Wickenburg's West Plaza and Glendale's Arrowhead Towne
Center in the West Valley. *By air:* **Wickenburg Municipal Airport** services
private planes. *By shuttle:* **Wickenburg Airport Express** (928-684-2888 or
866-245-5351) is available 24/7.

WHEN TO COME Wickenburg's high season runs from Nov. through Apr., when
the mild winter weather appeals to everyone. Some guest ranches close when
the warm weather hits in May, but the town has a large, and growing, year-round
population that encourages most businesses to stay open.

MEDICAL EMERGENCY Wickenburg Community Hospital (928-684-5421),
520 Beailler Road

⚲ **Desert Caballeros Western Museum** (928-684-2272), 21 N. Frontier St. Open Mon.–Sat. 10–5, Sun. noon–4; closed Mon. in July and Aug. Governor Napolitano named this western art and history museum one of Arizona's treasures. A collection of more than 400 pieces of western art includes works from Remington and Russell. Western life comes alive in the outstanding cowboy and Native American exhibits, street scenes, and dioramas. $7.50 adults, $6 seniors, $1 ages 6–16; under 5 free.

The Jail Tree, Tegner and Wickenburg Way. With the huge placer and lode gold discoveries going on around town, seems no one thought about building a jail. The powers that be merely chained scofflaws to the trunk of a mesquite tree. Now around 200 years old, the old mesquite could probably write a book on its times with some of the town's saltier characters who sat in its shade. Free.

The Wishing Well. Located next to the Hassayampa River bridge on US 60. Legend has it that once you take a drink from the Hassayampa River, you will never tell the truth again. You can read all about it at the Wishing Well. Free.

SCENIC DRIVES **Skull Valley.** This drive, about 50 miles one way, takes you through the mining town of Yarnell, then up to the green grasslands of Skull Valley along the historic Peavine Railroad. From downtown, head northwest on US 93 about 6 miles, then turn right onto US 89; go up the Yarnell Hill and through the town of Yarnell (stop at the **Cornerstone Bakery** for the richest pastries, good sandwiches, and homemade soups, or at **Buzzards Roost** for fresh-made barbecue) to Kirkland Junction (about 31 miles). Turn left onto Thompson Valley Rd., continue 4 miles to Kirkland, and turn right onto Iron Springs Rd. Go 7 miles to the town of Skull Valley. Just north of the railroad tracks, make a hard left onto 3-mile-long Old Skull Valley Rd. (unpaved after 0.5 mile, but graded) for a look at the countrified side of Arizona. This makes for a refreshing walk along a country road.

Stanton. See *Mining Adventures*.

* To Do

GOLF **Rancho de los Caballeros Golf Club** (928-684-2704), 1551 S. Vulture Mine Rd. This is not your traditional desert course with lots of forced carries. It's solid grass from tee to green, and the greens are some of the fastest in the state. This makes for a pace of play that hovers around 4 hours. Lady-friendly, only an hour's drive from Phoenix, and challenging to all abilities, the front nine present a classic layout of wide landing areas and ample greens. The hilly back nine

BACKCOUNTRY ROADS TAKE YOU INTO GORGEOUS PARTS OF THE SONORAN DESERT AROUND WICKENBURG.

will make you use just about every club in your bag. Hole 13 is consistently ranked as one of the most challenging par-5 holes in the state. What makes this par-72 course special, first, is the natural surroundings—Vulture Peak, the Bradshaw Mountains, and wildlife. Second, it's a deal. Such a wonderful deal, in fact, that it ranks among the world's best courses in popular magazine surveys. Driving range, putting greens, short game practice, and golf shop. $73–150.

Wickenburg Country Club (928-684-2011), 1420 Country Club Dr. The 50-plus-year-old course is called Wickenburg's best-kept secret. The newly rebuilt 18-hole green has a total yardage of 6,400. Par-71. $35 for 9 holes, $50 for 18 holes.

HIKING Some of the best desert hiking in the state is located in the wilderness areas surrounding Wickenburg. The popular **Vulture Peak Trail**, short and steep, is just outside town. Pick up a copy of *Wickenburg Adventures* at the chamber of commerce for other trails in the area.

HISTORICAL WALKING TOUR Get a map from the chamber of commerce for the self-guided tour to more than 30 historical buildings and other points of interest around Wickenburg.

JEEP TOURS BC Jeep Tours (928-684-7901) takes you out into the backcountry around Wickenburg for a short trip to see the local scenery or a day trip to historical mines and/or scenery. Call for reservations and prices.

ORCHARDS Date Creek Ranch (928-231-0704). Go 22 miles on US 93, and turn right (north) at milepost 177.5. Fruit trees in the desert? In the high desert, yes. You can pick your own pesticide-free peaches and summer apples from mid-July through August; Red and Golden Delicious apples in September and October. Check out their Apple Harvesting Fest in September.

DOZENS OF DISTINCTIVE HIKING ROUTES ARE LOCATED RIGHT AROUND WICKENBURG.

✳ Wilder Places

Hassayampa River Preserve (928-684-2772), 49614 US 60 (near mile marker 114 on the west side of the highway). Open mid-Sep.–mid-May, Wed.–Sun. 8–5; in summer, Fri.–Sun. 7–11. Trails close at 4:30; closed Thanksgiving and the day after, Christmas Eve and Christmas, and New Year's Eve and New Year's Day. Known as a bird-watchers' paradise, this is a spot where you can, and should, bring your binoculars, comfortable shoes, and a bird book—but not your pet. The area is a protected streamside habitat that attracts all kinds of wildlife. A marsh draws waterbirds and the endangered southwestern willow flycatcher. The preserve has some interesting cultural history as well. The headquarters building, built in the 1860s, is listed on the State Register of Historic Places. The property evolved from a working cattle ranch in 1871, to a guest ranch called the Garden of Allah in 1913, and then the Lazy RC Ranch. The Nature Conservancy finally bought and preserved the land and allowed nature to have its way once again. $5 per person.

✳ Lodging

🐾 ✎ ⅃ **Best Western Rancho Grande Motel** (928-684-5445 or 800-854-7235), 293 E. Wickenburg Way. This family-owned property is a guest-friendly favorite that gets repeat business. The property includes a pool and spa, horseshoes, volleyball, and a children's playground. Rooms have cable TV, complimentary high-speed Internet, free local calls under 30 minutes, coffeemaker, and refrigerator; many have kitchenette and microwave. Free breakfast included. Pets $8 per night. $80–94.

🐾 ⅃ **Super 8 Motel** (928-684-0808), 975 N. Tegner. The unique feature about this chain is it has corral space to board your stock. Laundry facilities on the premises. Rooms have cable TV, Internet access, and free local calls. Free Continental breakfast; fee for pets. $91.

⅃ **Los Viajeros Inn** (928-684-7099 or 800-915-9795), 1000 N. Tegner Rd. Rooms here are large, with Southwest appointments. King or queen beds, satellite TV, complimentary WiFi, mini fridge, and private balcony or patio. Pool and heated spa. Continental breakfast is included. No pets. $87–98.

BED AND BREAKFAST ∞ 🐾 ✎ ⅃
Robson's Mining World (928-685-2609) (see *To Do*). Open Oct.–May.

One of the most unusual B&Bs anywhere, this one is situated in the middle of a mining ghost town cluttered with the world's largest collection of old mining equipment. Located in a notch of the Harcuvar Mountains, the grounds exude a peaceful backcountry feel. In springtime, after a wet winter, wildflowers lavishly cover the grounds. This replica of an old timbered mining hotel has 26 rooms. Each room, simple but comfortable, has a private bath. No phones or TVs here—you're in the backcountry, remember? Plus, you won't need them with all there is to see and do on the property. Breakfast included. $87.50–105.

GUEST RANCHES Wickenburg's history as the Guest Ranch Capital of the World for more than 40 years makes it one of the best destinations for dude moments. The handful of ranches, though each different in style, offer an out-West experience as genteel or rugged as you want to go.

Flying E Ranch (928-684-2690 or 888-684-2650), 2801 W. Wickenburg Way. Open Nov.–May. Known as the Riding Ranch with its 20,000 acres of riding countryside, the Flying E is a small, informal operation. The property has a solar pool and hot spa, sauna, tennis, and horseback riding. Rooms have king or twin beds, heat and air-conditioning, wet bars, and

MINING ADVENTURES

Some of the richest gold strikes happened in and around Wickenburg: the Vulture Mine, Rich Hill, and all along the Hassayampa River.

🖉 ♿ **Robson's Mining World** (928-685-2609). From Wickenburg, travel west on US 60 about 24 miles, and turn right onto US 71; go 4 miles, turn left between mileposts 89 and 90, and follow signs to the parking area. Open Oct.–May 1st, Mon.–Fri. 10–4, Sat.–Sun. 9–5. Standing on the site of the Nilla-Meda Gold Mining Camp in the middle of the desert, you really get the feeling you've stepped back in time and entered the rough-and-tumble world of the old-time prospectors. There's a lot of fascinating stuff crammed into this compound, which includes thousands of pieces of antique equipment and 26 artifact buildings. A free guide explains what much of the equipment were used for. If you have a soft spot for history and machines, plan to spend the day. For more ancient history, you can hike a mile-long trail starting at the mine that crosses a pristine Sonoran Desert landscape on surrounding Bureau of Land Management acreage to a centuries-old Native American campsite. Robson's holds a birthday celebration in Jan. Admission gets waived, some of the old equipment gets fired up, top entertainment performs, local authors do book signings, and food is served. $5 per person, $4.50 for ages 55-plus; under 10 free.

Stanton. From US 60 in Wickenburg, go north on US 89 for about 18 miles to the signed turnoff to Stanton, then continue about 8 miles on the unpaved but graded road. You can see the buildings of this old ghost town where the

PETROGLYPHS ALONG THE TRAIL IN ROBSON'S MINING WORLD.

THE GHOST TOWN OF STANTON.

richest placer mining happened, and poke around Rich Hill a bit to see if you
might get lucky and find a golden nugget. In 1863, when gold was discovered serendipitously on the hill, the placer made for such easy pickings that
prospectors merely picked the nuggets, ranging from tiny grains to multi-
pound rocks, from their niches. Stanton soon became a true mining town
with a too-tough reputation. One local newspaper claimed that Stanton's
residents "drink blood, eat fried rattlesnakes and fight mountain lions."
Presently, a private prospecting group owns the town. When you drive by,
you can see original buildings still standing from the days when prospectors
plucked placer gold off Rich Hill and sifted the sands of Antelope Creek for
color. Ask for permission to get up close. In winter the place is abuzz with
modern-day prospectors who will tell you tales (true or not, who can tell?)
about where you can still find gold.

Vulture Mine (602-859-2743), 12 miles south of Wickenburg on Vulture Mine
Rd. Open fall and winter, Thu.–Mon. 8–4; spring and summer, Fri.–Sun. 8–4.
During the almost 80 working years from the time Henry Wickenburg discovered the state's most productive mine in 1863, its gold played a large part
in funding the development of Phoenix, spawned the town of Vulture City,
and allowed people to eke out a living during the Depression. The mine produced more than $200 million in gold, and people claim you can still find
smatterings. A self-guided tour takes you around the grounds where
prospectors lived, worked, and died. $7 adults, $6 seniors, $5 ages 6–12.

private baths. You get your meals served family style in a laid-back, homey atmosphere that's for guests only, and BYOL. Minimum stay; $285–350 for a double.

Kay El Bar Ranch (928-684-7593 or 800-684-7583). Open Oct.–May. Eight guest rooms—located in an authentic adobe building listed on the National Historic Register—have king, queen, or twin beds; no TV or phone. The property includes a pool and horseback riding. All meals are home-cooked from scratch and served in private dining room. Minimum stay; $340–380 per double.

⊗ ✍ ♿ **Rancho de los Caballeros** (928-684-5484), 1551 S. Vulture Mine Rd. Open from the second week of October through Mother's Day. With a name that translates to "gentlemen on horseback," the resort exudes class and over-the-top hospitality, from making notes of what pleases clients to ensure they experience the same on their next visit (guests from four generations are not uncommon) to the dinner dress code. This family-owned historic guest ranch thinks of itself as "high touch" rather than "high tech" by awakening the senses with basic pleasures. Like riding a horse. Though life doesn't always center on the corral around the resort today, the cowboy spirit reigns, and it certainly is in the blood of the owners and wranglers who work there. Love of the outdoors is celebrated here, with horseback riding, nature hikes, skeet shooting, cookouts, jeep tours, four tennis courts, swimming (in the hand-dug pool), golf (rated as some of the best in the country), and a spa (to massage out those sore muscles). Traditionally, guests congregated in the main lodge to unwind via card games,

billiards, and gossip. Handcrafted Santa Fe–style furniture and Mexican tilework make each of the 79 guest rooms and suites a different home on this 20,000-acre range. TVs and phones were begrudgingly added to rooms in the last two decades. Complimentary WiFi is available in the main lodge, but not allowed at the bar. Guests can no longer land on the private airstrip (they have to land in Wickenburg Municipal Airport), but they can pay with a credit card, circa 2004. One thing that hasn't changed is the running of the 100 or so horses in the morning and at dusk; that's enough to ignite the spirit of the cowboy in anybody. $468–490 per double.

Williams Family Ranch (928-308-0589). Open Sep.–May. Located about 20 miles north of Wickenburg at the end of a twisting mountain road on the edge of the wild and practically uncharted Hassayampa River Canyon Wilderness, this ranch will give you a valid taste of life on a working cow ranch. Nothing fancy here, just wild open spaces and real ranching. Minimum stay; $140 per person; no credit cards accepted.

✳ Where to Eat

🍴 ✍ **Anita's Cocina Family Restaurant** (928-684-5777), 57 N. Valentine. Open daily for lunch and dinner 11–9. The local gathering spot serves warm chips, salsa with a mild kick, and dependably good food. Make that big portions of dependably good food. Arrive late for lunch or early for dinner to avoid a wait. $5.95–12.95.

Cowboy Café (928-684-2807), 686 N. Tegner. Open daily for breakfast 6–11, lunch 11–2; call for dinner hours. This is where the real cowboys eat breakfast. The owners are rodeo

PRISTINE SONORON DESERT BACKCOUNTRY NEAR WICKENBURG.

riders, and meals are named for rodeo greats—such as the Bodacious Bacon Burger named for a famous bull. If you can't make breakfast, make sure you can come by for dinner and taste their famous chicken-fried steak. Entrées $7.95–8.95.

House of Berlin (928-684-5044), 169 E. Wickenburg Way. Open for lunch Wed.–Sun. 11:30–2, dinner Tue.–Sun. 5–9; closed Mon. Immerse yourself in a German atmosphere here, from the authentic German specialties to music with words recorded in German. Meals, large portions of homemade hearty dishes, include original bratwurst (white veal and pork sausage), Weiner schnitzel, Jaeger schnitzel, sauerbraten, and specials like *kohl roulade* (cabbage rolls). The salad is cucumber and tomato slices with a sweet vinaigrette, the (homemade) bread dumplings are wonderful, and the purple cabbage is seasoned with clove. If you grew up in a household that honored its Germanic heritage come mealtime,

you will feel right at home here. Entrées $11.95–17.95.

The March Hare (928-684-0223), 170 W. Wickenburg Way. Open Tue.–Sat. 11–2; dinner on Fri. (reservation required by Thu.) 5:30–7. This Victorian lunch spot might seem out of place in "Arizona's Most Western Town," but it fits like a glove. The Old West happened when Victorian was vogue. The small menu offers fresh-made quiche, salads (crab, chicken, or greens), and soups. Desserts come in half and whole sizes. Friday dinner is chef's choice. BYOB. Lunch $7.75; Friday dinner $16–20.

Rancho de los Caballeros (928-684-5484), 1551 S. Vulture Mine Rd. Open daily for buffet lunch and dinner October–May. Reservations required. Though it's part of a guest ranch where ranch life is celebrated, the restaurant truly leans toward the *Caballeros* part of its name rather than the *Rancho*. Chef Richard Lepree searches many corners of the world to fill his menus, which change daily, with rare and organic ingredients. Selections run the gamut from wild to mild, from traditional Old West to French, English, and East Indian. You might see quail with lavender butter, balsamic lamb loin with white truffle risotto, aalo ghobi, or white organic asparagus tips on beef carpaccio. The southwestern fare has a spiciness that keeps a low profile while making its presence pleasantly known. Aged beef is so fresh, it sees few stops between the ranch and the table. The breakfast buffet includes fresh foods, cereals, eggs, and more. The lunch buffet offers a couple of entrées, a large variety of salads, and breads, always the best quality. Keep a spot in your tummy open for dessert. There's a whole tableful of rich yummies—so big, a staff member stands by to answer questions regarding what's what in the sugary spread. Breakfast buffet $10; lunch buffet $14 weekdays, $16 Sunday; dinner $29 for starter, entrée, dessert, and coffee or tea.

Screamers Drive In (928-684-9056), 1151 W. Wickenburg Way. Open Mon.–Sat. 6 AM–8 PM (breakfast 6–10), Sun. 10:30–8. You don't want to be on a diet when you come to this classic drive-in. You do want to prime yourself for some good old-fashioned cooked-to-order fare: hand-packed burgers, delightful fresh fries, hot dogs, onion rings, malts, shakes, and cones. Sandwiches $2.50–5.50.

✳ The Arts

PERFORMING ARTS **Del E. Webb Center for the Performing Arts** (928-684-6624), 1090 S. Vulture Mine Rd. Often the preferred venue for artists performing in Arizona. People come from around the nation to see the talent in the 600-seat auditorium. Plus, the center provides free art camps for children from cities around the state. Call for schedule.

✳ Special Events

Call the chamber of commerce for more information on all events.

February: **Gold Rush Days**, a 60-year-old tradition that celebrates Wickenburg's heritage of cowboys and mining with a shoot-out, parade, rodeo, gold panning, mucking and drilling contest, vendors, art, and food. The Library of Congress in Washington, DC, recognized the celebration as one of the 100 Living Legacies in the United States.

April: The weeklong **Desert Caballeros Ride** brings cowboys from around the world to take part in a horseback adventure.

July: **Fourth of July Celebration** festivities include fun, games, food, and fireworks.

September: **Fiesta Septiembre** celebrates Wickenburg's Hispanic heritage with *folklorico* dancers, mariachi music, food, arts, and crafts.

October: **Wickenburg Fly-In & Classic Car Show** at the Wickenburg Airport features airplanes and classic cars.

November: The **Bluegrass Festival** draws thousands from the Southwest to a 3-day event that features the Four Corners states' championship contests for fiddle, flat-pick guitar, banjo, and mandolin.

December: Hear poems, songs, and stories about western heritage at the **Cowboy Christmas Poetry Gathering**. The **Christmas Light Parade** has lighted floats, Santa Claus, hot chocolate, carolers, and popcorn balls.

THE MOGOLLON RIM—WEST

When Zane Grey first experienced the Mogollon (pronounced *muggy-yown*) Rim, his poetic prose met its match as he "saw a scene that defied words. . . . For wild rugged beauty; I had not seen its equal." Enthralled with his new-found piece of wilderness, Grey settled down in a cabin there to write novels with heroes and heroines that traipsed the rim's enchanting countryside.

Called the backbone of Arizona, this 300-mile-long escarpment along the state's midsection—it extends into New Mexico—still casts a spell too mesmerizing for some people to untangle themselves. You have only to see its forested rampart where fluted limestone stacks upon blushing sandstone outcroppings, fill your lungs with pine redolence dripping in some of the cleanest air on the planet, or find yourself sealed in an envelope of silence in a remote section of the largest stand of ponderosa pines in the world to understand the rim's lure.

The Mogollon Rim draws those looking to escape the cities. Talk to the shopkeepers when you're there. Many will tell you about their former big-city-corporate-rat-race life. Like a mother comforting a child, the rim's tranquility and simplicity wrap you in security and peace. The sights, sounds, and smells of this backcountry saturate the senses.

In summer lush colonies of roses, ferns, and wildflowers cover the forest floor; wild grapevines drape the trees. Autumn ignites bursts of red, orange, and gold from big-tooth maples laced with aspens; russet from the Gambel oaks. Take a slow cruise down Colcord Road at twilight to view herds of elk, or watch a bald eagle splash into Willow Springs Lake in winter for a fish dinner to know how sweet a pine forest can get.

Do be warned, however, that Mogollon Rim weather is often at its worst in summertime. Daily thunderstorms rake across the escarpment, bringing afternoon wind, rain, and hail. Still, by day's end the swollen skies give way to an inky firmament sparkling with stars, and pine trees rock like ships lulled by a gentle wind as they toss their sweet aroma into the crisp night air. The campfire embers flare and pop, relinquishing their flame to ashes. And thoughts like Zane Grey's ". . . For wild rugged beauty; I had not seen its equal" creep into the mind.

GUIDANCE **Rim Country Regional Chamber of Commerce** (800-672-9766) is open daily and provides brochures, maps, directions, and area information.

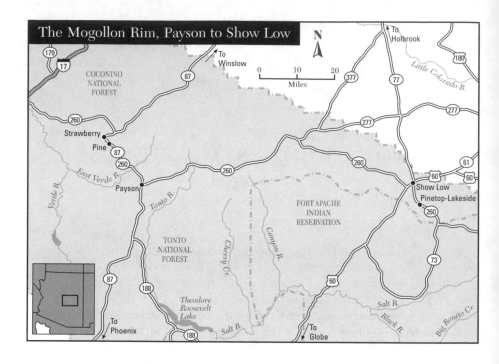

Payson Ranger District (928-474-7900), 1009 E. AZ 260, manages much of the beautiful spread of ponderosa pines on the rim along and south of AZ 260. For backcountry information for points north of the rim, contact **Mogollon Rim Ranger District** (928-477-2255) or **Happy Jack Info Center** (928-477-2172), located just north of the post office at Clints Well.

GETTING THERE From I-17, take AZ 260 east; from the east Valley, take AZ 87 north.

WHEN TO COME Summertime is high season on the rim. It's only about 90 minutes away from Phoenix and the Valley of the Sun—it's a major destination during summer. Be sure to plan ahead if you travel on weekends and holidays.

MEDICAL EMERGENCY **Payson Regional Medical Center** (928-474-3222), 807 S. Ponderosa.

✳ To See

Rim Country Museum (928-474-3483), 700 Green Valley Pkwy. Peruse the large collection of artifacts and memorabilia gathered from the early days of the rim and displayed in Payson's 1906 Forest Service ranger station. The museum has a bookstore and gift shop; you can also do guided archive searches. Free.

Shoofly Village Ruins. Contact Payson Ranger Station for more information. Located north of Payson off AZ 87, then east on Houston Mesa Rd. You can take a self-guided tour of the 3.75-acre site where a Native American village stood. Inhabited between AD 1000 and 1250, the village had 79 structures; only rock outlines remain from some. One of the larger structures had 26 rooms and was two stories high. Archaeologists from Arizona State University excavated the site, which is now on the National Register of Historic Places.

Strawberry Schoolhouse. Located 1.5 miles from AZ 260 on Fossil Creek Rd., Strawberry. Open May–Sep. on weekends and holidays, Sat. 10–4, Sun. noon–4. In 1884 county school superintendent Bucky O'Neill answered petitions from the territorial town of Strawberry and established School District 33 in the Strawberry Valley. When the Strawberry folks argued where this seat of higher education should reside, local cowboys employed some common sense to settle the matter: They used a calf rope to measure the lengths between the Hicks-Duncan cabin on the Valley's west end and the Peach cabin to the east, then established the midpoint by splitting the total down the middle. There the school was built with upscale materials and interiors, thanks to the political hob-nobbing between a resident and Bucky. It still looks pretty good after all these years (and a series of renovations). Free concerts and free demonstrations on summer weekends given by craftsmen such as a fiddle maker, basket maker, blacksmith, and saddle maker.

Tonto Creek Hatchery (928-478-4200). From Payson, drive about 21 miles east on AZ 260, then turn left (north) at the signed turnoff near Kohls Ranch Resort; drive 4 miles to this facility at the end of the unpaved road. Open 8–4 daily except Thanksgiving and Christmas. With a high-tech propensity and upscale equipment, Tonto Hatchery has practically perfected the art of raising fish. Stainless-steel raceways, a four-step water purification process, specially designed baskets for fry, and Tonto Creek's cold springwater add up to a survival rate as high as 92 percent. Tonto Hatchery's main products, rainbow trout, end up all along the Mogollon Rim and points northward, including Lees Ferry. The hatchery may have the best computer program in the western United States. You can tour the facility on your own, or call for a guided tour.

Tonto Natural Bridge State Park (928-476-4202), 10 miles north of Payson off AZ 87. Open Memorial–Labor Day, daily 8–8 (6 Apr., Sep., and Oct.); Nov.–Mar., daily 9–5; closed Christmas. Spanning Pine Canyon, a tucked-away chasm in the Mogollon Rim, the park looks more like it belongs in a coastal rain forest than a desert state: Vines climb up trees, mosses upholster rocks, and waterfalls drape into emerald pools. A travertine natural bridge inspired the park name. The bridge, probably the largest of its kind in the world, stands 183 feet high and 150 feet wide. Once a travertine dam built of calcium carbonate deposits from springwater flowing into Pine Canyon, it took on its current for-mation when Pine Creek eroded a tunnel through the travertine. You can explore the park on short hiking trails. $3 per person 14 and up; under 14 free.

SCENIC DRIVE **Forest Road 300**. The unpaved Rim Road (segments may require high clearance) travels about 43 miles through rich pine forests, to historic sites, and past exquisite views at the edge of the Rim. The side roads along the way provide scenic diversions.

✷ To Do

DOG PARK 🐾 **Payson Off-Leash Park** (928-747-5242), McLane Rd. next to the library. Open 24 hours. Trees, water, poop bags, and picnic area. Fenced area for small dogs.

FISHING Anglers claim that some of the best fishing anywhere takes place in the streams and lakes on the Mogollon Rim. Easy to reach, and often crowded, the **East Verde River** is only 4 miles north of Payson on AZ 87, just beyond Flowing Springs Rd. Turn left at East Verde Estates Rd., then turn right into the parking and camping area. **Christopher Creek** and **Tonto Creek** (above Kohl's Ranch, 22 miles east of Payson on AZ 260) are regularly stocked. To reach **Woods Canyon Lake**—an easy access on paved roads—drive 30 miles east of Payson on AZ 260, then left (north) onto Forest Road 300 and continue approximately 5 miles. It's the only rim lake with boat rentals and bait shop. **Willow Springs Lake** also enjoys easy access on paved roads and is located 31 miles east of Payson on AZ 260; head 1 mile past the Woods Canyon Lake turnoff, then go left (north). **Chevelon Canyon Lake**, the largest of the rim lakes, is also the most secluded and the most difficult to access. Drive 3 miles east of Payson on AZ 260 to Forest Road 300 and turn left (north); continue 10 miles to Forest Road 159, turn right, drive about 10 miles, then hike about a mile to the lake.

HIKING Rim Country has some of the best canyon hikes in the state. Some follow a maintained trail along a creek (such as the **Christopher Creek** and **Horton Creek Trails**); others, like **West Clear Creek**, are full-blown canyoneer adventures. Check out the **Woods Canyon Lake Trail** for scenery and watchable wildlife. Contact Payson Ranger Station or Happy Jack Information Center.

HORSEBACK RIDING **Kohl's Ranch Stables**, behind Kohl's Ranch Lodge, 15 miles east of Payson on AZ 260 on Christopher Creek. Open daily (except Christmas). Trail rides (offered 9–3) can last from 1 hour to half a day. Kids under 6 ride in the stable area only. $30 per hour per person.

LLAMAS 🦙 **Fossil Creek Llama Ranch** (928-476-5178). Located on Fossil Creek Rd., about 3.5 miles from AZ 87. Hum with the llamas on a hike in the ponderosa pine forest or just visit with them at this off-the-beaten-path ranch near Strawberry. Owners Joyce and John Bittner elucidate on these gentle creatures and their unique characteristics. They also have goats and turn their milk into goat cheese and fudge—both of which you get to taste if you stay for lunch. You can stay for the night in a yurt or tepee (Apr.–Nov.), too, and get hands-on experience in morning activities including barnyard detail and feeding and milking of the animals; something kids find fascinating, if not fun. Half-day hikes include lunch: $65 adults, $40 children under 12.

✳ Lodging

INNS ❧ Majestic Mountain Inn
(928-474-0185 or 800-408-2442), 602
E. AZ 260, Payson. High-country
ambience at a decent price. You'll
find an outdoor pool in the pines, a
meeting room, athletic club privileges, and complimentary coffee, tea,
cookies, and fruit all day. Rooms have
queen or king bed, TV-VCR, coffeemaker, and refrigerator; deluxe
rooms have cathedral ceilings and gas
fireplace; luxury rooms have spas.
$89–159.

**LODGES AND CABINS ❧ Strawberry
Lodge** (928-476-3333), Strawberry.
Homespun with a mountain-town
atmosphere, this lodge has been a
favorite for decades. Former owners
Jean and Dick Turner—who bought
the lodge after spotting a two-line ad
in the *Los Angeles Times* and making
one visit—used to say, "We didn't buy
this place to get rich, but to make a
place where people want to come."
And they did. Current owners Jan and
Adrian Marnell have kept this friendly
personality alive. The property
includes a restaurant. Rooms have
mostly double and queen beds, most
with fireplace, some with balcony.
$60–80.

❧ ♂ Christopher Creek Lodge
(520-478-4300), 21 miles east of
Payson. Christopher Creek, an off-
the-highway niche along the rim, has
been a mountain getaway of choice
for Arizonans since the 1950s, and
this lodge has the longest history of
family-owned status. This makes for a
more personal and personable experience. Rustic log and stone cabins with
modern features, shaded by ponderosa pines, bigtooth maples, and
Arizona walnut trees, cozy right next

to or near spring-fed Christopher
Creek. You can rent a motel room or
cabin here. All rooms have cable TV
and heat; cabins have cable TV, fully
equipped kitchen with oven, gas fur-
nace, wood-burning fireplace, cook-
ware, and utensils. $50–100.

Elk Haven Cabins (928-478-4582),
2 miles south of AZ 260 on Colcord
Rd. (1 mile east of Christopher
Creek). Located off the highway,
deep in the pine country that edges
along colonies of aspen trees, this
cluster of cabins rests in a peaceful
environment where wildlife feels
comfortable. Cabins include linens;
fully equipped kitchen with microwave, stovetop, and refrigerator;
gas log fireplace; love seat; air-
conditioning; BBQ; and satellite TV-
VCR with free movies. $85–110.

**BED AND BREAKFASTS ♂ Fossil
Creek Llama Ranch** (see *To Do*).
Stay in a tepee or yurt Apr.–Nov.;
breakfast included. $85.

Up the Creek Bed and Breakfast
(928-476-6571), 10491 Fossil Creek
Rd., Strawberry. Two words come to
mind when you first spot this property,
a contemporary farmhouse home
on 5 acres next to the national forest:
fresh and *simple*. The descriptive
becomes even more appropriate when
you get inside. The three guest
rooms, though ultracomfortable with
private bath, pillow-top mattress,
down pillows and comforters, CD
player, robes for two, and environmentally friendly amenities, have a
clean and uncluttered look. To make
your life even less complicated, the
rooms have no television, telephone,
fax machine, or computer hookup,
and the owners advise, "Your cell
phone probably won't work, either."

Breakfast included; children over 12 are okay, but no pets allowed. $95–165.

✳ Where to Eat

DINING OUT Cucina Paradiso (928-468-6500), 512 N. Beeline Hwy., Payson. Open for lunch Mon.–Fri. 11–2, dinner daily 3–8:30. The first thing you see when you walk into this classic Italian restaurant is the kitchen, with a brick oven as its star. All the baked meals, such as the popular chicken Parmesan and handmade pizza, find their perfection here. The wine list has some interesting Italian varietals from small vineyards, along with the requisite Californians and Australians. Lunch $7–10, dinner: $16–19.

🍴 ♪ **Mackys Grill** (928-474-7411), 1111 S. Beeline Hwy. (AZ 87), Payson. Open Sun.–Thu. 10–8, Fri.–Sat. 10–9. The unpretentious, *come-as-you-are* attitude and consistently good food here have made this a local favorite. The food, from Buffalo wings to the ranch house pie (both award-winning), with Black Angus hamburgers and juicy chicken in between, keeps Mackys on local best-of lists. $7–10.

The Randall House (928-476-4077), AZ 87, Pine. Open Tue.–Sat. 7–4, Sun. 8–2. One of the area's favorite, and best, restaurants serves freshly prepared breakfast and lunch, homemade pastries, gourmet coffees, and teas in the old Randall House, circa 1880. The food is fresh and healthy. The attention to aesthetic details, taste, and service has not changed over the years. Entrées $4–8.

Rimside Grill (928-476-6458), 3270 N. AZ 87, Pine. Open Wed.–Sat. 7 AM–8 PM (till 7 Sun.); summer hours, Wed.–Thu. 7–8 (till 9 Fri.–Sat.). Closed Mon.–Tue. all year. Best known for hearty and tasty breakfasts where everything is housemade, dinner specials, and a Friday fish fry where you can have the cod fried or baked. The dinner menu features steaks, chicken, and homemade sausages. Entrées $7.95–14.25.

The Small Cafe (928-474-4209), 512 S. Beeline Hwy., Payson. Open Tue.–Fri. 7–2 (1 Sat.–Sun.); closed Mon. The Small Café has always served good food, but recently a new owner—a graduate from Arizona Culinary Institute—has bumped the quality up a notch. All the meals are made from scratch, from pancakes and biscuits and gravy to eggs Benedict. Lunch sandwiches come with gourmet twists. The Lemon Surprise Pie, made from scratch from an historic recipe from the Heritage House, comes in a mandarin orange version, too. Entrées $6.25–9.75.

Strawberry Lodge Restaurant, (928-476-3333), Strawberry. Open Sun.–Thu. 7–7 (till 8 Fri.–Sat.). This long-standing favorite lures patrons from across the state for home-cooked meals. Their homemade pies are strong talismans. Breakfast includes classic egg dishes, hotcakes, and meats. Check out their hamburgers for lunch. Steaks, seafood, and specials for dinner. Meals are big, and pies legendary. Breakfast $3.25–9.75, lunch $5.95–9.95, dinner $8.95–16.95.

EATING OUT Pine Deli (928-476-3586), 6240 Hardscrabble Mesa Rd., Pine. Open Tue.–Sat. 11–8, Sun. 11–6. You can get ready-made sandwiches, hot or cold, here; or meats, cheeses, and salads by the pound.

Each day owners Mike and Debbie cook up a meal special you can take home after 4 PM; specialties include Italian dishes, stuffed cabbage with rice, brisket with egg noodles, and roast pork loin with stuffing. Pizza is served from 4 PM Tue.–Sat., noon on Sun. Entrées $6.95–8.99.

✳ Selective Shopping

The rim has an abundance of antique and collectible shops. In Pine, you just park your car and stroll the few blocks of shops. In Payson, go to the northern edge of town on AZ 87.

✳ Special Events

May: **Aero Fair** (928-978-4748) at the Payson Municipal Airport features aircraft rides and classic, older 4x4 vehicle displays along with food and merchandise. **Mountain High Days** (928-595-4397) celebrates arts and crafts in the Payson courthouse parking lot.

June: **Strawberry Festival** (800-672-9766), a weekend event in the Pine Cultural Center, serves treats from strawberry shortcake to strawberry salsa.

August: **Longest Continuous Rodeo** in Payson presents a classic rodeo weekend.

September: **Zane Grey Days** (928-595-4397) at Green Valley Park.

October: **Payson's Birthday Celebration** (800-672-9766). One hundred twenty-five years old and counting, Payson throws a mega party every year.

THE MOGOLLON RIM—EAST

W hen you enter the town of Show Low, you know you're getting deep into the heart of Rim Country: not quite in the White Mountains, but certainly high enough to lift you into the pines where life turns mild in summer. Show Low might be one of the best examples around of Old West pioneer spirit. The town got its name back when arguments were settled via fistfight, gunfight, or card game. As the story goes, soured partners Croyden Cooley and Marion Clark played an all-night card game to determine the ownership of some 100,000 acres of ranchland they shared. When Cooley needed just one point to win the marathon game of Seven Up, Clark blurted out: "You show low, and you win." Cooley cut the deck with the deuce of clubs showing. Show Low and its main street, Deuce of Clubs, memorialize this infamous 1870 moment.

Show Low has the essentials necessary for everyday life, while only a few miles down the road Pinetop-Lakeside exists for your recreational pleasure. In fact, Lakeside got its moniker when a handful of founding fathers spent an afternoon here lazing in the sun—a style of life you will find highly attractive in these parts. Must be the 40 lakes in as many miles surrounded by the world's largest ponderosa pine forest. Not surprisingly, Lakeside was recently named one of the most popular rim resort towns. Next-door Pinetop incorporated with Lakeside in 1984.

GUIDANCE **Show Low Chamber of Commerce** (928-537-2326), 81 E. Deuce of Clubs. **Pinetop-Lakeside Chamber of Commerce** (928-367-4290 or 800-573-4031), 102-C W. White Mountain Blvd., Pinetop. **Lakeside Ranger District** (928-368-5111), 2022 W. White Mountain Blvd., Lakeside, and **Black Mesa Ranger District** (928-535-4481) can give you information on backcountry hiking, fishing, mountain biking, and hunting.

GETTING THERE *By car:* You can reach both Show Low and Pinetop-Lakeside via AZ 260; the former sits at the intersection of US 60 and AZ 77. *By bus:* **White Mountain Passenger Line** (928-537-4539) commutes from Phoenix. *By air:* **Show Low Regional Airport** (928-532-4190), 3150 Airport Loop Rd., No. 100. Show Low has two runways (7,200 feet lighted and 4,000 feet unlighted), full taxiways, and commuter service to Phoenix via Arizona Express Airlines.

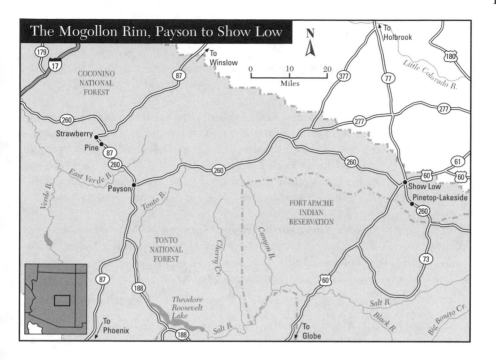

The Mogollon Rim, Payson to Show Low

WHEN TO COME Show Low and Pinetop-Lakeside open their arms all four seasons, but summer is the most popular here given the towns' elevations: 6,331 and 7,200 feet, respectively.

MEDICAL EMERGENCY Navapache Regional Medical Center (928-537-4375), 2200 E. Show Low Lake Rd., Show Low.

✳ To Do

FISHING Silver Creek Fish Hatchery (928-537-7513). From Show Low, go east on AZ 60 about 5 miles, turn left (north) onto Bourdon Ranch Rd., continue 5 miles to Hatchery Way Rd., and turn east to the facility. Open 8–4 daily except Thanksgiving and Christmas. The state's smallest fish hatchery raises a fish teetering on the edge of endangered species status, Arizona's native Apache trout. The hatchery sits right at the headwaters of Silver Creek, where 60-degree water flows without fanfare out of the ground. The fish raceways line up, end-to-end, at the spring's mouth, providing a habitat where Apache trout can grow quickly. It's a fascinating object lesson in fish management. Plus, Silver Creek has some good fishing down the creek (away from the hatchery, of course). See *Lakes* for more fishing hot spots.

GOLF Show Low Country Club (928-537-1564), 860 N. 36th Dr., Show Low. Located 2 miles west of Show Low on AZ 260 off Linden Rd., this 18-hole, par-70 course plays 5,702 yards and features grass fairways and bent grass greens.

One end plays in a pine forest, the other in open space. The semiprivate includes snack bar, lounge, driving range, and practice greens. $12–32.

Silver Creek Golf Club (928-537-2744), 2051 Silver Lake Blvd., Show Low. Gary Panks designed this 18-hole championship course that plays 6,813 yards at a par 71. You can play challenging black tees or regular. Semiprivate, the course has a restaurant, lounge, driving range, practice green, and airstrip. $27–45.

HIKING ⅙ The **White Mountain Trail System** comprises 11 loop trails ranging from easy to difficult in a variety of terrains. Several of the loop trails, designed for nonmotorized travel, connect. Contact the Lakeside Ranger Station for more information. **Woodland Lake Park** has short trails that work well for a family. The paved, barrier-free **Mogollon Rim Interpretive Trail** (contact the Lakeside Ranger District) runs along the edge of the rim for some great panoramas.

LAKES The **Rim Lakes Recreation Area** (see *Fishing* in "Mogollon Rim— West") includes Bear Canyon, Woods Canyon, and Willow Springs Lakes, where you can fish, swim, boat, and hike. Each pools in a highly scenic area and attracts lots of watchable wildlife, from elk in summer to bald eagles in winter. Contact the Black Mesa Ranger District.

MOUNTAIN BIKING The off-highway roads around here are perfect for exploring on a mountain bike. Get an Apache-Sitgreaves National Forest map and plan your route. The longer trails on the **White Mountain Trail System** are specially designed for mountain biking.PARK **Woodland Lake Park** (928-368-6700), Woodland Lake Rd. off AZ 260. More than 100 acres of open space with tennis courts, softball fields, hiking trails, equestrian trails, mountain biking, fishing, and ramadas with charcoal grills.

✳ Wilder Places

Big Springs Environmental Study Area (928-368-8696), Woodland Ave., 0.5 mile south of AZ 260. This outdoor study and recreation area features wetlands, wildlife, and short hiking trails. This is an excellent area for sighting watchable wildlife.

✳ Lodging

INNS & RESORTS 🐾 ✍ **Lake of the Woods** (928-368-5353), 2244 W. White Mountain Blvd., Pinetop. This private resort has its own lake in the pines to give you and the family a night in the forest with a cushion of comfort. Cabins come rustic to modern, each with a fireplace and kitchenette or full kitchen. The property includes a playground; a recreation hall with billiards, Ping-Pong, a video arcade, shuffleboard, badminton, and horseshoes; plus a Jacuzzi and dry sauna for adults. Fishing is free here, and you don't need a license. $99–309.

� **Mountain Haven Inn** (928-367-2101 or 888-854-9815), 1120 E. AZ 260, Pinetop. The rooms, all decorated nicely with their own theme from Victorian to Tree House, are clean and comfortable. Some have kitchens;

one has a covered porch. No pets. $59–99.

🐾 ♿ **Northwoods Resort** (928-367-2966 or 800-813-2966), 165 E. AZ 260. These Bavarian-style cottages have all the comforts of home, including queen or king beds, color TV, fully equipped kitchen, fireplace, and deck. The property has a playground, spa, and barbecue area. The resort has a loyal following—it's best to make reservations in summer. Low season $99–249, high season $139–339.

BED AND BREAKFASTS **Old Arizona Homestay** (928-367-0232), 551 Billy Creek Dr., Lakeside. Old Arizona Homestay really does bring a little of old Arizona to you. Owner-operator Lea Pace has pioneer Arizona roots that go deep, and the property reflects it. The two rooms and two cabins, all different, each have unique touches. The Indian room, for instance, includes a special display of Native American crafts and art, while the Cowboy has a collage of cowboy thangs. All feature queen bed, private bath, ceiling fan, drinking and shot glasses, refrigerator, complimentary sodas, soaps, and shampoo, a private deck with table and two chairs, and a Southwest family-style breakfast (that is casually described as able to fill a bronco buster's belly). The two cabins have fully equipped kitchen, TV, fireplace, washer and dryer, and porch. Rooms $85–95, cabins $95–190.

Pinetop Bed and Breakfast (928-367-0479 or 888-521-5044), 24444 Jan Lane, Pinetop. Three themed suites, each with its own bath. The Western has a wood-beamed ceiling and rugged decor, the Victorian drips with romance, and the Island features a fountain. You can sit in front of the

fireplace in the common area, or play billiards or video games in the game area. Innkeeper-owners Karen and Steve provide snacks to hold you through the night, then serve a gourmet breakfast come morning. No pets. $125 per couple; $15 for each extra person.

✳ Where to Eat

DINING OUT **Charlie Clark's Steak House** (928-367-4900), 1701 E. White Mountain Blvd. Open daily for lunch 11–3, dinner at 4:45. They say this rustic spot has accommodated the longest continuously operating restaurant in the state. That's if you count its start as a covert bar dispensing moonshine during Prohibition. When booze became legal, it evolved into Jake Renfro's Famous Log Cabin Café in 1933. Five years later Charlie Clark took over and made steak dinners for patrons—as long as they would tend bar while he cooked. You can get an excellent mesquite-broiled steak here, as well as chicken, prime rib, seafood, and classic house-made desserts. Afterward, keep up the ol' Charlie Clark tradition with drinks and dancing in the orchard (seasonal). Lunch $6.95–17.95, dinner $13.95–30.95.

La Casita Café (928-537-5179), 5000 S. White Mountain Rd., Show Low. Open Sun.–Thu. 11–8, Fri.–Sat. 11–9. An old house converted to a Mexican restaurant serves up great home-cooked meals. It's casual and family-friendly. Summer months are crowded at dinnertime. Entrées $6–11.

EATING OUT 🍴 **Eddie's Country Café** (928-367-2161), 1753 E. White Mountain Blvd., inside Eddie's Country Store. Open daily 7–7 (till 3 Wed., till 6 Sun.). This great little find serves up good food all day. Owned by Eddie Basha, Arizona's native son and food purveyor extraordinaire. Breakfast and lunch are the most popular meals here, and the 40-seat dining room gets filled fast. Weekends (Fri.–Sun.) become a special event when the deli manager, Roland, fires up the combination grill-oven-smoker in the parking lot and cooks some tasty barbecue (baby back ribs, chicken, and tri-tip). Breakfast $3.15–7, lunch $3–5, dinner $8–14.

⬥ **High in the Pines Delicatessen and Coffee House** (928-537-1453), 1191 E. Hall, Show Low. Open Mon.–Fri. 7–4, Sat. 8–3. It may be casual, but the food and beverages served here are upper crust. The recipes for breakfast and lunch fare originate from Europe and are made in-house, including the potato salad, chocolate candies, and truffles. Each dish has a special touch, from the steamed milk with the oatmeal (not instant), to the roast pork tenderloin sandwich with white cheddar cheese, to the charcuterie boards served in the European tradition with bread. Entrées $6–7.95.

✳ Special Events

May: **White Mountain Bike Rodeo** (928-367-1300) is a great kid's event with free food, activities, and equipment.

June: **Show Low Days** feature the **Still Cruzin' Car Show**. The **Annual Father's Day Fishing Contest** (928-368-8696) at the Woodland Lake Park Boat Dock awards prizes and trophies, then serves free hot dogs and soda. **National Trails Day Celebration** (928-368-6700, ext. 3) celebrates the outdoors with hiking, mountain biking, horseback riding, and interpretive activities in the White Mountain Trail System. **Annual "Best of the West" Fine Art Show and Sale** (928-368-8696) at Hon-Dah Conference Center brings the best of the western artists' works to the rim.

July: **Northeast Arizona Fine Arts Association Art Show & Craft Sale** (928-368-8696) in Charlie Clark's Orchard. **White Mountain Native American Art Festival** (928-368-8696) presents Native American art and crafts.

August: **White Mountain Bluegrass Music Festival** (928-368-8696) brings top bluegrass musicians to Hon-Dah Resort/Casino.

September: **Pinetop-Lakeside Fall Festival** (928-368-8696) has arts and crafts, a talent show, an antiques show and sale, a used-book sale, and entertainment.

December: **Show Low Main Street** (928-537-2326) features a Christmas tree lighting and electric parade.

Eastern Arizona 3

ROUTE 66 EAST: WINSLOW AND HOLBROOK

Two different towns with two different personalities—one traditional, the other whimsical. Both fill the pages of Arizona history—one with color, the other with class. But these cities, only 33 miles apart, have some strong commonalities. For one, they both make a good base for visiting Petrified Forest and Painted Desert National Parks. Both have smidgeons of Old Route 66 running through them. Both have interesting architecture. And they both love history. They just have different stories to tell.

By the 1930s Winslow had evolved into a renowned destination for a west-of-the-Mississippi adventure. The town, with its beautiful brick storefronts, exquisitely designed La Posada Hotel, vaudeville theater, and trading post, became the home base of choice for visitors who wanted to explore the surrounding reservations and natural wonders. When automobiles prevailed over railroad travel and I-40 bypassed Winslow, the world all but forgot about the town that brought a taste of culture to this rowdy land. The only attraction the town had to offer focused on a street corner where Jackson Browne might have seen a girl, my Lord, in a flatbed Ford.

Toward the end of the 20th century, the grande dame of Fred Harvey hotels where all the beautiful people stayed, the La Posada, caught the eyes of a handful of Californians who not only saved it from demolition but also lovingly restored the building to its former glory. Since then more of Winslow's beautiful historic buildings have gone through the restoration process. The resuscitation has pointed Winslow in the right direction, back to its more refined days.

Holbrook, on the other hand, was one of the reasons the West was called Wild. Before it was a decade old, the town experienced more than 20 deaths by gunfight. A shoot-out at the Blevins household evolved into the famous Pleasant Valley War, or Graham-Tewksbury feud, which lasted for years and would eventually be known the world over.

As the countryside around Holbrook filled with ranches, the tiny town surrounded by miles of open space became a modern-day trade route. Far from traditional, organized city life, eccentric personalities flourished. Rotgut whiskey provoked hair-trigger tempers into brawls and gunfights in saloons with graphic names such as the Bucket of Blood—which, by the way, is still in operation.

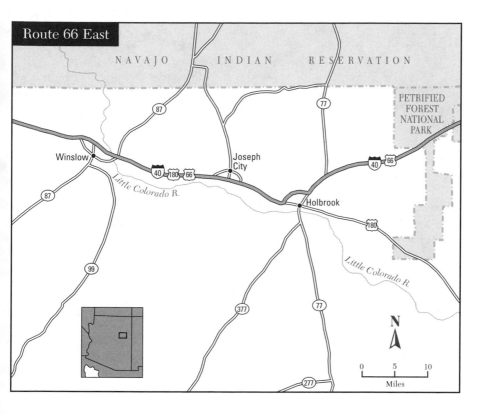

Cowboys, often fugitive outlaws feeling their oats and ready for a little fun, assembly-lined shots of whiskey. It took a lawman named Commodore Perry—a peacock of a man with attractive long locks who knew how to work a gun—to tame the town. Somewhat.

Cattle ranching grew big in Holbrook; some say there were up to 1.5 million head in the early 1890s. The area's big outfit, Aztec Land and Cattle Company, had the second biggest operation in the nation. The company, which also went by the name Hashknife, declared open season on rustling from inside the company and trolling the outskirts of the humongous herd. This led to the formation of the Arizona Rangers, a hard-bitten group described by state historian Marshall Trimble as "a bunch of rough-ridin' cowboys with a tough-as-nails reputation that made most criminals think twice about messing with them."

If the criminal activity wasn't enough, in 1899 the town carved a notch of notoriety for itself all the way back in Washington, DC, when Sheriff Frank Wottron sent out invitations for a public hanging. The invitation poetically stated that the soul of George Smiley, Murderer, "will be swung into eternity on Dec. 8, 1899 at 2 o'clock p.m. sharp. The latest improved methods of scientific strangulation will be employed and everything possible will be done to make the surroundings cheerful and the execution a success." A reprimand was quickly dispatched from President McKinley.

Things quieted down by the time Route 66 made its way through the town, and Holbrook took to its new role as a tourist destination. When I-40 came along, the town coyly kept itself up but never changed its style. Its retro tourist architecture is straight out of the 1950s. Plus, you can still see the buildings and businesses that made the town, hosted cowboy fights, and saw gun battles back in its rowdier days. Just like Winslow, history is big in Holbrook. It's just celebrated differently.

GUIDANCE Winslow Chamber of Commerce (928-289-2434), 101 E. 2nd St. The visitor center has an extensive selection of brochures, maps, and some souvenirs. **Holbrook Chamber of Commerce** (928-524-6558 or 800-524-2459) at the Navajo County Courthouse (100 E. Arizona) has a self-guided tour map of historic buildings gathered within a few blocks' area in the town. **Mogollon Rim Ranger District** (928-477-2255), HC 31, Box 300, Happy Jack, has information on backcountry use in the national forest.

GETTING THERE Winslow is located right along I-40 and intersected by AZ 87. *By train:* **Amtrak** (Los Angeles to Chicago) stops twice daily. *By air:* **Lindbergh Airfield** can handle just about anything from a little Cessna to a 747. You might get a special treat and see Bill Reesman's candy-apple-red Russian MiG jet stunt plane sponsored by Red Bull thunder into the ethers.

Holbrook not only straddles I-40 but also lies at the convergence of AZ 77 to the north and south, AZ 377 to the south, and US 180 from the southeast.

WHEN TO COME Most of the year these high-desert towns have a mild climate. Winds cool temperatures down a notch or two in summer.

MEDICAL EMERGENCY Winslow Memorial Hospital (928-289-4691), 1501 N. Williamson Ave.

RED BULL RUSSIAN MIG STUNT PLANE AT LINDBERGH AIRFIELD.

✳ To See

Homolovi Ruins State Park (928-289-4106). Located 1.3 miles north of Winslow on AZ 87. Visitor center open daily 8–5. Rich in artifacts and ruins, the park, located along the Little Colorado River, gives you a glimpse into how the Hopi Nation's descendants lived in the 13th and 14th centuries. A research center for archaeologists, the park has three main pueblo ruins that contain a rich array of scatterings of broken pottery and petroglyphs. $5 per carload, $1 for individuals on bicycle.

Hopi Mesas. From Holbrook, take AZ 77 north to AZ 264 and turn west;

from Winslow, go north on AZ 87 to AZ 264, then turn east or west. The Hopi Mesas jut out like three fingers from Black Mesa. The First Mesa has the views (no picture taking is allowed anywhere on the reservation) and artists' studios producing pottery, basketry, and kachinas. The artistry is generally handed down through generations and has deep spiritual connections. The Second Mesa has the **Hopi Cultural Center** (928-734-6650), open Mon.–Sat. 8–5. You can get a bite to eat, shop, and check into a room if you want to stay overnight. Check out the Hopi Museum to learn about Hopi traditions. Old Orabi, the oldest continually occupied village in North America, is located on the Third Mesa. Free.

La Posada Hotel (928-289-3873), 303 E. 2nd St., Winslow. Open 7 AM–9 PM. Arizona's great railroad hotel—designed by architect Mary Colter (of Grand Canyon fame) and built in the 1930s—was one of the finest in the Southwest and the most elegant Fred Harvey hotel built. Colter was a master at blending light, color, and materials. The world came to La Posada's door, and a Who's Who of the rich and famous stayed here, from Albert Einstein to Howard Hughes. The hotel briefly fell from grace when it was converted into generic office space and almost destroyed. After a total restoration, the stone and tile floors, glass murals, original furniture, and acres of gardens live once again. It's a remarkable place worth visiting even if you don't plan to spend the night there. Get a special tour led by the Winslow Harvey Girls by calling 928-289-9110 or 928-289-4160.

Meteor Crater (928-289-5898). Located 20 miles west of Winslow on I-40. Open Memorial Day–Labor Day 7–7, the rest of the year 8–5; closed Christmas Day. The world's first proven meteorite impact site has developed into a fascinating place to learn about the never-ending impacts in our solar system through interactive displays and exhibits in the Learning Center, a 10-minute movie in the big-screen theater, and guided tours and lectures (weather permitting). A collection of meteorites found at the site appears throughout the visitor center, including one that weighs more than 1,400 pounds. $15 adults, $6 ages 6–16, under 6 free.

Navajo County Courthouse (928-524-6558 or 800-524-2459), 100 E. Arizona, Holbrook. The rowdiest spot in town when it was first built in 1898, the old courthouse holds plenty of interesting memories, including all-night dances, notorious trials, and an invitation-driven hanging. Today the structure is quieter, describing through displays the historic events and cultures of its earlier days. In June and July, Native Americans hold dances in its plaza. Western and Native American art shows take place there throughout the year.

Old Trails Museum (928-289-5861), 212 Kinsley Ave., Winslow. Open Mon.–Sat. 9–5. Nicknamed Winslow's Attic, this two-room museum located in a 1920s building with its original tile floor, marble counters, and a classy vault has a nice compendium of artifacts, vintage clothing, bottles, and historic memorabilia collected from Indian ruins, the Santa Fe Railway, La Posada Hotel, and townsfolk. Free.

Remembrance Garden. Located on 3rd St. and Transcon Lane, Winslow. Two mangled beams from the World Trade Center, 14 and 15 feet tall and the largest pieces given to any community in the country, stand in a brick planter with the words UNITED WE STAND running across. It's an oddly placed memorial with an odd history. The project started when a Phoenix television station called Winslow to see what they planned for the one-year anniversary of the September 11, 2001, terrorist attack. The call spurred residents into action, and they took steps to create a memorial. They got two girders from the World Trade Center by signing a contract agreeing never to use the beams for profit. Next they had to transport them. One of the town's major businesses—Wal-Mart—picked up the beams. The truck entered Winslow on September 6, 2002, immediately starting an impromptu parade through downtown. At the site, everything was ready for placement: Residents had plucked weeds, installed a sprinkler system, and put up a flagpole. The beams were set in place just in time for the memorial's dedication ceremony at 5 PM on September 11, 2002, for all of TV-land to see. Free.

Rock Art Ranch (928-288-3260). From Winslow, go south on AZ 87 to AZ 99 and turn left; go to Territorial Rd., and turn left; go to the signed turnoff and turn right. It's 3 miles to the ranch. Reservations necessary. Open daily except Sundays and holidays. This working cattle ranch has a little bit of everything for the western aficionado. A museum has hundreds of southwestern artifacts, especially Anasazi pots and arrowheads. A centuries-old Hopi rock house and coral, Navajo hogan and sweathouse, and the last remaining bunkhouse of the Hashknife Outfit stands on the grounds. The star of this authentic western roundup is the 0.25-mile panel of rock art in Chevelon Canyon, one of the best such sites in the world. It'll match any national park or monument you may travel to, *sans* crowds. Call for admission and reservations.

Standin' on the Corner in Winslow, Arizona, Park. Kinsley Ave. and 2nd St. Back around the 1970s, Jackson Browne wrote a song about standin' on the corner in Winslow, Arizona, and seeing a girl (my Lord) in a Ford truck doing a double take. Winslow has memorialized this song—made famous by the Rock

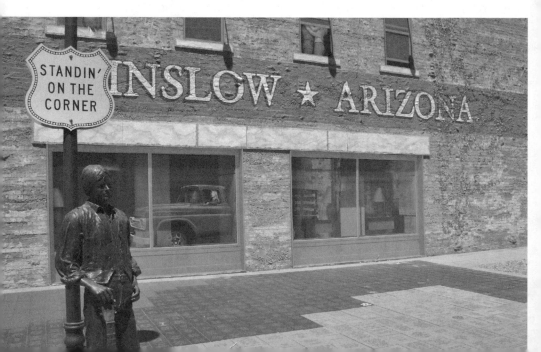

group, the Eagles—with a statue and a mural depicting the story. Winslow has a
Standin' on the Corner celebration every year. Whether or not Jackson Browne
did, indeed, get the eye from a girl in a flatbed Ford here, we don't know.
Flagstaff claims host to the event, but reliable sources say Browne's car broke
down in Winslow. The verdict's out whether or not anyone's willpower did, too.

PAINTED DESERT/PETRIFIED FOREST NATIONAL MONUMENT (928-524-3522).
Located 25 miles east of Holbrook off I-40 at exit 311. Open year-round except
Christmas Day: Nov.–Mar., daily 8–5; Apr.–Sep., daily 7–7; Labor Day–Oct., 7–6.
The Painted Desert actually spans from Cameron near the Grand Canyon to just
southeast of the Petrified Forest National Park. The short road here takes you
through a grand showcase of variety and colors typical of the desert. The various
layers of sandstone and mudstone in the Chinle Formation took on different colors from various minerals in the sediments and the rate at which the layers
formed. Red, orange, and pink hues (predominant at the north end of the park)
come from iron oxides and aluminum. When sediments rapidly build up—say,
during a flood—oxygen gets depleted from the soil and shades of blue, gray, and
lavender form, as you'll see in the south end of the park.

The **Painted Desert Inn Museum**, recently renovated, is open 9–5. The
museum, built in the 1920s, has wall murals painted by Hopi artist Fred
Kabotic. You may hike in the backcountry of the Painted Desert with a permit,
which is free and available at the museum. Access the wilderness via the mile-
long Wilderness Access Trail located at the northwest side of the Painted Desert
Inn. The wilderness area starts when you cross Lithodendron Wash.

Petrified Forest National Monument. The south end of the park contains the
state's colorful geological jewels of petrified wood. Actually ancient trees have
agatized into a rainbow of colors, some sprinkled with crystals, the petrified wood
lies pell-mell in "forests" along the ground. The park recently went through an
expansion doubling its size. However, the paved road that accommodates most
travel remains in the central part of the park, far from the extended boundaries.
Rainbow Forest Museum provides information on several ways to experience
the park: A 20-minute orientation movie runs every half hour, while the computer-
based Immersive Tour into the Triassic shows the ancient and present environ-
ments. You'll also find exhibits of dinosaurs, reptiles, and petrified wood; a bookstore and gift shop; and access to Giant Logs Trail. $10 per vehicle.

✳ To Do

CANOEING & KAYAKING McHood Park (see *Wilder Places*). If you have your
own craft, you can paddle down Clear Creek to secluded Clear Creek Canyon.

HIKING Several hiking trails are located on the national forest within day-trip distance. Contact Coconino National Forest. At **Homolovi Ruins State Park**, three
trails take you to different spots to view ruins, petroglyphs, and scenic vistas.
While all are short (0.5–1.3 miles long), they give you a sense of history and
scenery in this high-desert environment. **Petrified Forest National Monument**
has several short trails; experienced hikers can plan cross-country backpacks.

HOW WOOD GETS PETRIFIED

The dry, dusty tablelands in which the Petrified Forest National Monument lies give no immediate hint of their ancient status as a fern-stuffed flood-plain where dinosaurs roamed, marshes oozed, and volcanoes steamed. But fossils of ancient plants and dinosaur bones give its secret away.

The trees in the Petrified Forest came from a tropical forest atop an ancient chain of mountains once located to the south of the park. Trees died, fell, washed down to the floodplain, and over time were covered with silt, mud, and volcanic ash. The cover cut off oxygen and slowed the logs' decaying process. This allowed time for silica-laden groundwater to seep through the logs and replace their original wood fibers with silica deposits. Finally, the silica crystallized into quartz. Some pieces spangle with glitters of crystals; most are Technicolor beautiful.

You may be tempted to purloin a piece as you peruse the park. To dis-courage this, the Park Service has mounted a number of letters written by repentant wood thieves lamenting their actions by attesting guilty con-sciences, health problems, and broken marriages as a result of their swip-ing a fragment of petrified wood. It's clearly best to follow Leave No Trace ethics by taking only pictures.

HISTORIC WALKING TOUR Get a free self-guided map from the **Holbrook Chamber of Commerce** in the Navajo County Courthouse and take a look at some of Holbrook's more historic, and notorious, buildings. From the Bucket of Blood Saloon that withstood gunfights and brawls frequent enough to stain the floor to the Santa Fe Station.

ROCK CLIMBING **Jacks Canyon** is located 30 miles south of Winslow along AZ 87 at milepost 314.7; contact the Mogollon Rim Ranger District. This craggy spot, a climbers' wonderland, has almost 300 vertical to wildly overhanging routes on limestone, and sandstone cliffs have tons of pockets for monos to four-finger sinkers. Vertical walls have bubbly surfaces with edges and blocks. All routes are protected lavishly by cracks. One Winslow rock climber claimed, "Every rock climber in the world knows about Jacks Canyon except Arizonans." Now you know.

✳ Wilder Places

McHood Park and Clear Creek Reservoir (928-289-2434). Located 5 miles from downtown: Go south on AZ 87 to AZ 99, and turn left. The deep rock canyon of Clear Creek makes a magnificent setting with its redrock shelves brac-ing deep blue river waters. You can canoe, camp, swim, and fish here.

✳ Lodging

🐾 **La Posada Hotel** (928-289-3873), 303 E. 2nd St., Winslow (see *To See*). You get a gracious dose of history here, at one of the last great railroad hotels along the Santa Fe Railroad line. Each guest room has a full bath and a unique design that incorporates antiques. The 20-inch walls with acoustic insulation are thick enough to soften railroad sounds. The hotel has two tennis courts, a library, and gardens. Well-behaved pets and children are welcome. Pets must be registered at check-in and require an additional $10 fee. $89–175.

🐾 ✐ **WigWam Village Motel #6** (928-524-3048), 811 W. Hopi Dr., Holbrook. Not many franchise hotels are exclusive enough to warrant a patent like the WigWam Village. Frank Redford created the first village in Kentucky in the early 1900s to look like tepees he'd seen on the Sioux reservation.The model became a hit with travelers and evolved into a gathering place for the town as well. Redford realized he had a bankable product, patented it in 1936, and opened six more. Of the seven, only two remain: this one in Holbrook (listed on the National Register of Historical Places) and #2 in Cave City, Kentucky. In keeping with the prevailing retro theme of Holbrook, you will feel like you entered a time warp here. Check out the classic cars parked around the property. Tepees include bath with shower, cable TV, heat, and air-conditioning. $48–54.

✳ Where to Eat

Holbrook
Butterfield Stage Co. Steak House (928-524-3447), 609 W. Hopi Dr.

Open daily 4–10. It's casual, here, with a relaxing atmosphere. One of Holbrook's finer restaurants has people consistently commenting about the good food. The name implies steak (with filet mignon the favorite), but they also serve chicken (another favorite) and some good seafood. Salad bar included with the meal. $8.95–20.95.

Romo's Café (928-524-2153), 121 W. Hopi Dr., Holbrook. Open Mon.–Sat. 10–8; closed Sun. As in the rest of the town, the decor here is quintessentially retro—but the food is classic New Mexico. Savory red and green chili sauces, baked (not fried) chimichangas, and sopaipillas with soul. Entrées $7–16.

Winslow
E & O Kitchen (928-289-5352), Winslow-Lindbergh Regional Airport (take AZ 87 south to Airport Rd., then turn right to the parking lot). Open Mon.–Fri. 11–8, Sat. 10–6. Named for owners Estella and Oscar, this family restaurant does things a little different. The menu offers a couple dozen entrées with your choice of meat— *asada* (grilled beef), *machaca* (shredded beef), *picadillo* (ground beef), *carnias* (pork), *adobada* (pork in red chili), and *pollo* (chicken). Entrées $2.49–8.99.

✐ **Turquoise Room** (928-289-2888), La Posada Hotel, 303 E. 2nd St.,

Winslow. Open daily for breakfast 7–11, lunch 11–2, and dinner 5–9. Chef-owner John Sharpe has resurrected this restaurant—named for the famous Santa Fe Super Chief dining car—to the same level of excellence the original restaurant enjoyed at its finest. The Wild West still reigns here, menu-wise, with entrées such as elk, wild boar, and quail with prickly pear jalapeño glaze. These are nicely balanced with classics such as duck with raspberry brandy sauce and Angus steaks. Chef Sharpe slips creative twists into every course, from the yin–yang blend of cream of corn and smooth black bean soup, to crispy pork *carnitas* with papaya salsa, black beans in a red chile pool, polenta, and vegetables. The interiors are specially designed leather-and-wood chairs modeled after an original of La Posada, emerald brocade booths, Verne Lucero chandeliers, and a stained-glass mural of La Posada patron saints Ysidro, Pascual, and Barbara. Chef Sharpe gathers ingredients purchased and shipped from local farms or by overnight air express (fish, for example, is flown from New Orleans, Boston, and Nilinchic, Alaska) to produce a style of food he calls "Regional Contemporary Southwestern with an occasional trib-

ute to the great days of the Fred Harvey Company." Children's menu available. Entrées $19.95–26.95.

✳ The Arts

Snowdrift Art Space (928-289-8201), 120 W. 2nd St., Winslow. Open often. Dan Lutzick, once a partner in the La Posada Hotel, now devotes his time to producing big pieces of art (10-plus feet high) from industrial-grade materials. More than a dozen pieces stand in an old warehouse with a SNOWDRIFT PERFECT SHORTENING ad on the outside—hence the name. As of the time of this writing, Lutzick hasn't budged from his decision not to sell any of his art.

✳ Special Events

June: **City of Winslow Carnival** (928-289-2434).

September: **Standin' on the Corner Festival** (928-289-3434) in Winslow celebrates the Eagles' hit, along with a **Just Cruisin' Car Show**, Navajo County Fair (928-524-6407), 404 E. Hopi Dr., Holbrook. **Old West Days Celebration** (928-524-6558) in Holbrook includes a Wild West Art Show and Auction, Bucket of Blood Races, Old West reenactors, games, entertainment, a car show, a softball tournament, a chili cook-off, vendors.

December: **Holiday Tour of Homes** (928-289-8202) in Winslow presents four to six homes, decorated and open to the public.

ART IN THE SNOWDRIFT ART SPACE.

GREER

Located in an 8,500-foot-high valley along the confluence of the Little Colorado River and its West Fork, this hamlet holds as much beautiful scenery and wildlife as it does history. Here's where several pioneer families homesteaded. Farming reports about the hyperproductive land look like something straight out of Genesis, minus the grapes. One pioneer, E. R. Dewitt, recounted how in 1893 he raised "Thirty thousand pound of spuds from three acres, 330 bushels of oats, and 26 tons of oat hay on 12 acres." Farmers will understand how Mr. Dewitt must have welcomed the typical 200-plus inches of snow the area gets come winter.

As you peruse the streets around Greer, you might see relics from the old farming days, a truck from a logging business from back when, or historic cabins still standing but unused. But don't get the wrong idea. This is not Jeff Foxworthy territory, but rather well-heeled ranch country. Even though ranching no longer reigns (tourism does), the mind-set lingers, and in cowboy-land nothing gets thrown away. It's recycled, repaired, or displayed for posterity but never discarded.

Cozying up to the mixed conifers and aspens in the Apache-Sitgreaves National Forest, Greer hovers around 120 residents all year. The big draw today is the forest —for recreation, not logging. Big, beautiful, meadowed, and crossed by trout streams lined with wildflowers, the forest is at its best here in the White Mountains.

Mixed in among the memories and hidden-in-the-forest-coziness come signs hinting at more cosmopolitan times, such as huge new homes (mostly second) appearing on the mountain slopes and businesses that have become more accommodating to the more distinguished palate. Still, you won't find a gas station here, or a supermarket; only a string of independent businesses that offer food, shelter, and a smattering of gift shopping. Upscale accommodations make life easier in this rugged backcountry than at home. More importantly, there's the fresh air, clean water, and open space. That's enough to attract anyone looking for a great outdoor place these days. It was for the town's founding fathers.

GUIDANCE **Springerville-Eagar Regional Chamber of Commerce** (928-333-2123 or 888-733-2123), 318 E. Main St., Springerville. **Apache-Sitgreaves National Forest** (928-333-4301), 30 S. Chiricahua Dr. (open Mon.–Fri. 8–4:30), has information on backcountry use of the Apache-Sitgreaves National Forest.

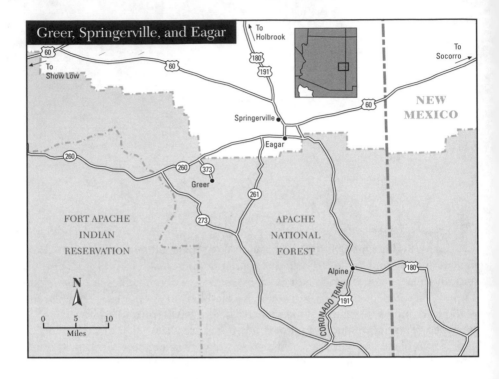

Greer, Springerville, and Eagar

To Holbrook

To Socorro

To Show Low

NEW MEXICO

Springerville

Eagar

Greer

FORT APACHE
INDIAN
RESERVATION

APACHE
NATIONAL
FOREST

Alpine

CORONADO TRAIL

N

0   5   10
Miles

GETTING THERE There's only one road to Greer: AZ 373 south of AZ 260.

WHEN TO COME The town's high season runs from Memorial Day through Labor Day, but most of the town stays open all year.

MEDICAL EMERGENCY White Mountains Regional Medical Center (928-333-4368; TDB, 928-333-7156), 118 S. Mountain Ave., Springerville.

✳ To See

Butterfly Lodge Museum (928-735-7414), AZ 373 and County Rd. 1126. Open Memorial Day–Labor Day, Fri.–Sun. 10–5. John Butler (husband of Molly Butler) built this rustic cabin in 1914 for the writer James Willard Schultz. The town's first tourist cabin is listed on the National Register. The fluttering butterflies around the meadows inspired the name. Schultz, a hunting guide and trapper from the Glacier Park area, and fighter for Native American rights, wrote dozens of books when he moved to Greer. Schultz's son, Lone Wolf, created the paintings and sculptures exhibited in the cabin. A number of special events and talks are scheduled throughout the season. $2 adults, $1 ages 12–17.

✳ To Do

CROSS-COUNTRY SKIING The national forest has developed a maze of trails in the **Greer Cross Country Ski Area** and nearby **Pole Knoll Recreation Area** just off AZ 260. Contact Apache-Sitgreaves National Forest.

DOWNHILL SKIING/SNOWBOARDING Sunrise Park Resort (928-735-7669). Located in McNary, 11 miles east of Greer on AZ 273, 7 miles south of AZ 260. One of the state's best ski areas has 65 runs for every level of experience. There's a snow half-pipe, implanted wood and metal rails, and a special-event area with jumps ranging from beginner to advanced for snowboarders. Lift tickets $35–45 adults, $30–38 youths, $25–26 under 12.

FISHING You need only step outside to the Little Colorado River to do some fly-fishing for rainbow trout. But why stop there when more than 600 miles of trout streams and more than 20 trout lakes lie within a couple of dozen miles of town? Check out *Fishing* in "Springerville" or contact Apache-Sitgreaves National Forest.

HIKING Greer is located in the national forest, and you have hikes with trailheads right in town: the mile-long **Butler Canyon Loop** and **Greer Cross Country Ski Area** (check out Trail No. 5) at Squirrel Springs Recreation Area, as well as the **West Fork** and **East Fork Trails**, both of which follow creeks. The **East** and **West Baldy Trails** travel to almost the top of Mount Baldy (the peak is sacred to the White Mountain Apache, and you need a permit to ascend it) are about 10 miles away. The **South Fork Trail** is just down the road off AZ 260. Contact Apache-Sitgreaves National Forest.

HORSEBACK RIDING Wiltbank Trail Rides (928-735-7454), 38735 AZ 373. Open Mon.–Sat. Rides run every 2 hours from 8 AM–4 PM on gentle and experienced horses. Travels trails on the national forest for 30 minutes to 2 hours and you can customize a longer ride with reservations. In the winter, a Belgian Trots team pulls a sleigh. $35 per rider from 6 years old and up.

MASSAGE Greer Massage (928-245-3037), 103 Main St. Call for an appointment. If the surroundings don't relax you enough, you can get a number of different massages here, from Swedish to hot stone, with reflexology, facials, and Thai yoga massage in between. Hatha yoga classes or private instruction offered as well. $75–105.

MOUNTAIN BIKING With all the unpaved roads in the national forest, most with little or no traffic, the area offers incredible possibilities for fat tires. This is not gonzo territory with steep, technical grades; rather, it's rolling hills (some with a kick) with awesome scenery in 8,000- to 10,000-foot elevations.

WILDFLOWERS In summer this area has the state's best show of wildflowers. Just head to a river- or creekside and hike. Hot trails are **Thompson Trail**, the

WHITE MOUNTAIN WILDFLOWERS DRAW MASSES OF BUTTERFLIES.

fisherman's trail (beaten path) along the West Fork of the Black River from the West Fork Campground, **West Baldy Trail**, and **East Baldy Trail**. Contact Apache Sitgreaves National Forest.

✳ Wilder Places

Apache-Sitgreaves National Forest has a variety of biomes, from ponderosa forests to subalpine meadows that take the look of a coastal rain forest in the wet summer months. All this water makes for excellent trout fishing, wildflower viewing in July and August, fall color from late September into October, and cross-country skiing and snowshoeing in the winter.

✳ Lodging

INNS & LODGES ⊗ 🐾 🐾 ♂ ♿ **The Amberian Peaks Lodge** (928-735-9977 or 800-556-9997). Located at the south end of Main St. The lodge is like a home away from home, providing most electronics—satellite radio, TV, DVD, VHS player, video games, and WiFi—in each room except a phone. Owner Ann Poyas explains that you don't have a choice about people calling you on the phone, but you do have a choice about turning on the TV. Rooms have king or two queen beds, private bath, microwave, and refrigerator. Some rooms have fireplace and/or whirlpool

THE WHITE MOUNTAINS FEATURE FORESTS, MEADOWS, AND LAKES.

tub. Yoga is available three mornings a week; there are also occasional murder mysteries (call for schedule)— both cost extra and are open to the public. Pets are welcome in the cabin. $95–240.

☙ ❦ Molly Butler Lodge (928-735-7226), 109 Main St. This historic lodge is where everything started in the town. Promoted as Arizona's oldest continuously operating lodge, its Longhouse, originally Molly's Bunk House, was built in the early 1900s. The rooms present a country decor with quilts, antiques, and barn wood furnishings, along with individual heat control and bath. If you want a quiet night's sleep, ask for one of the rooms adjacent to the lodge's porch; the activity from Butler's Bar, where many a tall tale has been told, starting with the owner, John Butler, gets lively. Two pets are allowed at $10 each per night. $55–80 for double occupancy; $5 a night for each additional person. Three-night minimum stays for holidays; 2-night minimum for weekends.

BED AND BREAKFASTS **Green Ranch & Stable Company** (928-735-9990), 38753 Hwy 373. The bed, breakfast, and stables cater to families, equestrians, fishermen, hunters, and outdoor lovers. The 5,000 sq ft building, originally a horse barn, has 3 rooms (all with WiFi and TV; 1 with a queen bed and private bath, 1 queen with a shared bathroom; and one with twin beds and a shared bathroom), a large grand room, full kitchen, and a national forest for a backyard. Guests get kitchen privileges, can use the washer and dryer, and can hang out in the grand room. You can rent a room or th whole lodge. Lodge $180 per day; Rooms $51–107 per day or $190–480 per week. Stable space also available for rent.

GUEST RANCH ∞ ❦ ✑ ♿ **Hidden Meadow Ranch** (928-333-1000 or 866-333-4080). This cluster of cabins located deep in the national forest has been likened to a camp for grown-ups. Kids will love it just as much. All your meals and most activities are included

in the price of your stay (horseback riding, archery, arts and crafts); overnight pack trips or fly-fishing outings incur an additional charge. The 10 log cabins—opulent, quiet, and cozy—provide enough of a lure to this serene setting that decompresses you from the outside world. Each cabin has a living room/dining area, wood-burning fireplace, oversized soaking tub, Aveda amenities, locally hand-carved wood furniture, and satellite radio. Three gourmet meals at the Ranch House are included with rates (see *Dining Out*). Two pet-friendly cabins provide dog dishes and fleece mat; proof of current vaccinations must be provided prior to arrival. Horse boarding available. $525–625 for two people in one cabin.

✳ Where to Eat

DINING OUT Amberian Peaks Restaurant (928-735-9977 or 800-556-9997). Located at the south end of Main St. Open for dinner Fri.–Mon. at 5; Memorial Day–Labor Day, breakfast 8–9:30, lunch 11–2:30. The menu lists rich entrées, with an appealing wine selection. Get classics with a twist, like mountain-baked Brie with a fruit compote or fried martini (breaded and deep-fried olives served in a martini glass) for appetizers, or entrées like buffalo steak Diane, chicken Wellington, and osso buco veal shank. Ahi tuna is a favorite, the crème brûlée is a trademark, and the strawberry napoleon "goes out the window" when available. Pizza is a local favorite. Entrées $22–32, pizza $18–22.

& **Molly Butler** (928-735-7226), 109 Main St. Open daily for dinner 5–9; breakfast and lunch served mid-May–Oct. Molly Butler cooked for her guests when she and her husband, John, opened the restaurant more than 90 years ago, and her food was not only known as some of the best around but reasonably priced, too. Things haven't changed in these two regards, and the restaurant continues as an area favorite, to the point that

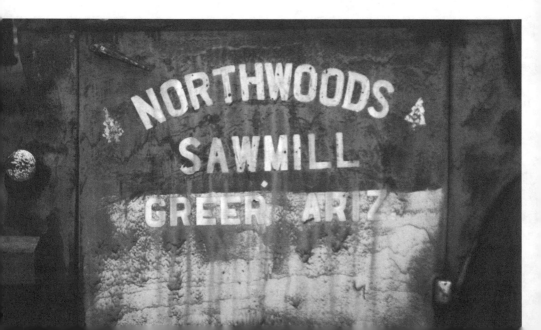

reservations are recommended. The prime rib is excellent, and fresh-baked bread a treat. Entrées $12–27.

The Ranch House (928-333-1000 or 866-333-4080). Open daily for lunch 11:30–2 and dinner 5:30–7 for families, then 7–8:30. The restaurant at Hidden Meadow Ranch (see *Guest Ranch*) opens its doors to nonguests for lunch and dinner if there's room available. Meals are special in this open-room log building, with bold touches that marry well. Pan-seared lump crabcake with avocado-corn salad and sweet chile aioli tastes extraordinary and is a favorite. Steaks and fish are generally excellent. Sides like roasted garlic truffled cream potatoes and campfire Vidalia onions make special accompaniments. Sticky toffee pudding is an unusual treat. Entrées $26–32.

EATING OUT ✿ **Rendezvous Diner** (928-735-7483), 17 Main St. Open Mon. and Wed. 7–4 (till 8 Thu.–Sun.); closed Tue. This local favorite serves up comforting grub that's done right and tastes good. Hamburgers are juicy, chicken-fried steak a favorite,

and pies homemade. The log cabin with a tin roof has loads of old-time memorabilia on the walls. You can eat out on the patio when the weather's right. Entrées $7–13.

✳ Special Events

Call 928-333-2123 for all events.

June: **Greer Days** has a parade, talent show, vendors, food, and drink.

July: **Chamber Music Concert Series and Art Show**. Residents open their home to chamber musicians from around the world.

SPRINGERVILLE, EAGAR, AND THE CORONADO TRAIL

T he two towns of Springerville and Eagar still carry the nickname *Valle Redondo* (Round Valley) given by founder Juan Baca, a Spanish sheepherder. The gorgeous expanse of open space has hills and dales formed by the Springerville Volcanic Field (the third largest of its type in the nation) covered by miles of grasslands that turn emerald in spring and summer after wet weather. Sheep herding, peacefully as it may have begun here in the valley, met with many a bloody battle with cattlemen as settlements developed. History says disputes between the two factions produced more than 50 deaths. Furthermore, bad men who flaunted money freely held a high reputation among the townsfolk, who graciously stayed out of their way. This did not bode well for peace and quiet, to the point that even lawmen wouldn't set foot in the two towns. Perhaps Uncle Pop Pace Wiltbank, who settled in Round Valley in 1879, summed it up the best: "Yah, but the code of living in them days was everybody mind your own business."

Cattle ranching prevailed and ended up having a big influence in the area for several decades. Though it's now on the wane, you may still feel the cowboy spirit in these twin towns—ranching doesn't just get into your blood, it becomes part of your heart and soul.

Springerville and Eagar are the last towns before you round the bend to head south on US 191 into the White Mountains. Once you pass Alpine, accommodations come sparingly, then not at all south of Hannagan Meadow until Clifton. The land along US 191 once dominated by outlaws and cowboys, now makes a place for outdoor lovers to explore. Wild when the cowboys roamed it, the land remains just the same today—if not more so, thanks to the reintroduction of the Mexican grey wolf.

GUIDANCE **Springerville-Eagar Regional Chamber of Commerce** (928-333-2123 or 888-733-2123), 318 E. Main St. Pick up *The Official Driving Tour of the White Mountain Region* here ($9.95 for tape; $15.95 for CD). The tour includes history and sites of the area and all the cultures that inhabited the land, from dinosaurs to outlaws. **Apache-Sitgreaves National Forest** (928-333-4301), 30 S. Chiricahua Dr. (open Mon.–Fri. 8–4:30), has information on backcountry use of the national forest.

GETTING THERE *By car:* You can reach Round Valley from several different directions: Take US 180/191 from the Navajo Nation in the north; US 60 east from New Mexico or west from Show Low; AZ 260 from the towns along the Mogollon Rim; and US 191 (the Coronado Trail) from the south. *By air:* **Springerville Airport** (928-333-5746), 905 W. Airport Rd., has a hard-surfaced, 8,400-foot landing.

WHEN TO COME Lying in the foothills of the White Mountains at almost 7,000 feet, the two towns keep comfortable from spring through fall. High season spans from Memorial to Labor Day, when the White Mountains get the most visitation.

MEDICAL EMERGENCY **White Mountains Regional Medical Center** (928-333-4368; TDB, 928-333-7156), 118 S. Mountain Ave.

✳ To See

Casa Malpais Archaeological Park and Museum (928-333-5375), 318 E. Main St. Open daily 8–4. Tours at 9, 11, and 2 (0.75-mile hike on a gradual climb that takes 1½–2 hours). One of the state's best archaeological sites features an astronomical observatory, great kiva, ancient stairways, and rock art. This museum takes a macrobiotic look at the area with not only artifacts from Casa Malpais ruins but also antiques from pioneer days and ancient relics from the days the dinosaurs reigned. The museum is free; admission to the ruins is $7 adults, $5 seniors 55-plus and students, kids 2 and under are free.

The Little House Museum (928-333-2286), X Diamond Ranch on South Fork Rd. off AZ 260. Open May 15–Labor Day; tour daily at 11 or by appointment. Wink Crigler, granddaughter of Molly Butler, created this small museum as a memorial to her late husband, a championship horse trainer. What started with a roomful of awards and memorabilia grew to a community repository, big on cultural history and packed with historical photos, unique musical instruments, antiques, and mementos from the pioneer days. $3 adults, $1 under 12; free to ranch guests.

A PIONEER WEDDING DRESS ON DISPLAY AT LITTLE HOUSE MUSEUM.

Renee Cushman Art Museum (928-333-4514), Church of the Latter Day Saints, Springerville. By appointment only. The story behind this museum is almost as interesting as its exquisite collection, such as an engraving attributed to Rembrandt, pen drawings by Tiepolo, and other art and furniture dating from the Renaissance to the early 20th century. Though not a member of the church, Cushman, a local rancher, willed the collection to the church as a way of acknowledging her friendship with a bishop who had assisted her in times of need. Free.

SCENIC DRIVES Take any of the nonpaved roads south of AZ 260 or west of US 191 to find extraordinarily scenic countryside of huge mountain meadows, aspen-fir forests, lakes, and streams. Many do not require high clearance or four-wheel drive. Purchase a map of the national forest from Apache-Sitgreaves National Forest. For a paved roadtrip, head south on the **Coronado Trail Scenic Byway**. Once called US 666, the forbidding stigma the triple-digit number implied conjured up a movement to save this segment of highway in Arizona (nicknamed the Devil's Highway) with a new numerical designation (US 191). The dramatic drive, which winds between Springerville and Clifton, doesn't exactly follow the historic route its namesake, Francisco Vásquez de Coronado, took during his 16-day pass through the White Mountains. But the road gets close.

With no services for the second half of the 120 miles, be sure to top off your gas tank and take a lunch or snacks. The scenery is heavenly, but full of devilish hairpin turns (420 by one Forest Service estimate). Take your time and enjoy the scenery.

✳ To Do

FISHING Located just outside the Apache-Sitgreaves National Forest with the most streams and lakes in the Southwest, you can head in practically any direction and find a stream or lake stocked with trout. Head 17 miles north to **Lyman Lake State Park** (928-337-4441) for quiet lake fishing. About 10 miles down US 191, **Nelson Reservoir** draws local residents for stocked rainbow trout, waterfowl, and migrating birds. **X Diamond Ranch** (see *Lodging*) allows five anglers at a time onto its segment of the Little Colorado River. Fees run $30–40 per person for half–full day. You can rent the river for $175. **The Speckled Trout** (928-333-0852), 224 E. Main St., offers guided trout fishing for $135–225 per day and casting/fishing lessons at $35 per hour (2-hour minimum). If you have your own rig and a sense of adventure, head into the Apache-Sitgreaves National Forest. Hot spots are the **West Fork of the Black River** (Thompson Trail), **Big Lake**, and the **West Fork of the Little Colorado River** (West Baldy Trail).

HIKING. Head west to Greer or south on US 191 for the best high-country hiking in the state. Along US 191, check out the first 3 miles of the **KP Trail**, which take you to a waterfall. The **Upper Fish Creek Trail** travels through an aspen-fir forest; the **Bear Wallow Trail** takes you into a remote wilderness.

HORSEBACK RIDING **K5 Outdoor Adventures** (see Reed's Lodge under *Lodging*). **X Diamond Ranch** (928-333-2286), South Fork Rd. The guest ranch offers rides to nonguests, too. You can spend an hour to all day in the saddle. Prices start from $25 an hour.

Contact **Apache-Sitgreaves National Forest** for information on the following.

Bear Wallow Wilderness Area. The Bear Wallow Trail in this wilderness is where guides take big-game hunters in the fall. With that in mind, don't be surprised to find bear tracks (it got its name from the bears that liked to wallow in the creek), mountain lion sign, prints of elk hooves sunken deeply into the trail, and Mexican grey wolf signs.

Blue Range Primitive Area (located south of Alpine and east of US 191). When mountain man James O. Pattie trapped beaver in the area in 1825, he marveled at its clear running streams, lush canyons, and abundant wildlife. Things haven't changed. The Blue, as locals affectionately call it, remains one of the nation's most unaltered areas of backcountry. Because the Blue never transitioned into a wilderness area, it stays out of books and reference pages.

As remote and lonely as the land remains, it has an extensive trail system that makes it highly accessible. Most of the trails have their roots as Indian paths. Later, ranchers developed the paths to run their cattle between the high country in summer and the Blue River in winter. Hikers can go weeks without seeing another human being in the Blue. If you travel any of these trails, bring a map, compass/GPS, layers of clothing, and a sense of adventure. Don't bring your dog. This is wolf country, where man's best friend is fodder for the territorial Mexican grey wolf.

Escudilla Wilderness. Located about 23 miles south on US 191. This small wilderness holds the state's third-highest peak. Two trails travel the area: the 3-mile-long Escudilla National Recreation Trail, which heads up to the top of Escudilla Mountain, and the 4-mile-long Government Trail that takes you on a side path firefighters used when a blaze burned the peak in 1951. Because the fire burned the mixed-conifer forests, aspens grew back with a vengeance. The mountaintop has the best autumn golds in the state.

Sipe White Mountain Wildlife Area (928-367-4281). Located 10 miles south of Eagar on US 191, then about 5 miles off US 191 on a gravel road. Arizona Department of Game and Fish manages this former streamside ranch. Wildlife-watching is big here, and Audubon considers it one of the better birding sites in the area, especially along Rudd Creek.

✳ Lodging

In and near town
🍴 **Reed's Lodge** (928-333-4323 or 800-814-6451), 514 E. Main St., Springerville. Family-owned by local ranchers and one of the favorite accommodations in the area, the lodge offers a rustic exterior with clean, comfortable rooms. Owners Roxanne and Galyn Knight also run

K5 Outdoor Adventures and will take you on guided hikes, SUV tours, and off-the-beaten-path places (all extra) privy to locals who have lived on the land for the last five generations because they like their guests to get to know the area a little deeper than just what you can see from the paved highway. Rooms have TV, phone, air-conditioning, and heat;

some have microwave and refrigerator. Ice is complimentary. $45–60.

Paisley Corner Bed and Breakfast (928-333-4665), 287 N. Main St., Eagar. An attractive restored home that catches your eye as you travel into Springerville keeps its image up on the inside with furnishings fit for the 1910 period in which it was built. Four large rooms have private bath and cable TV. The property has a hot tub and fireplace. Breakfast—always hearty with fruit, egg dish, meat side, and something sweet—is included. $75–95.

∞ ♫ ⟁ **X Diamond & MLY Ranch** (928-333-2286). From Eagar, go 5 miles on AZ 260 to the signed South Fork turnoff. Owner Wink Crigler has family roots on this land along the Little Colorado River that go back to 1890, when her grandparents Molly and John Butler homesteaded it. The property, 30,000 acres of grazing land, offers horseback riding, archaeological ruins you can view and even dig when the curator is on site, a museum, private fishing, and hiking. Wink is passionate about the land and gives several-hour tours of it. Kids will be drawn to the animals: horses, cattle, kittens, and glimpses of the wildlife that frequents the property. The grounds are impeccably kept and colored with wildflowers and several gardens. All of the six guest cabins, modern, neat, and clean, run 1,100–2,600 square feet with large, fully equipped kitchen (you just bring your own food), barbecue grill, and views. Most have wood or gas-burning fireplace, all have satellite TV/DVD and Jacuzzi tub; some have a phone or hot tub. $95–175 for two, $20 for each additional person per night. No pets or ATVs.

White Mountains

🐾 **Blue River Wilderness Retreat** (928-339-4426). Located about 20 miles south of Alpine near the confluence of the Blue River and Campbell Blue Creek and 10 miles from a paved road, this is where you go when you want to get away from it all. Three vintage motor homes and a cabin stand on an original 43-acre homestead in the Apache-Sitgreaves National Forest "not on the way to anywhere," as owner and artist Janie Hoffman describes it. Near three roadless areas and a few minutes' drive from trails in the Blue Range Primitive Area, the property is the perfect place for hikers, birders, and couch potatoes. Units are fully furnished, but bring your own towels and linens. Pets okay (bring a leash in case they make chase with owners' cats); use of corral $10 per night. A $25 cleaning fee is returned if your cabin is left clean. $200–250 a week.

♫ 🐾 **Hannagan Meadow Lodge** (928-339-4370). Located 23 miles south of Alpine on US 191 near mile marker 232. The only accommodations along US 191 between Alpine and Clifton. That's not the only reason to stay at the Hannagan Meadow Lodge. The rustic bed & breakfast, restaurant, and cluster of freestanding cabins are located in a gorgeous sub-alpine meadow. Rooms have antique furniture and private bathrooms. There is also a general store with gas station on the property. Breakfast is included with lodge rooms, but not cabins. Pets can stay in the cabins, but not in winter, and never in rooms. Rooms $65–90 (winter), $70–125 (summer); cabins $125–145 (winter), $150–200 (summer).

✳ Where to Eat

DINING OUT **Blue Bird Café** (928-333-2203), 746 E. Main, Springerville. Open for lunch Mon.–Sat. 11–3. This local favorite serves consistently good food and fresh ingredients from a menu that changes often. The name, inspired from the Bluebird of Happiness, stands for the simple things in your own backyard that give you pleasure (like their backyard patio). Luncheon fare includes salads, soups, and sandwiches. They serve French roast coffee, PG Tips English tea, and San Pellegrino sparkling mineral water and sodas. Homemade desserts include excellent pies. Entrées $7.25.

Café Beate (928-339-1965), 41633 US 180, Nutrioso. Open for dinner Apr.–Dec., Wed.–Sun. 4–8; Feb.–Mar., Sat.–Sun. 4–8; closed Jan. German-born Beate and Joerg make everything from scratch at their café, from sausage to dessert. Joerg does most of the cooking. Everything is splendid, and the locals know it. You usually cannot get a table as a walk-in; reservations are highly advised, especially in summertime. Favorites include sauerbraten, schnitzels, and sausage. At the time of this writing, alcohol is not available, but you can bring your own bottle of wine. Entrées $5.65–15.25.

EATING OUT **Java Blues Coffee Bar & Bistro** (928-333-5282), 341 E. Main St., Springerville. Open Mon.–Fri. 5 AM–7 PM, Sat. 6 AM–7 PM (11 if there's entertainment), Sun. 7–3. A meld of local diner, living room, and blues bar, this coffee bar has turned into all things to all people. You'll see everything from flip-flops to cowboy boots here as you sip on some of the best coffee this side of the Little Colorado River. Breakfast, lunch, and dinner served. Beverages include espresso drinks, smoothies, beer, wine, and the plain old cup o' java. Entertainment (most weekends) often includes well-known blues names. Free WiFi and Internet access. Breakfast $4.50–6.25, lunch $4.95–6.75, dinner $7.75–15.95.

✳ Special Events

Call 928-333-2123 for all events.

June: **Chrome in the Dome Classic Car Show** features classic cars, vendors, food, and live radio.

July: **4th of July Celebration** includes a parade, rodeo, barbecue, and fireworks.

August: **Eagar Daze** has a number of fun events that includes an ice cream social, talent show, youth rodeo, and logging activities, as well as vendors and food. **Valle Redondo Fat Tire Diesta Mountain Bike Festival** has trail rides, bike rodeo, and dinner.

December: **Electric Light Parade, White Mountain Historical Society Home Tour and Tea,** and **Christmas Eve Community Luminaria Lighting**.

SAFFORD

No longer willing to suffer the impetuous flooding of the Gila River, ranchers headed up the river valley in 1874, settled the first Anglo townsite, and called it Safford, after a visiting governor. The settlers worked the land and had a ready market for their goods in the mining country of Morenci just up river; life was good. Farmers and merchants in the mid-1870s pieced together a ragtag route called the Safford–Morenci Trail to pack their goods to the mining country.

Safford and the towns around have always ebbed and flowed with the activity of the mines. When the mines prospered, so did they. When layoffs came, the towns tightened their belts. Lately, the mines are prospering again, and life is bubbly along the Old West Highway.

Out in these parts life is down-home and grassroots. The restaurants have old-timer regulars lined up along the counter drinking their cups of Joe, shooting the breeze like they do every morning 'bout this time. You find that special something for your home from a thrift shop instead of a gift shop. The backcountry usually has little or no trace of the managing agency that supervises the land; exploring comes free in these parts.

Out here, the old-fashioned version of Arizona's independent spirit full of guts and gumption shows through in all its classic glory. They don't call US 70, the road along which Safford lies, the Old West Highway for nothing. The farther out in the country you travel, the more you, correctly, get the feeling things haven't changed all that much. The area oozes so much atmosphere and tradition, it's practically hallowed. Things sure are peaceful here. This calm assurance seems unusual for such a rough-and-tumble spot so full of raucous times and personalities. But a land this rich in culture often exudes such a soothing coziness —especially when the land itself remains unchanged and holds on to its history.

GUIDANCE **Graham County Chamber of Commerce** (928-428-2511 or 888-837-1841), 1111 W. Thatcher Blvd., has information about the town, area activities, and yearly events. **Bureau of Land Management Safford Field Office** (928-348-4400), 711 14th Ave., has information on public lands around the area. **Safford Ranger District** (928-428-4150) can tell you about backcountry use on Mount Graham. **Clifton Ranger District** (928-687-1301) has information on the backcountry north of Clifton.

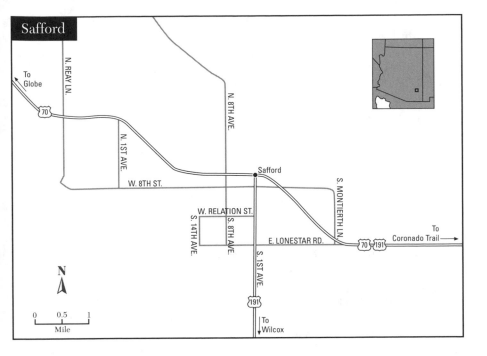

GETTING THERE *By car:* From Phoenix, go east on US 60 and US 70. *By air:* **Safford Municipal Airport** (928-348-0005), 4550 E. Aviation Way, has two well maintained paved runways, tie-downs for transient aircraft, a heliport, and 24/7 fuel service.

WHEN TO COME Safford has a lower Sonoran Desert climate—hot summers and mild winters. With so many outdoor enticements, it's best to plan your trip to match the activity. If you plan your activities on Mount Graham, wait until summer.

MEDICAL EMERGENCY **Mt. Graham Community Hospital** (520-348-4000), 1600 20th Ave.

✳ To See

Discovery Park (928-428-6260). Open evenings 6–10 on Fri. and 4–10 on Sat. Features the Governor Aker Observatory and its 20-inch reflecting telescope and Camera Obscura, as well as an exhibit gallery, gift shop, and educational facilities. A 20-minute simulated ride on the Shuttlecraft *Polaris* takes a "look" at the planets and their moons. $5 adults, $3 ages 6–11; under 6 with ticketed adult, free; train ride $3; *Polaris* Space Flight Simulator $6. You can pick up tickets for tours ($20) to the **Mount Graham International Observatory**, which take place Saturdays from early May until mid-Nov., as weather permits. Tours take you up Mount Graham and elucidate geology and natural and cultural history. At the observatory, you can see the Vatican Advanced Technology telescope, the Heinrich Hertz Sumillimeter Telescope, and the Large Binocular Telescope, the world's most powerful.

Fort Grant Historical Museum (928-828-3393). Located at the end of AZ 266 (go about 20 miles south of Safford on US 191, turn west onto AZ 266, and go 21 miles to Fort Grant). Open Mon.–Fri. 8–5. The drive alone is a scenic foray into the high-desert country full of unique boulders. The museum, a hidden-away cache of military items and photos and information about its history as a state reformatory and state prison, date back to the late 1800s. Free.

Pima Museum (928-485-9400), Main and US 70, Pima. Open Wed.–Fri. 2–4, Sat. 1–5. This great little museum has an interesting collection of displays from pioneer days to the present. You'll also find Native peoples artifacts from the region, an automotive display, and an agricultural museum. Donations accepted.

SCENIC DRIVES **Black Hills Backcountry Byway**. Contact the Bureau of Land Management. Located off US 70 east of Safford. Scenic and totally undeveloped, this 21-mile route winds through a countryside full of history and geology. If you like to rockhound, check out the Black Hills Rockhound Area. You may find some prized specimens of fire agate. High-clearance vehicles are recommended on this graded route.

Old West Highway, which starts at Apache Junction and travels on US 60 to Globe, then continues to Safford on US 70, takes you even deeper into the countryside and another 47 miles to Duncan at the New Mexico border. Check out the town of Virden on NM 92, then loop back on US 70.

Swift Highway. Contact the Safford Ranger District. Located off US 191, about 9 miles south of Safford. The 35-mile mostly paved road takes you up to the top reaches of Mount Graham. You travel through several different biomes, from desert to subalpine. It's full of hairpin turns and beautiful vistas.

Three Way. Take a look at where the Safford merchants sold their products by heading east on US 70, then north on US 191 to Three Way (a place on the map, not a town). Continue north to Clifton and Morenci. On the way back, take AZ 75 to US 70 and stop at Gimee's for a hamburger or classic Mexican food.

✳ To Do

BIRDING There are a number of hidden gems around Safford—ranging from wild and scenic to local ponds and lakes—where you can catch avian activity.

Cluff Ranch (928-485-9430) is located 10 miles west of Safford. Take US 70 northwest to Pima, turn left onto Main St., then left onto Cluff Ranch Rd. Open 24 hours. The ranch, maintained by the Arizona Department of Game and Fish, lies in the foothills of Mount Graham and presents several different habitats that attract a number of different species. The road leads to several ponds with trails that travel riparian woodlands. Free.

Discovery Park. The small pond behind the Graveyard Wash flood-control structure has a stand of cottonwood and willow trees that attract waterfowl, hummingbirds, hawks, falcons, and a number of neotropical migrants.

Gila Box Riparian National Conservation Area (NCA). More than 140 species of birds have been sighted here, including the common black-hawk, zone-tailed hawk, and yellow-billed cuckoo. Over 70 species nest right along the creek.

Roper Lake State Park. Park rangers and local birders post a daily list of birds sighted recently. Some of the more interesting you might spot there are brown pelican, black-crowned night-heron, and least bittern.

CULTURE Mexican roots go deep around here, and the town celebrates them with **The Salsa Trail**. Get a map at the Graham County Chamber of Commerce and visit a chile farm, a tortilla factory, and a handful of restaurants that serve this state's cultural favorite Mexican food.

FISHING Roper Lake State Park. In the cooler weather, bait your rig for rainbow trout and largemouth bass. Summer stocks include catfish.

HIKING Mount Graham. Check out the 5.1-mile **Arcadia Trail** for some great viewpoints. In summer follow the first few miles of the **Ash Creek Trail**. Or head up US 191 to the **Painted Cliffs** or **Spur Ranch Trails** (contact the Clifton Ranger District).

HOT SPRINGS Located on a lava field, the Safford area has several hot springs—all of different demeanor—where you can go soak yourself. Some require you bring your own towel, so come prepared if you plan to partake of the mineral water therapy. **Essence of Tranquility** (928-428-9312), 6074 S. Lebanon Loop. Open Mon. 2–9, Tue.–Sat. 8–9 (till 7 Sun.). The original owners of these hot springs called them "Lebanon" after the biblical Pools of Lebanon, where an angel occasionally agitated the waters and the sick and lame could get healed if they got into the pool when the waters stirred. The premises have six separate pools ranging from 103 to 106 degrees, and they still, many say, hold the healing powers of the Pools of Lebanon. Owner Clarrise Drake attributes healings to faith and the fact that the water has a lot of sodium, which draws out poisons and stress. Her spa's popularity comes from not only the water's health benefits but also its "funkified," homey atmosphere with plastic flowers and kitschy curios, decorative outside lights, and cozy sitting areas scattered around the spa's grounds. $5 per soak; bring your own towels. Camping, tepees, and casitas are available (see *Lodging*) for overnight stays. Body treatments (massage, reflexology, herbal detox wraps, hot mineral baths, herbal sea salt full-body scrub) are available.

Hot Well Dunes Recreation Area. Contact the Bureau of Land Management. Drive 7 miles east on US 70; turn south (right) onto Haekel Rd., and proceed 25 miles to the area. The road is well graded but not paved. Located 25 miles south of Safford, hidden in a gallery of mesquite trees surrounded by desert, the recreation area offers a wilder hot-springs experience. The 106-degree water flows at 250 gallons per minute from a well discovered by accident. Drillers seeking for oil instead hit a pocket of hot water 1,920 feet under the sand. From its two outdoor tubs, soakers can view the rolling sand dunes and the jagged peaks of the Peloncillo Mountains in the distance. One tub sits in the shade of a giant tamarisk; the other basks in the sun. At night bathers soak under a canopy of stars. And since you're surrounded by 2,000 acres of sand dunes, it's almost like a day at the beach. Picnic tables and camping available. Bring your own towels. $5 per vehicle per day.

Roper Lake State Park. See *Wilder Places*.

Kachina Mineral Springs (928-428-7212), 1155 W. Cactus Rd. Open Mon.–Sat. 9–4. Located at the base of Mount Graham in an area called Artesia because of its many free-flowing hot springs, Kachina Mineral Springs is fed by a hot thermal pool bubbling with 108-degree water. The spa has a large communal tub and several private mineral baths, which pour into Roman-style tubs cleaned and scrubbed after each use. You can also receive a body massage, sweat wrap, and/or foot reflexology treatment (reservations required) at very reasonable prices. $10 per person for a soak; treatments $55–90.

MINE TOUR ✿ **Morenci Copper Mine** (877-646-8687). Located 54 miles east of Safford. Tours are offered Fri.–Sat. at 9 and 1. You get a blend of information and entertainment when you hop on the $2 million haul truck normally used to carry about 270 tons of copper ore to take the 3-hour guided tour in the world's largest open-pit copper mine. The decommissioned truck has 12-foot-high tires and looks every bit like the ones still hauling raw ore for processing. Tours cost $8 for adults, $6 for seniors, $4 ages 9–17 (under 9 years old not allowed).

✳ Wilder Places

Gila Box Riparian National Conservation Area (NCA). Contact the Bureau of Land Management. Open 24 hours every day. The west end is located 20 miles northeast of Safford: Go east on US 70, then north on Sanchez Rd. near the town of Solomon; follow the road until the pavement ends, then continue on a graded road, following GILA BOX signs. The NCA contains 15 miles of Bonita Creek and 23 miles of the Gila River. Bonita Creek presents a beautiful riparian canopy of cottonwood, sycamore, walnut, ash, and mesquite trees in a narrow high-walled canyon. Beaver ponds pool the creek water. The Gila River is more open walled. A wildlife-viewing deck overlooks the confluence of the creek and river. If you explore along Bonita Creek, there's a good chance you'll see bear sign, if not bruin and javelina. Along the Gila, watch for hawks, eagles, and bighorn sheep. Free.

Mount Graham. The Pinaleño Mountain range, where Mount Graham is located, has a rich cache of wildlife and biological diversity. Scientists call the mountains a biologically unique area because 18 species and subspecies of plants and animals found here exist nowhere else on the planet. The diversity comes from the sky island principle; the range rises almost 8,000 feet above the desert floor. Its highest peak (and highest in southern Arizona), 10,720-foot Mount Graham, contains more life zones than any other single mountain in North America. Cacti cover the base of the mountains, and pine-oak forests the mid-section. Ponderosa pines blanket the upper realms, and old-growth fir and aspen forests on the mountains' tops. When you plan a visit to the Pinaleño Mountains, stay in their lowlands in winter, and head for the peaks in summer.

🐾 🏊 **Roper Lake State Park** (928-428-6760), 101 E. Roper Lake Rd. Open daily 6 AM–10 PM. The pleasant park has a lake stocked with fish, mineral hot springs, campground, restrooms, and showers. Ranger-led hikes provide information about the area and Native American petroglyphs and ruins in the park. $5 per car, $2 per bicycle. Camping $12–15 nonelectric, $19–25 electric.

❋ Lodging

INNS & LODGES 🏊 **Pioneer Lodge** (928-428-0733), 2919 US 70, Thatcher. Recently remodeled rooms have retained a rustic demeanor, which makes the lodge a little homier than a generic motel. Rooms have double beds, phones, cable TV, and dial-up Internet access; kitchenettes include two standard beds, full-sized refrigerator, stove, and sink. $40 and up.

BED AND BREAKFASTS **Olney House Bed and Breakfast** (928-428-5118 or 800-814-5118), 1104 Central Ave. The only B&B in the area was built in 1890 and is listed on the National Register of Historic Buildings as one of the finest examples of Western Colonial Revival architecture in the Southwest. The innkeepers, both retired from the US Air Force, have a veritable museum with all kinds of interesting memorabilia, antiques, and historic anecdotes about the home's first owner, Sheriff Olney. Breakfast included. No pets. $65–85 for two; $10 for each extra person.

OTHER LODGING **Essence of Tranquility Casitas and Camping** (928-428-9312), 6074 S. Lebanon Loop. After you've taken a soak in Clarice's

mineral tubs (see *To Do*), you'll probably appreciate the fact she has two casitas, several tepees, and space for tent camping to rest your wet-noodle-like body. The casitas have double and queen beds, microwave, mini refrigerator, air-conditioning, and heat. The tepees have cots and lights. You supply the shelter for the tent camping, but Clarice supplies a community kitchen and game room. Casitas $50–60, tepees and tent camping $15 per person.

🐾 🏊 **Roper Lake State Park Cabins** (928-428-6760). You're not exactly roughing it in these cabins, but you do need to bring your own bedsheets or sleeping bags. They're relatively new, with bunk beds or full-sized bed with mattress, and have a spacious, homey feel. But they don't have electricity, and open flames from candles and stoves are not permitted in the cabins. Each cabin has a charcoal grill and picnic table and lies within a short walk of the park's restrooms and showers. $35; pets $5 extra per night.

❋ Where to Eat

DINING OUT **The Branding Iron** (928-428-7427), 2344 N. Branding Iron Lane. Open Mon.–Thu. 5–9 (10 Fri.–Sat.). This local favorite serves up some pretty good steaks (and a great view of the sunset). Check out their specials: $1.25 tacos on Mondays, prime rib on Wednesdays, and ribs on Saturdays. Entrées $6.95–16.95.

El Chorro (928-428-4134), 601 W. Main St. Open Mon.–Thu. 11–3:30, Fri.–Sat.11–9:30. Located in the historic Reynolds & Jeters Building, this is the oldest continually owned and operated restaurant in the Gila Valley. They've been serving the green chili since 1955. The cook has worked here since the 1970s. History also shows up in the dishes, inasmuch as the older Hispanics often comment that the food tastes homemade, like it did when they were kids. The favorite is the *chalaca*, a fried masa bowl filled with beans and red or green chili, then topped with cheese, onions, and lettuce. $4.25–12.50.

La Paloma (928-428-2094), 5183 E. Clifton St., Solomon. Open for lunch and dinner Mon.–Thu. 10:30–8 (till 9 Fri.–Sat.). Located a few miles down the highway from Safford, this Mexican restaurant draws a following for a reason—fine food and service at great prices. All the food is good, and there's always a daily special. $4.99–9.45.

✳ Special Events

February: **Eastern Arizona Old-Time Fiddle Contest** (888-837-1841) presents fiddlers of all ages who compete for prizes.

May: **Gila Valley Family Festival** (888-837-1841) features a street fair, a classic car show, entertainment, and tours of the Mount Graham telescopes.

July: **Pioneer Days** (928-428-2511) includes a rodeo.

September: **Gila Valley Cowboy Poetry and Music Gathering** (888-837-1841) at the Graham County Fair Grounds draws cowboy poets, storytellers, and singers to a starlight concert followed by campfire jam session, performances, cowboy breakfast and barbecue, and Cowboy Church. **Graham County Fair** (928-428-7180) is a multiday celebration with animals, entertainment, competitions, and food. **Harvest Festival** (928-348-8514) has food, arts and crafts, and a fresh farmer's market.

November: **Cowboy Christmas Arts & Crafts Show** (928-428-5990) has more than 50 vendors at the Graham County Fairgrounds.

December: **Light Parade** (928-428-7435) in downtown Safford.

Southern Arizona 4

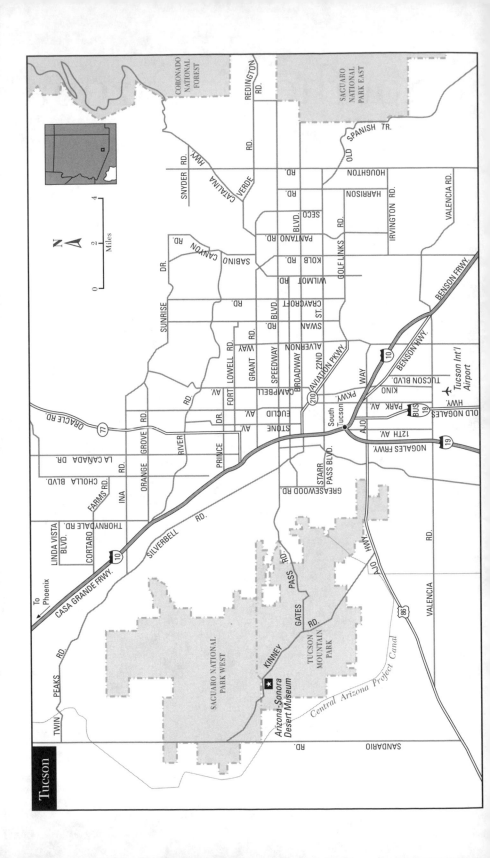

TUCSON

Dressed in Spanish and Mexican architecture, with a Wild West spirit and a Native American soul, Tucson brings visitors back to the state's cultural roots. The desert city, wrapped in mountain panoramas and natural Sonoran Desert scenes, takes visitors as close to the Wild West as they want to comfortably get or as far out into interstellar space as a telescope can take them.

Comfort is the key word here in Tucson, where even the toniest of resorts and restaurants add the word *casual* to *dressy* when defining their dress codes. The town's comfortable with its culture, cares about its surrounding landscape, and knows it has the edge when it comes to independent thinking. Many of its best businesses are homegrown independents that rack up awards and kudos.

As one of the oldest cities in the state, Tucson has blended tolerance with wisdom and comes up with a likable personality akin to that of a doting grandmother who can't do enough to make you comfortable but is able to teach you a new thing or two. The city, like much of southern Arizona, has been around the block a few times. Tucson has seen flags of three different countries and both sides of the Mason-Dixon Line during the Civil War flapping in its breeze.

Long before politics, the first signs of inhabitants roamed the area when mammoths did between 12,500 and 6,000 BC. Next, the Cochise culture built pit houses. By AD 300 the Hohokam farmed the valley. Spanish missionaries came on the scene in 1692 and built the Presidio of St. Augustin a year before the nation's founding fathers signed off on the Declaration of Independence. Tucson changed hands from Spanish adobe village to part of Mexico after the Mexican Revolution of 1821. Looking for railroad land, the United States negotiated the Gadsden Purchase, and Tucson finally flew the U.S. flag when Arizona became a territory in 1854. Of course, not all Washingtonians liked the idea. Some suggested the United States pay Mexico to take Arizona back, at double the original price.

Tucson spent a decade as the territorial capital but never could wrangle the title back after Arizona became a state. This ended up working for them, inasmuch as Tucson has always been able to favor the land and its culture over development. The result is a reputation as one of the state's most livable cities full of personality and a lot of soul.

GUIDANCE **Metropolitan Tucson Convention & Visitors Bureau** (520-624-1817 or 800-638-8350), 100 S. Church Ave. Open Mon.–Fri. 8–5, Sat.–Sun. 9–4.

A complete source for information on southern Arizona, from maps to brochures to magazine guides. The **Coronado National Forest** (520-388-8300), 300 W. Congress St., has recreation opportunity guides and sells maps of each ranger district managing the national forest surrounding the city.

GETTING THERE *By car:* I-10 travels through the city's west side. *By air:* **Tucson International Airport** (520-573-8000), 7250 S. Tucson Blvd., is served by 11 airlines, including American, Continental, Delta, Northwest, Southwest, and United. *By bus:* **Greyhound Bus Station** (520-792-3475), 475 W. Congress St. *By train:* **Amtrak** (520-623-4442), 400 E. Toole Ave. Check out this cool station even if you don't plan to use the rails.

GETTING AROUND Tucson's transit system, **Sun Tran** (520-792-9222), will get you around the town's major streets and to or from the airport. The downtown area has the free **Tucson Inner City Express Transit** (TICET). The **road bicycle** is big here, and drivers honor the bicycle's legal right to the road.

WHEN TO COME The weather is sensational from Oct. through Mar. High season runs Jan. through Apr. In summer, however, you get exceptional deals on resorts, golf, and spas. Surrounding mountains make cool getaways.

MEDICAL EMERGENCY Dial 911.

✷ To See

Arizona-Sonora Desert Museum (520-883-1380), 2021 N. Kinney Rd. Open every day of the year 8:30–5 (Oct.–Feb.), 7:30–6 (Mar.–Sep.). The Desert Museum has more than 300 species of native wildlife and 1,300 varieties of desert plants in exhibits designed to replicate natural habitats. Paths wind through Cat Canyon, Riparian Corridor, and a number of botanically correct habitats, from desert to woodland, that include the animals that dwell within. The Raptor Free Flight program demonstrates the natural inclinations of raptors in the Sonoran Desert. $9.95 adults, $1.75 ages 6–12; under 6 free.

♿ **Arizona Historical Society Museum** (520-770-1473), 140 N. Stone Ave. Open Tue.–Fri. 10–4. The Arizona Historical Society has several museums around the state, and a few in the city. This one has exhibits of life in 1870 Tucson; a history of medicine, including culture and science; the evolution of transportation in Tucson; and a Mining Hall. Donations accepted.

♿ **Arizona State Museum/University of Arizona** (520-621-6302), Park Ave. and University Blvd., University of Arizona campus. Open Mon.–Sat. 10–5, Sun. noon–5. The highly regarded, and oldest, anthropology museum in the nation features Southwest and northern Mexico cultures. The displays come from more than a century of research, and include the Wall of Pottery, the largest whole vessel collection of Southwest Indian pottery in the world. The museum rotates displays to showcase ancient and contemporary Native American culture. You won't find a better archaeological research center, with the world's top resident scholars and displays. $3 per person.

El Tiradito—**The Wishing Shrine**. Located on Main Ave. just south of Cushing St. in downtown Tucson. There are hundreds of shrines in Arizona, and many around Tucson. This particular one, however, comes with a promise. Legend has it that if, when you make a wish and light a candle, your candle stays lit through the night, you'll get your wish. Be careful what you wish for. Free.

Mission San Xavier del Bac (520-294-2624), 1950 W. San Xavier Rd. Open daily 8–5. The meld of Moorish, Byzantine, and late Mexico Renaissance styles in the mission is as delightful as it is captivating: angels, peering from the ceiling, wear checkered and striped skirts; statues wear real clothes; and deep, vivid colors—predominantly red, blue, and gold—splash across the ceiling and walls like a richly woven tapestry. The mission, built in 1783, is the oldest original building in the United States. Pilgrimages are common here; Masses are celebrated each Sunday. Donations accepted.

Old Tucson Studios (520-883-0100), 201 S. Kinney Rd. Coined Hollywood in the Desert, this working movie set was originally built in 1939 for the movie *Arizona*. Since then more than 200 films have been made here, including Lone Ranger films and *Tombstone*. The theme park features a re-creation of an 1880s frontier town with townsfolk dressed in period outfits reenacting life in the lawless Arizona Territory. $16.95 adults, $10.95 under 12.

♿ **Tohono Chul Park** (520-742-6455), 7366 N. Paseo del Norte. Open daily 8–5; Exhibit Hall, museum shops, and greenhouse 9–5; tearoom 8–5. The park weaves a mix of nature, art, and culture with botanical gardens, an Exhibit Hall in a renovated historic home, and excellent breakfast, lunch, or afternoon tea in the tearoom. You can shop in the greenhouse and museum shops. $5 adults, $4 seniors (62 and over), $3 students, $2 ages 5–12; free for members and children under 5.

Tucson Botanical Gardens (520-326-9686), 2150 N. Alvernon Way. As you tour its specialty gardens, you can see that this garden is big on education, with interactive touch carts allowing you to handle props about the desert. Horticulturists and gardeners interface with the public, a feature that makes you feel like you're talking to your next-door neighbor who happens to be an expert. Don't let the summer heat keep you from visiting this garden. During those hot days and warm nights the plants go nuts, especially during monsoon season. The garden gets a huge increase in butterflies during that time. $5 adults, $2.50 ages 6–12; children 5 and under free.

MEXICO Tucson is located only 60 miles north of the Mexican border on I-19, where mileposts are measured in kilometers rather than miles. You can simply drive down to Nogales (Arizona) park and walk across the border to shops and restaurants.

If you want to visit with a guided tour, **La Ruta de Sonora** (520-886-6555 or 800-806-0766) presents interesting trips to the borderlands, Gulf of Mexico, and into Mexico with an emphasis on the culture, landscape, and people. **Gray Line Tours** (520-622-8811 or 800-276-1528), 3594 E. Lincoln St., features a **Nogales Culinary Tour** where local celebrity chef Warren Weekes turns personal guide on a "true insider's look" into Nogales that includes local history, lore, facts, and food. $80 per person.

TIPS FOR VISITING MEXICO

- Drink bottled water, especially outside major tourist areas. Avoid eating fruits and vegetables from street vendors. However, these foods are generally safe at larger restaurants.
- The Mexican peso conversion runs approximately 11 pesos per U.S. dollar. However, merchants usually accept U.S. dollars, and many establishments accept major credit cards.
- Bartering is still a major part of the fun of shopping in Mexico. Compare prices before you start bargaining, and be ready to walk away if you want the best price.
- Carry proper identification with you, such as a birth certificate, voter registration card, current passport, military ID, alien resident card, or a notarized affidavit of citizenship.
- If you plan to drive in Mexico, buy Mexican insurance and carry proof of ownership of your car. If you rent a vehicle, make certain the rental car company allows it to go into Mexico.
- Bring cash to pay for gasoline. Mexican gas stations do not accept credit cards.
- If you are driving in Mexico, note that *alto* means "stop," and *peligro* means "danger." Also, Mexico has a few driving customs that are different than in the States. For instance, a left-turn signal doesn't necessarily mean the driver will turn left; it could also signal the driver behind that it's safe to pass.
- Safety decreases exponentially when you drive after dark.
- Pets are usually allowed into Mexico with verification of rabies vaccination within the last 6 months.
- Guns are not allowed.
- To reenter the United States, American citizens/residents must declare citizenship and purchases. Merchandise up to $400 per person is duty-free. You can bring back 1 quart of liquor and one carton of cigarettes duty-free. Purchases exceeding $400 will be taxed.
- You cannot bring back birds, natural wildlife and plants, unpacked food, fireworks, firearms, whale bones, or coral.

SCENIC DRIVES The preeminent road to scenery (and high-country cool) is the **General Hitchcock Highway**, locally known as the road to Mount Lemmon. Next, check out the saguaros taking Speedway all the way west up **Gates Pass** (the quintessential sunset vista) and then through the Saguaro National Forest—West.

THE ROAD TO MOUNT LEMMON.

✳ To Do

CAVE TOUR ✎ **Colossal Cave Mountain Park** (520-647-7275). Located off I-10 at exit 279. The cave has long wooed geology lovers, especially since the discovery of a chamber called La Tetera, which one researcher described as much more colorful than Karchner with "colors that are almost Disneyesque." The cave also drew robbers and other characters in decades past as a perfect hideout. A 45-minute tour that travels about 0.5 mile and includes 363 steps will give you information on the cave's natural, nefarious, and curious history. The after-hours Candle Tour experiences the cave by candlelight. Reservations are necessary. The Wild Cave Tour (for the physically fit) travels in the dark through rarely seen passageways that extend 0.25 mile deeper into the earth. The park also features a butterfly garden, a desert tortoise exhibit, a mining sluice that bags you gemstones and fossils, and an analemmatic (horizontal) sundial. You can camp in the park's picnic area. Trail rides are available. $5 per car. Tours $8.50 adults, $5 ages 6–12; under 6 free.

GAMING Casino del Sol (800-344-9435), 5655 W. Valencia. The Pascua Yaqui tribe's casinos features Mediterranean architecture, a fresh-air atmosphere, a 4,400-seat outdoor amphitheater, and restaurants. The casino has 1,300 state-of-the-art slot machines with the highest payout in the state and a 12-table poker room with tournaments.

Casino of the Sun (800-344-9435), 7474 S. Camino del Oeste. Another Pascua Yaqui tribe casino. This one has 400 slot machines, a live poker room, a 900-seat bingo hall, and big promotions for members, from cars to cash. An all-you-can-eat buffet attracts out-the-door lines.

Desert Diamond Casino (520-393-2700), I-19 and Pima Mine Rd. A Tohono O'odham Nation casino with slot machines, live keno and poker, a 2,000-seat entertainment center, and gourmet dining at **Agave restaurant and lounge**.

DOG PARKS 🐾 **Christopher Columbus Park** (520-791-4873), 4600 N. Silverbell. Open dawn–dusk. Enclosed area with Fido Fountain, scrambling area, shaded area with ramada, and pooper scooper dispenser.

🐾 **Palo Verde Park** (520-791-5930), 300 S. Mann Ave. Enclosed area (5-foot chain-link fence) for dogs with picnic tables, trash cans, doggy drinking fountain, and pooper scooper dispenser.

GOLF Arizona National Golf Club (520-749-3636), 9777 E. Sabino Greens Dr. Listed among top courses regionally and nationally, the former Raven Golf Club at Sabino Springs gives you a run for your money with challenges and decisions, as well as beautiful scenery in the Santa Catalina Mountain foothills. Robert Trent Jones Jr. designed the course to meld with the natural ruggedness of the land across arroyos and around craggy cliffs. Tee boxes show off views into Mexico. This is where the University of Arizona men's and women's collegiate golf teams play. $135–165.

The Gallery Golf Club at Dove Mountain (520-744-2555), 14000 N. Dove Mountain Blvd., Marana. If you can get in on the limited public time slots available, you will be playing where world championship games take place on courses designed exclusively for this club. The original **North Course** has a dramatic elevation change that gets up into the canyon. Its greens contour a bit differently, and they're loaded with 105 bunkers. The **South Course** is where championship games take place. Not exactly links style, the greens structure has a turtleback design—elevated off the fairway with a lot of possible roll-offs. Soft spikes okay, no denim, and shirts must have collars. Fees include cart and practice balls. $75 (summer)–195.

La Paloma Country Club (520-299-1500), 3666 E. Sunrise Dr. The premier luxury greens operated by Troon Golf touts an armload of awards, including one for being woman-friendly. The 27-hole Jack Nicklaus Signature golf course comprising the **Ridge**, **Canyon**, and **Hill Courses** spreads amid undulating foothills sheltering century-old saguaro cacti and showing off spectacular panoramic mountain vistas. PGA and LPGA golf staff professionals are available for private lessons; complete full-swing and short-game schools are available upon request. **La Paloma Dining Room** eyes the 19th hole. $50–75.

Starr Pass Country Club & Spa (520-670-0400), 3645 W. Starr Pass Blvd. This course goes back a couple of decades and has hosted some of the world's best golfers on its meticulous greens, including Arnold Palmer, Phil Mickelson, Payne Stewart, and Nancy Lopez. The course, part of a 27-hole Arnold Palmer Signature Golf Facility, has some features meant to challenge PGA Tour's great players. Back in the course's PGA days, hole 3 was ranked the most difficult hole on the PGA Tour in 1996, and hole 5 was ranked in the Top 5 Most Difficult. Bunkers and undulating greens remind you that the bogeyman is alive and well at this historic course. The three nines are named for the wildlife that has shown up at each one: **Rattler**, **Roadrunner**, and **Coyote**. $89–181.50.

Tucson Omni (520-297-2271), 727 W. Club Dr. Host to the PGA Tour's Tucson Open since 1976, this 36-hole desert course offers plenty of challenge. The pros rank the 18th hole (No. 9 on the Gold Course) as one of the most challenging finishing holes on the tour. The complicated shot—465 yards with water on both sides of the tee shot—has been the deciding factor of several tours. If you want a good score here, plan well on this par-4 trickster. Golf professionals and instructors provide playing tips and individual lessons. Long- and short-game practice areas, golf shop, and equipment rental available. $65–180.

Vistoso Golf Club (520-797-9900), 955 W. Vistoso Highlands Dr. This par-72 Tom Weiskopf course is carved right out of the mountains and is described as desert golf at its finest. Known for its outstanding course conditions and attention to detail, it always ends up on best-of lists, such as *Golf Digest*'s Best Public Course in Tucson as well as the Top 100 Places to Play. The Tucson Open Pro-Am, USGA Mid-Amateur Championship, and PGA Section Championship are played here. Dress code requires men to wear shirts with sleeves and collar; sleeveless is allowed for woman, as are midthigh shorts for men and women; no denim; nonmetal spikes only. Putting and chipping greens. $49–169.

HIKING Surrounded by four mountain ranges with several designated wilderness areas, this town is one great place to make a base camp if you like to hike. See *Wilder Places* for information.

HORSEBACK RIDING **Spanish Trail Outfitters** (520-825-1664), 8500 E. Ocotillo Dr. Rides are led by entertaining wranglers who impart fun and interesting facts about the Sonoran Desert. You travel a private trail system that winds through a particularly lush and pristine area of the Sonoran Desert, including streams, mesquite bosques, and stands of saguaro cactus. Watchable wildlife is big, especially during early-morning and evening rides. Of special interest are stops at ancient Hohokam village sites. $35–55 per person for 1–2 hours. Must be over 7 years old.

Walking Winds Stables at Hilton Tucson El Conquistador Golf & Tennis Resort (520-742-4422), 10000 N. Oracle Rd. One of the top stables in the basin takes you into the Coronado National Forest to secluded desert trails. You'll ride through saguaro cactus forests and past interesting rock formations while learning all about the fascinating Sonoran Desert. Call for reservations and prices.

MOUNTAIN BIKING Among all those mountains ranges ringing the city travel perfect single- and doubletrack trails. **Saguaro National Park—West** (520-733-5158) is a favorite. The trails in the **Santa Catalina Mountains** are long and steep, taking you more than 4,000 feet from the desert floor to the pine country. There are several wilderness areas that will keep you off these trails, however. You can purchase national forest maps from **Coronado National Forest** (520-670-4552). If you want to stay in town, **Fantasy Island** (Irvington and Houghton rds.) has a network of hand-built trails that twist and turn across the desert landscape on a tract of state trust land. Be sure to purchase a permit at the Arizona State Land office (520-628-5480), 233 N. Main, open 8–4:30. It costs $15 for an annual permit to carry and a hang tag for your car.

OBSERVATORIES With a strict ordinance against light pollution, Tucson's night skies facilitate stellar sky-watching, weather permitting. **Flandrau Science Center** (520-621-7827), 1601 E. University Blvd. Open Mon.–Sat. 9–5, Sun. 1–5; evenings Thu.–Sat. 7–9. This center was recently renovated to become a living and working laboratory with hands-on exhibits and programs. It has its eyes on the skies with a planetarium sky show (weather permitting) and its feet planted on terra firma in its Mineral Museum—one of the country's finest. $3 adults, $2 children.

Kitt Peak National Observatory (520-318-8726), AZ 86 (Ajo Way). Open daily 9–3:45. Closed holidays. This observatory houses the world's largest collection of optical telescopes. Two radio and 22 optical telescopes accommodate dozens of astronomical research projects at the observatory. You can take a docent-led or self-guided tour. At the National Solar Observatory exhibit gallery, you can see how scientists operate the world's largest solar telescope. Hour-long tours occur daily at 10, 11:30, and 1:30. $2 adults, $1 children. The **Night Observatory Program** (reservation required) is open daily, weather permitting, except during monsoon season (July 15–Aug. 31). Up to 20 people can observe the night sky through two of the observatory's telescopes. Light meal included. $39 adults, $34 children (8 years and older) through seniors; $10 deposit.

NOVEMBER'S TOUR DE TUCSON DRAWS ROAD BIKERS FROM AROUND THE WORLD.

ROAD BIKING In a town where professional road cyclists winter and Lance Armstrong trained for one of the earlier Tour de France races he won, you can understand how serious Tucsonans take road bicycles. The city rates as one of the most cycle-friendly in the West. Contact **Pima Association of Governments** (520-792-1093) for a map of the city and surroundings. Check out the country's largest road biking event, the Tour de Tucson (courses run from 30 to 100-plus miles long), which takes place the Saturday before Thanksgiving.

ROCK CLIMBING Granite rock walls, so absolutely perfect for scaling, await you here no matter what your experience. The **Catalina Mountains** (Santa Catalina Ranger District, 520-749-8700) have some sensational routes. If you like hanging out with the peregrine falcons (when the area isn't closed for raptor nesting), the **Dragoon Mountains** (see "Benson")

and their labyrinthine rise of balanced rocks will give you some sweet climbing
time. The **Santa Catalina Mountains** have a couple of books full of routes.
Contact Coronado National Forest or the outdoor outfitter Summit Hut (520-
325-1554) for information.

✳ Spas

Tucson gets special notice as one of the world's harbors for healthful revitaliza-
tion. The town has some of the most treasured health resorts/spas on the planet.
Client names are shrouded in confidence.

Canyon Ranch (see *All-Inclusive Resorts*) offers limited day-use packages based
on availability. $200–350.

Elizabeth Arden Red Door Spa (520-742-7866, ext. 7890), 3666 E. Sunrise
Dr. Open daily 8–8 (till 6 Sun.–Mon.). The staff dote on you here even before
you enter the decompression chamber—that would be the spa treatment area.
The over-the-top service continues in the form of roomy changing areas with
spacious vanities displaying quality amenities, and skilled therapists. The service
and setting befit the high-profile clients you are apt to see, and may recognize
behind dark sunglasses, from Vice President Cheney to Peter Fonda. Treatments
run the gamut from classic massages to energy therapies; water therapies to
body wraps; facials to foot treatments. The salon has hair services, waxing, makeup artistry, and a variety of manicures and pedicures. $100–173 for body treat-
ments and massages, $90–130 for facials, $55–215 for aqua treatments.

Hashani Spa (520-791-6117 or 800-503-2898), 3645 W. Starr Pass Blvd. They
say this spa is located on sacred ground, and a Tohono O'odham Native blessed
the premises. That may explain the peaceful, kind, and comfortable atmosphere
that permeates the facilities. Of course, the fact that every spa treatment starts
with a signature Hashani foot ritual that includes a rejuvenating foot reflexology
massage might have something to do with all that good feeling. It's a pretty spa,
too, with wonderful tilework and rich colors. The treatments blend ancient healing techniques with the latest in technology. The Petals and Leaves Body Ritual
is the signature treatment that combines a scrub, essential oils, and a full-body
mask of rose, lavender, or green tea to balance and rehydrate. When the therapist asks if you want the scalp massage while the body mask works its magic, take
it. The spa has a salon and fitness center ($25 a day); personal training runs $65
for 50 minutes. $120–220 for massage and rituals, $125–185 for facials.

Miraval Spa (800-363-0819), 5000 E. Via Estancia Miraval, Catalina. Open
daily 9–8. Known around the world to have an atmosphere so soothing, it calms
even the highest-strung Type-A personality, this spa goes delightfully beyond the
call of duty in providing a soul-stirring experience. Cutting edge in its therapies
(this is where the hot stone massage was invented), staffed with master practi-
tioners who explain the history and effects of your treatment, and permeated
with an accommodating atmosphere, Miraval can be described as magnificent.
The menu reads more like a book, with everything from the Blue Mint Foot
Repair Treatment for tired feet to Trager Psychophysical Integration to help
relieve you of chronic tension; exotic Ayurvedic and Oriental body treatments to

familiar Swedish and deep tissue massages; and facials from a gentle peel to deep hydration. Plan your spa experience early, because time slots get filled fast. The spa recommends making reservations at least 3 weeks in advance, and guests get first dibs. Call for prices.

The Sonoran Spa (420-917-2467), Westward Look Resort, 245 E. Ina Rd. Open daily 8–7:15. This boutique spa's whole property feels like a soothing garden. Maybe it's the outdoor pre- and post-treatment patio in which spa goers get to relax, looking at pretty views of the Sonoran Desert. Or the fresh fragrances that waft around the treatment rooms. The spa has a peaceful and gentle ambience, like a restful garden. The treatment menu grabs from every corner of the spa world—classic aromatherapy massages with oils for soothing tight muscles or relieving virus-riddled sinuses; popular hot stone massages; rituals such as the classic Shirodhara or lesser known Abyhanga; energy-oriented ones like Reiki; healing wraps; and facials for every season and skin type. Ingredients lean toward the natural, like aloe and blue corn, volcanic clay, and a blend of muds and clays. The salon has nail and waxing services. $99–149 for massages, body treatments, and rituals; $99–139 for facials.

Touch of Tranquility Spa (520-615-9608), 6884 E. Sunrise Dr., Suite. 150. Open Mon.–Sat. 9–7, Sun. 9–5. This day spa has a number of interesting and exclusive treatments as well as popular massages and facials utilizing products from Swiss goat butter cream to seaweed and Moor mud. Each treatment starts with a Welcome Ceremony where your feet are gently cleaned and dried. The most interesting part of your experience comes in the Brine Light Inhalation Therapy Room. Water gently cascades down a wall dripping with salt crystals, producing an infusion not unlike the salt air of ocean breezes so healing to the skin and lungs. Music and visuals soothe the soul as you lounge and breathe. The Alpine Herbal Steam Therapy replicates straw from a German meadow with an infusion of hay flowers, dried blossoms, seeds, and small leaves in a personalized warming booth—a tent of steam focusing on the lower extremities—excellent for sore muscles. $110–190 for massages and wraps; $125 for signature Rasul Oriental Ceremony Room treatments; $80 for facials.

✳ Wilder Places

Coronado National Forest (520-388-8300), 300 W. Congress St. This national forest—unique for its collection of mountain ranges that rise abruptly from the desert floor like a group of islands in a sea, called sky islands—spreads across southeast Arizona. The whole cluster is called the Madrean Archipelago. Each sky island has its own characteristics, but they all have incredible diversity and trails that often take you from the desert floor into the pines. The **Santa Catalina Mountains** have long, steep trails. **Marshall Gulch** is a favorite. The **Rincon Mountains** are more wild and remote, especially **Rincon Peak Trail**. The **Santa Rita Mountains** hold the highest peak around the Basin, Old Baldy. Take the **Super Trail** to its top. Bring rain gear during monsoon season (July to mid-September).

SOME SAGUAROS HAVE PERSONALITIES.

✏ ♿ **Sabino Canyon Recreation Area** (520-749-8700), 5900 N. Sabino Canyon Rd. Open 24 hours. One of the favorite backcountry destinations in the area. The canyon, cut deep into the Santa Catalina Mountains with a crystal stream embellished with granite boulders, is the quintessential natural desert oasis. The water and riparian area along the streambed attract wildlife and people. Up to 1978 you could drive up the 3.8-mile road, full of hairpin turns and nine stone bridges sometimes well underwater. Today you must walk, ride your bicycle, or take a tram up the road as it rises from 2,800 to 3,300 feet. You can duck onto one of several trails accessed along the road and get into a quiet corner of the backcountry in this altogether lovely canyon. Bicycles are permitted daily, except Wed. and Sat., before 9 or after 5. $5 per vehicle.

✏ ♿ **Saguaro National Park East** (520-733-5153), 3693 S. Old Spanish Trail. Open daily 7–sunset; visitor center open 7–5. Saguaro forests fill the slopes of the Rincon Mountains here and mix with more than 600 species of plants. In springtime, after a wet winter, dozens of species of wildflowers color the desert floor. In May cacti and trees bloom. Explore the park via the 8-mile **Cactus Forest** loop drive or several trails. Visitor center has maps and information. No pets. $10 per vehicle, $5 for motorcycles, $3 for bicycles.

✏ ♿ **Saguaro National Park—West** (520-733-5158), 2700 N. Kinney Rd. Visitor center open 9–5. You can drive, ride a bicycle, or walk on trails, unpaved roads, and paved highway through the most dense saguaro forest you'll find anywhere in the world. The **Wasson Peak Trail** is popular. If you don't want to climb much, take the **King's Canyon Trail** and stay in the wash. The visitor center has maps and information. No pets. Free.

✳ Lodging

INNS & RESORTS Arizona Inn (520-325-1541), 2200 E. Elm St. Built by Congresswoman Isabella Greenway to keep WWI vets in a job (they made furniture for the inn); her family carries on a spirit of community service by preserving the sumptuous era of Tucson's past when the inn was built. Formal but not stuffy, elegant but laid back, the inn attracts an often-celebrated clientele from around the world. The pink stucco walls aren't the only original feature you'll find on the property, listed on the National Register of Historic Places. Many of the furniture pieces, for which the inn exists, appear throughout the property. Each room has exquisitely crafted furniture, antiques, and unique pictures. The property includes the Main Dining Room, Har-Tru clay tennis courts, a 60-foot heated outdoor pool, an exercise facility, saunas, Ping-Pong, croquet, bicycle rentals, a gift shop, a DVD library, a laundry and dry-cleaning service, and business services. Each room has a 27-inch television, DVD player, complimentary high-speed Internet access, refrigerator, *New York Times* delivered daily, and turn-down service. Check out the complimentary afternoon tea or poolside ice cream and complimentary bottled water. Low season $279–389, high season $319–429; log onto www .arizonainn.com for special promotions.

∞ **Hacienda del Sol** (520-299-1501 or 800-728-6514), 5601 N. Hacienda del Sol. One of the more unusual inns in the state and a favorite on world-traveler lists, this Spanish Colonial compound built in the late 1920s has been around the block as it changed hands over the years. What started as a ranch turned into a college preparatory academy for young girls sporting surnames such as Pillsbury, Vanderbilt, and Westinghouse. Next the property became a guest ranch for folks like Clark Gable, Spencer Tracy, and John Wayne. Finally Tucson investors bought and restored the property in the late 1990s. The 30 historic guest rooms have thick adobe walls, original fireplaces, hand-painted tiles, exquisite views, and a down-to-earth comfort level. Each one, however, is decorated differently in classic hacienda-style colors, textures, and style. The property includes the Grill restaurant (see *Dining Out*), a local ʃ⎯rite that consistently makes best-⎯sts, a boutique spa offering spe-⎯ty and therapeutic treatments such

as craniosacral and shiatsu, and (by appointment only) the Wine Shop, where sommelier Dan McCoog personally selects 30 to 40 exceptional or hard-to-find wines each month that you can purchase in 6- or 12-packs at amazing prices (usually below wholesale . . . yes, Dan has connections). $99–495.

∞ ♨ ✂ & **Hilton Tucson El Conquistador Golf & Tennis Resort** (520-544-5000), 10000 N. Oracle Rd. Set right up against the Santa Catalina Mountains with the peaks between you and the city—you can't get a better backdrop or setting. Especially if you like outdoor sports. You'll find 45 holes of golf, 31 lighted tennis courts, regulation racquetball, basketball, and volleyball courts, four outdoor swimming pools (including an NCAA six-lane lap pool and a 143-foot waterslide), six hot tubs and a cold dip plunge, miles of trails for hiking, jogging, biking, and horseback riding, two major fitness centers, the Camp Quail for Kids, and a spa. This AAA Four Diamond resort has kept its rating just about forever; so expect consistency. Recently remodeled rooms are spacious and have gorgeous views (half have fireplace). In-room movies and Nintendo games come with all rooms, and WiFi is available. If it makes you tired just reading about all these opportunities for activities, keep in mind that the setting and panoramas are so nice, just lolling around to enjoy them is high on the activity list, too. $89–299. Optional sport and fitness facility fee $10 per day.

∞ ✂ & **Starr Pass Resort & Spa** (520-792-3500), 3800 W. Starr Pass Blvd. Tucson's resort scene remained unchanged for years until Starr Pass came on the scene in early 2005. And what a impressive scene it makes— tucked away in a box canyon of the Tucson Mountains on the city's west side, the golden-colored buildings, pattered after a pueblo, create a stunning scene when you first see them. The gold colors carry into the rooms, all of which have incredible views of the Tucson Basin. The property has 27 holes of Arnold Palmer Signature Golf; the 20,000-square-foot Hashani Spa, with fitness and movement studios; Rising Starr Kids Club; access to hiking and biking trails; two swimming pools; tennis courts; horseback riding; and seven restaurants, including its upscale and excellent Primo (see *Dining Out*). The rooms feature custom-made furniture, down duvets and tons of pillows on the bed, flat-screen TV, WiFi, and cordless phone. Optional sport and fitness facility fee $10 per day. $129–439.

⊘ 🐾 ✐ ✦ **The Westin La Paloma Resort & Spa** (520-742-6000), 3800 E. Sunrise Dr. Hard to believe a warehouse once stood where this Westin classic now spreads. The Mehl brothers negotiated hotly for the land, and once they got it, they built this hotel in 1986 to match the Biltmore in Phoenix. Standing in the foothills of the Santa Catalina Mountains, the resort has some of the most seductive views in the city. The mature landscaping with footpaths makes it a most pleasant place to amble around in. And you never know who you might see in the way of famous personalities at this AAA Four Diamond resort. The best in the business has been gathered onto these premises: local award-winning Janos restaurant (see *Dining Out*), the Red Door Spa, a 27-hole Jack Nicklaus Signature golf

course, a tennis and health center (10 courts, 4 clay and 10 lighted), indoor racquetball, five pools, sand volley-ball, a 177-foot waterslide, Westin Kids Club, and Children's Lounge. Rooms have WiFi, Starbucks coffee, and the famous Heavenly Beds and Heavenly Baths. Pets of 40 pounds or less are welcome when you sign a damage waiver. The Heavenly Dog Program provides an oversized pillow and a "doggy bag" filled with a plastic bag, glove, and food and water dish. $89–429.

⊘ ✦ **Westward Look Resort** (520-917-2476), 245 E. Ina Rd. The city's oldest resort is loaded with history, originality, and down-home comfort. What started as a homestead in 1912 evolved into a dude ranch and now a resort. For its AAA Four Diamond and Mobil Four-Star awards, it's incredibly unpretentious. The city favorite has beautiful nature trails lush with quintessential Sonoran Desert vegetation, open to the public, that wind through several gardens spread among the property's 80 acres. You'll also find tennis courts, a swimming pool, the Gold Room restaurant (see *Dining Out*), and the Sonoran Spa. Southwestern-style guest rooms each have balcony or patio, king or queen beds with pillow-top mattress, stocked mini bar, oversized bath, cable TV, and movies. $89–180.

ALL-INCLUSIVE RESORTS ✦ **Miraval Life in Balance** (800-232-3969), 5000 E. Via Estancia Miraval, Catalina. A favorite with savvy travelers who know the world, Miraval is one resort that can somehow be all things to all people. With its mantra of living in the moment, the resort aspires to heighten your senses and bring you into balance. And that it does,

🐾 ♿ **Canyon Ranch** (800-742-9000), 8600 E. Rockcliff Rd. The nation's first and the crème de la crème of health and wellness resorts lives up to every good thing you might have heard. It racks up awards continuously and consistently, even wowing *Gourmet* and *Bon Appétit* with its too-good-to-be-true spa cuisine à la chef Scott Uehlein. Basically, the whole idea behind the resort is to have a great vacation while receiving cutting-edge health therapies and/or medical treatments. The all-inclusive resort gives you spa time, three tasty squares, and a couple of dozen (mostly free) classes and seminars to fill your day. It's one of the few places on the planet where you can get an 80-minute physical and talk with the physician the whole time.

The adobe-style cottages—roomy, quiet, and pleasantly appointed—have spa amenities, television, and phone. The grounds have lush landscaping with streamlike water features. Art appears everywhere, inside and out. Still, it's probably the 80,000-square-foot spa (with such an extensive catalog of treatments, you might need a bit of counseling to determine which is perfect for you) that will lure you here.

Some people come to repair and recover after major operations because of the professional medical staff. Many come to kick a habit or enhance health and performance, though there's never a peep from the staff about who's who on the guest roster. There's even a program for teens (14 years and older, with some treatment restrictions). Up to two dogs less than 35 pounds each are allowed with current registration and vaccination records. They will pick up dog food, pet treats, and toys with 48-hour notice. Doggy massages are available. Four nights $2,333–5,030, 7 nights $3,890–8,100, 10 nights $5,060–11,030. Rates are per person, double occupancy.

SCULTPURES ON THE GROUNDS OF THE CANYON RANCH SPA.

whether you're a spa-goer looking for that unusual but enlightening treatment, a gourmand wondering how the meals can taste so good yet be so healthy, or closet Outward Bound type who needs a challenge to stay sane. Miraval embraces all with the warm arm of a friend. Laid out like a lush canyon with a stream traveling through it, the resort grounds look like a garden sanctuary. Rooms are warm Southwest. Amenities over the top. Service engaging yet professional. And what a variety of programs: bodymindfulness; challenge activities; cooking demonstrations; equine activities; golf; hiking; and, of course, the spa. Packages start at $570 per person per night. Log onto www.miraval resort.com for specials.

MIRAVAL LIFE IN BALANCE.

BED AND BREAKFASTS Adobe Rose Bed and Breakfast (520-318-4644 or 800-328-4122), 940 N. Olsen. The neighborhood myth holds that builders took the dirt from 2nd Street to make the adobe bricks for this property back in the 1930s. Located in the Sam Hughes District, the home has old Tucson character and style. The property earned the AAA Three Diamond award, highest for this category of lodging. Premises include a hot tub, pool, refrigerator stocked with soft drinks, juice, and water; and tons of sitting areas. Rooms have private bath, coffee, tea, hot chocolate, writing space, complimentary WiFi; cable TV, DVD, and functional fireplaces in two rooms. Breakfast, included with your room, means gourmet coffees, fresh fruit, and meals such as pecan French toast or Brie and apple omelets with fresh baked goods and coffee cake—and sometimes a tableful of astronomers taking advantage of the area's world-class astronomical environment. $95–185 peak season, $65–120 off-season.

Catalina Park Inn Bed and Breakfast (520-792-4541 or 800-792-4885), 309 E. 1st St. Closed mid-July to mid-Aug. This classy 1927 home features the quality craftsmanship characteristic of past eras. The inn's layout will have a familiar ring to Bostonians. Each of the six rooms is thoughtfully and impeccably arranged. At the same time, the home has a comfortable feel to it. It's the kind of place where the guests feel pampered, but can have a life—a trickle-down from the proprietors' casual yet professional attitudes. Gardens are big here, for secluded moments and outdoor relaxing. Breakfast (included in the rates) starts with European-roasted coffees and continues with specialties like papaya and lime scones and lemon ricotta pancakes. Complimentary WiFi; generally no pets. $106–166.

Hacienda del Desierto Bed and Breakfast (800-982-1795), 11770

Rambling Trail. Reminiscent of a Spanish hacienda with leanings toward luxury, you get something extra here that's sometimes hard to come by these days—privacy. The location is secluded on 16 acres in the eastern desert, where vistas look out on the Rincon Mountains and wildlife doesn't necessarily shy away. Owner-innkeepers David and Rosemary have a list of 40 bird species sighted on their property. They have a small nature trail marking desert vegetation. In Renaissance fashion David constructed most of the buildings. The landscaping is mature, aesthetic, and lush. Choose from one large room, two suites, and a two-bedroom casita, all with private bath and entrance, as well as complimentary high-speed Internet. Most have kitchenette,

THE OLD SWITCHBOARD AT THE HOTEL CONGRESS IS STILL IN USE.

antique wood-burning or gas stove, antiques, Mexican folk art, paintings, cable TV, DVD, and VCR. $135–269.

Natural Bed and Breakfast (520-881-4582), 3150 E. Presidio Rd. You may not find a bed and breakfast quite like this anywhere else in the Southwest. The property caters to clients with environmental sensitivities. No chemicals are used for house-cleaning, air purifiers and humidifiers are running, and no smoking or pets are allowed. Shoes come off as soon as you pass through the front door. Innkeeper Marc Haberman goes a step beyond the physical and has arranged the home to meet feng shui standards; he cleanses it with sage, has relaxing music going at all times, and offers plenty of interesting book and periodicals. Haberman, a holistic health practitioner and muscular therapist, offers massages. Breakfast consists of all-natural organic whole-grain cereals, toasts, jams, and juice. $65–75 for 2 or more nights; $10 more for 1 night.

HOTELS & LODGES ∞ 🐾 ♿ **Hotel Congress** (520-622-8848 or 800-722-8848), 311 E. Congress St. Even if you haven't been to this hotel for the last 40 years, you might feel right at home. The period antique furnishings (from iron beds to vintage radios), steam heat and evaporative cooling, and even the original switchboard ringing up your desired numbers are still here. Just to highlight the fact you could get lost in time here at the longest-operating hotel in the state, rooms do not have clocks. Wake-up calls come via live people who call your rotary phone. If you want to watch television, there's one in the lounge. The hotel, built in 1919, catered to the railroad and cattle industry, as well as (unknowingly) such nefarious folks as John Dillinger. A fire at the hotel flushed Dillinger and his gang out of their third-floor rooms, where they'd come to "lay low" after a series of robberies. Today the elegant hotel caters to those who love a sense of place and the original appointments, such as the Old West deco paintings on the walls created by Larry Boyce on a will-paint-for-room-and-board arrangement when he bicycled across the country and stayed for the summer. The **Tap Room** is *the* place to go for weeknight entertainment. All 40 rooms are located on the second floor and have private bath. Some even have ghosts. $69–109; pets $10 extra.

∞ ✿ 🐾 ♿ **La Posada Lodge and Casitas** (520-887-4800 or 800-810-2808), 5900 N. Oracle Rd. Correctly touting itself as Tucson's Best Kept Secret, you will get a sensibly priced room with a themed interior different from what a franchise would offer— Mexican (with tin headboards), southwestern (with tasteful furniture), or retro (with bold colors). The lobby has a Navajo mural that sets it apart from the norm. Amenities include a pool and workout facility. Rooms have a king, two doubles, or two queens, along with microwave, refrigerator, balcony, complimentary high-speed Internet hookup, and satellite TV. A complimentary full continental breakfast is included in rates. Pets are okay with $50 deposit. $89–169.

∞ ✿ ♿ **Viscount Suite Hotel** (520-745-6500 or 800-527-9666), 4855 E. Broadway Blvd. A true suite hotel— all accommodations are two-room suites with large living room, working desk, and separate bedroom. Rooms

include complimentary WiFi, cable TV, refrigerator, microwave, and complimentary full American breakfast buffet. The property has a heated pool, whirlpool, and fitness room. No pets. $119–150.

✸ Where to Eat

DINING OUT Acacia (520-232-0101), 4340 N. Campbell. Open daily for lunch 11–2 and dinner 5–9; Sun. brunch 11–2 with live jazz. When one of Arizona's best chefs, Albert Hall, decided to open up his own restaurant, his fans gave him no time to wonder if it would be a success. Crowned with a AAA Four Diamond award a year after opening in 2004, the restaurant has collected a phalanx of regal reviews. Combining some swank with a laid-back atmosphere, the dining room gives you room to relax while keeping in mind that this place, meals included, thrives on the aesthetic. Make that *ethereal*, especially if you chose the signature dish, Chilean sea bass with wasabi orzo. You may forever hold it as the benchmark against which sea bass meals are measured. The restaurant goes through hundreds of pounds of the fish in the high season, and Chef Hall returns fish not up to his standard. In fact, he's just as finicky about everything he serves. This includes the homemade frozen custard, that soulful treat midwesterners have been keeping to themselves. Entrées $19–32.

Café Poca Cosa (520-622-6400). Open Tue.–Thu. 11–9, Fri.–Sat. 11–10; dinner served daily at 4; closed Sun. Famous for having one of the most creative Mexican menus in the state, the restaurant itself is a unique meld of cosmopolitan cool filled with

AT THE CAFÉ POCA COSA.

Mexican folk art and world music. The familiar menu of innovative Mexican cuisine leans toward Mexico City fare. "No chimichangas here," chef Suzana Davila advises. The menu changes daily, but one entrée that stays put is the *plato poca cosa*, "where you give up all control to the chef," Davila says. This means that the chef chooses three dishes for you, perhaps *pastel de pollo* (shredded chicken layered with tortillas and mole sauce made with Godiva chocolate), *pescado* (slightly breaded cod), and tamale pie. Losing control is not a bad idea here. Entrées $17–22.

Café Terra Cotta (520-577-8100), 8500 E. Sunrise Dr. Open daily for dinner at 4. The only way Don Luria could keep his heartthrob, traveling Cordon Bleu–trained chef Donna Nordin, in town was to open this restaurant; it (and their resulting marriage) has been a success from the get-go, serving "innovative regional flavors" made with classical French contemporary cooking techniques. The results feature fresh ingredients native to the American Southwest and northern Mexico—chiles, corn, tomatoes, squash, and beans; sauces with more complexity, like those from the Yucatán, central Mexico, and Oaxaca; and elegant ingredients, such as goat cheese, Gorgonzola butter, lobster, and Maple Leaf duck. The fact that Donna is one of the Top 10 Chocolate Chefs in the nation adds fuel to any notion you might have to order the chocolate mousse pie. The dessert, described accurately as "rich and sinful" on the menu, appeared on the cover of *Bon Appétit*. Entrées $16–25.

Casa Vincente Restaurant Español (520-884-5253), 375 S. Stone Ave. Open for dinner Tue.–Sat. 4–10, lunch Thu.–Fri. 11–2. Vincente Sanchez, president of the Spanish Club in Tucson, opened this restaurant to bolster Spanish camaraderie and has re-created a piece of his Avila homeland with authentic food, entertainment, and atmosphere in the historic section of Tucson. Posters of Spain and area artists decorate the restaurant walls. A well-stocked lighted glass-block bar serves about 50 wines from Spain. Everything on the menu speaks of Spain: a variety of paellas (minimum of four diners, call ahead to reserve), dozens of tapas, several wonderful Spanish dinners, and *arroz con leche* and other Spanish sweets for dessert. Besides eating like you were in Spain, you can have some *Español*-style fun with tango dancing on Wednesday, live guitar music on Thursday, and flamenco dancing on Friday and Saturday. Entrées $10.95–23.95, tapas $4.95–9.95.

China Phoenix (520-531-0658), 7090 N. Oracle Rd., Suite 172. Open Mon.–Fri. 11–9:30; Sat.–Sun. 10–9:30 (dim sum 10–3). If your friends frequent your restaurant, you either have good food or very good friends. China Phoenix—very popular among the local Chinese community—has both. You'll get classic Chinese meals here, prepared well and without MSG. No tired seafood, and vegetables are fresh. Entrées $8–11.

Cup Café (520-798-1618), 311 E. Congress St. Open daily for breakfast Mon.–Fri. 7–11 (till 1 Sat.–Sun.), lunch Mon.–Fri. 11–3:30 (1–5 Sat.–Sun.), dinner Sun.–Thu. 5–10 (till 11 Fri.–Sat.). For a restaurant with such a simple name, the food is extraordinary. Gold, red, and cream colors accented with wood-paneled walls make a fitting setting for meals with tastes that take you around the globe. Everything's so elegant . . . and then you read the menu: Mary Had a Leg of Lamb (New Zealand lamb shanks braised in a rustic marinara, basil mashed potatoes, sautéed spinach with feta cheese); The Penne Is Spicier Than the Sword (garlic, corn, black beans, squash, carrots, tomatoes, fresh jalapeños, onions, and cilantro sautéed and finished with white wine and butter, topped with shredded Parmesan cheese); Two Thompson Automatics (shredded chicken marinated in Frank's original red-hot sauce, wrapped in an egg roll with Gorgonzola and deep-fried until crispy, served with Asian slaw). As slangy as it all sounds, it couldn't be classier. Bill Roberts boldly displays his award-winning homemade desserts in a showcase that steals the whole scene. Entrées $11–24.

The Grill at Hacienda del Sol (520-529-3500), 5601 N. Hacienda del Sol Rd. Open daily 5:30–10. Repeatedly on the list of favorites—of the community in general, and of gourmands at large. The courtyard leading up to the restaurant (part of the Hacienda del Sol Resort) colors with herbs, fruits, and vegetables used in the Grill's kitchen. The food is described as innovative American at its best, and it lives up to its reputation. The signature dish, Australian rack of lamb, has a scallop paired with truffle risotto and caramelized cippolini onion. Freshwater and ocean fish appear liberally, as does risotto. And game adds a rustic edge. The dessert menu mixes some classics (baked Alaska, crème brûlée) with the unique (peanut butter mousse, Guinness cake with whiskey icing, Baileys Irish Crème anglaise). The owners are oenophiles, and the wine list leans toward lavish. The Grill has a consistent run of earning *Wine Spectator*'s Award of Excellence since 1997; it has one of the top six wine menus in the country. Entrées $22–38.

⊗ ঙ **Janos** (520-615-6100), 3770 E. Sunrise Dr. Open for dinner Mon.–Thu. 5:30–9 (till 10 Fri.–Sat.); closed Sun., Thanksgiving, Christmas, and New Year's Days. Owner-chef Janos Wilder has played an integral role, nationally, in the use of organic produce and local, indigenous ingredients in restaurants. Janos, awarded Best Chef in the Southwest by the James Beard Foundation, marries the

CASA VINCENTE RESTAURANT ESPAÑOL.

sensible French style with the spicy American Southwest. What you get is a party—colorful, lively, and full of tastes and textures that titillate your palate. From appetizers like pan-roasted diver sea scallops with truffle salt, buttered leeks, cardoons, and tear drop tomatoes on lentil puree to entrées such as medallion of beef tenderloin on brioche toast with foie gras butter, truffle sauce, port-braised cipollini onions, fingerling potatoes, mushrooms, and leek puree, your palate will enjoy one savory evening. The restaurant interiors are as sensually intense as the food: The main dining room is red with a gold-leaf ceiling and beaded Moroccan fabric; art, mostly by local artists, decks the walls, along with a line of Mobil Four-Star, AAA Four Diamond, and DiRona Awards. The wait staff are in constant motion, tending to your needs and desires. Internationally known local musicians play on the patio during summer months. Entrées $24–50.

J-Bar (520-615-6100), 3770 E. Sunrise Dr. Open for dinner Mon.–Sat. 5–9:30; happy hour 5–6:30; closed Sun., Thanksgiving, Christmas, and New Year's Days. Owned by Chef Janos, and an extension of his namesake restaurant, the informal and lively J-Bar is the place to enjoy food, libations, and people. Janos patterned it after the parillas in Nogales. The food, with southern Arizonan, Mexican, Latin American, and Caribbean leanings, is created in an open kitchen and served family style. The highly original menu might have dishes such as achiote rock shrimp soft tacos with cilantro chili slaw, lemon crema, salsa fresca, pineapple rice, jicama orange relish, and chiles. On the other hand, steaks are simply grilled with salt and pepper. The bar serves some fun *bebidas*, such as a variety of mojitos and martinis, Sangria, and Liquado Del Dia (a nonalcoholic blend of fresh fruit and juices). Entrées $14.50–28.

The Gold Room at Westward Look Resort (520-297-1151), 245 E. Ina Rd. Open daily for breakfast Mon.–Sat. 7–11, lunch 11:30–2, dinner 5:30–10, Sun. brunch 10–1:30. Chef Jamie West just can't stop racking up accolades with his creative cuisine incorporating fresh ingredients and layers of flavor that play well together. West has received awards, honors, and respect from prestigious chefs around the world. Just over a decade in the California wine country taught him invaluable lessons from top vintners. The Chef's Garden supplies many of the fruits, vegetables, and herbs. Tried-and-true-mainstays such as filet mignon, pork tenderloin, and grilled salmon, find strange platefellows of blue spinach, mac and cheese orzo, and wasabi whipped potatoes. The homemade ice cream is to die for. The only thing that tops West's cuisine is the extravagant views of the Rincon Mountains and Tucson Valley twinkling with lights below. Entrées $19–30.

❦ Pastiche (520-325-3333), 3025 N. Campbell Ave. Open Mon.–Fri. 11:30 AM–midnight, Sat.–Sun. 4:30–midnight. Upscale yet casual, eclectic yet dependable, this locally owned bistro has a distinctive menu—American with global influences—that begs experimentation. To accommodate the process of ordering, they provide half and bistro portions (lighter versions of originals) that are perfect for sharing and sampling. For instance, you could get a bistro portion of the thyme-crusted sea bass and a half portion of the Pastiche baby greens and not miss out on either of these signature dishes. Comfort food appears in the form of baked mac and cheese (smoked Gouda, Parmesan, and white cheddar with mesquite-smoked bacon) and San Francisco–style "cioppino" with mussels, scallops, shrimp, calamari, and sea bass in a spicy tomato broth, served with grilled garlic sourdough bread. These, intelligently, do not come in smaller sizes. Since their next-door market has "bottles and bottles" of wine, you can imagine the wine list. Entrées $15.95–22.95.

Primo (520-791-6671), 3800 W. Starr Pass Blvd. Open daily for dinner 6–10. Casual, yes. Elegant, absolutely. *Casual elegance* is a perfect description for this fabulous Mediterranean-inspired restaurant named for chef Melissa Kelly's grandfather. A casual feel prevails with an open kitchen, expansive brick oven, and bread stations scattered throughout the room. The James Beard Award–winning Chef Kelly presents a fresh mélange of tastes that never clutter your palate. In back-to-basics style, the food is allowed to speak. That's why freshness is imperative, so the menu changes often to accommodate the best the market offers; this includes local organic produce and what grows in the property's own garden, tiered Italian style. Simple but memorable touches make the meal: Shellfish carry the sweet taste of the sea; the Farmer's Salad has coddled eggs and slabs of cheeses; cod fritters impart a bite of seaside heaven; and Lurisia sparkling water is lightly carbonated. Desserts, crafted by pastry chef Price Kushner, are in a class of their own. If you don't try the chocolate-dipped cannoli laced with amaretto cherries, do get the *Zepolis*. Consuming one of these Italian puff-doughnuts is like biting into eggy clouds coated with sugar—the half has not been told. Entrées $24–38.

EATING OUT Frost—A Gelato Shoppe (520-797-0188), 7131 N. Oracle Rd., Suite 101. Located in the Casas Adobes Shopping Center. This wonderful gelato shop raised the state's gelato standard to near perfection. With dozens of flavors to choose from—all made fresh daily, entirely from ingredients imported from Italy—your experience will not be easy until you get the product in hand and devour. $3.08–4.49.

❧ **Ghini's French Caffé** (520-326-9095), 1803 E. Prince Rd. Open Tue.–Sat. 6:30–3, Sun. 7–1; closed Mon. Exceptionally good food at low prices always draws a crowd. This popular albeit tucked-away gathering place serves French Provençal food in a most delicious way. Using locally grown ingredients when possible and La Baguette Bakery bread, the food is fresh, good, and downright comforting. Entrées $2.50–7.95.

Mama's Famous Pizza & Heros (520-319-8856), 4500 E. Speedway (and several more around the city). Open Mon.–Thu. 11–10 (till midnight Fri.–Sat.), Sun. noon–10. Created first in New York City, this family-owned pizzeria opened in Tucson in 1981, offering up quality food and good service with a good dose of thick New York accents. It's the place to go for a real New York pizza (round, traditional, hand stretched, and baked in a brick oven) or Sicilian square deep-dish pan. $9.95–23.95.

🍽 **Mi Nidito** (520-622-5081), 1813 S. 4th Ave. Open 11 AM daily; closed Mon.–Tue. Tortilla factory or restaurant? That was the question for the couple from Sonora, Mexico. They decided to open Mi Nidito (my little nest), and generations have been thanking them ever since. Their chiles rellenos are the best in town. You never know who you'll see in this small restaurant that serves up authentic Mexican fare so savory, it packs in clients from every rung of the social ladder, from students on a budget (that's the other excellent feature, low prices) to U.S. presidents. $7.95–10.90.

🍽 **Rocco's Little Chicago Pizzeria** (520-321-1860), 2707 E. Broadway. Open Mon.–Sat. 11–10. They live up to their name by serving truly authentic Chicago-style pizza (extra-thin crust). Plus, they serve deep-dish and stuffed. And Rocco's turns out such a good pizza, they end up on best-of lists in Tucson. Chose from 10 meat toppings and a couple of dozen veggies and such. $7.50–22.

DeGrazia Foundation Gallery in the Sun (520-299-9191), 6300 N. Swan. Open daily 10–4. Hypercreative Ettore DeGrazia, the artist who hung around with and painted scenes about Mexican and Apache peoples and cultures, embodied folk art. This gallery, once his 10-acre studio-retreat in the foothills of the Santa Catalina Mountains, was built by DeGrazia and friends from adobe and straw. It contains 15,000 original pieces of DeGrazia's art, from paintings to ceramics, and every other thing he could turn aesthetic, from tortillas to toilet floats. It's a fascinating place full of fascinating pieces created by an incredibly fascinating artist. Free.

THE DEGRAZIA GALLERY DISPLAYS THE FOLK ARTIST'S WORKS.

The Arts

Murals are rife around the Old Pueblo. About 34 mural projects cluster around the downtown area alone. The best public artwork appears at the downtown library on Church and Pennington.

Center for Creative Photography (520-621-7968), Speedway Blvd. and Olive St., University of Arizona campus. Open Mon.–Fri. 9–5, Sat.–Sun. noon–5. The world-class collection of photography represents nearly every 20th-century photographer of note and features the nation's foremost collections of Ansel Adams and Alfred Stieglitz. Free.

& Tucson Museum of Art & Historic Block (520-624-2333), 140 N. Main Ave. Open Tue.–Sat. 10–4, Sun. noon–4; closed Mon. This museum exhibits more than 7,000 pieces ranging from Western to European, modern to contemporary. Exhibits change almost monthly. The Historic Block represents five restored homes of the El Presidio Historic District built between 1850 and 1907 that surround the museum.

University of Arizona Museum of Art (520-621-7567), 1031 N. Olive Rd. Open Tue.–Fri. 9–5, Sat.–Sun. noon–4. This exquisite permanent collection was donated and purchased through the years. Pieces from the 15th-century Spanish Retablo of Ciudad Rodrigo, Georgia O'Keeffe, Picasso, Rembrandt, and Zuniga make a trip worthwhile. Free.

Selective Shopping

American Antique Mall (520-326-3070), 3130 E. Grant Rd. Open Mon.–Sat. 10–5:30, Sun. 11–4:30. The best thing about this huge mall is that

it's located in the heart of Tucson's Antique District (between Speedway Blvd. and Grant Rd.). So if the mall's 100 consigners don't have something to capture your fancy, you can continue the hunt to the surrounding antiques shops.

4th Avenue (520-624-5004), between University Blvd. and 9th St. It's exceedingly retro around 4th Avenue. The area has more than 100 shops, and most take you back to the 1970s. You can find antiques, imported gifts, vintage clothing, jewelry, and custom-made furniture. Cultural restaurants and popular bars dot the street as well. Street fairs in spring and winter bring thousands of shoppers.

The Lost Barrio, Park Ave. south of Broadway. They didn't give this shopping area its name out of whimsy. The out-of-the-way spot in the city might be likened to a type of Bermuda Triangle where people end up when they're lost. The locals dubbed it the Lost Barrio, and the nickname stuck. If you land here because you're lost, it may end up serendipitous. To make sure you arrive on purpose, the best way to get to the Lost Barrio from downtown is to go east on Broadway under the Rattlesnake Bridge (which rattles when you cross it), then turn south onto Park Ave. Looking more like a warehouse district than cool shopping haunt, the redbrick warehouses belies the cache of goodies— more global than border-town fare—inside them, antiques from China, lights from Italy, stonework from Morocco, and doors from everywhere else.

Old Town Artisans (520-623-6024 or 800-782-8072), 201 N. Court Ave. Open daily Mon.–Sat. 9:30–5:30, Sun. 11–5 (summer hours Mon.–Sat. 10–4,

Sun. 11–4). A large collection of local and regional art, fine crafts, trendy clothes and jewelry, and Native American art is presented in a historic 1860s adobe in the El Presidio District.

✳ Spectator Sports

Tucson Sidewinders Baseball (520-424-1021). Tucson's only professional team plays Apr.–Sep. at Tucson Electric Park (see below).

SPRING TRAINING Arizona's marvelous spring weather of clear skies,

SAGUARO CACTUS ARE UBIQUITOUS IN ARIZONA.

warm days, and cool nights lures teams from around the country. Check out the **Arizona Diamondbacks** and **Chicago White Sox** at Kino Sports Complex/Tucson Electric Park (420-434-1000), 2500 E. Ajo Way. The teams play about 30 games during Mar. and Apr., along with a compendium of activities to go along with the professional baseball action: theme days, concerts, sport tournaments, and community events.

Colorado Rockies Baseball Club at Hi Corbett Field (520-327-9467), 3400 E. Camino Campestre.

✳ Entertainment

Fox Tucson Theatre (520-624-1515), 17 W. Congress. The 1929 art deco theater is listed on the National Register of Historic Places as a historically significant building. It was a grande dame in its heyday but almost had a date with the wrecking ball in the 1970s. Now newly restored, the theater shows classic films and hosts the Puro Mexicano: Tucson Film Festival (the nation's first and only devoted to the best Mexican and Mexican American films) in November.

✳ Special Events

End of January–mid-February: **Tucson Gem, Mineral & Fossil Showcase** (800-638-8350). The world's largest marketplace, comprising more than 30 locations throughout town (at fine hotels and resorts, in shops and attractions, and under tents) featuring everything minerals and gems.

February: **Southwest Indian Art Fair** (520-626-8381). A high-quality Indian art fair hosted by Arizona State Museum, University of Arizona, featuring artists from around the Southwest, with musical entertainment. **La Fiesta de los Vaqueros: Tucson Rodeo** (520-741-2233). The Celebration of the Cowboys is an 8-day extravaganza centered on the Tucson Rodeo, one of the top 20 professional rodeos in the United States.

March: **Tucson Winter Chamber Music Festival** (520-577-3769). Nationally and internationally known groups perform at the Tucson Convention Center.

April: **Arizona International Film Festival** (520-628-1737). Independent films show in theaters around town, with opportunities to meet the filmmakers at workshops, seminars, and presentations at various venues. **Spring Fling** (520-621-5610) is the nation's largest student-run carnival, with fun rides, midway games, food, and amateur and professional entertainment, all at Rillito Raceway Park. **Pima County Fair** (520-762-9100) is an old-fashioned fair with exhibits, food, stage concerts, and live entertainment, carnival rides, educational exhibits at Pima County Fair Grounds. **Tucson International Mariachi Conference** (520-838-3908). This award-winning conference features mariachi music, *folklorico*

dancing, student workshops, a concert at Tucson Convention Center, and a community fiesta at Reid Park.

Late September–early October: **Oktoberfest on Mount Lemmon** (520-885-1181). Bring a blanket to relax on the pine- and aspen-forested slopes with German food and beer, music, dancing, and costumes atop Mount Lemmon.

October: **Tucson Culinary Festival** (520-488-8601). Wine dinners and seminars, plus the Grand Tasting at Westward Look Resort, with more than more than 70 wineries pouring wines and over 30 Tucson chefs presenting culinary specialties.

November: **El Tour de Tucson** (520-745-2033). Thousands of cyclists from around the world compete in this major annual event featuring a prestigious 109-mile perimeter race and 30- and 60-miles rides.

December: **Downtown Parade of Lights** (520-547-3338). Downtown Tucson's holiday parade begins at 6 PM. **Luminaria Nights at Tucson Botanical Gardens** (520-326-9686). Stroll down luminaria-adorned garden paths amid seasonal music after dark (5:30–11 PM).

TUBAC

Describing itself as the town "Where Art and History Meet," Tubac has evolved over the last two and a half centuries from Spanish presidio to true art town. Red tile roofs, ocotillo wand fences, latilla ceilings, and religious shrines—a meld of Old West and romantic Latino—gives the tucked-away town its inspiring charisma.

As the northern frontier of New Spain and first European settlement, this area of the New World was already happening when the American Revolution got under way. Tubac started in 1691 with the Tumacocori Mission (now a national park) and its Presidio defense post (now an Arizona state park) under the Spanish flag. Juan Bautista de Anza II carved a niche history by establishing a trail in 1775 that traveled all the way from Tubac to San Francisco. Decades before the Gold Rush, a third of the City by the Bay's residents named Tubac as their birthplace.

For the next 100 years Tubac roiled with Indian wars, served a stint as a Mexican colony, and wobbled with the rest of the state as a Confederate army pawn until Lincoln declared the Arizona Territory in 1863. With Tubac's war-torn history at a lull and its national status securely in U.S. hands by 1866 (after Geronimo's surrender), the town settled down into some serious peace and quiet. In 1948 artist Dale Nichols established the Artists School here. This eventually transformed the town into an artist community. By the 1960s Tubac became a respite for the East and West Coast crowds who doted on its arty élan. And thanks to Bing Crosby and his Hollywood cronies, Tubac even got itself a tony golf resort (recently remodeled, expanded, and better than ever).

Tubac has quietly developed its aesthetic propensities since its art colony days, expanding to a national art destination. During those decades, classic western art made room for modern southwestern artists. For a while abstracts and world art even showed up.

Where artists gather, shopping prevails; and galleries and specialty shops have multiplied. Over the years Tubac favored its free-spirited side and kept a laid-back ambience that visitors still find irresistible, never knowing what to expect. Shops rarely held to a schedule, while shopkeepers displayed their eccentricities. Recently, however, Tubac has started to flirt with sophistication: A number of fine-dining restaurants have opened their doors, and businesses have actually

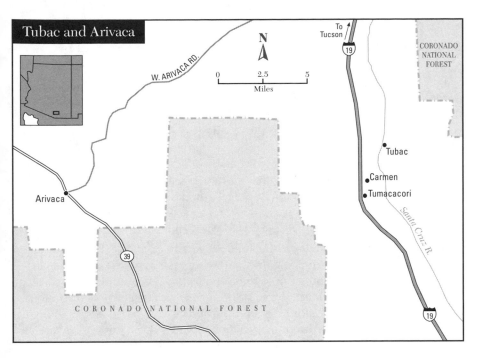

Tubac and Arivaca

CORONADO NATIONAL FOREST

W. ARIVACA RD.

To Tucson

Tubac

Carmen

Tumacacori

Arivaca

Santa Cruz R.

CORONADO NATIONAL FOREST

N

0   2.5   5
Miles

adopted hours of operation. Tubac may dally with a mañana attitude now and again, but it's definitely open for business.

GUIDANCE The official visitor center is located in **Tubac Presidio State Historic Park** (520-398-2252), Tubac Rd. and Burreal St. You can also contact the **Tubac Chamber of Commerce** (520-398-2704; assistance@tubacaz.com). **Nogales Ranger District** (520-281-2296), 303 Old Tucson Rd., Nogales, has information about the Coronado National Forest; open 8–4:30.

GETTING THERE Tubac is located on I-19 (this highway is measured and marked in kilometers rather than miles) at exit 34, about 20 miles north of Mexico.

WHEN TO COME Tubac's high season starts in December and ends in April. During the off-season, May through November, the art galleries and shops that open daily during the high season turn laissez-faire. Summer temperatures hover around 100 degrees during the day, but the nights drop into the 60s.

MEDICAL EMERGENCY Carondelet Holy Cross Hospital Inc. (520-285-3000), 1171 W. Target Range Rd., Nogales.

✳ To See

Santa Cruz Chili & Spice Co. (520-398-2591), 1868 E. Frontage, Tumacacori. Open Mon.–Sat. 8–5. The Santa Cruz Valley produces some of the best chile peppers around, and this company has grown special and distinctive chiles here since 1943. You can purchase their products, plus peruse memorabilia. Free.

Tubac Presidio State Historic Park (520-398-2252), 1 Burruel St. Open daily 8–5 except Christmas Day. Arizona's first state park showcases where Tubac got its start. The park celebrates the rich compendium of cultures through its history with static displays and living history events. If you start your Tubac visit with a tour, you get a strong overview of the area and its cultures. The park features an old schoolhouse, the Otero Community Hall (on the National Register of Historic Places), a museum, an underground archaeology display, and the trailhead to the historic Anza Trail. $3 per person 14 years and older.

Tumacacori Mesquite (520-398-9356), 2007 E. Frontage Rd., Tumacacori. Open Mon.–Sat. 8–5. Twisted, gnarled, and weathered to gray tones as a living tree, mesquite is the unsung hero of the wood world. When its outer wood is cut away, the wood's beauty comes through with hues that range from lemon, honey, and caramel to burgundy, and the grain from straight as a board (sorry) to highly ornate. The American Hardwood Association classifies this hardwood as rare and exotic. Oak, mahogany, and mesquite have equal status as the most stable hardwoods in the world. This mesquite mill specializes in all things mesquite, from milled wood to furniture, even utilizing the tough burls. Free.

Tumacacori National Historical Park (520-398-2341). Located just south of Tubac at 1891 E. Frontage Rd., Tumacacori. Open daily 8–5 except Thanksgiving and Christmas. Tumacacori is where everything started in Arizona. Father Eusebio Kino, a frequent face in Arizona history, established the mission here, indoctrinating the Pima Indians in the way of Roman Catholicism via ristras and rosaries. The mission led to the presidio in Tubac. You can tour the mission church, cemetery, and outlying structures. Check out the mission courtyard and garden just off the visitor center. $3 per person 17 and older.

✳ To Do

BIRDING The **Anza Trail** (see *Hiking*) follows the Santa Cruz River, a major birding thoroughfare. The riparian forest is a welcome habitat for passerines and an interesting variety of mammals, including an occasional jaguar.

Madera Canyon. Contact the Nogales Ranger District. One of *the* birding hot spots in the world accommodates one of the darlings of the avian world—the elegant trogon. About 240 species of birds live in the canyon.

GOLF The Tubac area has courses that rate among the state's best. With temperatures running warmer than Phoenix and Tucson, they make an excellent play in winter.

Rio Rico Golf and Country Club (520-281-8567), 1069 Camino Caralampi. This Robert Trent Jones Sr. golf layout hosts qualifying rounds for the U.S. Open and the Senior Open. Rye grass fairways and bent grass greens look gorgeous with the surrounding ridgelines rising all around. The front nine rates among the state's most challenging, and you'll find yourself in trouble if you don't have the skills right from the start with long yardages and sand traps. Private lessons, clubhouse, restaurant, and shop. $29–59.

Palo Duro (520-761-4394), 2690 N Country Club Dr., Nogales. Located along the border, this par-72 foothill course has views of Arizona's Santa Rita Mountains and the San Cayatano Mountains in Mexico. The course has a number of obstacles, from canyons and streams to doglegs all over the place. The 8th hole (par 5) has a 90-degree turn in the middle of the fairway with an optical illusion. From there, the entire back nine will test your mettle. Let's hope it's as tough as the wood of the tree for which the course is named. Restaurant and pro shop. $30–59.

Tubac Golf Club (520-398-2211 or 800-848-7893), 1 Otero Rd. History is a big thing in these parts, and this golf course has some interesting brushes with it. The historic Anza Trail passes through the 17th and 18th holes. More recent history was generated at the 15th hole, where Kevin Costner, aka the character Roy McAvoy in *Tin Cup*, sank his ball in the pond that fronts it. He then threw the golf ball onto Otera Road. This scene, to Hollywood's credit, is accurate. The bent grass greens are described as slick and tricky, and that pond is a troublemaker. As a counter to the Hollywood glitz, it's the only golf course in the state where you'll see cows on the fairways. The pastoral grounds include a line of giant eucalyptuses, lily ponds, and a couple of meanders of the Santa Cruz River. Excellent practice facilities and a shop. $59–109 (cart included).

HIKING **Anza Trail** (4 miles each way; easy). Trailheads located at Tubac Presidio State Park and Tumacacori National Historic Park. Juan Bautista de Anza blazed this trail along the Santa Cruz River on his expedition from Culican, Mexico, to San Francisco. A segment of this historic trail has been reconstructed into a maintained trail that follows the Santa Cruz River from Tubac down to Tumacacori. Free.

Atascosa Peak can be conquered via the **Atascosa Lookout Trail** in the Coronado National Forest. The 2.5-mile-long trail takes you to an enchanting panorama that looks into Mexico. Take I-19 to the Ruby Rd. exit, and go about 27 miles west to the trailhead.

Brown Canyon (520-823-4251, ext. 116). One of the state's best kept secrets has a trail that takes you into land where wildlife prevails. Reservations are necessary. Guided hikes, led by an escort from Buenos Aires Wildlife Refuge, take place the second Saturday each month Nov.–Apr. and cost $5 per person. Private tours cost $40 for up to 12 people, and it's worth the rare opportunity to see

THE TUBAC GOLF CLUB OFFERS A PASTORAL COURSE COMPLETE WITH COWS.

HISTORY IS VISIBLE ALL OVER TUBAC.

unspoiled grasslands and mountain slopes where jaguars roam. Call for reservations and directions.

Sycamore Canyon delves into the heart of the Pajarita Mountains. The 5.8-mile-long trail has an amazing array of botanicals not found elsewhere in the state. The perennial creek that flows through attractive geology also makes a big draw for wildlife. Take I-19 to the Ruby Rd. exit, and go about 29 miles west to the trailhead.

MOUNTAIN BIKING Singletrack trails are not the Tubac area specialty; rather, it's the network of remote back roads traversing some beautiful backcountry. Get yourself a copy of the *DeLorme Arizona Atlas & Gazetteer* and/or a map of the Coronado National Forest Nogales Ranger District, pick a route, and have some fun. Remember that designated wilderness areas (such as the Mount Wrightson Wilderness Area) do not permit mechanized vehicles, including bicycles.

✳ Wilder Places

Sonoita Creek State Natural Area (520-287-2791). From I-19, take exit 17 (Rio Rico), turn east (left) onto Rio Rico Dr., and continue to Pendleton Dr.; turn south (left) and go to Coatimundi; turn east (right) and drive to the parking area. The state's first natural area recently opened to the public, allowing visitors to see parts of the Sonoita Creek drainage as densely occupied by avian life as its cousin, the San Pedro River—one of the world's most biologically diverse areas. Seven distinct vegetative communities are present in the just-over-5,000-acre space. In addition, the natural area lies in a transitional zone between the Chihuahuan and Sonoran Deserts. Species from each zone interlope. Call for hours and admission.

✳ Lodging

BED AND BREAKFASTS AND INNS

ⓒ **Amado Territory Ranch Inn** (888-398-8684), 3001 E. Frontage Rd., I-19 exit 48, Amado. Rustic yet elegant, each of the nine rooms has historic southwestern decor kept to impeccable standards. Although the interiors edge toward rugged Victorian, and a traditional high tea is served in the guest ranch, amenities are modern. $95–135.

ⓒ **Hacienda Corona de Guevavi Bed and Breakfast** (520-287-6503), 48 South River Rd., Nogales. Bullfighter-turned-artist Salvador Corona inspired the name of this ranch-turned-B&B. Interior courtyard walls have murals painted by Corona 1944–1952 featuring indigenous scenes of Mexican culture. John Wayne used to stay here when rancher Ralph Wingate owned the property. Wingate loaned some of his cattle for the movie *Red River*, starring the Duke. Afterward, Wayne stayed several times at the ranch, and he and Wingate would play gin rummy for hours. Owner-innkeepers Wendy and Phil Stover have done an outstanding job renovating the ranch and each room to give guests over-the-top comfort with a casual atmosphere. There are five guest rooms and a 100-year-old casita available. Rooms don't have phone or TV, but guests can use the phone and computer in the library and watch TV in the bar. When it comes to breakfast, the Stovers' former lives as restaurateurs make a

strong presence. Innovative touches and homemade dishes make delicious and memorable meals. Guests can use the pool and the cabana and party house next to it. Children over 8 are okay; no pets. $175–225.

ⓒ ♿ **Tubac Country Inn** (520-398-3178), 13 Burruel St. Located right in town next to the Old Town shopping district in a peaceful garden setting. Innkeepers Ivan and April have thought of everything: queen bed, microwave, mini refrigerator, coffee, tea, hot chocolate, tableware, glasses, coffee grinder, WiFi, and TV. The rooms have a casual but polished southwestern elegance reflective of the town. The largest of the five rooms and suites available includes a workroom. A breakfast basket appears outside your door each morning with an assortment of cheese, fresh-cut fruit, juice, baked goods made that morning, and yogurt. The property features garden benches, a *chiminea* niche, and a barbecue; each room has separate access and porch space. $110–150 for up to two people per night; $25 per extra person. Children over 12 are okay, but no pets.

RESORT ⓒ ♣ ♿ **Tubac Golf Resort** (520-398-2211 or 800-848-7893), 1 Otero Rd. More caballero than cowboy, the resort stands on part of the former Otero cattle ranch located on the first Spanish Land Grant in the Southwest. Bing Crosby and partners bought the cattle ranch in 1959 and started the golf resort. Many of the original buildings still stand. It's one of the few resorts around that has a distinct gentlemen's appeal and estate feeling with tons of laid-back class. A relatively recent remodeling project has included the talents of area artisans down to the details: delicate handmade-paper wall sconces, entry doors fashioned from solid mesquite, latticed saguaro rib ceilings, hand-forged iron door handles, chairs upholstered with strips of serape, and cobblestone floors. The 70 guest rooms include high-speed Internet, robes, refrigerator, and coffee; 27 casitas feature separate living room and dressing area, fireplace and private patio; and 24 haciendas boast state-of-the-art sound system, flat-screen TV, jet tub, walk-in shower, sunken living room, fireplace, and patio. The Otero Suite in the historic Otero Hacienda has a bedroom, living room, den with kitchenette, fireplace, and private patio with golf course and mountain views. Casitas have richly crafted interiors that include leather furniture and Native American rugs. The 600-acre property has two restaurants, a swimming pool, chapel, golf course, spa, bicycles, croquet, volleyball, hiking on the Anza Trail, and meeting space. Oct.–Apr., $135–415; May–Sep., $99–275. Additional charges apply for additional guests; two-pet limit at $25 each.

✳ Where to Eat

DINING OUT **The Artist's Palate** (520-398-3333), 40 Avenida Goya. Open Tue.–Sun. for lunch 11:30–3, dinner 5–9. Relatively new, but gaining a respectful reputation for consistency, this themed restaurant leans toward the gourmet in menu selections. Carrying names pertaining to the arts, you can order Masterpieces (main courses) such as Renoir Filet Mignon and Chicken Cordon Louvre. Landscapes (salads) might be anything from Cézannes Caesar to Francis Bacon Baby Spinach Salad. Paints (soups) come in A Different Color Every Day. Multi-Media (pastas) could be as traditional as De Anza Lasagna or as avant-garde as Spaghetti and Warhol Meatballs made with saffron spaghetti. Mona Lisa's Pizzas are self-explanatory. Finishing Touches, like Death by Chocolate Cake and Windsor's Castle (A Royal Treat), make dessert an extravagant adventure. Water Colors (libations) are drinks from the full bar, with a menu of trendy cocktails. The lovely wine list ranges from Louis Jadot Pouilly Fuissé to St. Francis Old Vine Zinfandel by the glass or bottle; there are several very nice bottles ranging from Pezzi King (Dry Creek Valley, $35) to Roederer "Cristal" Champagne ($350). Entrées $18–26.

Border House Bistro (520-398-8999), 12-A Plaza Rd. Open daily 11–3 for lunch, 5–9 for dinner. Rustic and romantic, with a menu reminiscent of owner Benedetta Mattioli's Venetian homeland—but spiked with southwestern flavors. Lunch is special, from the handmade pizza cooked in a wood-burning oven to the fresh soups, salads, and hamburgers that leave an indelible mark on your memory. Steaks, chops, and free-range chicken make up the dinner menu. The Best Filet Mignon lives up to its name. The portions are big, with plenty of vegetables. Try the champagne mango salad in-season (May–Aug.). If you don't mind sharing, two can share a starter and entrée and leave the table full. Entrées $18–26.

Dos Silos (520-398-3737), 1 Otero Rd. Open Thu.–Mon. 11–9. Named for the two silos on the patio dating back to the original historic Otero cattle ranch. Inside, the decor is richly Southwest: copper-top tables with cobalt-blue glasses and plates. A mural on the wall depicts an agave farm, the plant from which tequila is made. The food is fresh with just the right touch of spices. Cilantro is one of chef George Bigley's favorites. The Baja-style fish tacos are excellent, and the *mole rojo con pollo*, described by the chef as "complicated to make but very rewarding," is just that. Cheese just gushes out the chile relleno *con queso*, and the corn casserole (included with entrée plates) is more than just cornbread with character—it's a signature dish. One of the special features of the restaurant is the real lime (or pomegranate) juice in every margarita. "Sweet-and-sour mix shouldn't be anywhere near a margarita," explains chef George Bigley. "Treat our margaritas like a martini. Half of it is alcohol." Entrées $11–13.

Melio's Trattoria Ristorante Italiano (520-398-8494), 2261 E. Frontage Rd. Open Wed.–Sat. 11:30–9 (till 8 Sun.); closed Mon.–Tue. Owners Elio and Melinda Trovarelli met in Rome and ran a trattoria there for a decade before moving to Arizona. *Melio* means "the best" in Italian, and it happens to be the combination of their two names. The restaurant lives up to its romantic genesis (with huge views of the Santa Rita Mountains by day and candlelight at night) and name. In a town where longevity is based on quality, Melio's has prevailed nicely for more than 10 years. The menu has classic dishes that taste much lighter than Sicilian—15 pastas; 10 meat, fish, and poultry dishes; and almost a dozen antipasti. Plus, they serve authentic Roman-style pizza, with a thin handmade and hand-rolled crust and an assortment of toppings. Popular dishes are the

homemade meat lasagna, filet mignon, and veal dishes. Desserts include tiramisu, pies, and fruit mimosa cake. Entrées $8.95–19.95.

Shelby's Bistro (520-398-8075), 19 Tubac Rd. Open daily for lunch 11–4, Wed.–Sat. for dinner 5–9. On a typical day in the high season, owner-chef Anthony can serve more than 200 people for lunch. His restaurant rates high among the locals. Anthony draws from his Mediterranean roots (southern France and southern Spain) for recipes. He makes nine different pastas and 10 different meat dishes. When he describes them as unique, he does so correctly, as he uses lavender, tarragon, fennel, and cilantro in these dishes and goes easy on the cream. Chef Anthony's creativity shows up in appetizers like baked Brie with fresh herb bread and pecans and oven-baked salmon artichoke spread; dinners such as Sonoran rubbed grilled pork chop and lobster with fresh spinach leaves. His pizza—European style with a thin crust and light sauce and cheese—is well-known in the area. Chef Anthony serves wines from California, Washington, Chile, and Argentina. Entrées $12.95–14.95.

EATING OUT **Las Trankas Mexican Food & Bakery** (520-377-7153), 1136 W. Frontage Rd., Rio Rico. Open Mon.–Sat. 7 AM–8 PM (till 6 Sun.). This restaurant feels right at home located *this close* to the Mexican border. It's real Mexican fare here, including the *queso*, chorizo, *machaca*, and menudo. On Sunday mornings mariachis serenade while you decide among breakfast dishes such as huevos rancheros, *huevos Mexicanos*, and *chilaquiles verdes y* *huevo motulenos*. Lunch entrées, available until closing, are classic Mexicana. Steaks are served 4:30–8. As the name says, this is also a bakery. The great display of pastries gives you a chance to decide which delectable Mexican treat is better than the other. Just get a bagful and be done with it. You won't be disappointed. Entrées $6.50–14.95.

Tubac Deli & Coffee Co. (520-398-3330), 6 Plaza Rd. Open daily 6:30–5:30. There are a lot of special things about this deli. Pastries are fresh baked every day. The pecan pinwheels can be hazardous if you're not known for moderation. The coffee is gourmet. Sandwiches include deli favorites like Reubens, tuna or turkey melts, and roast beef dip. And it's the only WiFi access in the area. If you're

LA PALOMA DE TUBAC.

a customer, you need only to open up your laptop and "plug in." Cash or checks only; no credit cards accepted. ATM machine available. Sandwiches $3.50–6.25.

✳ The Arts

The perennial art community has strong southwestern leanings. Several artists in town have galleries in their homes and open them by appointment. You can contact the chamber of commerce or Tubac Center of the Arts for information. Two native sons, both passed on, have galleries in town: **Hal Empie Studio & Gallery** (520-398-2811), 33 Tubac Rd., and **Hugh Cabot Studio & Gallery** (420-398-2721), 10 Calle Iglesia. **Karin Newby Gallery** (520-398-9662), 19 Tubac Rd., has a penchant for eclectic southwestern art. The gallery just opened up a sculpture garden, one of the largest in the Southwest.

&. **Tubac Center of the Arts** (520-398-2371), 9 Plaza Rd. Open Mon.–Sat. 10–4:30, Sun. 1–4:30; closed major holidays. The Santa Cruz Valley's major art organization exists to provide a venue for artistic activity. The center has three galleries with more than 3,500 square feet of exhibit space, a members' gallery, a performance stage, an art library, and a gallery shop. A number of exhibits run during the high season, as well as a performing arts series, art and cultural workshops for adults and children, an adult choral group, the Tubac Singers, and several benefit events. A monthlong arts program takes place in summer and culminates in July with a reception, exhibit, and performances. Donations accepted.

✳ Selective Shopping

More than 90 businesses line the village's Old Town area; it can easily take you a full day to peruse them all.

La Paloma de Tubac (520-398-9231), 1 Presidio Dr. Open daily 10–5. Like an open-air Latin American marketplace, this corner market has a collection of about 10,000 pieces of folk art handmade by more than 1,000 different artisans. The owners have dealt with the same families of Peruvian, Ecuadorian, Guatemalan, and Mexican artists for years, and you'll find an interesting collection of quality traditional crafts at good prices. If you don't plan to dip into Old Mexico, head here.

Old Presidio Traders (520-398-9333), 27 Tubac Rd. Open daily 9–5, except major holidays. Garry and Lisa Hembree have been here for 25 years, offering Native American crafts and jewelry. The Hembrees have traveled the reservations of northern Arizona and Mew Mexico for more than 30 years and are known for their authentic selection of Indian pawn at very reasonable prices, plus a large selection of fetishes,

✳ Special Events

January: **Santa Cruz Valley Car Nuts Car Show** brings vintage cars out of protective cover for all to adore.

February: **Tubac Festival of the Arts**, Tubac's big event, showcases the work of hundreds of visiting artists, craftspersons, and musicians from around the country and Canada.

March: **Art Walk** gives visitors a chance to take a look at artists' studios.

October: Tubac Presidio's **Anza Days** presents a Living History of the Indian, Mexican and Spanish Colonial Periods with military demonstrations, folkloric dancers, ethnic music, and food.

November: **Tubac, An Art Experience**, presents an object lesson in art: Village artists demonstrate their works to the tunes of local musicians.

December: During the annual holiday celebration of **Luminaria Nights/ Fiesta Navidad**, luminaries line the streets and stores stay open until 9.

ARIVACA

T he saying goes: *You know you're lost if you end up in Arivaca*. The community, located on a secondary road off I-19, is isolated, but not necessarily insular. If you want to drop out of the fray of life, check out this interesting townsite that has all the comforts of home—a general store, a few restaurants, a bakery, gas station, artists' co-op, coffee shop, library, and two bars.

Tucked away and tiny, but with a big personality that celebrates individualism, Arivaca still holds fresh memories of the independent ranchers and miners who lived here in the olden days. The land, especially, still looks much the way it always has: wild, beautiful landscapes and big skies. The last federal township has roots tied to the Hohokam Indians. Now the area hosts an interesting compendium of artists, outdoor lovers, astronomy buffs, and birders who don't seem to mind living off the beaten path.

The little town actually has quite a connection with the outside world. People pass through all the time on their way to the Buenos Aires National Wildlife Refuge, Arivaca Lake, the ghost town of Ruby, and trails in the Coronado National Forest. Plus, they grow 20,000 pounds of certified organic produce each year that's sold to local communities and distributed to residents in need.

GADSEN COFFEE, THE HEART OF ARIVACA.

Whether you're lost, just passing through, or looking to stay, Arivaca makes an interesting place to explore.

GUIDANCE Community web site: www.arivaca.net. If you plan to visit anywhere in the Coronado National Forest, contact **Nogales Ranger District** (520-281-2296), 303 Old Tucson Rd., Nogales, for information.

GETTING THERE From Tucson, drive south on I-19 about 30 miles to Arivaca Rd. (exit 48) and head west; or take AZ 86 west to AZ 286 south, then continue east on Arivaca Rd.

WHEN TO COME It's best to head here from October through April. If you plan to visit in summer, consider taking a siesta in midafternoon when the day's heat reaches its highest temperatures in these desert lands.

MEDICAL EMERGENCY Arivaca Clinic (520-398-2621). Call for hours.

✳ To See

SCENIC DRIVES You can pick just about any back road in the area and have yourself a scenic drive. However, the **Road to Ruby** (about 44 miles long) is one of the more memorable. The sedan-friendly route (time and weather may change road conditions; the first 9 miles are paved) starts in Arivaca and twists and turns through some of the most scenic countryside this side of the border on its way to I-19. Volcano-formed peaks contain stunning colors and shapes. Just beyond Montana Mountain at about mile 15 are the ruins of Ruby. The town's present owners charge $12 for visitors to tour the well-preserved ghost town started in 1912.

✳ To Do

BIRDING Arivaca Lake and **Buenos Aires Wildlife Refuge** (see *Wilder Places*) present some of the best birding in the state. The refuge has Arivaca Creek (located about 2 miles west of Arivaca on Arivaca Rd.) and Arivaca Cienega (0.25 mile east of town on Arivaca Rd.) to attract avian guests. A free, guided bird walk takes place each Saturday at 8 AM, Nov.–Apr., at Arivaca Cienega.

CANOEING & KAYAKING Quiet little Arivaca Lake is located about 7 miles from Arivaca, on Ruby Road. Originally built to water local cattle, the lake is managed by the Nogales Ranger District. Gas engines are prohibited here, and wildlife likes that, too.

HIKING Just outside town you can choose from Arivaca Creek (located about 2 miles west of Arivaca) and Arivaca Cienega (located 0.25 mile east of town).

LABYRINTH WALK The **Desert Light Labyrinth** is open to the public regularly. It's an eight-circuit labyrinth (eight being the number of the unknown) built in the view (and energetic shadow) of Baboquivari, a mountain sacred to local tribes, who believe it is the source of creation. You can walk the labyrinth or meditate. Silence is golden here, where healing and self-inquiry happens. Turn left onto Ruby Rd., go 2.25 miles, then turn right onto Old Stage Rd. and continue to the road's end. Free.

MOUNTAIN BIKING Locals call the area Moab South because of the incredible cache of bikable terrain. Jeep trails provide the track, and you can wind around the backcountry on them for hours without crossing paths with a vehicle—or a human. You might see some wildlife, however. These roads accommodate riders from gonzo to timid. All you need is a map of the Coronado National Forest Nogales Ranger District or a copy of *Arizona Atlas & Gazetteer* and a sense of adventure. Bring plenty of water, sunscreen, and a helmet.

✳ Wilder Places

Arivaca Lake (520-281-2296). Go west on Arivaca Rd., and turn south onto Forest Road 216; go about a mile and turn east onto FR 39; go about 5 miles to a road that turns left (east) to the lake. As isolated as the town for which it's named, the lake has but a toilet and a primitive boat ramp. With only single electric trolling motors allowed on the lake, it's a great place to get some R&R and/or bird-watch. Free.

Buenos Aires National Wildlife Refuge (520-423-4251, ext. 116). From Arivaca, go west about 2 miles on Arivaca Rd. to reach the refuge boundary and another 10 miles to AZ 286 to reach the western boundary. To reach the headquarters, drive north about 8 miles on AZ 286. Once a ranch named Buenos Ayrees, Spanish for "good air," this refuge in southeast Arizona's Altar Valley has recaptured the native characteristic that inspired its name—a sea of rolling grasses that wavers in gentle high-desert breezes. The rich grassland attracts a variety of watchable wildlife, including an occasional jaguar and the masked bobwhite quail. A walk along the Arivaca Cienega or Arivaca Creek gives glimpses of some of the 340 species of birds sighted in the refuge.

✳ Lodging

BED AND BREAKFASTS AND INNS

Arivaca's Country Bed and Breakfast (520-399-9219), 16225 Universal Ranch Rd. No dirt roads to get to this B&B, which is a little different for Arivaca. The property has a one-room kitchenette, simple and clean, with bath, telephone, microwave, refrigerator, and toaster. A full breakfast is included. $75.

BirdHouse Lodgings (520-398-2944), 15750 W. Universal Ranch Rd. Owner-innkeepers Laura and Eric named their property for its former life as a parakeet barn and chicken house. It has undergone a major renovation with no clue, other than their word, that birds once prevailed there. Laura did a great job decorating the interiors with touches of rustic elegance. Eric installed butcherblock counters. Choose from two options:

GUEST RANCH

Rancho de la Osa (520-823-4257 or 800-872-6240), Sasabe. With a history dating back to the celebrated Father Kino's Jesuit priests, the cantina in this old adobe compound is said to be the oldest building in the state. The compound itself, made of hand-formed adobe (mud) bricks, is one of the last great Spanish haciendas still standing in America. Even though all the buildings, and many of the guest rooms, have experienced centuries of use, the property is neat, clean, and highly aesthetic. Color, art, and memorabilia make each room a point of interest. Each has handcrafted pillows and bedspreads, a private bath, porch, and separate entry. Most have a wood-burning fireplace. Original artwork, Mexican antiques, and whimsical designs capture the colorful spirit of the desert Southwest. Wranglers manage a corral of horses for guest to ride; you'll also find a pool, heated to 83 degrees in winter, and lots of peace and quiet under the shade of a forest of eucalyptus trees more than 100 years old. Three meals described as "Southwest fusion" are included. $220–250 per person, double occupancy.

THE RANCHO DE LA OSA RESORT IS ONE OF THE OLDEST ADOBE BUILDINGS IN ARIZONA.

an 1,100-square-foot living space that has a kitchen, laundry privileges, king bed, and three-quarter bath with shower; or an adobe cottage with two rooms and a bath and a half. $75–100.

✳ Where to Eat

Arivaca Sourdough Bakery (928-398-9239), 16725 W. Arivaca Rd. Open Wed.–Mon. 10–5:30. *Somebody had to do it.* That's the reason Jeanie, the present owner of this popular bakery, gives as to why she took it over. The bakery only serves yummies and sourdough bread. You can also buy Oaxacan wood carvings at a great price.

Gadsen Coffee Co. (520-398-3251), 22 Arivaca Garden Way. Open Mon.–Thu. 9–3, Fri.–Sun. 9–5. Catch up on counterculture news with a very fresh-roasted cup of organic coffee here. The owner, Tom Shook, is particular about his coffee. He serves only traditionally farmed coffee and religiously roasts it himself every Mon., Tue., and Wed. Besides a good cup of coffee and gossip, you can also pick up some great baked goods, soups, salads, sandwiches, and smoothies here. Listen to live music on Friday nights and sometimes on Sunday afternoons. Entrées $4.95–7.

Grubstake Saloon (520-398-9130), 16785 W. Arivaca Rd. Open daily 8–5 (till 7 on Fri.–Sun.). You might have noticed how Arivaca has two business districts along the Arivaca Rd. The original town started on the east end of the road. John Fry, who owned the Grubstake Mine in nearby Warsaw Canyon, bought this building on the west side—originally intended to be a hardware store—because he was peeved at the town. You can learn all kinds of local history here, as well as enjoying some Oriental food Fri.–Sun.

✳ The Arts

Arivaca Artists' Co-op (520-398-9488), Main St. next to the Mercantile. Open Wed.–Sun. 11–4. You'll get a good feel for the talent floating around Arivaca and neighboring communities where the artists who exhibit here come from. The community has only about 1,200 residents, but creativity and independence run high on their lists of characteristics. The co-op has everything from tie-dyed clothing to mesquite furniture; photography to pottery.

BENSON

A classic example of the saying *Good things come in little packages*, this small town has a number of niche-type museums and points of interest on subjects you might find in a Trivial Pursuit game. It's a doorway for several points of interest in Cochise County and always has been.

The town started as a stage stop for the Butterfield Overland Stage mail delivery route. When prospectors struck it rich in Cochise County mines, the Union Pacific Railroad laid tracks through the stage stop to cozy up to the silver boomtown of Tombstone. Thanks to the railroad, Benson was born.

Benson became a railroad hub with a global population of Mexicans, Chinese, and Anglo cowboys, miners, and railroad workers, mostly men. As the town grew, so did the saloons, gambling houses, and cache of ladies of ill repute. Oftentimes the town would try its hand at respectability, ridding itself of undesirables, but it took churches and schools to bring stability. By 1913 the railroads expanded to other cities, and by 1920 mine production slowed. Ranching and farming followed, and the wild bachelors of the cosmopolitan hub of the mining towns and camps either moved on to seek their fortunes elsewhere or finally settled down into connubial bliss. Benson's had a few brushes with ghost-town status but has always endured.

GUIDANCE **Benson Visitor Center** (520-586-4293), 249 E. 4th St. For information on the Coronado National Forest, contact the **Douglas Ranger District** (520-364-3468), 3081 N. Leslie Canyon Rd., Douglas. **Bureau of Land Management** (520-439-6400) has information on the San Pedro Riparian National Conservation Area.

GETTING THERE *By car:* With I-10 running through the town, you need only head east from Tucson or west from Willcox to get there. AZ 90 drops to the south from Benson, as does AZ 80, only a few miles east. *By air:* **Benson Municipal Airport** (520-586-2245) is located 2 miles north of the AZ 90/I-10 interchange for private craft. *By bus:* The **Greyhound Bus** stop is located at Benson Flower Shop (520-586-3388), 680 W. 4th St. You cannot acquire tickets from this stop, but you may call the Greyhound Telephone Information Center at 800-231-2222. *By train:* **Amtrak** (800-872-7245).

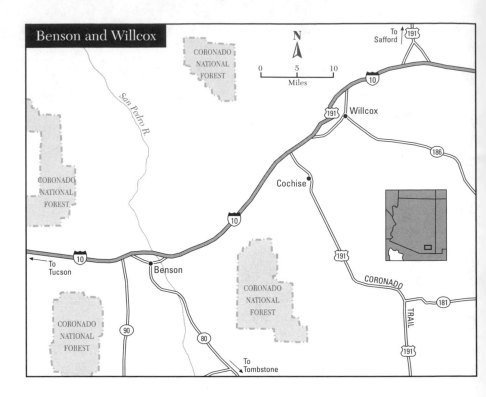

GETTING AROUND Southwestern Aviation (520-586-3262) offers rental cars starting at $25 per day.

WHEN TO COME Even with its 3,585-foot elevation, Benson sizzles in the high 90s in summer. Fall and winter calm down to agreeable levels, and winter, comfortable to many, averages about 62 daytime degrees.

MEDICAL EMERGENCY Benson Hospital (520-586-2261), 450 S. Ocotillo.

✳ To See

The Amerind Foundation (520-586-3662), 2100 N. Amerind Rd., Dragoon. Open Tue.–Sun. 10–4; closed Mon. and major holidays. One of Arizona's more unusual museums gets its name from a contraction of *American Indian*, to which the foundation devotes itself through art, artifacts, and research. New Englander William Fulton started the foundation, a result of his love of archaeology. The museum, a compound of Spanish Colonial Revival–style buildings built in 1930–1959, houses Fulton's private collection of ethnographic and archaeological materials, one of the best private collections in the world. $5 adults, $4 seniors (60-plus), $3 ages 12–18, under 12 free.

Gammons Gulch Ghost Town Movie Set (520-212-2831). Open Wed.–Sun. 9–4. Jay Gammons bought the land to set the stage for this living museum 35 years ago, then started collecting historical buildings from ghost towns to re-create an

1890s mining camp. The whole town is authentic, from the shingle nails on the roofs to the old-time machines and outhouses; and everything has a story. You might see parts of the town in a movie or commercial. $7 adults, $3 under 18.

Holy Trinity Monastery (520-720-4642). Located off AZ 80 south of St. David between mileposts 302 and 303. This Benedictine monastery glows with a halo of peace, harmony, and beauty. This is where people living in an Andy Warhol painting retreat when they want to experience a Monet world; where the curious come to find out just what goes on in a monastery (usually prayer or meditation, so you won't see many people milling about here). Nevertheless, you can explore the bird sanctuary, Prayer and Meditation Garden, museum, and even join the padres for breakfast, lunch, or dinner. Just don't expect engaging conversation, as most of the meals follow the monastic tradition of silence. You can even spend the night in the simple visitor quarters ($40–60).

✔ ♿ **Kartchner Caverns** (520-586-2283). From I-10, take exit 302 (Benson) and drive 9 miles south on AZ 90 to the signed entrance. Open daily 8–5 except state holidays. One of the world's premier caverns gives you the chance to walk through a live cave still in the process of evolving and growing. The air hangs thick, like a sultry night in a Louisiana swamp; water drips arbitrarily all around. Kartchner is among the top 10 caves in the world for unusual minerals. It contains colorful and diverse formations such as fragile crystalline rods, flowstone walls, and quartz needles. The park includes a discovery center that features a makeshift underground journey plus a video explaining the history of the cave; you'll also find a gift shop, picnic areas, ramadas, restrooms, hummingbird garden, and the 4-mile (aboveground) Guindoni Loop trail. There's a park entrance fee of $5 per car (up to two adults), or get in free with a tour reservation. Rotunda/Throne Room Tour $18.95 adults, $9.95 ages 7–13, free for children 6 and younger; Big Room Tour $22.95 adults, $12.95 ages 7–13; no children under 7.

San Pedro Valley Art & Historical Society (520-586-3070), 180 S. San Pedro. Open Wed.–Fri. 10–4 (till 2 Sat. and in summer). When the old mercantile store, built in the early 1920s, changed hands more than 20 years ago to become a museum, some of its inventory went with it and remains on display here. The museum houses a variety of historic items, from an 1900 horse-drawn school bus to a steam engine, maps, and historic memorabilia of Benson. It showcases changing displays and exhibits highlighting local cultures. Donations accepted.

Singing Wind Bookshop (520-586-2425), 700 W. Singing Wind Rd. Open daily 9–5. If you have any bibliophile blood flowing in you, this bookshop will captivate you. Located off the beaten path a mile north of town on a working cattle ranch, it's known the world over. Books about the West and Southwest prevail, but don't be surprised to find a few anomalous niche subjects. The shop, more a social happening than a bookstore, has scheduled events throughout the year.

✳ To Do

BIRDING **City of Benson Wastewater Ponds and Birding Trail** (520-586-4293). The ponds are located north of I-10 on Darby St. (follow signs to the animal shelter). The Birding Trail is found on 4th just past the visitor center: Go left on San Pedro, right on Pearl, and pass under the interstate to the San Pedro River. **San Pedro Riparian National Conservation Area** (Fairbanks BLM Headquarters, 520-586-3467). One of the premier birding sites in the world stretches from St. David to Naco, Mexico, along the upper San Pedro River. At the Fairbanks area, located about 26 miles south of Benson, you'll find flycatchers, red-tailed hawks, Gambel's quail, and buntings.

GOLF **San Pedro Golf Course** (520-586-7888), 926 N. Madison. Bluegrass fairways with bent grass greens gives you a true links experience. The 18-hole championship course stretches 7,313 yards from the tips and plays along the banks of the San Pedro on the front 9; the back 9 presents four canyonlike settings and finishes with the 457-yard par-4 split-fairway signature 18th hole. Five sets of tees give you a fighting chance no matter what your experience level. Still, less experienced players may end up wanting to throw an iron or two into the San Pedro River. Grill, golf shop. $44.95–45.95.

HIKING The **Dragoon Mountains** (see *Wilder Places*) present a unique landscape to explore. If you want to know what the basic lay of the land looks like, hike the popular 5-mile **Cochise Stronghold Trail**. For a more intimate look, take the tucked-away 3.5-mile **Slavin Gulch Trail.** Contact the Douglas Ranger District.

ROCK CLIMBING The **Dragoon Mountains**, one of the best climbing spots in the state, have more than 100 routes in their labyrinthine maze of granite formations. Contact the Douglas Ranger District.

✳ Wilder Places

Dragoon Mountains. Located about 25 miles south of Benson. Contact the Douglas Ranger District. Lying like a lazy dragon stretched across the high-desert grasslands floor, the Dragoons evoke an aura of fantasy with their strangely sculpted peaks and outcroppings. Their curious granite landscape of towering pinnacles, boulders precariously balanced atop one another, and spiny peaks that look like fingers pointing every which way makes a perfect hideaway. The confusing jumble of rocks became the last stronghold of Cochise and his loyal band of Apache. Cochise always retreated to these mountains after bloody battles over his coveted land. Like an impenetrable rocky cocoon, the Dragoons never failed to protect him as he turned southeast Arizona on end. The Dragoons still keep watch over Cochise, never telling where his fellow Apache buried his body in the labyrinthine formations.

✳ Lodging

✎ **Cochise Stronghold Bed and Breakfast** (520-826-4140 or 877-426-4141). Located in a canyon amid the mountains to which legendary Apache leader Cochise retreated, this nature retreat has a special atmosphere steeped in the legends and lore of its colorful past. Tranquil yet wild, the land around the canyon still defers to nature and wildlife. Owner-innkeepers John and Nancy Yates note that any stress guests bring with them dissolves overnight. The Yates built environmentally savvy casitas full of amenities to make your stay as comfortable as the landscape will make it memorable. Straw-bale casitas have a fully equipped kitchenette or kitchen, king or queen beds, private bath, and patio with barbecue grill. For a wilderness experience kids will love, you can stay in the B&B's tepee. It has a double and two single beds, Franklin wood-stove with plenty of wood, outside running water, fire pit, and hot shower station. You can rent the whole ranch for a totally intimate stay. A full break-fast, served in your casita or tepee, is included; and you can order steaks or salmon to make your own dinner or have John and Nancy get groceries for your stay. Double occupancy for casitas $159–189; tepee $89; add $25 for each person. Rent the whole ranch for $439 plus base rate.

Down by the River Bed and Breakfast (520-720-9441), 2255 Efken Place, St. David. This newly built Santa Fe–style B&B has views from all angles. Four rooms have king or queen beds; two have whirlpool and beehive fireplace. The great room, open to all guests, has 12-foot ceilings with ponderosa logs and latilla. Oversized pool table and barbecue open for guest use. No children under 8, and no pets. June–Oct., $85–95, Nov.–May, $105–130.

✳ Where to Eat

Horseshoe Café (520-586-3303), 154 E. 4th St. Open daily 7 AM–8 PM. The two-story building, home to one of the area's most enduring and endearing western restaurants, has had the same menu for the last cou-ple of decades. The southwestern fare is decent, and the café is famous for its chicken-fried steak and liver and onions. The western decor makes a great ambience. Entrées $6.25–19.95.

Ironwood Grill (520-586-2525), 926 N. Madison St. Open Mon.–Thu. 10:30–5 (till 7 Fri.), Sat. 7–7, Sun. 7–4. Located in the San Pedro Golf Course. One of the town's popular venues serves the perfect hamburger cooked to your temperature specs and a tasty Caesar salad for lunch. Dinner happens on weekends, and the entrée of choice is the prime rib. Cheesecake desserts (with banana, coconut, and rum sauce or turtle divine) are the diet wreckers here. Entrées: lunch $5.25–8.95, dinner $8.95–14.95.

Ruiz's Family Restaurant (520-586-2707), 687 W. 4th St. Open Mon.–Sat. 7 AM–9 PM. A local favorite that serves up authentic Mexican food, this family-owned restaurant has been around for more than four decades here, and travelers make repeat visits when passing through. $7.25–8.25.

✳ Special Events

Contact 520-586-2842 unless noted elsewhere.

February: **Territorial Days** (520-586-9706). Entertainments, food, ven-dors, and a carnival.

May: **Bluegrass in the Park** is a 2-day festival featuring the top blue-grass bands in the nation with food and craft vendors and music work-shops taught by bluegrass masters.

July: **July 4th Celebration** has a parade, entertainment, and fireworks.

October: **Butterfield Overland Stage Days** spans 2 days that start with a parade; also entertainment, food, art and crafts, rodeo, and fireworks.

December: **Christmas on Main Street**. Shopping, Santa, and a lighted parade.

WILLCOX

There are a few towns in Arizona that don't seem to budge much when it comes to change. Willcox is one of them. The old cattle capital still celebrates cowboy history. The late cowboy movie star Rex Allen has a monument and festival dedicated to him. The mercantile store still sells western wear and equipment. And the railroad station is still a focal point in the town. Willcox, like many of the cities in southeastern Arizona, has recently become an ecotourism destination. Birds are big here, specifically the sandhill crane. Even better, a number of one-of-a-kind wilderness areas lie just a short drive away. When you get hungry, Willcox and its environs hold around a dozen U-pick orchards, and just down the road in don't-blink-your-eyes-or-you'll-miss-it Kansas Settlement are salt-of-the-earth farms run by Mennonites. It's an interesting mix of Old West meets ecotourism surrounded by orchards and farms run by people that still believe the best things in life are natural and simple. That alone makes it a truly special place.

GUIDANCE **Cochise Visitor Center** (520-384-2272 or 800-200-7727), 1500 N. Circle I Rd. Located on the eastern side of Willcox. You can watch a video on Willcox's history and the building the center is housed in, a historic railroad station. Pick up a free map and details of a self-guided tour in Willcox, as well as brochures on farm produce and birding spots. A small gift shop has books and maps. **Douglas Ranger District** (520-364-3468), 1192 W. Saddleview Rd., Douglas, has information on backcountry use of the Coronado National Forest. Open Mon.–Fri. 7:30–4:30.

GETTING THERE Willcox straddles I-10, and you can reach it by driving 81 miles east of Tucson or 40 miles west from the New Mexico border. The city also lies at the top of the Cochise Circle Route (AZ 186, AZ 181, US 191, and I-10) that takes you past some great history and scenery.

WHEN TO COME The prime tourist season runs from fall through spring. Fruit and nut orchards ripen late July through September.

MEDICAL EMERGENCY **Northern Cochise Community Hospital** (520-384-3541), 901 Rex Allen Dr.

✳ To See

Willcox Commercial Store (520-384-2448), 180 N. Railroad Ave. Open Mon.–Sat. 8:30–6:30. Built in the early 1880s, this claims to be the oldest continually operating store in the state. It's seen some interesting characters in its heydays. One, for instance, was the great Apache freedom fighter Geronimo. So distrustful of Anglos was the Apache champion that he would risk coming out of hiding to buy a pound of sugar. Why? As the story goes, he didn't trust the white man's pound. He knew how a pound in the hand felt, and Geronimo would hold the sugar in his hand to feel the weight of it. You can still get a pound of sugar (true weight), as well as hats, cowboy boots, and western wear, just like the good old days when Geronimo did his shopping here.

Chiricahua Regional Museum & Research Center (520-384-3971), 127 E. Maley St. Open Mon.–Sat. 10–4. This relatively new museum contains artifacts of the Chiricahua Apache culture as well as frontier memorabilia and a rock collection. The museum covers Apache history from Animas Valley to San Carlos Reservation and the San Pedro Valley to Fronteras, Mexico. Donations accepted.

Fort Bowie National Historic Site (520-847-2500). Go 20 miles south on AZ 186 to unpaved Apache Pass Rd. and turn left; continue 8 miles to the trailhead. Open daily 8–5, except Christmas. The 1.5-mile-long trail to the fort gives you a chance to stretch your legs through some isolated countryside full of colorful history. This was the land where the Apache lived their last days in freedom. The fort, built in 1862 on a mail route, played a big part in quelling the tribe. The Fort Bowie Visitor Center displays military photos and memorabilia. For nature lovers, it has a virtual computer program featuring natural history of the area. Free.

Headquarters Saloon on N. Railroad Ave. While Wyatt Earp made his mark all around the state, especially in Tombstone, his lesser-known youngest brother, Warren, ran a stage route in the area. Warren wasn't as sharp a shooter with a gun; he was shot and killed here in July 1900 carrying nothing but a half-opened pocketknife. Poor Warren rests in peace in the Old Willcox Cemetery.

Rex Allen Museum and Willcox Cowboy Hall of Fame (520-384-4583), 150 N. Railroad Ave. Open 10–4 daily except Thanksgiving, Christmas, and New Year's Day. The legendary country-western singer made a big impact on his beloved Willcox. This museum celebrates the legend's career with memorabilia, including some flashy outfits the silver screen star wore. $2 per person, $5 per family, $3 per couple.

SCENIC DRIVES The **Cochise Circle** (about 87 miles of AZ 186, AZ 181, US 191, and I-10) makes an excellent day trip. Clockwise, you pass through the ghost town Dos Cabezas with its adobe ruins; the turnoff for Chiricahua National Monument; the cemetery where the homesteaders who discovered the monument and lived near it rest; scenic ridges around the junction of AZ 181 with US 191; the turnoff for the little ghost town of Pearce; and Willcox Playa.

✳ To Do

APPLE ORCHARDS The Sulphur Springs Valley provides the requisite climate for apple orchards: sunny days and cool evenings.

Apple Annie's Orchard (520-384-2084 or 800-840-2084), 2081 W. Hardy Rd. Open July–Oct., 8–5:30; Nov., 10–4:30. You can start picking apples here at the beginning of July. The harvest includes Gala, Red and Golden Delicious, Fuji, Rome Beauty, and Granny Smith. If you don't want to labor for the fruits, you can get already picked apples, pies, cider, or an apple-smoked hamburger. The family-run orchard has the largest cider mill in the state.

Stout's Cider Mill (520-384-3696), 1510 N. Circle I Rd. Open daily 9–5 except Thanksgiving and Christmas. From apples to ostrich eggs, you get all unadulterated products here. Known as "that apple place in the desert," the orchard has more than 10,000 apple trees and 18 varieties, including Granny Smith, Gala, Fuji, Jonathan, and Red Delicious. Almost 1,000 apricot, peach, pear, and cherry trees provide fruit for preserves. You can pick apples July–Oct.

BIRDING Willcox labels itself as Arizona's Mecca for Wintering Sandhill Cranes, Raptors, and Sparrows. It's the wide swatches of open-space grasslands that attract many of these species. More than 5,000 sandhill cranes winter at the **Willcox Playa Wildlife Area** (520-628-5376), located southeast of Willcox; go 6 miles east on AZ 186, turn south onto Kansas Settlement Rd., and go 4 miles to the wildlife area. You can hike 1.5 miles to the crane roosting area. **Lake Cochise/Twin Lakes Golf Course** (800-200-2272) draws wading birds and shorebirds during migration and for the winter. Go south on AZ 186 to the signed turnoff for the golf course and follow the birding signs. The **Apache Station Wildlife Area** (520-384-4256) also draws wintering sandhill cranes, and other birds year-round. From I-10 east of Willcox, go south on US 191 for 8.5 miles.

THE WILLCOX TRAIN STATION.

HIKING One of the more fascinating places to hike in the state is **Chiricahua National Monument**. **Chiricahua Wilderness** offers trails less traveled and very beautiful. See *Wilder Places*.

ROAD BICYCLING Most of the highways around here are perfect for road biking—there's little traffic, many have good shoulders, and you'll wheel past tons of open space. Services are limited, however; bring plenty of food, water, and a repair kit. **Kansas Settlement Road** travels flat and scenic farmlands. **AZ 186** traverses a wild and wonderful landscape full of history and rollers. **Dragoon Road**, a little-known niche, travels past acres of fruit and nut orchards with a tease of the Dragoon Mountains' curious rock formations.

Chiricahua National Monument. Contact the National Park Service at 520-824-3560. This national monument has some of the most unusual geology in the state. Formed by a cataclysmic act of volcanism, the lava that makes up the strange formations here was catapulted from its subterranean flow, scientists say, some 25 million years ago as incandescent ash and molten pellets of pumice. As the thick layer of stuff cooled, vertical joints appeared and separated over time, then allowed erosion to have its artistic way, forming the rock spires, totem poles, hoodoos, and bridges in the monument. Head for Massai Point for the best panoramas.

As if this spectacular geological history weren't enough, the flora and fauna is askew as well. The monument is a crossroads for plants and animals. It's a mixed-up area, not only because of the sky island concept, but it has Rocky Mountain, Sierra Madre, Chiricahuan, and Sonoran Desert plants and animals living on the fringe of their natural environment. The **Heart of Rocks Trail**, which so typifies the geological landscape of the monument, lives up to its name. The **Echo Canyon Trail**, spiritually important to the Apache, is the soul.

Chiricahua Wilderness. Contact the Douglas Ranger District. This designated wilderness lies on the sky island range of the Chiricahua Mountains. Its 13 trails cross some of the most attractive mountainscapes in the Southwest with precipitous canyon walls, pine forests with deciduous tree stands along mountain streams, and slopes colored with wildflowers. Avian sightings are legendary. Check out **South Fork Trail** for birds from May through Sept. and fall color in Oct. The **Crest Trail** has dozens of wildflowers in summer. **Rucker Canyon Trail** has some of the most distinctive scenery.

❋ Lodging

HOTELS 🏨 **Cochise Hotel** (520-384-3156 or 877-344-3156), 5062 Cochise Stronghold Rd., Cochise. Built in 1882 and listed on the National Historic Register, this adobe hotel comes with plenty of history. Originally a Wells Fargo office and mail stop, the hotel provided room and board for Southern Pacific Railroad workers. It also saw the likes of Wyatt Earp, Big Nose Kate, Alan Ladd, and John Wayne over the years. The whole town, population 24, is a page from the past, actually. Advertising "honest beds" and home ranch cookin', it's a fun place to stay with a sense of humor. The suites and rooms, clean and comfortable but authentic enough, fit in at the turn of the 20th century, have private bath and period furnishing with antiques dating well into the late 1880s; beds range from double to king. A full breakfast is included in the rates. If you want dinner (comfort ranch food for $17.50 extra—glass of wine included), you must make a reservation. Carla will "gladly and gratefully serve dinner to non-guests with 24 hour notice." $65–95.

GUEST RANCHES ∞ ♿ **Sunglow Ranch** (520-824-3334 or 866-786-4569), 14066 S. Sunglow Rd. Closes mid-May and reopens on Labor Day. Located on 400 acres in the Chiricahua Mountains, next to 300,000 acres of open-space national forest land, the property feels more like retreat grounds. It does in fact host several events through the season. The property has a truly unexpected scene more European than southwestern: an open meadow ringed by mountains with a pond owned by a gaggle of geese. Nine casitas, crafted by neighboring Mennonites, have a colorful and fresh decor. One-bedroom casitas have a queen bed; two-room casitas have a bedroom with two queen beds, living room, fireplace, and futon; and casita grandes have same with two bedrooms. All come supplied with Harney & Sons tea and organic coffee. Healthy gourmet foods for breakfast and dinner are included in the rates. Prime rib and salmon dinners on Saturday nights are open to the public with reservations (see *Where to Eat*). $162.50–212.50 per person, and $70 for each additional guest; casita grande, $325 for two people and $70 per additional guest ($40 for children).

✳ Where to Eat

Burger Barn at Apple Annie's Orchard (520-384-2084), 2081 W. Hardy Rd. Open for lunch mid-July–Oct., Sat.–Sun. 11–3. As you can imagine, apples are big here and appear in everything from pies to apple-smoked burgers. Pancake breakfasts take place about six times through the season. Entrées $5.59–7.59.

Rodney's (520-384 5180), 118 N. Railroad Ave. Open Tue.–Sun. 11–8. Looking like an eatery in Bayou Country, this tiny restaurant is where food happens in Willcox. Rodney, owner-chef, cooks up some excellent meals culled from a variety of cultures, from Cajun to Southwestern to South Side Chicago. His grandmother was the cook in the family, and he inherited her talent for cooking with-

out a recipe. "We were the kids with pulled taffy and homemade egg rolls," Rodney explains. "Mom was the recipe person, I just watched and could cook without one. We call it passing the spoon." The sign on the restaurant says, HOME IS WHERE THE FOOD IS. Consider this your second home. Entrées $5.99–7.99.

Sunglow Café (520-824-3334 or 866-786-4569), 14066 S. Sunglow Rd. The Sunglow Ranch's restaurant is open to the public for dinner on Saturday only. It's the best place around for fine dining, and the food is excellent. The interiors, a mix of Mexican and Provençal enriched with plants and water features, create a harmonious ambience. The food (you get a choice of prime rib or salmon) is healthy gourmet, and the portions are hearty. Call for prices and reservations (required at least the day before).

✳ Special Events

Call 520-384-2272 for more information.

January: **Wings Over Willcox** celebrates the winter migration of thousands of sandhill cranes to the area, as well as birding in general, with birding tours, seminars, workshops, photo contest, and banquet.

September: **Magic Circle Bike Challenge**. This road biking event takes place on Labor Day.

October: **Rex Allen Days**. Events include the induction of a new cowboy into the Willcox Cowboy Hall of Fame, softball tournament, turtle race, rodeo, country music concert, western dances, and country fair.

December: **Christmas Apple Festival** includes a judged arts and crafts show, bazaar, and local entertainment.

SIERRA VISTA

L ocated in a biome-crossed area of the state, Sierra Vista has become one of the destinations of choice for ecotourism in Arizona. It has the best of both worlds—civilized comforts and watchable wildlife. Species from Mexico's Sierra Madre feel just as at home as those dipping down from the Rocky Mountains and in from the Sonoran and Chichuahuan Deserts. Plus, the city lies on a major avian migration path along the San Pedro River. Hundreds of species of birds pass through the city during their seasonal shifts. Premier watchable wildlife areas lie within a stone's throw from the city limits—it's that close to the backcountry.

The San Pedro River flows only a few miles from the city, and the remnants of centuries of history remain along the riverbanks. This history is not exactly the kind you find in a textbook. It's full of color and cuss thanks to the mining camps along the river and the tenacious courage of Native Americans who refused to give up their extraordinary homeland. Which brings us to the reason Sierra Vista exists—Fort Huachuca. The fort was established to protect settlers and travel routes in this corner of the state, then a territory, from attacks by resident Native people. That particular spot was selected because it had fresh water, an abundance of trees, excellent observation in three directions, and high ground. Many of the same reasons the birds like this area so much. And once again, we come full circle back to why you might want to visit Sierra Vista—it's the best of both worlds.

GUIDANCE **Sierra Vista Convention & Visitor's Bureau** (520-417-6960 or 800-288-3861), 3020 E. Tacoma St. You can pick up an official visitor guide, an information brochure about birding and watchable wildlife, and a *Cultural Heritage Tour* brochure, as well as specific information on things to do in the area. Check out the *How the West Was Fun* CDs, full of information on the famous people—Cochise, Geronimo, Buffalo Soldiers, and pioneers—who made the area their home. The late Rex Allen and local rancher and cowboy poet Bud Strom tell you all about these charismatic personalities. Call 520-417-6960 for information, 800-288-3861 to order. The **Sierra Vista Ranger District** (520-378-0311), 5990 S. AZ 92, Hereford, has information, maps, and descriptions of trails for hiking and mountain biking in the Huachuca Mountains. The **Bureau**

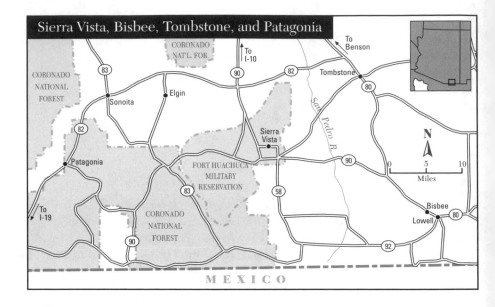

of Land Management (520-439-6400) has information on the San Pedro Riparian National Conservation Area.

GETTING THERE *By car:* Sierra Vista is located right on the curve of AZ 90, about 24 miles south of I-10. *By air:* **Sierra Vista Municipal Airport** (520-459-1581), 1800 Airport Dr.

WHEN TO COME High season is spring, when the weather is mild and major bird activity starts. The birding doesn't slow until October. Then the secondary birding season begins and lasts through winter.

MEDICAL EMERGENCY Sierra Vista Regional Health Center (520-458-4641), 300 El Camino Real.

✳ To See

Arizona Folklore Preserve (520-378-6165). Go 6 miles south on AZ 92, then turn west onto Ramsey Canyon Rd.; go 3.5 miles. State balladeer Dolan Ellis first thought of opening the preserve in the Phoenix area. And then he experienced Ramsey Canyon in the Huachuca Mountains, fell in love with the canyon's beauty, and thought it the perfect place to fulfill his dream of creating a venue where the songs and stories celebrating Arizona and western heritage and culture could be performed and preserved. The preserve is nonprofit, and admission charges are considered a donation. $12 adults, $6 ages 17 and under.

Fort Huachuca Historical Museum (520-533-1107), Buildings 41401 and 41305, Fort Huachuca. Open weekdays 9–4, weekends 1–4; closed Thanksgiving, Christmas, and New Year's Day. This national landmark and old (established 1877) military complex still operates. You can peruse the grounds and check out two museums. This one tells the story of the U.S. Army on the southwestern frontier. One of the most endearing parts of the history is the segment of the Buffalo Soldiers—African American regiments who patrolled the frontier and its rawboned characters. The Buffalo Soldiers also fought in Mexico and trained infantrymen for World War II combat. Today the fort has evolved into the army's intelligence center. **The U.S. Army Intelligence Museum** (Building 41411) presents the axiom that *Intelligence Is for Commanders*, currently the cornerstone of U.S. Army intelligence doctrine. Exhibits discuss how the idea developed over the past 200 years. Both museums are free.

Murray Springs Clovis Site (520-458-3559). Take AZ 90 about 5 miles east of town, then turn north onto Moson Rd. and follow the signs. When a University of Arizona excavation team found a Clovis Point (a fluted spear point crafted by the Clovis Culture more than 11,000 years ago) here, they had no idea it was only the tip of the iceberg. The site turned out to be an undisturbed cache of a stratigraphic record in time. The team found 15 more Clovis Points dating back some 11,000 years, along with bones of several extinct animals, tools, and a hearth. Free.

Our Lady of the Sierras Shrine (928-378-2950). Located in Hereford off AZ 92; turn west onto Stone Ridge (near mile marker 333), and right again onto Prince Placer; turn left onto Twin Oaks Rd. to the parking area. You might notice the shrine's 75-foot-high Celtic cross in the foothills of the Huachuca Mountains from the highway. You can view it up close at its 5,300-foot elevation when you walk the steps up several hundred feet to the shrine inspired by a religious event in Medjugorje, Yugoslavia. The shrine provides an inspiring view and a quiet place to contemplate—even experience a miracle. Some visitors have noted unexplained healings. A stone chapel includes an antique Spanish cross, wooden beams hand hewn in the 1830s over the doors and windows, vigil candles, chairs, and an altar. Free.

AN ANGEL STATUE AT SIERRA VISTA'S OUR LADY OF THE SIERRAS SHRINE.

✳ **To Do**

GOLF Pueblo del Sol Country Club (520-378-6444). The bent grass fairways and greens here top the list in southern Arizona. They also are known to be the fastest in the state; watch your putts!

GHOST TOWNS Fairbank Historic Townsite. Contact the Bureau of Land Management. Located on AZ 82 at the San Pedro River. Open 24 hours. At this historic railroad stop, you'll learn that the history along the San Pedro is just as prevalent, and colorful, as the birds. Mills that once operated 24 hours a day—as did the brothels and bars—kept the river a lively place. The spot is now quiet, with abandoned adobe buildings and the foundation remains of the post office, a general store, the Montezuma Hotel, a schoolhouse, and a saloon. You can only imagine what life might have been like. Free.

Charleston and Millville. Contact the Bureau of Land Management. Located just downriver (north) of the Charleston Road bridge along the San Pedro River. The river's present peaceful demeanor gives no clue of the raucous mining-town life here in the 1880s, the heyday of silver mines in nearby Tombstone. While the West's legendary heroes, bad men, and brazen ladies converged in Tombstone, a rougher breed rumored to be even more ruthless congregated here in the adobe ruins of Charleston. If, as the saying goes, Tombstone was "too tough to die," Charleston was too mean to live. Farther upriver at Brunkow's Cabin, the bloodshed got worse. The tiny shack known as the Bloodiest Cabin in Arizona hosted at least 21 murders.

HIKING Arizona Trail (602-252-4794). The 800-mile trail gets its start at Coronado National Memorial on the Crest Trail, located across the parking area at Montezuma Pass. Contact the Sierra Vista Ranger District for trail conditions.

The **Huachuca Mountains**, among the great hiking spots in the state, have a beautiful network of trails that take you through canyons and up mountaintops. Check out the **Hamburg Trail** for one of the most scenic hikes in the area, **Comfort Springs** and **Carr Peak Trails** for excellent wildflower activity from mid-July through Aug., and the **Scheelite Canyon** and **Miller Canyon Trails** for spectacular autumn color in late Oct.

HORSEBACK RIDING Buffalo Corral Riding Stables (520-533-5220), located in Fort Huachuca. You can rent a horse by the hour or the month. Guided tours into the Huachuca Mountains are available as well. The stable has a horse for all skill levels. If you're around in Oct. and an experienced rider, you can join the annual ride to Tombstone. Call for more information.

HUMMINGBIRD BANDING Sierra Vista, the Hummingbird Capital of the United States, has a wealth of hummers sipping on the incredible diversity of vegetation in the area. You can watch the fascinating process of banding these little ones at several places July–Oct. **San Pedro House** (520-508-4445) is 6 miles east of Sierra Vista on AZ 90 at the San Pedro River; call for dates and times. Donations accepted. **Fort Huachuca** (520-792-0980). Every other Sunday morning

BIRDING

One of the five hottest birding spots in the nation, and constantly showing up on the radar of bird-watchers around the world, Sierra Vista sees birders flying in at the mere mention of a sighting. The spring migration peaks between late April and early May. The best time span to see tropical species such as hummingbirds, trogans, warblers, and flycatchers is from mid-April through September. In late summer monsoon storms coax a wide array of wildflowers that attract hummingbirds and butterflies. Migrating birds pluck seeds, fruits, and insects from the area.

Hot spot canyons include **Ash Canyon** and its namesake trail. The **Ash Canyon B&B** (520-378-0773) (see *Lodging*) opens its birdfeeding area to the public from dawn to dusk daily for a donation (the hummingbirds here burn through 7 pounds of sugar a day during peak season). You might catch sight of a plain-capped starthroat or Lucifer's hummingbird here. Owner-innkeeper Mary Jo Ballator will tell you about the birds at the feeders and in the area.

Miller Canyon and its namesake trail have harbored a number of rare birds, too, and **Beatty's Guest Ranch** (see *Lodging*) holds the record for greatest variety of hummingbird species in a day (15 in 2002)—they like to sip from the property's public hummingbird feeders. The white-eared hummingbird makes an exclusive appearance here.

Carr Canyon (520-378-0311). Take AZ 90 to Carr Canyon Rd., and turn west; go 8.5 miles to the campgrounds. **Carr House Visitor Center** has exhibits, trails, and native plantings for hummingbirds and butterflies. The **Southeastern Arizona Bird Observatory (SABO)** conducts regular bird walks in spring and summer. Call for dates and times.

San Pedro Riparian Conservation Area (see *Wilder Places*). Everything they say about birding here is true, especially if you come during migration times when you'll see a variety of the more than 330 species of birds recorded here. Bring your life list.

Ramsey Canyon Nature Preserve (520-378-4952) (see *Wilder Places*) has been a favorite haunt of birders and other naturalists for more than a century.

Sierra Vista Wastewater Wetlands (520-458-5775 or 800-288-3861). Take AZ 90 for 3.1 miles east of Fry Blvd. Open Mon.–Fri. 7–3:30. Three ponds—part of a pilot project to test natural treatment of secondary sewer effluent—attract thousands of waterfowl, shorebirds, rails, raptors, and songbirds with their lush aquatic vegetation.

Mar.–Oct., banding begins at dawn (4:45–6) and continues for about 5 hours. Call ahead for dates and specific details. **Ramsey Canyon Preserve** (520-378-4952) sees banding Mar.–Oct., usually 6–11 AM. Call ahead for dates and times.

MOUNTAIN BIKING The area has a number of dirt roads and singletrack routes to explore, especially in the Huachuca Mountains. Contact Sierra Vista Visitor Center for a map, and the Sierra Vista Ranger Station for information. The **Dawn to Dust Mountain Bike Club** (520-458-0685; www.dawntodustmountainbike club.org) leads medium to difficult rides.

MULTIUSE PATHS The city has several 10-foot-wide paved trails for walking, running, and biking. Check out the paths along Buffalo Soldier Trail, Martin Luther King, Avenida Cochise, and AZ 92. Contact the visitor center for more information and maps.

BIRD WALKS **Casa de San Pedro** hosts tours guided by SABO every Tues. morning during Apr. and May; reservations required for nonguests. The **San Pedro River Inn** offers guided bird walks every Wed. and the second Sun. of each month. Call in advance. **San Pedro Riparian National Conservation Area** (520-459-2555) has guided bird walks Jan.–Apr. Call for dates and times. **Ramsey Canyon Nature Preserve** (520-378-4952). Call for scheduled walks. **Sierra Vista Wastewater Wetlands** (520-458-5775 or 800-288-3861). Take AZ 90 for 3.1 miles east of Fry Blvd. Guided bird walks on Sun.

Also see *Hummingbird Banding*.

NATURE WALKS **Interpretive River Walks** (520-459-2555). Walk 2–3 miles along the San Pedro River and learn about the river, its natural history, and its endangered existence. Meet at **San Pedro House**. Donations accepted.

Ramsey Canyon Preserve (520-378-4952) offers walks Tue., Thu., and Sat. at 9 from Mar.–Oct. The preserve opens at 8 to public. Call ahead to confirm walk dates.

STARGAZING The members of the Huachuca Astronomy Club of Southeastern Arizona own and operate 15 observatories, several of which are open to the public. **Desert Coyote Observatory** (520-432-4433) has one of the largest telescopes in the area, 12 feet tall with a 20-inch mirror, as well as several others; all are available to rent. Call for more information. The president of the Huachuca Astronomy Club opens up his **Palominas Star Haven Observatory** (520-366-5788) when conditions (weather and his schedule) are right. Free. Call for information.

✳ Wilder Places

Huachuca Mountains. The sky island range of the Huachuca Mountains, part of the Madrean Archipelago, has a rich mélange of wildlife activity: birds, insects, butterflies, and animals. These peaks draw rare plants and animals that thrive there while they struggle in other locations.

MISS LITTLE BIT

"She's a wiggler," declares Sheri Williamson, research director at San Pedro House, as she gently maneuvers a squirming runt of a hummer in her hands. "She's a survivor."

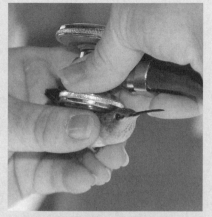

Miss Little Bit will have to be. During the routine examination and recording of gender, weight, beak and fat measurements, and overall health, Williamson discovers that the top and bottom parts of the bird's bill don't match. This will

LISTENING TO MISS LITTLE BITS HEARTBEAT

make sipping from flowers impossible. "She'll need feeders to accommodate her scissor bill, and they're hard to come by in Mexico where she's heading for the winter."

Nevertheless, Miss Little Bit continues to amaze Williamson as much as she fights her. The tiny bird has more fat than usual, and weighs 3.9 grams—several hundreths of a grams more than most of the other birds banded that day. Her heartbeat, which sounds like static at 1,000 beats per minute, is strong.

The little bird absolutely charms all who watch. The banding process has everyone absorbed and happy.

"Who wants to release her?" Williamson asks as she stations Miss Little Bit at a feeder.

Everyone does. Williamson eyes a little girl and puts Miss Little Bit in her hand for release. The crowd watches as the antsy bird takes off immediately then sends up a cheer in hopes that the handicapped bird will do well on the difficult journey of life ahead.

You can hike all but the mountains' uppermost trails, which get snow in winter, through most of the year. But certain seasons have different attractions—birds migrate in spring and fall, butterflies and hummingbirds proliferate in summer when wildflowers peak, and late autumn brings exquisite color to the canyons and mountaintops.

Coronado National Memorial (520-366-5515). Visitor center open 9–5. From Sierra Vista, go south on AZ 92 and turn south onto Coronado Memorial Rd. The visitor center has a small museum with exhibits explaining the history of the Coronado expedition. The scenic overlook at Montezuma Pass shows great panoramas of the San Pedro and San Rafael Valleys as well as Mexico. Several hiking trails start in the park. Free.

Ramsey Canyon Preserve (520-378-2785). From Sierra Vista, go south on AZ 92 for about 7 miles, past Fry Rd., and turn west onto the signed turnoff. Open Mar.–Oct., daily 8–5; Nov.–Feb., Mon–Fri 9–5, Sat.–Sun. 8–5; closed Thanksgiving, Christmas, and New Year's Day. Owned by the Nature Conservancy, where land protection reigns. The 300 acres located midmountain present excellent birding opportunities from Apr. through Sept. You can access the **Ramsey Canyon Trail** here. $5 adults, under 16 free, and the preserve is free to all on the first Sat. of every month. A pass is valid for 1 week from the date of purchase.

San Pedro Riparian National Conservation Area. Contact the Bureau of Land Management. This sanctuary, located on the upper San Pedro River, is the most extensive riparian ecosystem remaining in the desert Southwest. The river still nurtures a lively lineup of wildlife influenced by the Rocky Mountains and Sierra Madre. Almost 400 species of birds, 180 species of butterflies, 87 species of mammals, and 68 species of amphibians and reptiles give the San Pedro the greatest diversity of vertebrate species in the continental United States, and the second greatest diversity of land mammals in the world (the mountains of Costa Rica rank first). You can see an incredible array of these mammals in the 40-mile-long segment of this natural area. Free.

✳ Lodging

SUITES 🐾 ♿ **Sierra Suites** (520-459-4221), 391 E. Fry Blvd. This southwestern-style inn is packed with amenities, including a pool and spa, fitness center, and meeting space. Each room has refrigerator, microwave, free local calls, free WiFi, pay-per-view TV, and coffee. Continental breakfast included. $59–79.

BED AND BREAKFASTS **Ash Canyon Bed and Breakfast** (520-378-0773), 5255 Spring Rd., Hereford. You're pretty much in the center of birding activity at this B&B. Located on an Important Bird Area, it's one of the hot spots where more than 144 species are sighted through the year. It's also located near several hiking trails, and plenty of wildlife congregates around the 6.5 acres the straw-bale casita sits on. The casita has a kitchenette, dining area, queen-sized bed, sofa, and bath. The kitchenette is fully stocked, from coffee grinder to electric frying pan, and includes an assortment of breakfast foods to create your own breakfast whenever you want it. Reverse osmosis provides water for drinking and ice. Well-behaved children are welcome, but no pets. $135.

Beatty's Miller Canyon Guest Ranch & Orchard (520-378-2728), 2173 E. Miller Canyon Rd., Hereford. Beatty's claim to fame is the variety of hummingbirds that gather at the property's public feeders—the most species (15) ever sighted in the area in 2002. Plus, the property sits right above the trailhead of the Miller Canyon Trail—one of the more beautiful routes in the Huachuca Mountains. Six cabins are available, three turn-of-the-20th-century and three newly built, with breakfast. $65–120.

∞ ঙ **Casa de San Pedro** (520-366-1300 or 800-588-6468), 8933 S. Yell Lane, Hereford. Located away from the city along the San Pedro River, this distinctive property is a favorite among bird-watchers and guests seeking peaceful and natural accommodations. Xeriscaped gardens contain colorful flowers to attract hummingbirds and butterflies, so you need not venture far to see them. Each of the 10 guest rooms has hand-carved Mexican furniture, a private bath, a patio, a king-sized or two double beds, telephone (local calls free), and complimentary high-speed Internet access. The property has a ramada with a gas barbecue open to guest use. Out front, you can walk the Four Elements Labyrinth. Breakfast starts with shade-grown coffees and herbal teas, then progresses into a full-blown gourmet meal complete with fresh-baked goods, entrée, fruit, and juices to the sounds of Gershwin (or other classical favorites) in the background. Afternoon goodies include home-baked pies and assorted beverages. $109–145.

Adobe (520-378-2762), 5043 S. AZ 92. Open Wed.–Sun. 5–9. Chef Donald Libasci creates a new genre of southwestern cuisine with entrées like adobe spiced duck (with blue corn and Hatch chile waffles), grilled New Mexico–style BBQ salmon (with sweet corn polenta and tequila lime butter), and poblanos rellenos (fire-roasted poblano chiles stuffed with smoked chicken or pork, goat cheese, white cheddar, and a roasted tomato sauce). The latter is a true labor of love, since rellenos take time and talent, not to mention burned fingers from handling the hot peppers. Desserts are fresh and house-made. Tequila aficionados will have lots to choose from on the list of premiums. Entrées $14–24.

Delio's Italian Restaurant (520-378-1066), 3637 S. AZ 92. The local Italian favorite has some excellent pizza available in delicious combinations along with good classic Italian food. Bread is delightful. Entrées $5.99–14.99, pizzas $9.95–16.95.

The German Café (520-456-1705), 1805 Paseo San Luis. Open for lunch Tue.–Sat. 11–2, dinner Thu.–Sat. 5–8. Owners Peter and Brigitte Volger present a totally German experience in a town where the world meets (because of Fort Huachuca). The menu lists items in German with an English translation: *Bratwurst mit Katoffelsalat und Sauerkraut* or fried sausage with potato salad and sauerkraut, and *Berliner Gulasch mit Spätzle* or Berlin goulash with noodles. You can get sides of all the German favorites (noodles, red cabbage, sauerkraut, bread and butter), and desserts (from cheese to rum cake). The Volgers make everything in-house. Entrées $8–13.

The Outside Inn (520-378-4645), 4907 S. AZ 92. Open Mon.–Fri. 11–1:30 and 5–9, Sat. 5–9. Located in a restored home and set back from the highway, it's a favorite fine-dining spot for the locals. The low-lit dining room retains a bit of elegance when the place gets lively, which is often. The food, generally good and thoughtfully prepared, has gourmet touches. Salmon and filet mignon are favorites, as well as chicken champagne and Mediterranean chicken. $12.95–15.95.

❧ **Peacock Authentic Vietnamese Cuisine** (520-459-0095), 80 S. Carmichael Ave. Open Tue.–Fri. 11–9, Sat.–Sun. 4–8. One of the town's best restaurants (family-owned and -operated) serves a variety of Asian fare. Mom cooks each of the 90 items on the menu from scratch; Dad and the kids serve. The most popular dishes include a variety of curries and sautéed chicken with lemongrass. Entrées $8.95–16.95.

✳ Selective Shopping

Fort Huachuca Thrift Store (520-458-4606). Located in Fort Huachuca. Open Tue. and Thu. 9:30–3, and first Sat. of the month 9:30–1:30. One's man's treasure is another one's trash, but at this thrift shop treasures come from military families who have lived all over the world. The store has a loyal following, and some folks spend the whole day seeking their treasures here, which often come at bargain prices. The store is run completely by volunteers and all profits go to local schools, groups, and charities.

✳ Special Events

January: **Sierra Vista Senior Games** (520-458-7922). If you're 50 or older, you're welcome to partake in the competition events.

February: **Cochise Cowboy Poetry & Music Gathering** (520-249-2511). The Old West comes to life through song, poetry, and stories.

October: **Art in the Park**. The premier art event of Sierra Vista, this fine art and crafts show features more than 200 booths of original artwork, furniture, jewelry, clothing, and sculptures.

November: **Festival of Color**. Around 30 brightly colored balloons participate in this hot-air balloon rally.

December: **Holiday Parade** (520-458-6940). Family-oriented fun to start the mood for the holidays. **Holiday Tour of Historic Homes** (520-417-6960). View beautifully decorated homes built at the turn of the 20th century at Fort Huachuca. Soldiers dressed in period uniforms greet visitors at each historic home. No children under 10 years of age.

BISBEE THE COPPER QUEEN

The first Distinctive Destination Award given by the National Trust for Historic Preservation to an Arizona town went to Bisbee. The terraced community is a bundle of Old World culture and Old West individualism. Counterculture influences play pleasantly with the classic beauty of Greek, Romanesque, Renaissance Revival, Mediterranean, Victorian, and art deco architecture to produce a quirky charisma that actually invites visitors to join in the fun.

Known as the Queen of the Copper Camps, the mineral-rich mining town didn't stop at copper, not its biggest draw even at 8 billion tons. The area produced more gold, silver, and lead than any other mining district. It took little more than a couple of decades for this fast-living mining town to find its place among the nation's cosmopolitan cities. Soon after the turn of the 20th century, Bisbee ranked the largest city between St. Louis and San Francisco. Its Brewery Gulch mining camps won the distinction as the liveliest spots between El Paso and San Francisco with nearly 50 saloons and who knows how many shady ladies.

By the mid-1970s, though, large-scale mining had hit the skids in Bisbee, and the town's glory started to evanesce—a denouement some liken to Rome in its last days. The counterculture, drawn by affordable housing with beautiful architecture, breathed life back into the city with their art, however homespun it might have seemed at the time. What looks hippie retro to the present-day visitor is actually the town's prevailing personality from the '70s, not a retro movement.

The National Trust for Historic Preservation put Bisbee on its 2005 list of America's Dozen Distinctive Destinations, honoring unique and lovingly preserved communities in the United States. Though Bisbee has reclaimed some of the culture for which it was famous a century ago, it's still quirky after all these years.

GUIDANCE The **Bisbee Visitor Center** (520-432-3554 or 866-224-7233) has information on Bisbee's events, attractions, and accommodations. Stop by for a brochure detailing two self-guided, historic walking tours that feature historic buildings and architectural influences. One tour goes up Brewery Gulch, where the miners' shadows came out to play; the other features the downtown area where they boasted openly about their riches.

GETTING THERE Bisbee is the southern point of AZ 90 and almost at the tail end of AZ 80. Just head south on either road from I-10 to reach the town a few miles north of the Mexican border.

GETTING AROUND **Bisbee Trolley Tours** trace the path of the Warren-Bisbee Railway, which began operating in 1908. As the trolley traverses the steep streets, guides recount anecdotes about historic times in Bisbee and its outskirts. Tours depart Copper Queen Plaza (just south of the historical museum) at 9:30, 11, 1, 2:30, and 4 daily. $10 adults, $7 ages 10 and under.

WHEN TO COME Located at 5,300 feet, Bisbee is comfortable just about any time of year. Late fall through spring is high season, but summer is the best-kept secret. Highs may hover around 90, but afternoon thunderstorms cool things down and add some atmospheric drama, then the nights settle into the 60s. Couple that with fewer tourists and lower rates, and you might end up preferring the low season.

MEDICAL EMERGENCY For hospital services, **Copper Queen Community Hospital** (520-432-7450), 7 Bisbee Rd.; for outpatient services, **Chiricahua Community Health Center** (520-432-3309), 108 Arizona St.

✳ To See

Bisbee Mining and Historical Museum (520-432-7071). Open daily 10–4. This museum was the first western affiliate of the Smithsonian Institution. Take a look at how Bisbee got started through changing exhibit displays that showcase numerous artifacts from the mining days explaining the macrocosm of Bisbee: why it happened, who lived here, and what the social issues of the day were. History starts to make sense here. Once you learn about daily life in Bisbee, you'll never again complain about having to walk up a steep hill or an endless set of concrete steps to get around town. $7.50 adults, $6.50 over 60, $3 under 16.

Copper Queen Library (520-432-4232), 6 Main St. Open Mon. and Wed. noon–7, Tue., Thu., and Fri. 10–5, Sat. 10–2. Opened when Arizona was still a territory in 1882, not only is this the state's oldest library, but it may have the most interesting inception as well. As the story goes, when mining magnates showed up in town one day and saw a hung corpse swaying in the breeze, they swiftly decided the town needed a strong dose of Christian and cultural distractions. The opening of the Copper Queen Library in a corner grocery store promptly followed. It worked. By 1920 more than 260 people visited the library each day.

Queen Mine Tour (520-432-2071). Tours available daily at 9, 10:30, noon, 2, and 3:30. A cool 47 degrees year-round, the bonanza copper mine comes alive in this tour, given by retired miners who lend an air of authenticity as they describe working conditions and relate personal anecdotes about working in the mine. A mini train takes you, clothed in yellow rain gear, helmet, and headlamp, into the bowels of the mountain via the Queen Mine Shaft, and you see firsthand how they blasted and stabilized the mine while they excavated ore. They'll tell you how old-timers made a life underground. You'll view the cars, the drilling equipment, and the vertical shaft with its cage, aka elevator. $12 adults, $5 ages 4–15.

St. Patrick's Church (520-432-5753), 100 Quality Hill Rd. One of the remedies for the bawdy behavior in Bisbee's early years, this Roman Catholic Gothic Revival church (listed on the National Register of Historic Places) copies St. Mary's Catholic Church in Whitehaven, England. Of special interest are the 27 windows designed in 1917 by Emil Frei, the world-class master designer of Victorian-style stained glass. Each, a masterpiece, is created from lead crystal glass.

✴ To Do

BIRDING The Southeastern Arizona Bird Observatory (SABO) (520-432-1388), a nonprofit scientific and educational organization, leads tours, workshops, seminars, and trips throughout fall and winter that share the fascination of winged creatures. Feeding areas attract birds for an up-close-and-personal experience. The organization offers half-day and full-day guided walks, tours, and personalized guide services. Take AZ 80 West (north) 2 miles past the Mule Pass Tunnel to the turnoff on the left.

Wezil Walraven Bird Tours (520-432-4697). Wezil Walraven, a professional bird guide, leads you on owl and bird-watching tours in the area throughout the year. Call for information.

COOKING SCHOOL You can create you own homemade masterpieces at the **Bisbee Cooking School** (520-432-3882) under the direction of owner Helen Saul, a professional chef. She teaches four styles of cuisine—French, Italian, Cajun, and Creative Southwest. Only six people participate in each class, which emphasizes the background of recipes, the ingredients that go into them, and having fun. The best part is indulging in the dish you've created at a sitdown meal, including the appropriate wine. Prices include all materials. Call for class schedules. $40 per class.

GOLF Turquoise Valley Golf Course (520-432-3091), 794 W. Newell St., Naco. Open every day but Christmas. This course takes you way back in Arizona golf history; it's the oldest continuously run course in the state. Built in 1937, the course features undulating bent grass greens and rolling Bermuda fairways. Holes 10 through 18, built in 1999, head into the high-desert terrain for some challenge and true desert course action. Watch for the par-6, 727-yard Rattler (said to be the longest golf hole in Arizona) and water hazards on holes 1 and 16. Bar, restaurant, and pro shop on the grounds. $25.

THE OLD STREETS OF BISBEE.

JEEP TOURS **Lavender Jeep Tours** (520-432-5369), 1 Copper Queen Plaza. Bisbee's history is fascinating enough inside its city limits, but once you get outside, you experience a whole other form of wild. It doesn't take long to get into the backcountry, and these jeep tours teach you all about the areas they take you to: the Sky Island Adventure takes you through several biological zones as you climb up to 7,400 feet; the Back Roads of Bisbee winds 90 minutes on the narrow, twisting back roads; the Mining Landscape Tour explores the whole Warren Mining District. $35–45 per person.

✳ Spas and Massages

Monsoon Face and Body (520-432-6868), 33 Subway. This spa offers a compendium of therapies: therapeutic massage, shiatsu, Reiki, facials, and 90-minute yoga classes. Hair care includes styled cuts and Goldwell color treatment. Asian-inspired boutique. Massage $55–75, facials $45–65.

Mary Walker Massage Therapy (520-432-4829), 101 Clawson Ave. Open Mon.–Sat. 9–5. A member of the Medical Team at the 1984 Olympics in Los Angeles, Walker practices a number of therapies for sore muscles, stress, relaxation, and general health maintenance. Call for rates and appointments.

✳ Lodging

HOTELS AND SUITES **Copper Queen Hotel** (520-432-2216), 11 Howell Ave. Built by Copper Queen Consolidated Mining Company to accommodate its East Coast executives, the hotel was the most elegant of its time. Some of its guests from decades past still roam the three floors. Julia Lowell, one of three ghosts who show up occasionally, has a namesake room on the third floor. The hotel management thinks she might be the strange lady in a long black dress and veil who stops clocks, appears half naked on the grand staircase clutching a bottle, whispers to men in the elevator, tinkers with lights, and opens windows. Each room's decor remains historic, and each is different. Some have clawfoot tubs, while all have heat, air-conditioning, telephone, cable TV, and private bath. The property includes a second-floor outdoor swimming pool as well as the **Winchester Restaurant** and **Old West Saloon**. Low season $75–145, high season $144–176.

Letson Loft Hotel (520-432-3210 or 877-432-3210), 26 Main St. Located in the Letson Block—the oldest brick building and only authentic Victorian structure in Bisbee—this relatively new hotel has a well-done blend of Old World interiors with modern amenities. The second-floor hotel has four rooms in front with bay windows to watch the street scenes below, a kitchenette, and a suite. Some have authentic skylight or clawfoot tub; all are spacious. Antique furnishings give a period feel. Rooms have private bath, complimentary WiFi, flat-screen TV, air-conditioning and heat controls, authentic wood floors, and 11-foot ceilings. Light breakfast (such as Brie, apricot, and apple phyllo pockets, coffee and tea) are included with your room. $120–145.

San Ramon Hotel (520-432-1901), 5 Howell Ave. The big and bright rooms at this renovated hotel give you plenty of space, even if you spend some time in them. Each room has several big windows or skylights. Rooms have private bath, complimentary WiFi, complimentary bottled water, and air-conditioning and heat. Snack on fresh-baked cookies in the lobby. Double occupancy $75–129; $10 for each extra person.

BED AND BREAKFASTS AND INNS

☀ **Mayberry's Place** (520-234-1252), 318 Tombstone Canyon. Mayberry's Place, built in 1906, was named for the previous owner of the building and town barber Eskar Mayberry. Eskar lived on the top floor of the building and had his barbershop on the bottom floor. In like manner, current owner Donna Burke runs her Red Shoes Hair Salon on the bottom floor. The two-bedroom cabin has queen beds, washer and dryer, full kitchen, cable TV, VHS library, and a small private rear yard and balcony overlooking Tombstone Canyon. $95; $25 per night for each additional guest; no charge for children under 10 years; small pets okay. Cash or check.

❀ **School House Inn** (520-432-2996 or 800-537-4333), 818 Tombstone Canyon. This old brick schoolhouse, built in 1918, is located in a residential neighborhood, yet close enough to Old Bisbee's shops and restaurants. The classrooms-turned-guest-rooms and -suites are big, with 12-foot ceilings and private bath. Rooms have full- or king-sized beds, complimentary WiFi, and great views of Tombstone Canyon. Guests can use cable TV in the family room and have plenty of off-street parking. Full breakfast included in the rates. $60–90.

☀ ♿ **Sleepy Dog Guest House** (520-432-3057), 212A Opera Dr. Local artist Tad Cheyenne Miller restored this miner's cabin perched on a hillside. The one-bedroom cabin is simple but elegant, full of art and collectibles and gorgeous views. It sits on an acre of land, which makes it quiet and very private. It also makes it perfect for dogs with its enclosed yard, large Frisbee lot, off-leash trails, and designer doggy bowls. For your comfort, the cabin has a king-sized bed, down and feather beds, luxury linens, and clawfoot bathtub. Informal breakfast and coffee and tea are included in the rates. $125, cash or check only, for 1 night; or $95 for 2 nights or more. Weekly and monthly rates are available upon request.

❀ **Walker Guest Apartment** (520-432-4829), 101 Clawson Ave. Owner Mary Walker calls this her "bed and make your own breakfast," which you can do in the apartment's fully equipped kitchen. The 1910 home is located directly across the street from Old Bisbee High School. The last class to graduate was 1958, and the old school building now holds the county library and other county offices. The Walker House has a queen bed, clawfoot tub/shower, cable TV/VCR, phone, air-conditioning/gas heat, and off-street parking. Walker provides massages on the premises. No pets. $75 per night. One child is okay. $15 for an extra adult.

OTHER LODGING ❀ **Shady Dell RV Park** (520-432-3567), 1 Old Douglas Rd. The Shady Dell opened in 1927 as a trailer park and campground for travelers on AZ 80, which runs from San Diego, California, to Savannah, Georgia. You can still hook up your

BISBEE STREETS.

own RV here, or you can stay in one of a collection on the property, including a 1949 Airstream, 1950 Spartanette, 1950 Spartan Manor, 1954 Crown, and 1951 Royal Mansion. Trailers have a propane stove, refrigerator, electric percolator, dishes, and linens; cassette tapes of big band, early rhythm and blues, and favorite old radio programs you can play in reproduction vintage radios; and period magazines and books. Some trailers have a bath or vintage black-and-white TV and phonographs with vinyl records. $40–125.

✳ Where to Eat

DINING OUT **Bisbee Grille** (520-432-6788), 2 Copper Queen Plaza. Open daily 11–9. One of the few "late-night" venues serves dependably decent food. The menu leans toward the Southwest with steaks, seafood, and vegetarian entrées. Fine dining starts at 6 PM. Entrées $8.99–21.99.

Café Roka (520-432-5153), 35 Main St. Open at 5 PM for dinner Thu.–Sat. Jazz on Fridays. This local favorite

always gets great write-ups thanks to consistently good food at reasonable prices—the only AAA Three Diamond restaurant in this rural town. Without reservations you may be able to get a seat at the bar, where you can order dinner. Chef Rod Kass grabs a bit from Italian, California, and new vegetarian cuisines to create his Modern American menu. This is one of the few restaurants in the nation to serve four-course meals (soup, salad, sorbet, and entrée) without going prix fixe. Tastes teeter-totter—crunchy/soft, tangy/sweet, spicy/muted, or subtle/rousing—to keep your palate's attention. The changing menu has several vegetarian dishes that will capture your attention. Desserts are made in-house. Entrées $13.50–23.50.

Santiago's (520-432-1910), 1 Howell Ave. Open daily 11–9. Located at the gateway to Brewery Gulch, where wild and raucous life happened in Bisbee's prime. The brightly colored decor fits the personality of the town. A variety of Mexican provinces inspire the menu, and the food is fresh and good. The signature Rocky Point (fish tacos with corn and rice) is excellent, the Sonoran enchilada has a fried flat masa dough, and the fajitas come in pork, chicken, shrimp, or beef. The margaritas have a stellar reputation and may add a bit of old-time Brewery Gulch conviviality to the meal. Entrées $7.99–12.99.

EATING OUT **Alley Café** (520-432-3733), 17 Main St. Open 10–4. Grab a quick bite here in the form of a hot dog, homemade meat loaf or chicken salad sandwich, or chili. If Seth, owner of Bisbee Bean Coffee, is around, you might get a free shot of espresso. $2–5.75.

❧ **Bisbee Breakfast Club** (520-432-5885), 75A Erie Street, Lowell. Open Thu.–Mon. 7–3. You have to travel just outside Old Town to get to this fabulous breakfast/lunch spot that looks straight off the cover of Super Tramp's *Breakfast in America.* "This is the kind of building that's disappearing in America," says owner Heather Grimm. She and husband (and chef) Pat put sweat equity into the open and airy diner with distinctive glasswork created by a local artisan. The building, once an old Rexall Pharmacy, may insist *diner,* but the food says it's a special one. It's a local favorite, and people come from all over the state to eat here. Entrées $3.95–6.95.

❧ ♪ **Dot's Diner** (520-432-1112), 1 Old Douglas Rd. Open Wed.–Sun. 7–2. Located in the Shady Dell trailer park, this authentic 1950s diner was built by the Valentine Manufacturing Co. in Kansas. The company manufactured diners since the 1930s and didn't sway much in its design. Consequently, Dot's has a deco decor that features a black-and-white checkerboard floor, red stools, and lots of chrome. John Hart originally opened the diner in 1957 at the corner of Ventura and Topanga Canyon Boulevards in Los Angeles. After his retirement, and 13 years of decline, Dot Bozeman moved the diner to Bisbee via a flatbed truck in 1997. She retired, but the legend of good, home-cooked food in a cozy atmosphere lives on. Entrées $3.25–5.95.

Mimosa Market (520-432-3256), 215 Brewery Gulch. Open weekdays 7 AM–9 PM, weekends 7–7. This eclectic market has prevailed for the last century as the neighborhood grocery store. Their motto is posted on a sign in the store: NOT EVERYTHING ALWAYS, BUT MOST OF IT A LOT OF THE TIME. It stocks the makings for a perfect picnic featuring the freshest of produce, better beer and wine, and homemade deli items. There are several salads, great cheeses, and wonderful homemade breads. You can also pick up baked chickens, homemade meat loaf, and desserts, or get sandwiches made to order.

Prickly Pear Café (520-432-7337), 105 Main St. Open Mon.–Thu. 11–8 (till 9 Fri.–Sat., 4 Sun.). This small restaurant serves up fresh salads, cold and hot wraps, and "Cubans"— hot-pressed sandwiches on flat bread. Just about everything has a distinctive touch, from the wasabi deviled eggs to the Harney's Gourmet hot teas. On Monday, arrive by 7 PM and see a movie with dinner for $8. Entrées $5.50–6.25.

✳ **The Arts**

You can find art all over the city— from cosmic murals to colorful window covers on the old miners' homes teetering on the steep hillsides to well-polished galleries. Professional and philanthropic **Beeleza Fine Art Gallery** (520-432-5877), 27 Main St., is owned and operated by the Women's Transition Project, a port in the storm for homeless women and their children. The gallery features local favorite, established, and emerging artists.

✳ **Special Events**

February: **Chocolate Tasting** (520-432-3554) in the Copper Queen Library gives you a chance to indulge in the most decadent of chocolate desserts for $10.

March: **Art Auction** (520-432-3765) presents a collection of some of Bisbee's finest artists at the Bisbee Convention Center.

April: **Copper Classic Car Show** (520-432-5421) has food, music, drawings, and lots of dazzle and chrome. **La Vuelta De Bisbee** (520-432-5795) presents a 3-day staged bicycling event that includes time trials, a circuit race, and a road race.

July: **4th of July** (520-432-6016) gives you a chance to take part in mining activities of old, such as mucking and hard rock drilling. Coaster races, parade, and fireworks.

August: **Southwest Wings Birding and Nature Festival** (520-432-3554), Arizona's longest-running birding festival has 4 days of birding and nature workshops and programs.

September: At the **Brewery Gulch Daze** (520-432-3554) you get a taste of the lively atmosphere that once prevailed on Bisbee's liveliest streets—family style, with a pancake breakfast, pet parade, chili cook-off, recycled-art show, children's carnival games, and skateboard competition.

October: **Fiber Arts Festival** (520-432-4474) displays more than 30 artists' works made from natural fibers. You can get hands-on fiber experience, too, at workshops. Test your stair-climbing mettle at the **Bisbee 1000 Stair Climb** (520-432-1585), where you get firsthand knowledge of the endurance Bisbee gives its residents via those steep and endless flights of stairs. The **Wine Tasting Festival** (520-432-3554) allows you to taste about 50 different varietals in Brewery Gulch. **Halloween in Bisbee** (520-432-3554) is big; it's one of the city's favorite holidays.

November: The holiday season kicks off at the **Festival of Lights** (520-432-3554). Get an up-close look at some of Bisbee's showcase homes at the **Historic Home Tour** (520-432-3554).

TOMBSTONE

L ike many small Arizona towns, Tombstone got its start from precious metal. A relentless, and generally unlucky, prospector named Ed Schieffelin changed his destiny when he poked around the limestone bluffs along the San Pedro River, an area then inflamed with battles among Native Americans, Mexicans, and Anglos. As the story goes, a soldier warned Schieffelin he'd find nothing but his own tombstone. Instead he found a silver lode, big enough for the assayer to say, "You're a lucky cuss." Schieffelin's Lucky Cuss Mine drew a crowd of treasure seekers to Ed's cleverly named town of Tombstone.

The passel of personalities that lived during Tombstone's decades of decadence created a reputation so infamous, the town refuses to die. Many of the main players in Tombstone traveled the whole state following the flow of money to rack in riches from gambling, mines, and business deals. But in Tombstone, where winks, nods, and tolerance allowed outrageous transgressions, the convergence provoked a perfect storm. It's the stuff that creates romance and history today, but at the time could be described as simply raucous and ruthless. Bravado ruled in Tombstone, and its personality grew too big for its own britches. Its aura—a meld of mystique, taboo, and excitement—still wafts from the old buildings and the stories they hold.

GUIDANCE Tombstone Chamber of Commerce (520-457-9317 or 888-457-3929), 105 S. 4th St. You can pick up a variety of information brochures and purchase tickets for tours at the **Tombstone Visitor Center** (520-457-3929), 4th and Allen Sts.

GETTING THERE From I-10, go south on AZ 80 about 20 miles to the signed turnoff. From Sierra Vista or Bisbee, go east or north, respectively, to AZ 80, turn north, then go 15 miles to the turnoff.

TOMBSTONE STREETS ARE STILL DUSTY AFFAIRS.

GETTING AROUND The **Tombstone Pharmacy** (520-457-3543), 516 E. Allen St., rents wheelchairs; the **Tombstone General Store** (520-457-3997), 512 E. Allen, rents strollers; and the **American Legion** (520-457-2273), 225 E. Allen, provides free use of wheelchairs to American Legion or VFW members.

WHEN TO COME The season spans Oct. through Mar. With big celebration events going on in Oct., it's best to make reservations if you plan to stay then.

MEDICAL EMERGENCY Sierra Vista Regional Health Center (520-458-4641), 300 El Camino Real, Sierra Vista.

☀ To See

Bird Cage Theater Museum (520-457-3421), Allen and 6th. Open daily 8–6. No self-respecting women would be seen anywhere near this dance hall bordello licensed to "Dutch Annie" Smith in 1881 by Cochise County. Anyone with a strong attachment to his or her life stayed away, too. During the bawdy bar's 8-year life, it saw 16 gunfights and 26 deaths; it has 140 bullet holes shot into the walls to prove it. On the other hand, randy-minded cowboys, miners, and gamblers gladly paid $25–40 for a bottle of liquor and a gal. The joint was named for the "cages" suspended from the ceiling, where the ladies entertained their customers. You can see part of the bar and get an oration on the history for free. A self-guided tour of the whole building costs $6 adults, $5.50 seniors, $5 ages 8–18, $17 for a family with children up to 18.

Boothill Graveyard (520-457-3300), AZ 80 just north of Tombstone. Open daily 7:30–6. Some of the town's roughest residents lie here, including the slower draws from the OK Corral shootout. Donations accepted.

OK Corral & Tombstone Historama (520-457-3456 or 800-518-1566), 3rd and 4th Sts. Open daily 9–5. This is where the event took place that made Tombstone immortal: the shoot-out at the OK Corral between the notorious cowboys and the famous faction of lawmen. You can peruse the museum (the largest in town) and watch a 25-minue multimedia presentation, narrated by Vincent Price, explaining the true history of the town every half hour 9:30–4:30. At 2 PM (and for $2 extra) you can watch a re-creation of the gunfight that took place near the spot. $5.

THE TOMBSTONE COURTHOUSE—NOW A MUSEUM—WAS ONCE A BUSY PLACE.

Rose Tree Museum and Books (520-457-3326), 116 S. 4th St. Open daily 9–5. The 120-plus-year-old Lady Banksia rosebush, which sprawls over 9,000 square feet, has a listing in the

Guinness Book of World Records as the largest on record. $3.

Tombstone Courthouse State Historic Park (520-457-3311), Toughnut and 3rd St. Open daily 8–5 except Christmas Day. Built in 1882 to accommodate county officials, courts, and criminals, the courthouse buzzed with activity during the town's heyday. Tombstone kept the county seat until another bonanza mineral strike moved it to Bisbee, about 29 miles down the road. The museum has an

THE *TOMBSTONE EPITAPH* IS STILL PRINTED.

intriguing collection of artifacts and memorabilia from the height of the era. $4; $3 in summer.

Tombstone Epitaph Museum (520-457-2211), 9 S. 5th St. Open daily 9:30–4:30. Founded in 1880, this notorious and long-running paper published some unique tongue-in-cheek articles (such as cattle sweating gold dust and nefarious bees taking, instead of making, honey) over the years. It also blared sensational headlines the town generated. The office still has its original presses and equipment, plus archives. Free.

Schieffelin Monument. Located 2.3 miles west of town on Allen St. The man who started all the action lies in repose far away from all the action. The founding father of Tombstone and the Lucky Cuss Mine specifically requested a burial atop the granite hills west of town with "a monument such as prospectors build when locating a mining claim" marking his grave.

Tombstone Western Heritage Museum (520-457-3800), Fremont and 6th St. This private museum has a collection of Earp personal memorabilia, rare and unique guns, and historic photos. $5 adults, $3 ages 12–18.

✳ To Do

HISTORIC TOURS In a place as well preserved as Tombstone, you might want to get the facts via a tour. John Rose of **Tombstone & Thunder Valley Tours** (520-378-2539) offers historically accurate tours full of fun and action. Call for information.

Old Butterfield Stage Lines (520-457-2278) takes you on tours around town in a stagecoach or covered wagon with a guide announcing the historic high points of the wild times of Tombstone. Tours run 9–5, and you can board them on Allen St. between 4th and 5th Sts. $10 adults, $5 children.

HORSEBACK RIDING **Badger Creek Riding Stables** (520-457-2567), Tombstone Livery, just past AZ 80 on AZ 82. Trail rides head to spots in the local backcountry, such as Indian rock art and ghost towns. Call for times and prices. **Tombstone Range Riders Horseback Riding** (520-349-9312), Tombstone Rangeworks General Store & Feed, 116 S. 4th St. Trail rides last half an hour in town, or you can take a 1- to 3-hour trail ride into the Valley of the Mines or the hills of Tombstone. The horses have saddlebags, ropes, scabbards, and rifles—in the style of the late 1880s. $15–60.

✳ Lodging

BED AND BREAKFASTS ◯◯ 🐾

Tombstone Boarding House Bed and Breakfast Inn (520-457-3716 or 877-255-1319), 108 N. 4th St. The town's first boardinghouse carries some interesting history. Practically all the six rooms, decorated in 1880s style with country antiques, have a tale to tell, from bullet holes outlining Buckskin Frank Leslie's wife's silhouette to legends of a gunfighter taking his last breath. If the walls could talk, you might be up all night. A three-course breakfast is included in the property's Lamplight Room restaurant (see *Dining Out*). One room has a mini fridge and is ideal for families. A guest center has WiFi. Pets okay. $79–99.

Tombstone's Victorian Gardens Bed and Breakfast (520-457-3156), 211 Toughnut. Frilly, fancy, and altogether Victorian, this inn presents the elegant side of Tombstone with vintage Victorian interiors, antiques, and history. And ghosts—perhaps holdovers from when the home was a

gambling venue? All three rooms have private bath, cable TV, bottled water, snacks, and robes. Breakfast included. $80–125.

✳ Where to Eat

DINING OUT **The Lamplight Room** (520-457-3716 or 877-225-1319), 108 N. 4th St. Open Mon.–Thu. 11:30–8:30 (9 Fri.–Sat., 7 Sun.). The town's first fine-dining establishment (since the turn of this century) serves excellent Mexican food and some decent classics (Parmesan-encrusted salmon, chicken cordon bleu, fettuccine Alfredo). They are known for their chiles rellenos and great margaritas. Spanish guitarist Juan de Granada plays classical, *folklorico*, and flamenco guitar Fri.–Sat. 6–9.

The Longhorn Restaurant (520-457-3405), 501 E. Allen St. Open Mon.–Sat. 7 AM–9 PM, Sun 8 AM–9 PM. Originally the Bucket of Blood Saloon. Virgil Earp (who was shot from the second floor of this building) probably would never believe the establishment has gotten enough respectability to earn repeated awards for their ribs. Specialties include shredded barbecue beef and pork. It's comfort food to the max. Entrées $8.95–18.95, sandwiches $6.50–8.95.

EATING OUT **The Patio Restaurant at Big Nose Kate's Saloon** (520-457-3107), 417 E. Allen St. Open 11–8. What started as the Grand Hotel, and *the* place to stay, has evolved into a National Historic Landmark. The bar

ARIZONA SHOPS HAVE SOME INTERESTING OFFERINGS.

has an atmosphere that takes you back 125 years. It serves a light menu and is famous for its giant overstuffed Reuben sandwich, huge hamburgers, and tons of legend and lore about the town. $7–8.

✳ Special Events

Contact 520-457-2458 unless noted elsewise.

March: **Territorial Days** honors the town's founding father, Ed Schieffelin.

April: **Rose Festival** celebrates the bloom of the town's floral mascot, the Lady Banksia rosebush, with a social and parade.

Memorial Day weekend: **Wyatt Earp Days** honors the famous lawman with gunfights, a chili cook-off, mock hangings, an 1880s fashion show, street entertainment, and a Wyatt look-alike contest.

August: **Vigilante Days** (520-457-3495) features Tombstone's unique heritage.

Labor Day weekend: **Rendezvous of Gunfighters** (520-457-3548). Gunfighter groups from around the nation show their talents and costumes.

Third weekend of October: **Helldorado Days** (520-457-3291) started as the town's golden anniversary in 1929 and has since become a yearly event.

November: **Clanton Days Rendezvous** has a costume contest, historical walking tours, and a ghost tour.

PATAGONIA, SONOITA, AND ELGIN

When Arizonans who travel the state talk about their favorite places, the Mountain Empire is invariably high on the list. Folks adore this beautiful countryside of rolling hills with galleries of oaks in a sea of golden or emerald (depending on the season) grasses.

It doesn't take long to experience the classic reaction to open space when you stand in this Empire's countryside, with views so big and far reaching, they swallow you up. At first you feel cloistered. Then your soul relaxes into the reality that there are none of the boundaries city folks feel—buildings, privacy fences, strip malls, and sundry responsibilities—restricting you. Highly charismatic with laid-back manners, the place grows on you. Especially if you like to take your days slow and easy, yet fill them with interesting things to do.

The rich grassland landscape bordered by picturesque mountains captured the attention of Hollywood often over the years. More than half a dozen movies were filmed here, as well as two television series. This rich range country sent thousands of head of cattle a day by train to markets in the East decades ago. The cowboy spirit, so attractive to visitors, lingers on the land and just gets more intense when you see it from horseback.

You don't have to be a cowboy, or an equestrian to take to this area. But it helps if you love the outdoors, because there's lots of it. Even if you don't, you can feel at home on this range.

It's now a bird-watcher's paradise, an oenophile's dream, and an artist's mecca with cutting-edge environmentally sensitive dwellings and organic farming on the rise.

At the end of the day, when thousands of stars seem to swirl in the black ink night sky and the coyote lives up to its nickname of song dog, you can feel as good as the cowboys who ranched here dozens of years ago did—right at home on this classic grassland range.

GUIDANCE The **Patagonia Area Visitor Center** (520-394-0060 or 888-794-0060), 307 McKeown, Patagonia (www.patagoniaaz.com), has a cache of information on this special area, including maps of historic buildings, a vineyard map, area maps, and brochures. The **Nogales Ranger District** (520-281-2296), 303 Old Tucson Rd., Nogales, is open 8–4:30, and can supply information about backcountry use in the Coronado National Forest.

GETTING THERE The only paved highways that approach and travel through the Mountain Empire are AZ 82 and AZ 83.

WHEN TO COME Most visitors wait for winter to travel to this area. However, the land doesn't necessarily have its spring–summer verdancy then. Casual visitors should consider traveling during spring through fall: After a wet winter the grasslands are gorgeous, summer rates are attractive, and fall colors turn riparian forests along the creeks golden. If you plan outdoor activities and are from a cooler climate, wait for winter, late Nov. through Mar.

MEDICAL EMERGENCY Dial 911.

✳ To See

Heartland Ranch Alpacas & Country Store (520-455-5701). Open Fri.–Sat. noon–2. Mark and Rachel Hendrickson raise one of the planet's most warm and fuzzy (and pricey) species here. You can visit the ranch on their open-house dates (call for dates) and view alpacas, Tennessee Walker horses, guanacos, llamas, and Dorper sheep. The Country Store has items made from the soft, silky alpaca fur.

SCENIC DRIVES This highly romantic landscape begs for a leisurely drive or two. You can travel these routes via sedan, road bicycle, or motorcycle. Just remember to include in your driving time extra moments for gawking; the routes are

THERE'S GORGEOUS SCENERY IN THE SAN RAFAEL VALLEY.

that scenic: **Patagonia-Sonoita Scenic Byway** (AZ 82: 52 miles from I-10 to Nogales), **road to Parker Canyon Lake** (AZ 83: 32 miles from Sonoita to Parker Canyon Lake), and **San Rafael Valley** (approximately a 50-mile loop on paved and graded gravel roads).

✳ To Do

APPLE PICKING You can pick some pretty tasty apples at **Douglas Apple Orchards**. The orchard has about 1,500 different apple, pear, and peach trees. Pick your own organic apples for a cost of about 30 cents a pound. Sampling encouraged. Located on Lower Elgin Rd. Open Aug.–Oct.

BIRDING Wherever you are in the area Apr.–Oct., especially the spring and fall migration, you're in for a treat. Located right next to and near flyways where 300 to 400 different species of birds have appeared, the area gives birders a chance to check off a few from their life lists. Your best bet for sightings is to get right into the middle of the action in the **Patagonia-Sonoita Creek Preserve** or one of the area's lakes (see *Wilder Places*).

FISHING Parker Canyon and Patagonia Lakes (see *Wilder Places*) get stocked with a variety of fish.

HIKING The nearby **Santa Rita Mountains** have a large network of trails that travel in oak woodlands up to pine forests. Contact the Nogales Ranger District.

Arizona Trail (www.aztrail.org). You only have to travel 3 miles outside Patagonia to access the historic Arizona Trail, which runs from Mexico to Utah.

The **Patagonia-Sonoita Creek Preserve** has a couple of trails that are especially good for bird-watching (see *Wilder Places*).

HISTORIC WALKING TOUR Pick up *A Walk Through Time* map at the **Patagonia Area Business Association Visitor Center** and meander around town to the marked spots of historic interest in Patagonia.

HORSEBACK RIDING **Arizona Horseback Experience** (520-455-5696 or 866-844-7444), 16 Coyote Court, Sonoita. Ron and Marge Izzo have more than 25 years' trail-riding experience and offer trips that last from 3 hours to several days. You won't get a nose-to-tail experience with their horses. These animals are healthy, responsive, and energetic, and they like to move out. People come from around the world to ride with the Izzos. Call for prices and reservations.

Coronado Outfitters (520-394-0187) in Patagonia can take you on hours-long trail rides, day rides, or days-long pack trips. The extended rides are catered and guided. Their **Cherry Creek Campground** can accommodate your horse and tent camping. Call for prices and information.

MOUNTAIN BIKING The president, at the time of this writing, of the Patagonia Area Business Association moved from Colorado for the scenic quality of the mountain biking in the area. This is comparable to a Napa Valley vintner moving to Elgin (not a bad decision, either). The back roads are exquisite for tour or mountain bike rides that last from several hours to all day. **Patagonia Cyclery** (520-394-2794; patagoniacyclery@theriver.com) offers guided tours Oct.–May and rents bicycles, as well.

ROAD BIKING You can travel the same paved highways listed in *Scenic Drives*; all of the routes if you have a tour bike.

SWIMMING **Patagonia Lake State Park** (see *Wilder Places*) gives you a chance to commune with nature and humanity. It's very popular with the locals come summertime, and closures are not unusual. Call before heading out at that time.

WINE TOURS Oenophiles will be delighted to know the Mountain Empire has land perfect for producing award-winning wine. The area's fertile soil compares to that in Burgundy, France, and the appellations produce some of the best wines in the country—some have been served at the White House. A map of the wine country leads you to the area vintners. The area's most consistent and notable producer is **Callaghan Vineyards** (520-455-5322), 336 Elgin Rd., Elgin. Open Fri.–Sun. 11–3. Vintner Kent Callaghan produces wines that have captivated the palate of the single most influential wine critic in the world, Robert Parker, and the consistent attention of the *Wall Street Journal*. Wine aficionados on the lookout for something different wait with interest for Callaghan's next harvest to come of drinking age. $3 for tastings.

Sonoita Vineyards, Ltd. (520-455-5893), 290 Elgin Canelo Rd., Elgin. Open daily 10–4 except holidays. Owner Dr. Dutt opened the winery in 1983 and has collected a string of awards through the years. Varieties grown on the estate include Chardonnay, Sauvignon Blanc, Cabernet Sauvignon, Merlot, Pinot Noir, and Mission. The Mission grapes date back to the Spanish missionaries from the 16th century.

✳ Wilder Places

🐾 ☁ ♿ **Parker Canyon Lake** (520-388-8300). Located southeast of Sonoita at the end of AZ 83. The ride to this secluded lake is worth each of the 32 miles it takes to get here from Sonoita for a lakeside picnic. Fishing is the main draw here. You can catch cold- and warm-water species, including stocked rainbow trout and resident bass, sunfish, and catfish, from a boat, the fishing pier, or the lakeside paved area and a graveled path. A country store has last-minute supplies. You can buy a fishing license or rent a boat at the store, too. Free.

🐾 ☁ ♿ **Patagonia Lake State Park** (520-287-6965), 400 Patagonia Lake Rd., Patagonia. Open daily 8–10. Once a canyon through which the Southern Pacific Railroad ran a route from Benson to Nogales, now 2.5-mile-long Patagonia Lake laps against clumps of cattails and masses of smooth bluffs. Formed by the damming of Sonoita Creek to supply water to Nogales, Patagonia Lake makes a picturesque recreation spot in the rolling hills of southern Arizona. The best way to experience the lake is to get in the water. Unsupervised Boulder Beach provides a protected area no more than 6 feet deep from its sandy shore to its corded buoys for swimmers to use; the marina store rents rowboats, paddle boats, and canoes to explore the quiet coves and side canyons along the lake. Water-skiing (prohibited May 1–Sep. 1), fishing, camping (72 developed sites and 12 lakeside boat access sites; 32 hookup sites), picnicking, and hiking trails are available at the park. Weekdays $7, weekends $8. Lakeside and electric hookup camping $22 per night, tent camping $15 per night.

Patagonia-Sonoita Creek Preserve (520-394-2400), 150 Blue Heaven Rd., Patagonia. From AZ 82 in Patagonia, turn west onto 4th Ave., then turn south onto Pennsylvania; cross the creek and go 1 mile to the entrance. Open Oct.–Mar., Wed.–Sun. 7:30–4; Apr.–Sep., 6:30–4. A rare, streamside habitat along Patagonia-Sonoita Creek presents one of the planet's best birding habitats. About 300 species of birds have been sighted here, including the gray hawk, green kingfisher, thick-billed kingbird, northern beardless-tyrannulet, violet-crowned hummingbird, and rose-throated becard. Two and a half miles of hiking paths take you into the world-class bird land. Guided nature walk every Saturday at 9 all year with seasonal birding and natural history programs. $5 admission is good for 7 days from date of purchase; Patagonia residents and children under 16 are free. No dogs permitted.

✳ Lodging

🐾 ♿ **The Duquesne House Bed and Breakfast** (520-394-2732), 357 Duquesne Ave., Patagonia. More than a century ago this adobe building housed rough-and-tumble miners. Now fixed up with harmonious colors and textures, the rooms make a comfortable and pleasing stay with appointments such as Mexican folk art, hand-stitched samplers, and quilts. Gardens and patios attract avian life. One room has a kitchenette and large shower for handicapped accessibility. Breakfast leans toward healthy gourmet with fresh ingredients made by the owner. Pets are okay with a deposit. $99.

⌒ 🐾 **An Enchanted Garden Villa** (520-394-0272), 136 Forrest Dr., Patagonia. All the native trees, flowers, and birds on this property give it the look and feel of an arboretum. On the rustic Zen side, the outside garden is cozy and secluded and lives up

to the property's name. The interiors are simple, clean, and environmentally friendly for allergy-sensitive travelers. Continental breakfast of fruit, fresh-baked breads or muffins from in-town bakery, and organic coffee. Polite pets are okay with a $15 extra charge. $109.

⌒ 𝄞 **La Hacienda de Sonoita** (520-455-5308), 34 Swanson Rd., Sonoita. Built as a bed and breakfast, so you have the privacy of a hotel but the camaraderie of the hosts and other guests if you like, the hacienda has a warm, laid-back atmosphere. Four themed guest rooms keep the spirit of the West in mind—fully tiled, wooden ceiling beams, and decorated in cowboy legacy. The great room has a library, game table, piano, sitting area, and two fireplaces. All the guest rooms have a private bath: One has a fireplace and full tub and shower; another twin beds; and two have queen beds. A full, delicious breakfast is included with stay. No pets. Equestrian accommodations available (bring your own feed). $100–115.

La Frontera Gallery and Guest Cottages (520-394-0110), 340 Naugle Ave., Patagonia. Art plays a big part in La Frontera's two guest cottages. Innkeeper-owner Kathleen James was an art dealer and shares her love of art and her husband's photography. One cottage, a two-bedroom, two-story studio loft with a kitchen and bathroom, has Mexican decor. The other, a catalog home shipped on the train with bead board and Victorian nuances, has a bedroom, sitting room, bath, and kitchen. The cottages have regional touches with fine textiles, rugs, territorial antique furniture, and folk and contemporary art. Coffee and tea are included in the cottages, and Kathleen can stock the refrigerator with breakfast food. Breakfast for two—large and regional Mexican—is available on request for $25. Children are okay, but no pets. $125; $15 for each additional person.

☙ **Spirit Tree Inn** (520-394-0121), 3 Harshaw Creek Rd. Patagonia. Located on a 52-acre inholding right in the Coronado National Forest, you get pretty secluded here, though only a few miles out of town. The property got its name from the majestic 150-year-old cottonwood tree in the front meadow. Its 300-inch girth puts it in the top 10 in the world. Native peoples believed large trees, such as this cottonwood, held the spirits of their ancestors. Originally the Rocking Horse Ranch headquarters, the historic building drips with rustic ranch character—sturdy but unpretentious. The three guest rooms in the home and two casitas have

private bath and WiFi. The casitas have kitchenettes and can accommodate pets. Breakfasts, thanks to Thomas Barholomeaux's career working with some of the world's finest chefs and in five-star restaurants, definitely have gourmet leanings. He also shares his talents in the afternoon social hour with light delights and local wines. Gourmet breakfast included in rates. Dogs are accepted on individual basis; horse facilities for haul-ins. $110–220.

✳ Where to Eat

DINING OUT ☙ **Café Sonoita** (520-455-5278), 3280 AZ 82, Sonoita. Open Wed.–Thu. 5–8, Fri.–Sat. 11–2:30 and 5–8; closed Sun.–Tue. The restaurant has trademarked their "creatively delicious" fare, which originally was displayed on a Famous Changing Chalkboard Menu. Today

THE SPIRIT TREE INN TAKES ITS NAME FROM THIS HUGE COTTONWOOD.

the menu is printed and handed out tableside. Beef in this cattle country restaurant comes served six ways to Sunday—in a steak or roast, on a salad, or in a half-pound burger. The food has a rich, and certainly creatively delicious personality, so more refined palates will not go unsatisfied. Desserts are house-made and creatively delicious. A wine list features area varieties along with favorites from around the world. Entrées $7.95–14.50.

Canela (520-455-5873), 3252 AZ 82, Sonoita. Open Thu.–Mon. 5–10. The husband-and-wife team of Joy Vargo and John Hall—both experienced chefs who met at the New England Culinary Institute in Vermont— display their innovative talents through a delicious menu big on local foods and wines. The menu changes daily, offering a strong variety of meats, a fish dish, and a vegetarian entrée. The appetizers can range from albondigas soup with A bar H beef meatballs, pickled serrano chiles, and cilantro, to a salad, to *calabacitas* (squash, roasted garlic, cotija, and cilantro). The meat entrées are excellent—such as the hanger steak with roasted potatoes and onions, cilantro garlic butter, and a baby salad with coriander vinaigrette. The grilled pork chop comes with fresh herb spaetzle, roasted red pepper and cucumber relish, and green chili sauce. Joy specializes in fish (a holdover from her Seattle days), which seems to be catching the interest of the local beef eaters. Desserts are house-made and special, from the chocolate truffles to made-to-order sorbet and honey tuilles. The coffee is from Seattle and much of the wine from area vineyards. Entrées $13–24.

EATING OUT Gathering Grounds (520-394-2097), 319 McKeown Ave., Patagonia. Open daily 7–5, Sun. 8–5. Like most coffee shops, this one gathers the locals to its side. While you get your buzz from espresso and other coffee drinks, ice cream delights, or Italian cream sodas, you might hear the buzz the locals have about organic gardening, Qi-Gong in the town park across the street, or the Mississippi Soul Meets West Coast Blues event for the Humane Society. The establishment also serves deli foods for a meal to stay or go.

The Grasslands Bakery-Café (520-455-4770), 3119 AZ 83, Sonoita. Open Thu.–Sun. 8–3. Totally organic and "natural from seed to table," you can get a rich, homespun breakfast and lunch here, as well as some delicious homemade breads and baked goods. The salads (Greek, avocado, grasslands, fruit plate, and European potato) are organic, as are the warm pasta salads. Deep-dish pies, which

change daily, range from broccoli to mushrooms and cheddar, portobello, aubergine, and hearty Hungarian. Sandwiches come on croissants. Each variety of quiche comes in a spelt and olive oil crust. The coffee comes from organic beans, and the cream is heavy; wines come from area vineyards, some without sulfites; and the desserts are stellar (remember, this is a bakery). On the way out, pick up some fresh-made canned goods. Entrées $10.95–12.95.

❧ **Santos Mexican Café** (520-394-2597), 328 W. Naugle Ave., Patagonia. Open Mon.–Wed. 7–3 (till 8 Thu.–Sat.); closed Sun. Some say Santos' serves the best Mexican food in the state. Those who can't live too long without a Mexican food meal will consider Santos' heaven—a likely place for saints to dwell, as *santos* means "saint" in Spanish. From the menudo to the flan, the food is fresh, homemade, and classic. Entrées $4.25–8.25.

Velvet Elvis Pizza Company (520-394-2102), 292 Naugle Ave., Patagonia. Owner Cecelia St. Miguel celebrated the opening of this venerated pizza place with a procession to Our Lady of Guadalupe. Since then the restaurant, which serves food made from recipes with 70-year-old roots in a Brooklyn, New York, restaurant, has appeared in international magazines and newspapers. Arizona's Governor Napolitano declared the tiny place filled with paintings of Elvis (on velvet, of course) and our Lady of Guadalupe an Arizona Treasure. You'll find everything from vegetarian soups to organic salads, calzones to pizza, lemon-herb baked chicken to BBQ back ribs. Freshly blended juices, microbrewed and imported beers,

and wines are available. Designer pizzas $20–35, entrées $11.99–14.99.

✳ The Arts

The Mountain Empire has evolved into an artists' enclave. You'll find all kinds of talent and media, from crafts to collectible pieces, lining the two main streets (Naugle and McKeown) in Patagonia. The **Mesquite Grove Gallery** (371 McKeown) opened more than 20 years ago—the town's first gallery—as a local artists' venue. The gallery continues to support the local arts, as well as works from outside the region.

✳ Selective Shopping

The word *franchise* does not exist in the Mountain Empire. Words like

PUBLIC ART ABOUNDS IN PATAGONIA.

vine. Appoint a designated driver, turn wine imbiber, and stock up the cellar.

Nogales, Mexico. Only 20 miles south across the border, you can shop till you drop in Mexican markets. Just remember to bring a valid form of identification for your return into the states. (See the *Tips for Visiting Mexico* sidebar on page 216.)

✳ Special Events

April: **Blessing of the Vine Festival** (www.arizonawines.com). Special blessings and celebrations at Sonoita Vineyards.

July: **4th of July Celebration** (520-394-0060) in downtown Patagonia and Town Park.

September: **Blessing of the Harvest Festival** (www.arizonawines.com). Special blessings and celebrations at Elgin vineyards. **Sonoita Rodeo** (520-455-5553) is an Old West rodeo along with steak fry and dancing at Santa Cruz County Fairgrounds on Labor Day weekend. **Santa Cruz County Fair** (520-455-5553) features open exhibits, vendors, and entertainment the last weekend of the month.

October: **Patagonia Fall Festival** (520-394-0060 or 888-794-0060). Art and crafts, music, food booths, and a dance in Town Park.

unique, one-of-a-kind, original, independent are more befitting this land of the self-made man/woman. The gas station in Patagonia declares itself politically incorrect, and the market does not take credit, except for a fee. The dot-on-the-map business area in Sonoita along AZ 83 has a few interesting shops worth checking out. Elgin's heart belongs solely to the

Western Arizona 5

ROUTE 66: ASH FORK TO
CALIFORNIA

LAKE HAVASU CITY

YUMA

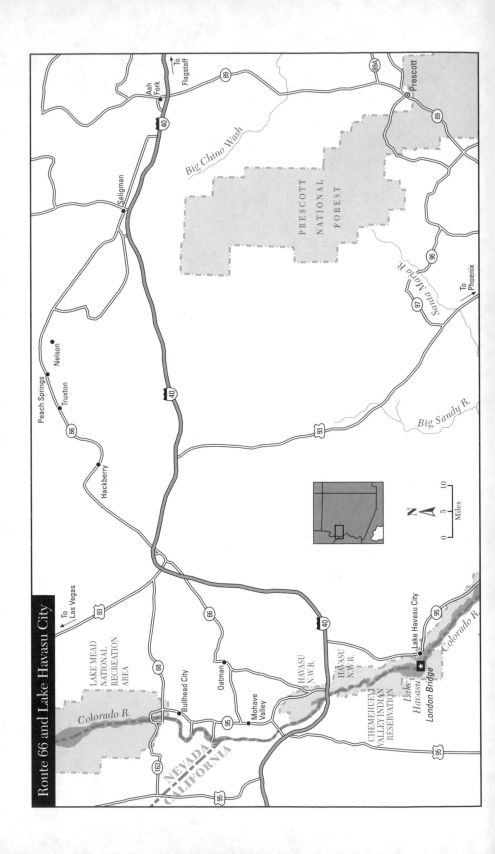

Route 66 and Lake Havasu City

ROUTE 66: ASH FORK TO CALIFORNIA

K nown as the Mother Road, the Main Street of America, and the Will Rogers Highway, Route 66 has an endearing reputation. The 2,448-mile-long highway, commissioned back in 1926, became the epitome of freedom, linking the strong-shouldered Chicago with the free-spirited Santa Monica. It took more than 10 years to get the whole highway paved, and some of the segments of the route that still exist (not replaced by an interstate) in Arizona feel like they belong right back in the pre-paved days. This western segment that crosses Arizona (dubbed the Heart of Route 66 because it contains the longest original stretch left) starts in Ash Fork and crosses some wide-open spaces with little in the way of luxury. It's the simple life, where extravagance shows up in scenery rather than amenities. The grand finale of Arizona's stretch of Historic Route 66 takes you through the Black Mountains into Oatman, and then on to a segment designated a Scenic Back Country Byway that winds down to Topock at the edge of the Colorado River.

Oatman looks much the same as it did in its heyday from the early 1900s to its bust in 1942. Boardwalks line storefronts along the mile-long main street. The buildings' blend of wood and corrugated metal, sometimes shaky with age, adds a ramshackle demeanor. Foot-thick old adobe buildings, answers to the 2,700-foot-high town's searing summers, brand Oatman as unmistakably southwestern. The town exudes a cagey twist of mischievous fun and history.

The whole highway is the stuff that William Least Heat Moon's classic *Blue Highways: A Journey into America* is about. Here, along Old Route 66, you find out where life really happens. Interestingly, it usually happens to be your own.

GUIDANCE **Ash Fork Chamber of Commerce** (928-637-2442), 616 Lewis Ave., Ash Fork. **Powerhouse Visitors Center** (928-753-6106), 120 W. Andy Devine Ave. (Route 66), Kingman. **Oatman Chamber of Commerce** (928-768-6222). **Hualapai Office of Tourism** (928-769-2230). Located in Hualapai Lodge in Peach Springs. Get permits for and information about traveling on the Hualapai tribal lands. Contact the **Havasupai tribe** (928-448-2121), P.O. Box 160, Supai, AZ 86432 for information on Havasu Canyon.

GETTING THERE You can approach Route 66 from Flagstaff via I-40 and exit at Ash Fork; from Prescott, go north on US 89 to Ash Fork; from California, take I-40 east to the Topock exit.

WHEN TO COME Peak season for most of this stretch of high-desert highway runs from Mar. through Nov. However, Oatman, located in a lower desert zone, is flip-flopped: High season is Oct. through Mar.

MEDICAL EMERGENCY Dial 911.

✳ To See

Seligman
Delgadillo's Route 66 Gift Shop and Museum (928-422-3352), 217 E. Route 66. Open daily 8:30–6. The Route 66 Gift Shop hasn't changed a bit since the time it was Angel Delgadillo's barbershop, back when people were getting their kicks on Route 66. Delgadillo, born and raised in Seligman, lobbied the Arizona legislature to designate and preserve Route 66 in Arizona as a historic highway. The unofficial spokesperson who calls himself the "Guardian Angel" for Route 66, he loves to talk about his passion. Peruse the memorabilia, add a business card to the collection on the wall, and pick up a *Walking Tour Guide to Historic Seligman*.

Peach Springs
Grand Canyon Caverns (928-422-4565). Located 2 miles west of Seligman. Open daily except Christmas. The limestone walls of the natural cavern were formed in prehistoric times by an inland sea. On the 45-minute (0.75-mile) tour, an elevator transports you 210 feet underground. Besides limestone formations, you see fossils and the bones of long-extinct animals. $12.95 adults, $9.95 ages 4–12.

Kingman
Mohave Museum of History & Arts (928-753-3195), 400 W. Beale St. Open Mon.–Fri. 9–5, Sat.–Sun. 1–5. This collection of historiana from the northwest corner of Arizona features the cultures that played a part in settling the area: Native American tribes, missionaries, miners, ranchers, railroad workers, soldiers, steamboaters. There are a number of exhibits, murals, and dioramas, plus an outdoor display. If you have time and would like to dig a bit deeper into the area history, check out the museum library and its collection of documents, manuscripts, and photographs centering on Mohave County and the Southwest (open Mon.–Fri. 9–4:30). $4 adults, $3 seniors (over 60); children under 12 are free when accompanied by adult. The admission fee also allows access to Route 66 Museum.

Route 66 Museum (928-753-9889), 120 W. Andy Devine Ave. (Route 66). Open daily 9–6 (9–5 Dec.–Feb.). This well-organized museum unfolds the historical evolution of travel along what became Route 66 with murals, dioramas, and photographs. $4 adults, $3 seniors (over 60), children under 12 are free when accompanied by adult. The admission fee also allows access to Mohave Museum of History and Art.

GRAND CANYON SKYWAY

The Hualapai tribe has been promising to develop a skyway over a segment of the Grand Canyon (marketed by the tribe as Grand Canyon West) for more than a decade. The idea was spawned out of Las Vegas by a developer named David Jin in 1996. The tribe agreed to the fantastic project, as long as they could own the skyway and Jin take a percentage of the income.

Construction, much to some people's chagrin, started in 2005. Tribe members got second thoughts when construction efforts unearthed several Hualapai burial grounds. Plus, they remembered, the canyon holds sacred status with the tribe. Environmentalists thought it a travesty. Others simply wondered.

At the time of this writing, the 1.07-million-pound, $30 million skyway had just finished completion. The U-shaped walkway juts 70 feet from the rim. Here's the thrilling part—it has a 4-inch glass bottom. If you get a little woozy looking down from the top of the Empire State Building or Chicago's John Hancock Center, take your required dose of Dramamine™ before you look down from this attraction. You're 4,000 feet above the canyon floor for the whole 20-plus yards.

Like Navajo Bridge, building the Skyway was a masterful feat. To safely lay it in place, engineers perched this bridge at the canyon's edge via a pulley system connected to four tractor-trailers. Hydraulic braces lifted the Skywalk from underneath above a cement track, maneuvered the walk (balanced by about half a million pounds of steel cubes at land's end to keep it from forming another set of rapids in the river below) over a web of metal rods, and positioned it onto four steel anchors previously drilled deep into the canyon rock. Workers finished the procedure, described by a spokesperson for Grand Canyon West as "Just smooth as glass," by welding the walkway onto the anchors.

If you go, you can rest assured the walkway can withstand 100 mph winds as well as 8.0 earthquakes up to 50 miles away; shock absorbers should keep it from shaking while you walk. Contact the Hualapai tribe for information on getting there and total cost of admission (including transportation and admittance onto the walkway).

Oatman

Oatman's most charming attraction is the group of wild burrows that roam the streets carte blanche. Their lineage comes from the mining days when prospectors used them as beasts of burden. Around a dozen of the burros' descendants mosey around town, greeting visitors and chomping carrots—the only legal treat allowed the animals and sold by the bagful by shop owners. The burros basically have a sweet demeanor, but they do have their moody moments, and some may kick or bite if provoked. About 1,500 wild burros hang out in the surrounding mountains.

Oatman Hotel (928-768-4408), 181 Main St. Open daily Mon.–Fri. 10:30–6, Sat.–Sun. 8 AM–9 PM. The hotel, built in 1902, was the happening place during the town's boom. Miners spent much of their off time in the hotel, and the premises hold plenty of memorabilia from the gold-mining past. Thousands of signed and dated dollar bills cover the walls and ceilings of the bar and restaurant (open until 9 PM). The tradition originated with the miners. When they had money, they tacked up a dollar. If they ran out of cash, they knew they could still buy a bottle of beer with their dollar. If you look hard enough, you might see one signed by late President Ronald Reagan. When Carole Lombard and Clark Gable tied the knot in 1939, they spent their wedding night at the Oatman Hotel. They liked the atmosphere so much—she the peace, and he the card games with miners—that they made repeat visits. Used to be, until a few years back, you could stay the night until someone realized 17 rooms (that never got much attention, anyway, in the way of upkeep) and one bathroom down the hall wasn't convenient. Today Gable and Lombard's Honeymoon Suite, and other rooms, are part of a museum. Donations accepted.

Oatman Museum (928-768-4871), Main St. Call for hours. The small museum has a decent collection of mining memorabilia. Donations accepted.

SCENIC DRIVES **Peach Springs Road**. From Peach Springs, turn south onto Diamond Creek Road. This is the only place where you can drive down to the Colorado River in the Grand Canyon. The 20-mile drive (high clearance recommended) travels some pretty spectacular countryside, *and* you can picnic or camp right alongside the river. Purchase a $10-per-person-per-day permit from the Hualapai Nation.

✳ To Do

Peach Springs
HIKING **Havasu Canyon** (see *Wilder Places*). This classic hike, with pilgrimage status, ends at the hotel in the tiny town of Supai (mile 8) or the campground (mile 10), often drawing repeat visits. From Supai, you can hike another 8 miles to the Colorado River. The hike to the river requires experience with long distances and remote areas. The first 5 miles travel the Havasupai reservation; the last 3, Grand Canyon National Park. The segment has one technical spot and must be done as a day hike since the tribe does not allow overnight use on the reservation outside the campground, and the National Park Service does not allow overnight use in that portion of the park. Contact the Havasupai tribe (see *Guidance*) for permits.

Oatman
GOLD-MINE TOUR **Gold Road Mine** (928-768-1600). Located 2.5 miles east of Oatman on Route 66. Tours run 10–4. A $16 grub stake got the Gold Road Mine started. You find out all about the mine's history and hardships of gold mining on

an hour-long tour given by mine workers. The mine tunnel, which travels under Route 66, follows a milky-white vein of quartz containing rich amounts of the yellow metal. You even get a handful of quartz chipped from the precious vein. At the end of the tour, you head to a small room with special lights that illuminate gold veins like a green fluorescence. You may not strike it rich, but you might come away with a smattering of the precious metal that put Oatman on the map. $12.50 adults, $6 ages 12 and under.

HORSEBACK RIDES Oatman Stables (928-768-3257). Closed in summer. Head out into the rough-and-ready countryside of the Black Mountains down old cavalry trails on horseback. The rugged desert mountains provide a beautiful Wild West landscape. Guides take you out on 1- ($25) or 2-hour ($45) rides, cookouts, cattle drives, and overnighters. Call for information and reservations.

✳ Wilder Places

Havasu Canyon. The trailhead is located 60 miles from Peach Springs on Hualapai 18. Sacred to the Havasupai people and so distinctly beautiful, the poetic canyon draws people from around the world. The liquid turquoise flow of Havasu Creek through the redrock cliffs of Havasu Canyon is the big draw; the waterfalls along the creek's course to the Grand Canyon are some of the most celebrated in the state. The remote town of Supai, 8 miles from the trailhead at Hualapai Hilltop on the bottom of the canyon, has no cars and very little in the way of modern conveniences besides a hotel, small market, and cafeteria restaurant. Two miles downcreek, you can camp. The only ways in to this Edenic piece of nature are hiking, horse, or helicopter—making this a trip to remember. Contact the Havasupai Nation (see *Guidance*) to obtain permits.

WILDER PLACES—HAVASU CANYON.
© Scottsdale Convention & Tourism Bureau

Hualapai Mountain Park (928-757-3859). From Kingman, go east on Andy Devine Ave. (Route 66), and turn right onto Hualapai Mountain Rd.; go 14 miles to the signed park entrance. Open daily 5 AM–9 PM. While not a wilderness, the park is a neat little niche in the mountains in which to picnic, camp, and view wildlife, hike, or mountain bike on several multiuse trails.

✳ Lodging

Seligman
🐾 **Canyon Lodge** (928-422-3255), 114 E. Chino Ave. You can get a comfy and clean room here and watch the world go by on the balcony lounge. Rooms have double or California king beds, refrigerator, microwave, TV, and phone. Continental breakfast included. $42–46.

Peach Springs
🐾 **Hualapai Lodge** (928-769-2230 or 888-255-9550), 900 Route 66, Peach Springs. The Hualapai tribe, owners and operators, have accented the lodge with their culture. The property has a restaurant, gift shop, meeting facilities, laundry, Jacuzzi, pool, and fitness room. Rooms—oversized, comfortable, and clean—have phone and cable TV/movies. $79–109.

Kingman
🐾 ✐ **Hualapai Mountain County Park Cabins** (928-681-5700). It's BYO here regarding linens, dishes, food, and the like, but otherwise the cabins (some stone) are fully furnished with beds (double, twin, and/or bunk), table, cooktop stove, refrigerator, heater, electricity, bath and shower, and hot and cold water; some have fireplace or woodstove. Plus, each has a barbecue grill and picnic table outside. Rustic, but fun. Three-day holiday minimum. $45–110.

✳ Where to Eat

Seligman
Snow Cap Drive-In (928-422-3291), 301 E. Route 66. Open daily 9–5; closed Nov. 22–Mar. 1. Owner and general practical joker Juan Delgadillo has a host of gimmicks for the unsuspecting traveler. The drive-in itself looks as zany as the owner's personality. All the food is made to order; the most popular items are the tacos and burritos, but a red chiliburger and soft ice cream treats makes a great meal, too. $1.95–5.25.

Westside Lilo's Café (928-422-5456), 415 W. Route 66, Seligman. The best restaurant in town serves good food at good prices. Breakfast is served all day. Soups are made fresh each day, hamburgers have Black Angus chuck, french fries are fresh cut, salads are fresh, and desserts are house-made. All the fried foods are prepared in a low-saturated-fat blend with no cholesterol. Wiener or Jaeger schnitzels are dinner favorites. Entrées $4.25–7.25.

Kingman
Mr. Dz's Route 66 Diner (928-718-0066), 105 E. Andy Devine Ave. Open daily 7 AM–9 PM. You can't miss the building—turquoise and pink—standing right on the town's main drag. This is soda shop classic, where you order burgers, a "tower" of onion rings, and a root beer float (made from Mr. Dz's own special recipe) to the sounds of the jukebox in the background. Take your meal outside, make yourself at home on one of the benches, and watch motorcycles and vintage cars cruise by. $5.50–12.

Oatman
Oatman Hotel (928-768-4408), 181 Main St. Open daily Mon.–Fri. 10:30–6, Sat.–Sun. 8 AM–9 PM. This is the place where all the nightlife happened during the town's high times; and it still is, inasmuch as it's the only place open after dark on weekends. You can get a decent meal here in a historic atmosphere. Afterward, peek

THIS IS THE REAL THING ALONG RTE 66 PASSING THRU OATMAN.

upstairs to see where people stayed. Entrées $6.95–8.95.

🦞 🍨 **Olive Oatman Restaurant and Ice Cream Saloon** (928-768-1891), 171 Main St. Open daily 8:30–4:30. Named for the daughter of a pioneer Illinoisan family sold as a slave to Mojave Indians. Her incredible story is on the back of the menu. You can get a hearty breakfast here and sandwiches for lunch. Specialties include Indian frybread, Navajo taco, and peach frybread (with ice cream). Local musician Tom Woodard plays old country music from noon until closing almost every day. Entrées $4–6.50.

✳ Special Events

January: **Polar Bear Dip** (928-757-7919). Start the year off with an icy plunge into Kingman's Downtown Pool.

February: **Wild West Days** (928-768-6222) in Oatman celebrates the town's wild history.

May: **Historic Route 66 Fun Run** (928-753-5001) brings hundreds of classic cars to Seligman to travel Arizona's western stretch of Historic Route 66.

July: **Sidewalk Egg Fry** (928-753-2636) is Oatman's caricature attempt to celebrate the sear of summer by giving participants a chance to fry an egg at high noon.

August: **Hualapai Mountain Arts & Crafts Festival** (928-757-3545), high in the pines at the Hualapai Mountain Resort.

September: **Gold Camp Days** (928-768-6222) is Oatman's Labor Day weekend celebration with a parade, crazy hat contest, beard contest, and fun-filled Burro Biscuit Throwing contest. **Mohave County Fair** (928-753-2636) presents livestock and crafts exhibits, shows, carnival rides, and games. **Andy Devine Days** (928-757-7919) honors the late western actor Andy Devine and Kingman's western heritage all weekend, including a rodeo.

October: **Kingman Air & Auto Show** (928-692-9599) takes place at the Kingman Airport with aerial acrobatics and static aircraft displays, classic car show, dragster races, vendors, and food.

December: **Very Merry Parade of Lights** (928-753-9095) in downtown Kingman celebrates the holiday season with lighted floats and vehicles.

LAKE HAVASU CITY

I n summer, when desert temperatures run amok, most denizens stay clear of the sun's sizzle. Animals slink into the shadows, and humans head for air-conditioned shelter. This is not true, however, along the lower Colorado River. This near-sea-level segment of the trans-state river passes through some of the hottest spots in the nation, where only 3 inches of rainfall hits the ground each year and temperatures toy with the 120-degree mark.

In this land where record temperatures are more novelty than nuisance, the river becomes the center of attention for man and beast. Where animals depend on the river for sustenance, often stealing sips during the twilight hours, man relies upon it for recreation. When the temperatures rise, the residents of Lake Havasu City simply migrate to the water. They find a cool pocket in the lake, grab a cold drink, don a life jacket, and bob in the refreshing currents.

From springtime to autumn the lower Colorado River around Lake Havasu City roils with activity. With river temperatures hovering in the 80s, the glug-a-lug of racing boats, nasal buzz of personal watercraft, and whoosh of water-skiers prevails through the daylight hours. The hot, humid, and mostly sunny days draw people into the river channel near London Bridge. They wave to the vessels that parade past all day.

When temperatures relax back into double digits from autumn through early spring, so does the activity, at least from a human standpoint. From a wildlife point of view the river, a major migratory route, becomes one popular place. Birds travel all the way from the Arctic to winter along the river while resident waterfowl loll along the shore and a variety of mammals become visible. Fishermen take to the quiet lake to catch the trophy fish that might lurk in the blue-green water. At twilight geese honk their way across the sky and great horned owls hoot cross-canyon to each other.

Hot or cold weather, the river stays busy year-round. It just depends what type of migration you're interested in.

GUIDANCE **Lake Havasu City Convention & Visitors Bureau** (928-453-3444), 314 London Bridge Rd. Open daily 9–4. **Bureau of Land Management** (928-505-1200 or 888-213-2582), 2610 Sweetwater Ave. **Lake Havasu State Park Windsor Beach** (928-855-2784 or 800-285-3703), 699 London Bridge Rd.

GETTING THERE *By car:* AZ 95 takes you right to the riverside city from either 305
direction (north or south). *By air:* **Lake Havasu City Municipal Airport** (928-
764-3330), 5600 AZ 95, is serviced by U.S. Airways.

WHEN TO COME Because of the lure of the water, summertime is high season
here. Make sure you have reservations, especially on holidays, when the boats
get so concentrated on the lake that you can walk from one to the other without
getting wet.

MEDICAL EMERGENCY **Havasu Regional Medical Center** (928-855-8185),
101 Civic Center Lane.

✳ To See

Lake Havasu Museum (928-854-4938), 320 London Bridge Rd. Open
Tue.–Sat. 2–4. The museum has a number of interesting exhibits related to the
area: mining, steamboats, the London Bridge, and Native peoples. You can even
do some research nosing through their collection of old newspapers. Catch a
classic film at 1:30 Tue., Thu., or Sat. $2 adults, children under 12 free.

London Bridge. Coined the most expensive antique in the world, England's
London Bridge got a new home in Lake Havasu City in 1971. The Brits put the
famous bridge up for sale in the early 1960s because the granite span started
sinking into the Thames River's clay bed. City father Robert McCulloch Sr. part-
nered with C. V. Wood Jr. (the largely unknown brains behind Disneyland) to
buy the bridge for $2,460,000. The duo had the bridge dismantled, coded each
granite block with a set of numbers, shipped the pieces to the States, and reconstructed the bridge over Lake Havasu by matching the code numbers. The
bridge has become Arizona's second biggest tourist draw. In summertime up to
20,000 boats cruise underneath; it's the place to see and be seen.

✳ To Do

BEACHES If you don't have a boat in which to cruise the river, lounge beside it
on one of several beaches in town. **Cattail Cove State Park** is located 10 miles
south on AZ 95. It has camping, a boat launch, picnic area, marina, swimming
beach, and hiking trail.

Lake Havasu State Park Windsor Beach, centrally located (near London
Bridge) and busy with activities, has camping, a boat launch, swimming beach,
nature trail, and events. $9 per vehicle; $2 for an individual on bicycle.

London Bridge Beach. Located along the Bridgewater Channel (access
through the public parking lot on the south side of McCulloch Blvd.), this is
more a riverside park with picnic ramadas and barbecues, swimming area, play-
grounds, and restrooms. It's where everyone not in a boat likes to hang out.

BOAT CAMPING Boat camping is allowed by permit only on a first-come,
first-served basis. Arizona State Parks sites located between Red Rock Cove and
Cattail Cove cost $14 each night. Sites maintained by the Bureau of Land

Management south of Cattail Cove cost $10 for day use and $10 for camping. Most boat camps have table, grill, and outhouse, but no drinking water. For more information, contact Lake Havasu State Park or the Bureau of Land Management (see *Guidance*).

BOAT TOURS BlueWater Jetboat Tour (928-855-7171), 501 English Village, Lake Havasu City. Sep.–May, the *Starship 2010* cruises at 28 miles per hour northward through Havasu Natural Wildlife Area to a petroglyph site in the Topock Gorge. Along the way a guide narrates natural and cultural history. The jetboat slows down for animal sightings—which, during the cooler months, can be often. Call for tour times and prices.

Dixie Belle **Tour Boat** (928-855-0888 or 866-332-9231). Located in the English Village. Open daily, weather permitting; call for reservations and tours times. For a quick lowdown on Lake Havasu's high points, take an hour-long tour on this paddlewheel boat around the Island, a human-made isle with lodging, restaurants, and London Bridge Beach. As the paddlewheel chugs around the Island, the captain shares fun facts about the lake, the town, and the lower Colorado River while identifying popular places and activities on the lake. $15 per person. Dinner cruises available.

GOLF Emerald Canyon Golf Course (928-667-3366), 7351 Riverside Dr., Parker. The 18-hole, par-72 championship course gets the nod from regional and national golf gurus. Described as raw, rugged, and ravishingly beautiful, it's the site of Southwest Section Senior PGA Championship games. The course has a putting green, driving range, practice green, beverage cart, snack bar, and pro shop. $55.

KAYAKING If you have your own kayak, you can launch from Cathedral Rock, areas along Windsor Beach, and Cattail State Park. Vendors also rent vessels along the beaches. If you want to go on a guided tour or paddle from Topock Gorge, **Jerkwater Canoe & Kayak Co., Inc.** (928-768-7753 or 800-421-7803), will outfit and shuttle you. Call for information and prices, or log onto www .jerkwater.com.

DOG PARKS 🐾 **Lion's Dog Park** (928-453-8686), 1340 McCulloch. Open 6 AM–10 PM. Lion's Park follows along the Colorado River. Fenced area with a dog fountain.

FISHING Famous for its striped bass, Lake Havasu holds the state Colorado River record for black crappie, green sunfish, and redear sunfish. One of the best times to cast for stripers is in summer when they're actively chasing the shad in the surface waters of the lake. Take a pair of binoculars to spot seagulls. Where seagulls gather (right above schools of shad), stripers aren't far away. Neither are the anglers; they just go from boil to boil.

WALKS Bridgewater River Walk. Located on Rotary Park Beach. Anytime of year is perfect for a walk along the river. In winter you have your choice of time of day. In summer get out in the cool freshness of the early morning—or wait for sunset, when you see a poetic side to the fast-paced lake. The lake shimmers ice blue under the jagged ridgeline of California mountains purpled against a backdrop of fiery fluorescence. Temperatures relax back into the double digits. And the lake action settles down long enough for everyone to catch their breath. Tomorrow, the fun starts all over again.

✳ Wilder Places

Like just about everything else, these wilder places are centered on water, and you will need a boat, canoe, or kayak to travel them. If you don't have your own, see *To Do* for information on rentals or tours.

Havasu National Wildlife Refuge (760-326-3853). Just over half a dozen decades ago the banks along the lower Colorado River had galleries of cottonwood and willow trees that formed a rich riparian habitat. After Parker Dam tamed this segment of river in 1941, pooling Lake Havasu, the water submerged the cottonwood galleries and formed a waterlog of marshes. The ecosystem transitioned into a waterfowl dream. As one of the best bird-watching spots on the lower Colorado River, the federal government designated the 30 miles between Needles, California, and Lake Havasu City as a wildlife refuge. Clucks, peeps, and chirps continually rise from thickets of tules—8- to 15-foot-high bulrushes—that border the river where you might hear the infamous *kek-kek-kek* of the elusive Yuma clapper rail, one of the four endangered bird species found in the refuge. Southwestern willow flycatcher, peregrine falcon, and southern bald eagle are the others.

Topock Gorge. Take AZ 95 north to I-40; go west on I-40 to the Golden Shores exit, turn left, and go under the railroad bridge to the marina on the left. If you want to locate the heart of the western Colorado River, you might find it beating in its lower reaches near Yuma, where riverboat commerce had its heyday and colored the history of the river. Its soul, however, would hover in Topock Gorge. At times moody and introspective, then deeply inspirational, the gorge has evoked legends and lore from the different cultures that have passed through it. Rows of needlelike hoodoos, arches, and curious formations carve the gorge's copper ridges leaning pell-mell into one another. In the late 1800s riverboat captains had moments of difficulty and tragedy navigating its midsection, cluttered with serpentine writhes and sandbars, prompting names of landmarks like Devil's Elbow. The jagged ridgelines in the upper gorge inspired the name for Needles, California. Spindly and pinprick-sharp, the hoodoos pocked with arches akin to needles' eyes create a strange beauty. Free.

✳ Lodging

⅁ **Agave Inn** (928-854-2833 or 866-854-2833), 1420 N. McCulloch Blvd. The guest rooms and suites, both spacious, have simple interiors with European flavor. Luxury touches, like floor-to-ceiling river views and whirlpool baths, make nice additions.

Rooms have large TV, DVD/CD player, Internet access, mini fridge, microwave, and 300-count sheets. No pets. $139–399.

∞ ✎ ⅁ **London Bridge Resort & Convention Center** (928-855-0888 or 800-624-7939), 1477 Queens Bay.

The resort, with its English-castle exterior, has an atmosphere of casual elegance. The property—in the middle of everything at the English Village next to the London Bridge—includes three pools, a golf course, a fitness center, and laundry facilities. Suites have fully equipped kitchenette, coffee service, TV and stereo, multi-line cordless phone, robes, and fine linens. No pets. $59–289.

✄ & **Nautical Inn Resort & Convention Center** (928-855-2141 or 800-892-2141), 1000 McCulloch Blvd. The only beachfront accommodation has heated pool, hot tub, and conference center. Rooms have queen or king beds, TV, refrigerator, private patio or balcony. $79–350.

✳ Where to Eat

Angelina's Italian Kitchen (928-680-3868), 2137 W. Acoma Blvd. Open for dinner Tue.–Thu. 4–9:30 (10 Fri.–Sat.). This local favorite, located away from the din of boat motors and tourists, serves up some good Italian classics. It's best to make reservations on weekends. $8–14.

Barley Brothers Brewery & Grill (928-505-7837), 1425 McCulloch Blvd. Open daily 11 AM–1 AM. You can get a decent sandwich or meal here, including dinner salads and pastas, or create your own wood-fired pizza. Plus, they make award-winning microbrews to quench your thirst, from lemon-tinged blond ale to double-espresso stout. Entrées $9.95–24.95.

ChaBones (928-854-5554), 112 London Bridge Rd. Open daily 11–10. The name (actually the nickname of one of the owners' son) sounds soul food, but it's more food for the soul: Angus beef, fresh seafood, back ribs,

and prime rib in a relaxing atmosphere. The most popular fare is the prime rib French dip at lunch and black eye prime rib (with shrimp and special sauce) for dinner. You can BYOBB (Build Your Own Bones Burger—from hand-formed Angus beef) or BYOB Pizza (handcrafted with pan-sauce-infused oils and fresh toppings). Appetizers (20 different tapas) are excellent, and half price during happy hour 3–6. Entrées $9.99–28.99.

Javelina Cantina (928-855-8226), 1420 McCulloch Blvd. Open Sun.–Thu. 11–10 (till 11 Fri.–Sat.). Grab a beverage (they make specialty margaritas, the newest being pomegranate, from a stash of 90 different tequilas) and find a spot on the back deck, where you can watch boaters and Jet Skiers cruise by. The Sonoran cuisine menu has some excellent fish tacos, fajitas, and rellenos. Grilled salmon is a favorite entrée. It's a hot spot on summer weekends; best to make reservations then. Entrées $12–17.

✳ Selective Shopping

Stroll the **English Village** next to London Bridge. This shopping area celebrates the bridge's heritage with an English theme. Shops sell souvenirs, food, and specialty items.

✳ Special Events

February: **Winterfest Festival** (928-855-4115) has a lineup of vendors and activities.

March: **Juried Springs Art Show** (928-855-6340) at the Aquatic Community Center.

July: **4th of July Fireworks Display** off the Island at dusk.

October: **London Bridge Days** (928-855-4115) celebrates the dedication of London Bridge with a parade, fun, and festivities.

December: **Festival of Lights** (928-855-0888) displays more than one million lights under London Bridge. **Boat Parade of Lights** (928-855-8857) presents the Lake Havasu Yacht Club's finest decked out in lights.

YUMA

S ince its start in the mid-1800s, Yuma's quiet prominence has popped up throughout the West's history. Yuma's claim to fame grew from an anomalous geological feature that made it the crossing of choice over the impetuous pre-dam Colorado River. Two granite outcroppings—Indian Hill and Prison Hill—forced the river to cut a deep channel, narrowing the flow to 400 yards just south of its confluence with the Gila River.

This passage became known as Yuma Crossing, and over the years it has brought waves of peoples through the city. First came the steamboats and their colorful cargo and crew. When Native peoples saw the first steamboat, they surmised it was the devil approaching with all its fire-and-brimstone glory. Though the steamers always seemed to have a swell of chicanery about them, their payload supplied the growing frontier. Next, fortune seekers made their way via Yuma to gold-rich mountains in California. In 1877 the railroad laid tracks on a bridge at the crossing, allowing trains to enter the state for the first time. Decades later the Ocean-to-Ocean Bridge allowed auto traffic to cross the Colorado River, linking San Francisco with New York. The crossing provided a chance for thousands of immigrants to find a new life in California during the Dust Bowl and Great Depression.

Though Yuma's farming foundation started with cotton and citrus, its date farms got the attention of Middle Eastern date growers. Since the late 1970s, the farmland around Yuma has produced more than 90 percent of the vegetables sold in a U.S. winter. Practically frost-free and sunny, it's a perfect winter climate for veggies and people, too, not to mention the birds that migrate from points north along the Colorado River. Once World War II ended and the buzz from military personnel at the Yuma Proving Grounds quieted down, that great winter weather led the whole city into a cyclical rhythm. The city accommodated human and avian snowbirds and crops in winter, then turned ghost-town empty when summer arrived.

Since the turn of the 21st century Yuma has developed a number of areas, including its spot along the Colorado River, an international business scene, upscale riverfront work and living properties, and some great new eating venues. For a city that feeds the nation, is an international hub, and serves as a major wintering spot for avians and humans, Yuma may not get the prominence it deserves, but it sure does have some great winter weather.

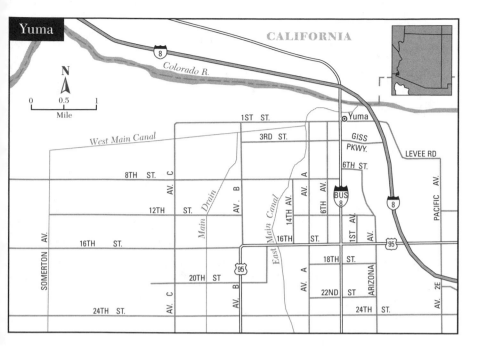

GUIDANCE The **Visitors Information Center** (928-783-0071 or 800-293-0071), 377 S. Main St., Suite 102, has maps of the historic section and information to get you around town. Open Nov.–Apr., Mon.–Fri. 9–6, Sat. 9–4, Sun. 10–2; Mar.–Oct., Mon.–Fri. 9–5, Sat. 9–2.

GETTING THERE *By car:* Yuma lies at the southern end of AZ 95 and on I-8 on the western border of Arizona. *By bus:* **Greyhound Bus** has a station at 170 E. 17th Place. *By air:* **Yuma International Airport** is serviced by United Express and America West Express and can handle any craft up to a 747.

WHEN TO COME With Yuma known as the city with sunshine 95 percent of the year, you can understand why the city's population doubles in winter when temperatures average in the 70s. Summers linger in the triple digits; many businesses take a seasonal siesta.

MEDICAL EMERGENCY **Yuma Regional Medical Center** (928-344-2000), 2400 S. Avenue A.

✳ To See

Sanguinetti House Museum (928-782-1841), 240 S. Madison Ave. Open Tue.–Sat. 10–4 year-round. You don't see a lot of old adobe buildings in Yuma because of the propensity of the Colorado River to flood before the river was dammed. Pioneer merchant E. F. Sanguinetti's home, however, still stands and is the headquarters of the Rio Colorado Chapter of the Arizona Historical Society. You can see artifacts, photographs, and furnishings from life during the territorial days. The home features gardens and aviaries with exotic birds. $3 adults, $2 ages 60 or older and 12–18, under 12 free.

Saihati Camel Farm (928-627-2553), Avenue 1E and County 16th St. Open daily Oct.–May; tours at 10 and 2 Mon.–Sat. and 2 on Sun. If the romantic silhouettes of palm trees in date gardens against an ice-blue or fluorescent sky at twilight aren't enough to make you feel like you're in the Middle East, check out this camel farm with one of the largest camel herds in North America. Livestock includes Arabian camels, Arabian oryx, African pygmy goats, Asian water buffalo, scimitar-horned oryx, and Watusi cattle. $3.

Yuma Crossing National Heritage Area (928-373-5190). Located at 1st St. and 4th Ave., the Heritage Area actually consists of several different projects— some still a work in progress. **Gateway Park** got its start in the mid-1990s by the residents of Yuma when they cleared vegetation along the river; historic and recreational improvements will follow. The **West Wetlands** is an amazing example of how to turn garbage into something precious. Once the town dump, the 110-acre natural preserve has been transformed into a natural wetlands and nature area. It includes a butterfly garden, burrowing owl apartments, and a millennium tree grove. Future plans include a children's park designed by children. The **East Wetlands** is one of the projects in process—a 1,400-acre reserve located between the confluence of the Gila and Colorado Rivers and the Ocean-to-Ocean Bridge. So far 70 acres have been cleared and 2,000 trees planted. All free.

Yuma Crossing State Historic Park (928-329-0471), 201 N. 4th Ave. Open daily 9–5, except Christmas. The compelling stories of all the cultures that lived in the sultry riverside heat gets told at the site of the Quartermaster Depot—a compound made up of the commanding officer's quarters, office of the depot quartermaster, quartermaster's storehouse, water reservoir, and corral house. Displays feature military and cultural artifacts, pictures, and animated quotes from past residents describing life along the river. $3 for ages 14 and up.

Yuma Territorial Prison State Historic Park (928-783-4771), 100 N. Prison Hill Rd. Open daily 8–5; closed at 2 on Thanksgiving and all day on Christmas. The state park gives you insight into why this infamous prison was called the Hell Hole of the West. A tour of the solid-iron cages ensconced in granite gives a vivid idea of life in the succinctly nicknamed prison. The dark cell, dungeonlike and reportedly haunted, still gives people the creeps even with sunlight streaming in its open door. A museum has pictures, stories, and artifacts elucidating the sordid side of life during Arizona's territorial days. $4 for ages 14 and up.

✳ To Do

BIRDING Located along the Pacific Flyway, Yuma and points along the Colorado River, such as **Imperial National Wildlife Refuge**, **Mittry Lake**, and **Martinez Lake**, constitute a major birding area. Waterbirds, waterfowl, and passerines drop in from fall through spring, when more than 200 species of migrating birds travel the flyway. Wintering waterfowl—flocks of Canada geese and a variety of northern ducks—start appearing in Dec. and don't leave until late Feb.

Betty's Kitchen (928-317-3200). Take US 95 to Ave. 7E, turn left, go 9 miles past Laguna Dam, and turn left at the sign. Located just south of Mittry Lake, a 0.5-mile loop trail managed by Bureau of Land Management tunnels inside a forest of trees along the Colorado River near Laguna Dam. Named Betty's Kitchen for a restaurant that once stood in the residential area before getting wiped out in a 1983 flood, now it's a hot spot for birds and wildlife to gather.

DATE RANCHES Since the 1920s farmers from the Yuma area and Egypt have been visiting one another, swapping farm technology. Like the Nile River Valley, the Coachella and Bard Valleys have date trees. The area is the world's largest producer of Medjool dates. The trees, imported from Middle Eastern countries such as Algeria, Tunisia, and Morocco, produce the world's oldest-known cultivated crop of dates. The date stands present a misplaced, but exotic, scene. You can watch the harvest Sep.–Nov. The produce gets transformed into yummy delights, from dried fruit to date shakes.

Ehrlich's Date Garden (928-783-4778), 868 S, Avenue B. Open 9–5 daily during harvest. This date garden has about 10 different varieties totaling more than 300 trees. Their harvest begins in Aug. and continues through Oct.

Imperial Date Gardens (760-572-0277), 1517 York Rd., Bard, CA. Take 4th Ave. north into California; turn right onto S-24 and go about 6 miles; turn right

THE ENDURANCE FLIGHT

The military had a big influence on Yuma during World War II. When the war ended, the servicemen left and the town quieted down. In an attempt to lure the military back, a handful of community leaders decided to convince the military that Yuma made a great airspace, and they did so via the Endurance Flight in 1949. The plan: have a plane circle Yuma continuously to demonstrate the flight-friendly skies. To keep the flight continuous, a Buick convertible assisted with refueling. The process required a man to stand on the convertible while it was moving and pass a gas can (a tall metal creamer can with a strap welded to it that had a filter and a piece of chamois to make the liquid ultraclean) up while the plane flew low enough to track with the auto. The flight could have gone longer than its 1,056 straight hours, but one of its taillights went out, which forced the pilot to land. The flight made history as the longest ride at the time in the world.

The Marine Corps was indeed impressed and moved its air station to Yuma. Today allies from around the world test equipment at the Yuma Proving Grounds. Fly Field, named for Colonel Benjamin Fly, has the longest runway in the state.

onto Ross Rd., and continue for about 12 miles to the gardens on your left. Open Mon.–Fri. 9–5; Nov.–Feb., also open Sat. 9–5 and Sun. 10–5.

FISHING Martinez Lake Resort (928-783-9589 or 800-876-7004) rents boats, has a kayak and canoe shuttle, and offers guided fishing. From Yuma, go north on US 95 for 25 miles, turn left (west) onto Martinez Lake Rd. and drive 13 miles to the signs directing the way to the lake. For every mile of river flowing through Martinez Lake, there are five miles of backwater ponds. This is fisherman heaven. One feature Martinez Lake has over most all other waterways in the state is an abundance of private docks. These wooden structures built on underwater stilts make perfect hideouts for bass. Anglers can cast their bait under the docks just as if they were skipping a rock across the water's surface . . . and get a bass surprise. Catfish grow huge here, too—bigger than an ocean fish—requiring tackle fit to fight marlin.

GAMING Cocopah Bingo and Casino (928-726-8066), US 95 and County 15th St. Bingo is big here, with a choice of Bonanza and Mini Bonanza games and Letter E progressives every weekend. The property also has slot machines, video poker machines, and video keno machines.

GOLF Recently rated as the seventh best city in the country for golf by *Golf Digest*, Yuma might surprise you with its golf options. Especially attractive are the incredibly reasonable prices on well-maintained courses that you can use year-round (just be sure to finish your game by midmorning in summer).
Desert Hills Municipal Golf Course (928-344-4653), 1245 Desert Hills Dr. Open sunrise or 6 AM. Considered one of the best municipal facilities in the state, the par-72 championship course hosts several professional events. The property has a driving range, restaurant, and pro shop. Jan.–Mar., $13–44.
Mesa Del Sol Public Golf Club (928-342-1283), 12213 Calle del Cid. A par-72, 18-hole champion course designed by Arnold Palmer with a number of par-3s to give your game some kick. Driving range, restaurant, and pro shop. $21–43.

HIKING You can take a 1.5-mile loop hike on the **Painted Desert Trail** in **Imperial National Wildlife Refuge**. Across the river in California, experienced hikers can get a wilder taste of the area at **Kofa National Wildlife Refuge**.

MEXICO A 10-minute drive can take you to the Mexican border, where you can park your car and dip into the little village of Algodones to shop, refresh yourself at a cantina or restaurant, and visit a pharmacy, doctor, or dentist. Algodones reciprocates the business with two festivals: Welcome Winter Visitors Festival in Dec. and Thank You Festival in Mar. See page 216 for tips on visiting Mexico.

RIVER TOURS In a land that only gets about 3 inches of rain a year, a waterway as significant as the lower Colorado River creates a lush contrast with the desert environment. The best way to get to know the Colorado and its wildlife is to travel it by tour boat. **Yuma River Tours** (928-783-4400) offers 2-hour to all-day tours. Tours depart from Fisher's Landing at Martinez Lake (see *Fishing*).

✴ Wilder Places

Imperial National Wildlife Refuge (928-783-3371). From Yuma, go north on US 95 for 25 miles; turn west onto Martinez Lake Rd., continue for 13 miles, and follow signs to the visitor center. Open daily. The 25,768-acre Imperial NWR protects and enhances a 30-mile section of the lower Colorado River in Arizona and California, including its associated backwater lakes and wetlands. These marshy areas have given the refuge the nickname of Arizona's Everglades.

Imperial Sand Dunes (760-337-4400). From Yuma, head west on I-8 for about 20 miles. Like a scene from a science-fiction movie, the barren-looking dunes here rise more than 250 feet. Anything but barren, you can find unusual plants and animals unique to this area. The movie-set look worked perfectly for *Star Wars: The Return of the Jedi* and *Stargate*. The admission fee of $25 is good for 7 days.

Kofa National Wildlife Refuge (928-783-7861), 356 W. 1st St. (office). From Yuma, take US 95 north toward Quartzite, Arizona, to refuge entrance signs. Hot, dry, and rugged, the Kofa National Wildlife Refuge has a surprising native, the California fan palm, flourishing in its mountains. This is one of the few spots in Arizona with native California fan palms, likely descendants from glacial-era palms growing in the area. If you're lucky, you might spot another of the refuge's main attractions: one of the desert bighorn sheep rambling over the refuge's rocky outcrops. The 665,400-acre refuge has a herd of about 800 bighorns, which traipse the area's rugged Kofa and Castle Dome Mountains. These rhyolite peaks have the kind of precipitous landscape sheep like.

Roads and trails are few and far between in this large refuge. You can explore the hillsides further on foot, but not by vehicle. The best time to visit is late fall through early spring, when temperatures remain mild.

Mittry Lake Wildlife Area. Just downriver from the Imperial National Wildlife Refuge, between Imperial and Laguna Dams, pools a backwater paradise that has become all things to all beings. Fish and fishermen, birds and birders, wildlife and its watchers all find what they're looking for at Mittry Lake Wildlife Area, jointly managed by the Arizona Department of Game and Fish with the U.S. Bureau of Land Management and U.S. Bureau of Reclamation.

YUMA'S POST OFFICE IS IN A HISTORIC BUILDING.

While largemouth bass, channel catfish, flathead catfish, crappie, and bluegill lurk in the marshy waters of the dredged lake, a variety of birds take to its labyrinth of bulrushes and cattails. During a winter's visit to the shallow lake, you might see grebes, cormorants, herons, and pelicans, all of which commonly make appearances. Target birds to sight include the western warbler, Crissal thrasher, and Abert's towhee. You might also see, or at least hear, a least bittern or Virginia rail.

✳ Lodging

✿ 🐾 ✎ **Coronado Hotel** (928-783-4453), 233 4th Ave. This Best Western property carries a bit of history: It was the first motor hotel in Yuma. The rooms—large king, queen, or family suites—have a clean, friendly retro decor. The property includes two swimming pools and a laundry facility. Rooms have datajack phones. Your stay includes breakfast at next-door **Yuma Landing Restaurant**. This eatery, located on the spot where the first airplane landed in Arizona in 1911, has a pictorial transportation museum featuring planes, trains, and automobiles along with quirky memorabilia. Pets are welcome, with no deposit charged. $79.50–89.50.

∞ ✎ **Hampton Inn** (928-329-5600), 1600 E. 16th St. The newest hotel in Yuma. The decor is fresh and pleasant, and you'll also find an outdoor pool and spa, 24-hour business center, and 24-hour fitness room. Rooms have free WiFi, free local calls, complimentary *USA Today*, refrigerator, and microwave. A hot breakfast is included with your room. Service pets only. $99–149.

Hotel Lee (928-783-6336), 390 S. Main St. This 1917 Colonial Revival hotel is the only one in Yuma on the National Historic Register. The city's first radio station, KUMA, broadcast from the hotel, and General Patton took it over during World War II. The hotel became the place of choice for married-on-the-fly servicemen during the war. The property has historically themed rooms with Victorian antiques and three ghosts, all friendly. Guests can make themselves at home in the downstairs kitchen. Rooms have refrigerator, microwave, and DirecTV. No pets. $29.95–69.95.

∞ ✿ 🐾 ✎ ♿ **Shilo Inn Hotel** (928-782-9511), 1550 S. Castle Dome Ave. You get a great deal here—a basic, clean room with tons of amenities, free high-speed Internet access, a complimentary hot buffet breakfast, two complimentary drinks, an outdoor pool, a fitness center with sauna and steam room, and fresh coffee, fruit, and popcorn in lobby. Children 12 and under stay free. Pets are okay with a $10 deposit.

THE HOTEL LEE HAS PERIOD FURNISHINGS —AND GHOSTS TO BOOT.

✳ Where to Eat

DINING OUT Ciao Bella Ristorante Italiano (928-783-3900), 2255 S. 4th Ave. Open daily 11–10; closed Sun. Chef Able Garcia found his calling with this wonderful Italian menu. The dining area ranges from packed to cozy-cramped; people have been known to feign reservations to slip in without one. All the food is good, from the classic spaghetti and lasagna to True Cod Olivia grilled with olive tapenade over lemon risotto, or signature rack of lamb with berry froth. Several of the desserts are made in-house. You get to choose from more than 100 different labels of wine at reasonable prices. Lunch $7–10, dinner $13–25.

Garden Café (928-783-1491), 250 S. Madison Ave. Open Tue.–Fri. 9–2:30, Sat.–Sun. 8–2:30. Closed May–Oct. Just walking down the brick corridor to the all-outdoor seating area is a treat. The walkway has potted plants, colorful birds, and bougainvillea. It's the place of choice for breakfasts with such fare as specialty quiches and pancakes. The Kamman sausage—a spicy Yuma specialty—makes eggs snappy. The breakfast salad combines granola, low-fat yogurt, and fresh fruit, then tops the mix with raspberry sauce. For lunch, it's sandwiches and homemade soups. Grilled tri-tip entrées make popular, heartier meals. Save room for rich desserts. Sunday brunch buffet presents a gourmet lineup of egg and meat dishes and sides, fruit, and homemade breads and muffins. Entrées $6.25–8.95.

Julieanna's Patio Café (928-317-1961), 1951 W. 25th Place. Open Mon.–Sat. for lunch 11–3, Mon.–Fri. for dinner 4:30–9 (till 10 Sat.); closed Sun. On a warm evening, you might feel you're in a rain forest what with up to half a dozen macaws squawking among the gush of greenery on the patio. Owner Julie Fritz Fienberg envisioned a tropical patio restaurant where she'd unwind at the end of the day, sipping on Chardonnay and eating steamed clams on the patio. The menu, correctly described as eclectic, has everything from classic BLT to Thai fried noodles; traditional Caesar to coconut chicken salad; fresh fish to lobster. A platter of fresh, house-made desserts finishes the meal. You can also sit at the sushi and martini bar. Entrées $15–48.

River City Grille (928-782-7988), 600 W. 3rd St. Open for lunch Mon.–Fri. 11:30–2, dinner every night 5–10. The menu leans toward seafood here, flown in fresh from the

Pacific Northwest, presented with several different cultural influences. Seared ahi with wasabi cream, Oregon bay scallops with chanterelles, and crabcakes Thai style give you an idea of the East-meets-West style of cooking. The food's good for you, too—leaning toward low fat and using all-natural beef, wild-river salmon, and Denver lamb. Half a dozen vegetarian entrées are available. The two outdoor brick patios make pleasant dining alternatives. Entrées $15.95–24.95.

EATING OUT ❧ **The Chili Pepper** (928-783-4213), 1030 W. 24th St. Open Mon.–Sat. 8–8. This Yuma staple has locals who have been away for any length of time heading straight

YUMA'S ANNUAL BICYCLE RACE DRAWS CYCLISTS FROM AROUND THE WORLD.

for its cafeteria-style dining room to indulge in very basic, very good Mexican food. The smell of homemade tortillas greets you in the parking lot. Breakfast burritos are served until 10. From then on, it's rolled tacos, tortillas, burritos, and a small variety of dinners. Entrées $3.85–4.60.

Lutes Casino (928-782-2192), 221 S. Main St. Open Mon.–Thu. 10–8 (till 9 Fri.–Sat., 6 Sun.). The state's oldest pool hall and domino parlor makes an entertaining stop for a hamburger as legendary as the establishment's reputation. Its motto, "Where the Elite Meet," refers to such folks as Clark Gable, who played poker at the now tamed and family-oriented business at a time when pool games lead to wild fights. The wildest thing to happen these days is the Special—an interesting combination of hamburger and hot dog with melted "orange" cheese on a bun said to have been dreamed up when Bobby Lutes imbibed too much tequila. Be sure to douse this half-breed critter with hot sauce. Without a doubt, the hamburgers are king here. Entrées $3.75–5.50.

Mi Rancho (928-344-6903), 2701 S. 4th Ave. Open Mon.–Thu. 11–9:30, Fri. 10–10, Sat. 8–10, Sun. 8–9:30. Mi Rancho mirrors the flavors and ambience of Old Mexico. You can order classic fare such as enchiladas, tacos, tortas; or traditional seviche, *camarones*, *machaca*, menudo, and beef tongue. It's all excellent. Entrées $7.99–12.99.

✳ **Special Events**

Contact 928-783-0071 for more information.

January: **Old Town Jubilee** in historic downtown on Main St. The **Lettuce Festival** celebrates Yuma's status as the country's number two producer of lettuce.

February: **Silver Spur Rodeo** at the fairgrounds. **Marine Corps Air Station Air Show** at the marine base. **Yuma River Daze/Yuma Crossing Days Festival** takes place along the river with a block party on Main Street.

Late February or early March: The **North End Classic** (928-373-0700; www.northendclassic.com) is one of the first pro road biking events of the year and draws more than 400 participants from all over the world.

March: **Midnight at the Oasis** is a car show and concert featuring national artists.

April: The **Yuma Birding and Nature Festival** features birding tours, slide shows, and nature tours.*May:* **Cinco de Mayo Parade and Celebration** on Main Street.

INDEX